Praise for the first edition of *A History of the Ancient Near East*

"This extremely readable account will provide an historical and political framework for the student and the general reader who wish to get to grips with this vast and significant area of human history. Assuming no prior knowledge of the region, it moves swiftly to a detailed engagement with the material. Its two special strengths are the strong forward thrust of the historical narrative, and the emphasis on the range of sources available for the reconstruction of that narrative." *Jeremy Black, University of Oxford*

"This text deserves a place on the shelves of ancient historians and archaeologists, and it will certainly have pride of place in reading lists for courses in Mesopotamian history." *Norman Yoffee, University of Michigan*

"An excellent introduction for general readers and students at all levels. Highly recommended." *R. P. Wright, New York University*

"Marc Van De Mieroop's introduction to the history of Iraq and the Asiatic Near East is suited to first-year undergraduates in ancient history, the archaeology of Western Asia and ancient Near Eastern studies generally, and to all others who need an up-to-date summary of what happened before the Greeks." *Times Higher Education Supplement*

"At a time when authors have created sweeping positivist histories and dubious claims built on questionable connections . . . the book demonstrates the potential for responsible and critical historical analysis. Van De Mieroop's aim, of 'inviting [readers] to explore further,' is more than amply met by this book." *Bulletin of the American Schools of Oriental Research*

"The treatment of the subject is based on sound philological competence, an up-to-date knowledge of sources and of related debates, in the framework of a very advanced historiographic approach . . . I do not know of any other handbook of similar size that can compete with Van De Mieroop's book in philological competence, in historiographic method, and in expository clearness." *Mario Liverani, in Orientalia*

Blackwell History of the Ancient World

This series provides a new narrative history of the ancient world, from the beginnings of civilization in the ancient Near East and Egypt to the fall of Constantinople. Written by experts in their fields, the books in the series offer authoritative accessible surveys for students and general readers alike.

Published

In Preparation

A History of the Ancient Near East

ca. 3000–323 BC

Second Edition

Marc Van De Mieroop

Blackwell
Publishing

BLACKWELL PUBLISHING
350 Main Street, Malden, MA 02148-5020, USA
9600 Garsington Road, Oxford OX4 2DQ, UK
550 Swanston Street, Carlton, Victoria 3053, Australia

First edition published 2004
Second edition published 2007 by Blackwell Publishing Ltd

9   2011

Library of Congress Cataloging-in-Publication Data

Van De Mieroop, Marc.
A history of the ancient Near East, ca. 3000–323 B.C. / Marc Van De
Mieroop. – 2nd ed.
    p. cm. – (Blackwell history of the ancient world)
Includes bibliographical references and index.
ISBN 978-1-4051-4910-5 (printed case hardback : alk. paper)
ISBN 978-1-4051-4911-2 (pbk. : alk. paper)
1. Middle East–History–To 622.   I. Title.   II. Series.

DS62.2.V34 2007
939'.4–dc22

                                                        2006006920

A catalogue record for this title is available from the British Library.

Set in 10$^{1}/_{2}$/12$^{1}/_{2}$pt Plantin
by Graphicraft Limited, Hong Kong
Printed in Singapore
by Fabulous Printers Pte Ltd

For further information on
Blackwell Publishing, visit our website:
www.blackwellpublishing.com

Contents

Illustrations

Charts

Maps

Boxes

Documents

Preface to the Second Edition

Perhaps because of the tragic events that have happened and continue to happen in the heartland of ancient Mesopotamia, Iraq, the first edition of this book sold remarkably well for a work on the ancient Near East. My editor, Al Bertrand, asked me thus whether I would be interested in writing a second edition. His staff conducted a survey of teachers of ancient Near Eastern history and related fields to inquire how the work could be improved as a textbook. Meanwhile, my own students at Columbia University in New York were also critical judges of the text. With their comments and the (unfortunately few) published reviews in mind, I decided to undertake revisions primarily aimed at making the book more accessible and useful as an introduction to ancient Near Eastern history. At the suggestion of several people, I expanded the guide to further reading drastically and increased the number of maps slightly. I also integrated new research that convinced me to revise earlier opinions or guided me to a better understanding of issues. It is my hope that readers familiar with both editions will find the revisions improvements. The intent of the book has remained the same as before: to introduce as many people as possible to the fascinating world of the ancient Near East.

Preface to the
First Edition

In the year 334 BC, a young king from Macedonia and his well-trained army crossed from Europe into Asia, confronted the vast empire of Persia, and conquered it in the course of a few years. Alexander's troops marched through an antique world that contained evidence of thousands of years of earlier history. Their previous encounter with Greece could not have prepared them for what they saw in the Near East and Egypt. They entered cities like Uruk that had existed for three millennia, and saw pyramids and temples that had stood for almost as many years. This was a world steeped in history, not a world in decline, waiting for fresh inspiration. The city-dwellers knew their traditions were so ancient that they claimed they dated from the beginning of time itself. People wrote in scripts that had been used for almost three thousand years, they read and copied texts that were hundreds of years old. These were not idle claims, as for centuries their lands had indeed been home to the most advanced cultures in the world, well before Greece had developed its great classical civilization.

It is in the Near East and north-east Africa that many of the elements we associate with advanced civilization first originated, such as agriculture, cities, states, writing, laws, and many more. Because this region lies at the juncture of three continents, practices and concepts from many and diverse people came together there, inspired and complemented one another, and were used by the inhabitants to manipulate their surroundings. They created their environment rather than reacting to it. This had happened over many centuries, indeed millennia, through processes that saw developments both smooth and abrupt, reversals of fortune, and false starts. Today we are naturally attracted to finding out how and why such things happened, and who was involved. Nineteenth- and early twentieth-century scholarship used to trace the roots of modern civilization in the ancient history of this region, but an approach of this kind is no longer acceptable as we now realize that world history is not just a long and uninterrupted evolution from a single source. We can assert, however, that in the Near East and north-east Africa, we are able to study for the first time in history how humans lived, in circumstances that include many of the elements of our own culture. This can be studied on the basis of a written record as well as from material remains, since the first literate societies in history are found there. And this study acquires greater poignancy because we often see the indigenous creation of cultural factors here, rather than elements borrowed from elsewhere.

The Near East and Egypt encompass a vast area, stretching from the Black Sea to the Aswan Dam, and from the Aegean Sea to the highlands of Iran, an area that was densely inhabited throughout its history. The multiplicity of cultures and histories in this entire stretch is immense, too vast to describe in a single book. Therefore I shall deal only with the Near East, that is, the regions of the Asian continent, and shall exclude Egypt from the discussion. This still leaves us with an enormous variety of peoples, cultures, languages, and traditions with which to deal. There is a certain unity in this diversity, however, that makes combined study desirable. In the variety we can see many similarities. Political and military circumstances at times brought many of these people together under a single system, and we can see almost constant processes of social and cultural interaction and exchange that connected the varied regions.

Near Eastern history should not be one of beginnings only, or of interest solely because it provides the earliest evidence on questions the historian can ask. Many other aspects are involved. It is a history of some three thousand years, a period somewhat longer than that which separates us from Homer. This long time span, with its numerous people, can be studied through a continuous historical record that enables us to see changing circumstances and human reactions with a detail that exists nowhere else in the ancient world. The past has been described as a foreign country, and to study it is like traveling: we meet people who are much like us, but also distinctly different. As when we travel, our access is restricted and we do not get to see everything. We are nevertheless provided with an abundance of information for the ancient Near East, and that abundance enables us to see a great deal more than for many other cultures of the past.

As visitors to a foreign country we do not comprehend all we see, because we are not full participants in the lives and cultures we encounter. Hopefully, however, we learn to appreciate differences as responses to challenges and opportunities that are as human as our own, whatever our circumstances. We learn that our habits of behavior and thinking are not the only ones that make sense. Historians are like travel guides: claiming greater familiarity with the foreign countries than their readers, they point out what they find interesting, and phrase their enthusiasm in ways they find comprehensible and logical. They hope to inform readers, while inviting them to explore further. That is the aim of this book, too: it provides an introduction to a rich and fascinating subject that can be examined in many ways, and from many different perspectives.

Since the material at hand is so abundant and diverse, a summary book like this one will necessarily present the author's personal view on the subject, and my interests and prejudices are clearly reflected in the topics I address and the interpretations I suggest. The intent is not to write a definitive history of this region and era of human history, but to inspire readers to travel ahead on their own through this ancient Near Eastern world

Acknowledgments

My greatest debt is to Al Bertrand at Blackwell who has continued to be an ideal editor and who, with his staff, has facilitated my work enormously. I still owe gratitude to the people who helped me in the preparation of the first edition of this book: J. A. Brinkman, Bob Englund, Ben Foster, Steven Garfinkle, Avery Kastin, and Seth Richardson. I would like to remember above all Jeremy Black, whose untimely death in 2004 was a great personal loss.

For illustrations I am thankful to Joan Aruz and Kim Benzel (Metropolitan Museum of Art), Andrew Gessner (Columbia University, Department of Art History and Archaeology), Ulla Kasten (Yale Babylonian Collection), Helen Whitehouse (Ashmolean Museum), Ralph K. Pedersen (Institute of Nautical Archaeology), and Geoff Emberling (Oriental Institute of the University of Chicago). Susan Pollock, Paul Zimansky, and especially Zainab Bahrani kindly gave me photographs from their private collections and enabled me to include objects and sites inaccessible to me.

As always, I could not have written this book without the moral support of Kenan and Zainab.

Marc Van De Mieroop
Oxford
December 2005

Author's Note

I have rendered the names of places and persons with the intent to make them as easily recognizable as possible to the reader. Thus I use familiar English forms whenever they exist, e.g., Nebuchadnezzar instead of the more accurate Nabu-kudurri-usur, Aleppo instead of Halab, etc. My colleagues will be aware that there is inconsistency in my practice, but they will know what the various renderings of such names are. For others, I hope it will facilitate the consultation of other books on the subjects discussed here. I have not attempted to render some phonetic forms of the ancient Near Eastern languages, such as the emphatic s, pronounced ts, which is rendered as a simple s here. Long vowels are not especially indicated except when an entire term is in Akkadian.

In the translations of ancient Near Eastern texts, restorations of broken passages are not always indicated, in order to increase legibility of the text. When they are indicated, they appear between square brackets. When a word is partly inside the brackets, partly outside them, it indicates that part of it is still legible. Uncertain translations are in italics.

1
Introductory Concerns

1.1 What is the Ancient Near East?

The term "Near East" is not widely used today. It has survived in a scholar-ship rooted in the nineteenth century when it was used to identify the remains of the Ottoman empire on the eastern shores of the Mediterranean Sea. Today we say Middle East to designate this geographical area, but the two terms do not exactly overlap, and ancient historians and archaeologists of the Middle East continue to speak of the Near East, as I will do in this book. Already this habit gives a certain vagueness to what constitutes the ancient history of this area of the world, and the geographical boundaries of the region can differ substantially from book to book. Some definitions, then, of what is intended here are in order.

In this survey of history, Near East designates the region from the Aegean coast of Turkey to central Iran, and from Northern Anatolia to the Red Sea. Egypt, whose history intersects with that of the Near East at many times, will be excluded, except when it extended its empire into Asia in the second half of the second millennium. These boundaries are deliberately somewhat indeterminate. This results from the fact that we study primarily the history of a set of core areas, whose reaches extended over shifting zones in different periods. Foremost among them is Mesopotamia, the area between the Tigris and Euphrates rivers, from which we have the most abundant documentation and whose history thus dominates any study of the Near East. For instance, at times Mesopotamian states reached into the Arabian peninsula. Consequently, that region became part of the Near East while hitherto it remained otherwise unknown. When some other states in central Anatolia, south-west Iran, and northern and western Syria expanded, they drew additional regions into the orbit of Near Eastern history. As historians, we rely on sources; their extent, both in geographical terms and in what facets of life they document, fluctuates

enormously over time. When they report on activity somewhere, that place becomes part of the Near East; when they do not, histories have little to tell. The
ancient history of the Near East can be likened to a dark room with isolated
points of light, some brighter than others, provided by the sources. They shine
especially clearly on certain places and periods, but leave much else concealed.
It is the historian's task to try to make sense of the whole.

The chronological boundaries of ancient Near Eastern history are also ambiguous, and authors of different books on the subject use a variety of dates.
Both the beginning and the end dates of this history are flexible. History is
traditionally considered to rely on written sources, and the origins of writing
in the Near East, around 3000 BC, can then be seen as the start of history. Yet
script was just one of several innovations that had its roots in earlier times, and
the earliest texts contain no "historical" information that we can understand
beyond the fact that people had the ability to write. Thus, most histories of the
Near East start in prehistory, oftentimes in the tenth millennium, describing
in more or less detail the developments that took place before the historical
period. During these seven millennia, so many important changes happened in
the lifestyles of humans in the Near East that they deserve separate in-depth
treatment, using archaeological and anthropological methodologies and sources
different from historical ones. There is not enough room in this book, which
intends to discuss the historical periods thoroughly, to do full justice to all prehistoric developments. Hence the chapters of this book will start with the "Uruk
revolution" of the fourth millennium, while earlier developments will only be
cursorily outlined in this introduction. It seems appropriate to begin a history
of the Near East around 3000, as several prehistoric processes culminated
simultaneously at this time, and writing appeared, dramatically changing the
nature of our source material.

History rarely knows clear-cut endings. Even when states are definitively
destroyed, they leave an impact, the duration of which depends on whether
one looks at political, economic, cultural, or other aspects of history. But the
historian has to end somewhere and the choice of when needs a rationale.
Various dates are commonly used to end ancient Near Eastern history, most
often either the fall of the last native Mesopotamian dynasty in 539 or the
defeat of Persia by Alexander of Macedon in 331. I have chosen to take
Alexander as the last figure of the political history of the ancient Near East,
because while the changes he instituted were probably not momentous for
most of the people at that time, our access to the historical data is transformed
starting in his reign. The gradual shift from native to external classical sources
necessitates a different historiographical approach. The arrival of Hellenism is
a fitting borderline because the historian's understanding of the region changes
significantly.

The years from around 3000 to 331 involve some twenty-seven centuries,
which is a very long period. Few historical disciplines engage themselves with
such lengths of time. We can compare it to what is covered in survey books of
the whole of western civilization, which link Homeric Greece to the present day.

While we can see clearly distinct periods in that western evolution and appreciate the pivotal changes that took place over time, it is harder to do so for ancient Near Eastern history. Our distance from the Near East, both in time and in spirit, sometimes leads to a view that blurs distinctions and reduces everything to one large static mass. On the other hand, one can take a diametrically opposed view and fragment this history into short, coherent, and manageable segments. Discontinuity then becomes the focus. The latter attitude lies at the basis of what is usually presented as the periodization of Near Eastern history. A sequence of phases, mostly defined in dynastic terms based on events in Mesopotamia, is strung together as a historical continuum. Each phase experiences its cycle of rise, prosperity, and decline, as if it were a biological entity. In between fall the so-called Dark Ages, moments of historical silence.

I shall take an intermediate stance here. While continuities should not be overemphasized, some basic patterns of Near Eastern history are visible. In political terms, for example, the Near East was a region of fragmented power with relatively short-lived periods of centralization under rulers or dynasties (usually Mesopotamian) whose territorial reach became increasingly wider. While I shall maintain the traditional subdivisions into dynastic periods, I shall group them into larger units. This book is thus divided into the ages of city-states, territorial states, and empires, each with their moments of greatness and disruption (if we equate power with greatness). The city-state was the primary political element from 3000 to approximately 1600, territorial states dominated the scene from that point on to the early first millennium, and empires characterized later ancient Near Eastern history. Mesopotamian states usually demonstrate these stages of development most conclusively, but it is clear that they also occurred elsewhere in the Near East.

In the end, the availability and extent of the sources define the ancient Near East as a historical subject and subdivide its history. Extensive written and archaeological documentation is available in certain places at certain times, and those regions and moments form the core of the subject. The cultures of Mesopotamia dominate in this respect. They were often the leading civilizations of their time, and their histories had an impact over the entire Near East. When they influenced or controlled non-Mesopotamian regions, those areas became included in Near Eastern history; when they did not, we often lose track of what happened outside Mesopotamia. In the last three decades, it has become increasingly apparent that other regions of the Near East experienced developments independent of Mesopotamia and that all cultural innovations cannot be credited to that area. Still, it remains impossible to write continuous histories of those regions without reliance on a Mesopotamia-centered model. Mesopotamia provides the geographical and chronological unity to Near Eastern historiography. Its use of an age-old script, its continuation of religious practices, and its cultural continuity from the third to the first millennia allow us to look at its long history as a unified whole. The study of the other cultures in the region is mostly pegged to that of Mesopotamian culture, but we should not ignore their contributions to the history of the Near East.

Box 1.1 *Dating Near Eastern history*

Following the practice of the large majority of histories, this book uses absolute dates to indicate when events took place. These dates are set within the artificial construct of the Christian or Common Era, and since the entirety of ancient Near Eastern history took place before the start of that era, all are B(efore) C(hrist) or B(efore) C(ommon) E(ra), the higher numbers preceding the lower ones. That is merely a convention to enable us to comprehend the sequence of events and their distance in time, even if the era has an ideological basis without relevance to the ancient Near East. All dates in this book thus have to be read as BC.

I have also stated these dates absolutely, giving a false impression of certainty. The absolute chronology of Near Eastern history is a vexing and controversial problem. The Mesopotamians were very good at providing sequences of rulers, for example, but the difficulty for us is to establish a firm point in time to which they can be attached. The tools employed derive from multiple disciplines (e.g., astronomy, archaeology, philology) and the scholarly debates are very technical. Since they are so complex, I will not discuss them here but only indicate the system I have used. First-millennium chronology is secure because of several reliable data, including the record of a solar eclipse that took place on June 15, 763, and allows us to anchor a long sequence of Assyrian eponyms (see chapter 6). The absolute chronology of the second millennium and before is uncertain, however. Scholars have reconstructed a reliable relative sequence, primarily based on Mesopotamian lists of kings, but that sequence cannot be absolutely dated with certainty. Different systems are in use and one called "Middle Chronology" has been the most popular, although it has often been justifiably attacked. It dates the reign of King Hammurabi of Babylon from 1792 to 1750. I have taken over this system without comment, or even a belief that it is superior to alternatives, because it is the most commonly used, which should make it easier for readers to consult other scholarship.

1.2 The Sources

As pointed out above, the availability of sources determines the confines of ancient Near Eastern history. Fortunately, these sources are incredibly abundant and varied in nature for the whole of this long history. Texts, the primary source for the historian, have survived in the hundreds of thousands. From early on, kings carved inscriptions on stone monuments, many of which were among the first archaeological finds made in Mesopotamia. More important, however, was the clay tablet, the medium of writing that developed in southern Mesopotamia and was adopted by all Near Eastern cultures. It has amazing durability in the dry soil of the region, and texts from the mundane receipt of a single sheep to literary works such as the Epic of Gilgamesh are plentiful. The survival of numerous documents of daily use distinguishes the ancient Near

East from other ancient cultures. In Egypt, Greece, and Rome, similar things were written, but on parchment and papyrus, materials that have survived in unusual conditions only. The writings from the ancient Near East are rich not only in number but also in what they cover: the economy, royal building activity, military campaigns, government business, literature, science, and many other aspects of life are abundantly documented.

Archaeological material has become increasingly important as one of the historian's tools. Not only do excavations allow us to determine that the Hittites were present in northern Syria in the fourteenth century, for instance, but they also permit us to study the material conditions of their lives there. The Near East is covered with artificial mounds that were formed over the centuries by the debris of human occupation. Those are called *tell* in Arabic, *tepe* in Persian, and *hüyük* in Turkish, terms we find in the names of most archaeological sites. The possibilities for archaeological excavation in the Near East are so great that we have only scratched the surface so far, despite 150 years of work. Major cities such as Uruk, Babylon, Nineveh, Hattusa, and so on, have been explored over many years and have yielded enormous numbers of buildings, monuments, objects, and texts. But when one compares what has been uncovered with what remains hidden, it is clear that this is only a beginning. There remain thousands of unexplored sites, not all of which can be systematically investigated. Since numerous dams, roads, and agricultural developments are constantly being built and threaten to annihilate ancient sites, the selection of what is excavated is often determined by rescue efforts.

We should not underestimate the importance of the vicissitudes of archaeological exploration in determining our outlook on Near Eastern history. Modern political developments in the Middle East control where one can excavate. Imperial competition between Great Britain and France in the mid-nineteenth century led their representatives to focus on the massive sites in northern Iraq, the region of Assyria. There they found the most impressive monuments to be displayed in national museums, which led to the early interest in Assyrian history. Only later in the century, when concerns about origins peaked, did archaeologists explore the south of Iraq systematically, in search of the earlier Sumerians. More recently, after the Shah of Iran invited western archaeologists to his country, the results of their research led to significant revisions of the history of the Near East. The revolution of 1979 suddenly terminated that research, however. Likewise, the Iraq Wars of 1991 and 2003, and the subsequent instability of the country, have fully choked off access to the heartland of Mesopotamia. Archaeologists sought new terrain, and many turned to northern Syria and southern Turkey. It is no surprise that the finds from these regions force us to rethink their impact on ancient Near Eastern history. The most important repercussion of these changes has been the shift away from Mesopotamia to what used to be called the periphery. Syria, Anatolia, and western Iran are much better known than before, and the documentation of cultural evolutions there has forced us to reconsider the primacy and dominance of Mesopotamia in many aspects of history.

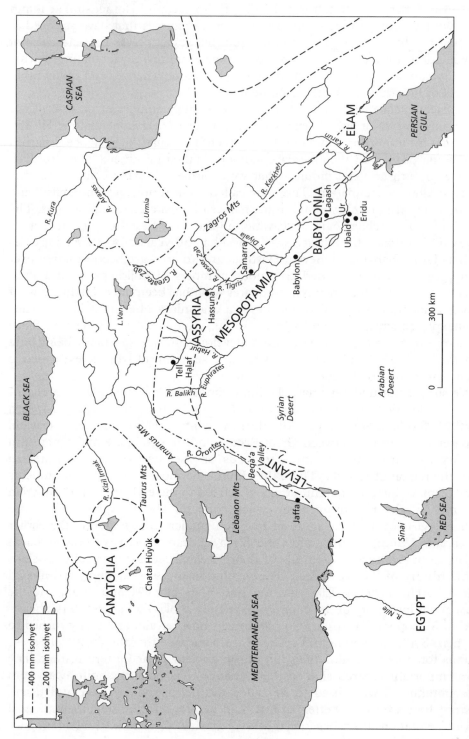

Map 1.1 The ancient Near East

A final point needs to be made about the distribution of sources. In the ancient Near East, there is a direct correlation between political centralization of power, economic development, the construction of monumental architecture, and the increased production of written documents of all types. Thus the sources, both archaeological and textual, accentuate moments of political strength. History is by nature a positivistic science (meaning that we discuss what is preserved), and necessarily focuses on those moments for which the sources are most plentiful. In between are what we call the "Dark Ages." The historian observes and interprets points of light, discontinuous in time and regional coverage. While the distant past is usually less well documented than the more recent one, the ancient Near East presents an exception to that rule. Although uneven, the coverage of our documentation is almost continuous for the three millennia of its history, and at times there is an abundance of sources. What is available for twenty-first-century Babylonia, for example, surpasses in number and scope the written documentation from many later periods in history. The ancient Near East provides the first cultures in human history in which true and detailed historical research can take place.

1.3 Geography

The Near East is a vast landmass situated at the intersection of three continents: Africa, Asia, and Europe. Three tectonic plates meet there and their movements determine the geology of the region. The Arabian plate presses to the north underneath the Iranian plate, pushing it upwards, and is itself forced down. Where the two plates meet, there is a long depression stretching from the Mediterranean Sea to the Persian Gulf in which the Tigris and Euphrates rivers flow, turning a desert into highly fertile land wherever their waters reach. The African and Arabian plates meet at the western edge of the Near East and are separated by the Great Rift, which runs parallel to the Mediterranean coast and creates a narrow valley lined by the Amanus and Lebanon mountains. There is little room for coastal settlement except in the south, where the plain widens. The north and the east of the Near East are also dominated by high mountain ranges, the Taurus and Zagros, which contain the sources of all rivers in the region. The south of the region is a huge flat landmass, containing the Syrian and Arabian deserts. These become more mountainous the further south one goes and are almost entirely deprived of water.

Geological phenomena, earthquakes and volcanic eruptions, as well as the effects of wind, rain, and water, have created a highly diverse area. Quite in contrast to the popular view of the Middle East as a flat monotonous expanse, the variation in natural environment is enormous. This is true not only for the varied wider regions (coastal areas, deserts, alluvia, etc.), but also on a local scale, where great ecological variations exist in distinct micro-environments. Two examples demonstrate this. Babylonia, the area between the Persian Gulf and modern-day Baghdad, may seem an area with little diversity, relying on irrigation by the Euphrates and Tigris rivers for its survival. The two rivers run through a narrow plain that is extremely flat: it rises less than 30 meters above sea level some 500 kilometers inland. But very different geographical zones are contained within that stretch. In the north is a desert plateau where agriculture is only possible in the narrow river valleys. Somewhat downstream the rivers enter the alluvium, but still have clearly defined channels. South of the city of Babylon, however, they break up into numerous branches that run almost on top of the land, and their courses shift constantly. Finally, south of the ancient cities of Ur and Lagash, the region becomes completely marshy, and agriculture is impossible.[1] Several ecological zones are present in close proximity to one another. The far north is uninhabitable, the northern plain allows an irrigation agriculture of square low fields over large areas, while the southern plain requires elongated fields lined with furrows. The south had access to varied resources from the marshes: fish, reeds, and so on; the north relied more on animal husbandry. Great differences are thus visible in the area we summarily call Babylonia.

In the mountains of the Lebanon there was an even greater variety of natural environments. The Beqa'a Valley in the rift between the Lebanon and Anti-Lebanon ranges is some 100 kilometers long by 25 kilometers wide. On a map this small area looks uniform, but there are numerous local differences in its ecology. The high mountains cause plenty of rainfall on the western side; the area to the east is consequently dry. Springs, while numerous, are unevenly dispersed through the region and the Orontes River is not a good source for irrigation water. Hence, wetlands alternate with very dry areas, zones of intensive horticulture with zones where only animal herders can survive. The valley is thus a collection of what has been called micro-ecologies, each enabling different lifestyles.[2]

Within the vast area of the Near East, we have to recognize great variability in natural environments. However, there are certain basic characteristics with important repercussions for the livelihood of the inhabitants. Agriculture, the prerequisite for the permanent settlement of populations, is difficult. Rainfall is scarce almost everywhere because the high mountains in the west leave large parts of the Near East in the rain shadow. Agriculture that relies on rain, so-called dry farming, requires at least 200 mm of water annually. The 200 mm isohyet, that is, the line that connects those points of equal rainfall, runs through the Near East in a great arch from the southern Levant to the Persian Gulf. The mountains and foothills receive more rain, the plains less to almost none at all. But the line on the map is misleading: annual variability is great and there is a large marginal zone which at times receives sufficient rain, at times does not. Rainfed agriculture is only guaranteed when one reaches the 400 mm isohyet. The effect on human settlement is drastic. South of the 400 mm isohyet, agriculture is possible only if rivers are available to provide irrigation water. The Tigris and Euphrates rivers afford a lifeline to the Mesopotamian plain where rainfall is scarce and erratic. These two rivers and their tributaries, the Balikh, Habur, Greater and Lesser Zab, Diyala, Kerkheh, and Karun, originate in the mountains of Turkey and Iran where rainfall and snow feed them. As perennial rivers, their water can be tapped to irrigate the crops with careful management and using techniques that will be discussed later in this chapter.

Long periods of drought could easily have occurred in the time span we study here, however. While we can assume that over the last 10,000 years the climate in the Near East has not fundamentally changed, it is certain that even marginal variations could have had serious consequences for the inhabitants. The question arises as to whether the so-called Dark Ages resulted from a drying of the climate which made rainfed agriculture impossible in zones usually relying on it, and which lowered the rivers to such an extent that irrigated areas were substantially reduced. Or should we focus on human factors in trying to explain such periods? So far, insufficient data on the ancient climate are available to serve as a historical explanation for the drastic political and economic changes we observe.

A second important characteristic of the geography of the Near East involves the question of boundaries. These are created by mountains, seas, and deserts, which could all be crossed, although in limited places and with special technology only. The Zagros and Taurus mountains were massive barriers to the states of Mesopotamia, and could only be entered through the river valleys. Military expansion was thus always restricted there, even by such mighty powers as Assyria. The mountain ranges in the Levant left a narrow corridor only for movement from northern Syria to Egypt, and control of individual valleys denied passage between the two. Mountains were also the habitat of many uncontrollable groups that often tried to enter the states we will study. To the dwellers of the plains, the mountains must have presented a fearful and inhospitable sight.

Seas form a very different kind of boundary, the Mediterranean and the Persian Gulf being the most important. They do create a border, but once crossed, they provide access to regions at great distances. Thus the Persian Gulf and the span of marshes at its head form the southern border of Mesopotamia, but from the fifth millennium on, inhabitants of Mesopotamia sailed in primitive crafts to regions along the Gulf coasts. In the late fourth millennium sailors may have reached Egypt that way, and in the third and early second millennia direct seaborne contacts with the Indus Valley were common. The Mediterranean was a different prospect. Only a few harbors existed along its coast, none south of Jaffa. By the late third millennium, however, Aegean sailors had ships that could reach the Syro-Palestinian coast, and in the second half of the second millennium, shipping throughout the eastern Mediterranean was common. Around 1200, technological innovations on boats enabled people from Syro-Palestinian harbors to sail long distances, and the entire Mediterranean came within their reach. First-millennium Phoenicians established colonies as far west as Spain and the Atlantic coast of North Africa.

More formidable as a border was the great desert stretching between Mesopotamia and the Levant. For millennia, people from Mesopotamia could only make their way along the Tigris or Euphrates river valleys and cross the northern Syrian steppe to reach the Mediterranean. With the domestication of the camel around the year 1000, direct passage became possible, although infrequent. Even when small companies of people could cross directly through it, the lack of water still forced armies to take the age-old roundabout route through the Levant and northern Syria to get from Egypt to Mesopotamia. The desert, like the mountains, was home to groups feared and hated by the settled people, nomads whose lifestyles were despised and who were impossible to rule. Even if the desert could be crossed, the states of the Near East could not overpower its inhabitants.

This permeability of boundaries not only allowed Near Easterners to move outward, but also enabled outsiders to enter the region. The Near East's position at the juncture of three continents is unique in the world. Populations from Africa, Europe, and Asia have moved into the region from early pre-history till today, causing interaction, exchange of technologies, and increasing pressures on the natural resources. This may explain why so many "revolutions" in the lifestyles of humans have taken place there: the emergence of modern humans, of farming, of cities, and of the first empires. It is certain that popula-tion movements took place during ancient Near Eastern history, but to study them is difficult. While we can say with confidence that the Mongol and Turkish tribesmen who invaded Iran and Iraq in the thirteenth century AD came from inner Asia, we are not so certain about the origins of the Hittites, for instance. Perhaps, as speakers of an Indo-European language, they indeed came from a region north of India and arrived in Anatolia in the early second millennium, as many historians used to think. But the presumed Indo-European home-land north of India could be a pure phantom, and speakers of Indo-European languages could just as easily have resided in Anatolia from prehistory on, only entering the historical record in the early second millennium. The same is true for so many populations – Sumerians, Hurrians, Sea Peoples, Israelites, and so on – who once were thought to have invaded parts of the Near East. To reprise the earlier metaphor, the Near East is this one area of light in a world of prehistoric darkness. People suddenly appear in its spotlight. It may be impossible to establish whether such people came from far away or nearby – or if they had always been in the region where they first appear in the documentation.

1.4 Prehistoric Developments

We must undertake the study of the long cultural evolution of prehistory from a perspective that takes the entire Near East into account. Despite the great ecological diversity in the region, we see simultaneous developments in several places. The absolute chronology of events is still uncertain and debated, but we have a good idea about overall trends. Especially with the beginning of the Neolithic period around 9000, important cultural developments occurred that established the setting for the later historical Near Eastern civilizations.

The most crucial technological development was agriculture, which enabled the existence of societies in year-round settlements. This evolution took place over several millennia and involved the domestication of plants, primarily cereals, and of animals. The archaeological sites where we see these changes occur are usually located at the borders of different ecological zones, whose occupants took advantage of varied plant resources and hunted different animals. The ecological variety of the Near East described above may in fact have been one of the reasons why agriculture evolved there so early. People became so used to having access to a variety of food resources that they sought to guarantee the supply by interfering in the natural growing cycles of preferred crops and animals.

For millennia, humankind had lived by gathering its food from local resources, and moving when these were exhausted. The hunting of wild animals probably complemented a diet that relied primarily on wild cereals, fruits, legumes, fish, shellfish, and whatever else the environment provided. Small groups were forced to move around seeking shelter in caves and the like. Their lifestyle should not necessarily be considered as harsh and difficult. Ethnographic studies have determined that the life of early farmers was more arduous than that of hunter-gatherers, especially in the resource-rich area of the Near East, where food could be readily collected without much effort. The question of why people moved toward agriculture thus remains difficult to answer. Settled life in larger communities may simply have been more socially appealing. Also, many of these changes in the interaction between humans and their natural environment may have been unintentional, their effects only noticed gradually after many seasons.

Direct control of the food supply via cereal agriculture was achieved through a series of probably inadvertent steps from the eleventh to seventh millennia as humans became more practiced at sowing, husbandry, harvesting, and storage. Wild cereals have two characteristics that cause problems for human consumers – they have weak stems so that their seeds easily disperse and fall to the ground before they are harvested. Also, it is hard to get at their seeds, which are covered with strong husks in order to prevent premature germination. When harvesting, people would gather more seeds that had not fallen to the ground from plants with stronger stems, and such plants would be promoted once seeds were sown. More consciously, people may have selected grains with thinner husks for sowing, hence propagating such species. Over many centuries, through selection and cross-breeding with wild grasses, the einkorn and emmer wheats that grow wild in the Near East mutated to develop into the modern bread and club wheats.

Selective hunting of wild animals also replaced previous indiscriminate killing. Wild herds were culled to procure a proper age and gender balance, and were protected from natural predators. Sheep and goats became the most common domesticates, and among them preference was given to breeds that provided the most resources, such as sheep with thick wool coats. Over time, humans became responsible for all aspects of the animals' existence, whose behavior had now totally diverged from that of their wild progenitors and whose physical attributes had become very different as well.

Thus there was not a sudden change from hunting-gathering to farming, but rather a slow process during which people increased their reliance on resources they managed directly, but still supplemented their diets by hunting wild animals. It is clear that the process was not irreversible. Sometimes populations had to return to a hunter-gatherer existence or increase their intake of wild resources when the domesticated supply did not meet their needs. We have to keep in mind that both lifestyles existed in the same geographical area: agriculture developed where wild resources were abundant.

Agriculture enabled an increase in continuous settlement by people. The various archaeological cultures we can distinguish between the years 9000 and 5000 demonstrate a greater permanence of residence, larger communities, and an increased usage of domesticated over wild resources. The house is the attribute of sedentary life that is best distinguished in the archaeological record. In the Levant, houses were built of stone or with stone foundations; elsewhere in the Near East their walls were of piled mud, and later of mudbrick. The settlements became increasingly large, which demonstrates the ability to provide food for greater numbers of people. A shift from round to rectangular houses took place in the ninth millennium, showing the cohabitation of larger groups of people with some type of social hierarchy and a specialization in room use. In the earliest villages of the ninth millennium, people used clay storage bins to keep wild and domesticated cereals, but in the eighth millennium they developed fired pottery. Although perhaps not a major technological breakthrough, since it was merely an extension of earlier storage practices and work with clay, it was useful for cooking and enabled people to store goods safely. Coincidentally, pottery provides the archaeologist with an extremely useful tool for dating excavated remains, in part because it was a constantly developing technology (see box 1.2).

By 7000, completely agricultural villages existed throughout the Near East, all of them located in areas with sufficient rainfall for farming. In Anatolia and the Levant, there was an abandonment or contraction of earlier sites and a return to less complex societies, however. The focus of subsequent cultural developments shifted at this time to the east, especially the region below the dry-farming area, namely the plains of Mesopotamia. Shortly after 7000, farming communities developed in areas of northern Mesopotamia with insufficient rainfall, consequently relying on irrigation. The technology of leading water from rivers and basins to crops had already been used much earlier in areas such as the Levant, but with the move of settlements into arid zones, irrigation became essential and better organized. Unlike the Nile in Egypt, which provides water in the late summer just when it is needed to prepare wet fields for planting seeds, the Tigris and Euphrates rivers rise in the late spring when almost full-grown plants can be damaged by too much water. The rivers in Mesopotamia are at their lowest when the sowing season arrives. A system of canals and storage basins had to be developed to control the water and

Box 1.2 *The use of pottery in archaeological research*

Ceramic remains provide an important tool to the archaeologist. Pottery is ubiquitous in the archaeological record, the shards are almost indestructible, and styles of decoration as well as pot shapes change relatively rapidly over time, indicating the tastes of distinct groups of people. Just as in our day the shape and decoration of soda bottles develop over time and we can date a photograph by the shape of the bottle in a person's hand, so the changing styles of pottery in antiquity can be used as a way of dating sites and the archaeological levels within them. Consequently, prehistoric cultures are often named for the type of pottery that represents them: Hassuna, Samarra, Ubaid, and so on, whose pottery styles were first identified in the sites with those names (see figure 1.1). When several ceramic assemblages are found in a stratigraphic sequence, we can establish their relative chronology. All *tells* of the Near East are covered with potsherds that represent the periods of occupation. Thus even without excavation, the archaeologist can determine when a site was inhabited on the basis of pottery remains.

allow it to enter the fields only when needed. The system did not have to be elaborate and could be managed by small communities, but still there had to be an awareness of the cycles of the rivers and the crops, and planning and organization were required to irrigate using the Mesopotamian rivers.

Small irrigation systems were created first in the foothills of the Zagros, and probably also at the edge of the marshes in southern Babylonia. Before the technology could be extended into southern Mesopotamia, however, it had to be further developed. The extreme flatness of the plain readily exposed fields to floods, especially from the Euphrates, which has almost no valley at all. The river, with its many branches and human-created canals, had to be carefully managed. Any time it overflowed, a natural levee developed from the deposit of silt left behind by the water losing its speed. While these could be reinforced artificially and turned into dikes, sedimentation between them often led to riverbeds being higher than the fields around them. There was no natural drainage of water deposited in the fields, and the high temperatures in the region led to evaporation and a high level of salt in the soil, arresting the growth of plants. Moreover, the water table rose after irrigation, damaging roots when it came too near the surface. Over the millennia, inhabitants of southern Mesopotamia developed the technology to irrigate increasingly larger areas, but it is important to remember that the practice started on a small scale, using the many branches of the Euphrates. Between 6000 and 5500, permanent settlement in the lower Mesopotamian plain became common and remained a constant feature.

Primarily on the basis of pottery styles, archaeologists delineate a sequence of cultures in the period from 7000 to 3800: Proto-Hassuna and Hassuna in

Figure 1.1 Samarra period decorated bowl from Tell al-Sawwan, Iraq. Courtesy of Columbia University, Department of Art History and Archaeology

Chart 1.1 Chronology of the prehistory of the Near East

date BC	Levant	Anatolia	N. Mesopotamia	S. Mesopotamia
9000				
	Proto-Neolithic (PPN A)			
8500				
	Aceramic Neolithic (PPN B–C)			
7000				
	Pottery Neolithic		Proto-Hassuna	
6500		Chatal Hüyük		
	Amuq B		Hassuna/Samarra	
6000				
	Halaf	Halaf	Halaf	Early Ubaid
5500				
5000				
4500	Ubaid	Ubaid	Ubaid	Late Ubaid
4000				Early Uruk
	Chalcolithic			
3500			Uruk	Late Uruk

the rainfed areas of northern Mesopotamia in the seventh millennium, and Samarra in the irrigated zone of the north in the late seventh millennium. The west of the Near East was characterized at the time by a less-developed culture identified as Amuq B. The sixth millennium saw a massive expansion of the north Mesopotamian Halaf culture that ranged over the entire rainfed zone abutting the Mesopotamian plain and extended into the Levant. Areas previously occupied by the Samarran culture have not yielded archaeological remains, but southern Mesopotamia became permanently settled by people using a cultural assemblage we call Ubaid. Around 4500, this Ubaid culture replaced the Halaf in the north and in the Zagros Mountains.

The most remarkable aspects of these cultures are their wide geographical spread and their long-distance contacts. Keeping in mind the fact that these were small communities without any organization beyond the village level, the spread of a cultural assemblage such as that of Halaf from the central Zagros to the Mediterranean coast is astonishing. There are limited remains and local differences are blurred, but aspects of Halaf's material remains are quite specific, such as the unique layout of its houses which stands out as a marker of this culture. At the same time, we observe that luxury materials were obtained from very distant regions. For instance, obsidian was only naturally available in central Anatolia, but it is found in sites throughout the Near East. The success of Chatal Hüyük, a large site in central Anatolia that existed from ca. 7200 to 6000, is often thought to have resulted from its trade in this volcanic stone. Less prestigious goods were obtained in distant regions as well. Ubaid pottery produced in southern Mesopotamia was found along the Persian Gulf as far south as Oman, and scholars have interpreted this as the remains of fishing and pearl-diving expeditions.

Another characteristic of these early cultures is their longevity. The Halaf culture lasted almost a millennium and was gradually infiltrated by that of the southern Ubaid. The latter's durability over almost two millennia, and the high degree of cultural continuity it demonstrates, are startling. These factors seem to suggest that once communities had settled in lower Mesopotamia, they retained a stable and local development. They preserved the same material culture throughout their existence, only gradually becoming more extensive and complex.

Primary among the social developments were the rise of a hierarchy and the centralization of powers and functions, a result of the growth in size of communities. There are fundamental differences visible between the north and the south of Mesopotamia in this respect. In the southern Ubaid culture, some members of the communities had a distinct status, as indicated by the larger size and the particular layout of the buildings they inhabited or supervised. The power of these newly developed elites seems to have derived from control over agricultural resources. Among the families forming communities, one would emerge to supervise the storage of harvests in a central location. This is already visible in the south, whereas the contemporary Halaf culture in the north exhibits a high degree of social homogeneity. When the Ubaid culture spread into Halaf territory after 5500, social differentiation arrived there as well. The new elites are visible to us in their claim to rare and exotic foreign goods. Possibly they were immigrants from the south who imposed a type of political authority over the weaker local families and controlled long-distance trade. Only late in the Ubaid period did they start to exercise the type of local agricultural dominance visible earlier in the south.

The physical focus of these centralized functions seems to have been a building that may already be called a temple. Starting in the mid-sixth millennium, the site of Eridu in the far south of the region shows a sequence of increasingly larger buildings on the same spot, culminating in a great temple of the late third millennium. Projecting the function of early historical temples back in time, it is likely that from the early Ubaid period onward, this building functioned both as a centralized place of worship and as a center for the collection and distribution of agricultural goods. In some of Eridu's archaeological levels, masses of fish bones have been found, which seem to be the remains of offerings made to the deity of the temple. A social organization beyond the individual household was thus developing within communities, with all families of the settlement contributing to the temple cult. There also developed a hierarchy of settlements in the far south of Mesopotamia, a few measuring 10 to 15 hectares surrounded by smaller ones that were usually only 0.5 to 2 hectares in size. This demonstrates that individual communities became integrated into a wider cooperative territorial organization.

The prehistoric evolutions summarily sketched here demonstrate that many of the cultural aspects of later Near Eastern history developed over long periods. A culmination of these processes occurred in the fourth millennium, when the coalescence of several innovations led to the establishment of Mesopotamian civilization. These events will be discussed in more detail in the next chapter.

NOTES

1   P. Sanlaville, "Considérations sur l'évolution de la basse Mésopotamie au cours des derniers millénaires," *Paléorient* 15/2 (1989), pp. 7–9.
2   Peregrine Horden and Nicholas Purcell, *The Corrupting Sea: A Study of Mediterranean History* (Oxford: Blackwell, 2000), pp. 54–9.

Part I
City-States

2
Origins: The Uruk Phenomenon

3500	3000	2500	2000	1500	1000	500

3500–3100	Late Uruk period
3400–3100	Uruk IV level, Eanna precinct, Uruk
3100–2900	Jemdet Nasr period
3100–3000	Uruk III level, Eanna precinct, Uruk

The fourth millennium was a crucial time in the history of humankind. During this period we see the culmination of several cultural processes leading to many innovations of seminal importance, including states, cities, and writing, all of which reveal the existence of a complex society organized by a hierarchy and with specialized labor. While these developments occurred in the south of Mesopotamia, their influence had considerable effects throughout the Near East.

In the early fourth millennium, a new type of pottery style appeared throughout the Near East. The carefully fashioned and decorated vessels of the previous cultures were replaced by rough and undecorated wheel-made plates, bowls, and jars which seem to be purely utilitarian (see figure 2.1). Rather than the result of the arrival of new populations, this development more likely reflects a change in attitudes toward these utensils. More people living together needed more pots, and these were mass produced in order to fulfill the increased demand. Indeed, in the Uruk period, which lasted for the whole of the fourth millennium, social changes of such magnitude took place, entirely as a result of indigenous forces, that they used to be referred to as "the urban revolution," on a par with

Figure 2.1 Beveled-rim bowls from the Uruk Mound at Abu Salabikh. Courtesy of Susan Pollock

the industrial revolution of the nineteenth century AD. The term revolution might be considered a misnomer for a process that occurred over one thousand years, but the importance of the changes should not be underestimated. They did not only comprise the origins of cities. Many other innovations were visible in other areas of society, the economy, technology, and culture that were equally significant for humanity. Anthropologists, for instance, often focus on the development of the state at this time, emphasizing the relationship between settlements and their surroundings. Historians often stress the origins of writing, which provides us with a whole new means of access to the people we study. Art historians often focus on the appearance of monumental art, signifying a completely new relationship between art and society. That these changes coincided was certainly not accidental. We will discuss some of them separately to understand what happened more clearly.

2.1 The Origins of Cities

The geographical center of developments in the Uruk period is in the extreme south of Mesopotamia, at the head of the Persian Gulf. Ironically, that area has yet to be thoroughly excavated for this period. The site after which the culture is named, Uruk, is really the only one where there is a meaningful exposure of archaeological remains, allowing us to reconstruct the physical appearance of the settlement. At that site two areas with important Uruk period remains were excavated. Most significant is the Eanna precinct, which was leveled and abandoned early in the third millennium and whose fourth-millennium remains were close to the surface. The archaeological exposure remains limited but sufficient to reveal the important functions of the Eanna complex, providing an understanding of social and economic developments. The stratigraphy of the Eanna complex excavations is highly complicated. It includes a sequence of layers numbered as Eanna XIV (the earliest) through III (the latest), which demonstrate changes in the material assemblage. As compensation for the lack of excavations of Uruk period sites in southern Mesopotamia, scholars have turned to an archaeological technique called settlement survey for a better understanding of developments. This technique allows us to identify the locations of sites and to calculate their sizes. Using size as an indicator of importance, it permits us to establish a hierarchy of sites. The largest and central sites can be considered to be cities, smaller ones villages.

While a simple, straightforward definition of a city is elusive, we intuitively associate it with certain characteristics: a substantial number of people living in close proximity to one another and having many occupations, including a variety that are non-agricultural. Historical circumstances determine to a great extent what can be regarded as a city and what not. The number of residents is not an absolute measure. For example, 30,000 inhabitants in today's world would indicate a town, but in classical Greece a city with this many people would have been considered large.[1] The size of a settlement is an important indicator of its status as a city, as well as the level of labor specialization by its inhabitants. In a city, the individual or individual family is not self-sufficient but relies on others for certain goods and services. The services provided are not limited to the inhabitants of the same settlement, however, and this provides perhaps the most important criterion of what constitutes a city. A city acts as a mediator between people, both those living inside its limits and those in permanent or seasonal settlements in the surroundings; it acts as a point of collection and redistribution of goods and provides a number of central services. The city is a center in its geographical setting, the focal point both for its own inhabitants and for the people living in the countryside.

It is this latter characteristic that allows us to ascertain the growth of cities in southern Mesopotamia in the fourth millennium. Starting in the Ubaid period, we can see an increase in the number of settlements there, with a beginning of differentiation in their size. Some may have had a small circle of subsidiary villages around them. Throughout the Near East, the end of the Ubaid period was characterized by a regression of the number of settlements, and some of the prominent sites were destroyed and abandoned. But in the early fourth millennium, with the start of the Uruk period, the number and size of sites vastly increased, especially in two regions of southern Mesopotamia – central and southern Babylonia. The number of people seems to have been almost equal in both regions, but in central Babylonia they lived in three centers of 30 to 50 hectares, while in the south one settlement alone dominated, with a size of some 70 hectares: Uruk (see map 2.1). The rapid increase of settled population at that time cannot be explained with certainty. It seems too fast to have been the result of indigenous population growth alone, even if the new agricultural conditions promoted demographic expansion. There may have been an increased sedentarization of semi-nomadic people previously unrecognizable in the archaeological record, or outsiders may have entered the region because of climatic changes or other reasons.

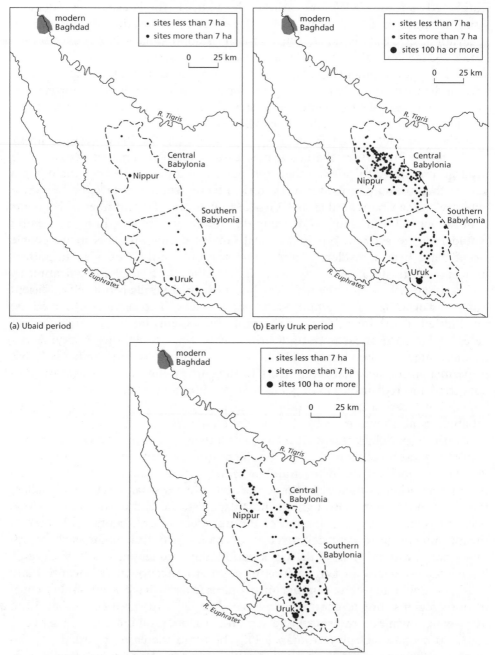

(a) Ubaid period

(b) Early Uruk period

(c) Late Uruk period

Map 2.1 Changing settlement patterns in Babylonia during the Ubaid and Uruk periods (based on Susan Pollock, *Ancient Mesopotamia: The Eden That Never Was* [Cambridge: Cambridge University Press, 1999], pp. 56–8)

The process of urban growth continued in the Late Uruk period with a difference between the center and the south of Babylonia. In the center of Babylonia, the increase of the permanently settled population was minor and can be explained as the result of natural growth. In the south around the city of Uruk, however, there was an enormous escalation in the area occupied by permanent settlement, from 81 to 210 hectares. A large part of that increase took place in Uruk itself, now 100 hectares in size, which became a real urban center surrounded by a set of secondary settlements. While population estimates are notoriously unreliable, scholars assume that Uruk inhabitants were still able to support themselves from the agricultural production of the fields surrounding the city that could be reached in a daily commute. But Uruk's dominant size in the entire region, far surpassing that of other settlements, indicates that it was a regional center and a true city. Indeed, it was the first city in world history.

The question of why these developments took place in the far south of Mesopotamia can only be answered tentatively. The variety of ecological niches nearby seems to have been a crucial factor. Uruk was located just inland of the marshes at the head of the Persian Gulf. Its agriculture relied on irrigation water provided by a branch or branches of the Euphrates, enabling abundant cultivation of cereals and orchard fruits, especially dates. In between the irrigated areas was the steppe, where animal husbandry of sheep and goats took place in addition to hunting. Nearby were the marshes, with a plentiful supply of fish and fowl, and where water buffaloes were herded for their milk. The great differentiation of food provided by each ecological niche led to labor specialization among the producers: fishermen, farmers, gardeners, hunters, and herdsmen were more productive if they devoted most of their time to the care of the resources closely available to them. Certain technological developments may also have made specialization more desirable. Thus the invention of the seed-plow, an instrument that deposits seeds in the furrow while it is being plowed, may have made farming more difficult and required the hand of an expert. Those people who specialized in the production of one resource were no longer self-sufficient, and a system of exchange was required to feed them. That service was provided by the center of the region, the city of Uruk. Other factors could certainly have contributed to the growth of that city. It is possible that changes in the climate and in watercourses led to the necessity for larger irrigation canals and an increased need for cooperation in agriculture, but it still seems that the need for exchange was the most crucial single element in the establishment of the city.

The vast majority of the population remained active in agriculture, even those living within the city itself. But a small segment of the urban society started to specialize in non-agricultural tasks as a result of the city's new role as a center in its geographical surroundings. Within the productive sector, there was a growth of a variety of specialist craftsmen. Already early in the Uruk period, the turn to undecorated utilitarian pottery was probably the result of specialized mass production. In early fourth-millennium level XII of the Eanna sequence at Uruk, a pottery style appears that is most characteristic of this process, the so-called beveled-rim bowl (see figure 2.1). It is a rather shallow bowl, which was crudely made in a mold, hence in only a limited number of standard sizes. For some unknown reason, many were discarded, often still intact, and thousands have been found all over the Near East. The beveled-rim bowl is one of the most telling diagnostic finds for identifying an Uruk period site. Its use will be discussed later. Of importance here is the fact that it was produced rapidly in large amounts, most likely by specialists in a central location.

A variety of documentation indicates that other goods were made by skilled artisans as well, while earlier on their production was undertaken as one of many duties by a member of the family. Certain images depict groups of people, most likely women, involved in the weaving of textiles, an activity we know from later third-millennium texts to have been vital in the economy and to have been centrally administered. A specialized metal smelting workshop may have been excavated in a small area at Uruk. It contained a number of channels lined by a sequence of holes, ca. 50 centimeters deep, all showing burn marks and filled with ashes. This has been interpreted as the remains of a workshop where molten metal was scooped up from the channel to be poured into molds in the holes. Some type of mass production by specialists was involved here.

Objects themselves suggest that they were the work of skilled professionals. In the Late Uruk period, there first appeared a type of object that remained characteristic for Mesopotamia throughout its entire history: the cylinder seal. This was a small cylinder, usually no more than 3 centimeters high and 2 centimeters in diameter, of shell, bone, faience, or a variety of stones (e.g., carnelian, lapis lazuli, crystal), on which a scene was carved in mirror image. When rolled over a soft material – primarily the clay of bullae, tablets, or clay lumps attached to boxes, jars, or doorbolts – the scene would appear an indefinite number of times in relief, easily legible (cf. figure 4.3). The cylinder seal was an important administrative device and will be discussed later. The technological knowledge needed to carve it was far superior to that for stamp seals, which had appeared in the early Neolithic period. From the first appearance of cylinder seals, the carved scenes could be highly elaborate and refined, indicative of the work of specialist stonecutters. Similarly, the Late Uruk period shows the first monumental art, relief and statuary in the round, made with such a degree of mastery that only a professional could have produced them.

The specialization of productive labor led to the need for an authority to organize the exchange of goods, as individual families were no longer self-sufficient. This authority required an ideological foundation shared by the participants in the system to make it acceptable for them to contribute part of their production in return for something else in the future. In Uruk-period Mesopotamia, that ideology was provided by religion: goods were received by the god of the city and redistributed to the people. The temple, the house of the god, was the central institution that made the system work. Continuing a trend that had started in the early Ubaid period, temples in the Late Uruk period became the most monumental buildings in the settlements, constructed at great expense of labor as physical indicators of their prominent role within society. Two temple complexes existed simultaneously at Uruk, the Eanna precinct and the less-explored Anu-ziggurat (temple tower). The structures of the Eanna complex were the most elaborate and were rebuilt several times in the Uruk IV period (we distinguish the earlier IVb from the later IVa levels). Within an area surrounded by a perimeter wall, several enormous buildings were in use simultaneously. These were not only large, in the order of 50 by 80 meters, but also extensively decorated with a technique that was typical for the Late Uruk period. Within the walls were stuck clay cones colored white, black, and red, which formed mosaics in geometrical patterns on the surface. In one building these cones were of stone, a material more difficult to obtain in the region of Uruk than clay.

The buildings presented an impressive sight and a visual focus for the sur-roundings of Uruk, which was located in an extremely flat region. They had a cultic role in that goods were offered to the god(s). One of the major works of art of the period, the Uruk vase (see box 2.1), pictorially expresses the role of the Eanna temple complex in Uruk society: it collected the produce of the land as if it were an offering to the goddess. A human, more prominent than the others surrounding him because of his height and dress, acts as an intermediary. We can most likely identify him with the head of the temple organization, perhaps referred to by the title "lord," EN in Sumerian.

Box 2.1 *The Uruk vase*

Found in a deposit of cult objects from Uruk III levels was an almost 1-meter-high alabaster vase, the surface of which is entirely carved with an elaborate scene (see figure 2.2). It depicts a procession of naked men carrying bowls, vessels, and baskets containing farm produce. Ears of grain and sheep and goats in the bottom register summarily represent the agriculture of the region. The high point of the relief's story is where a female figure faces the human ruler, who is ornately dressed with an attendant carrying the train of his garment. At some later date the depiction of the ruler was excised from the scene, but we can reconstruct his appearance from con-temporaneous representations on other objects. The female can be identified as the goddess Inanna by the symbols standing behind her: two so-called reed-ring bundles, which acted as doorposts in the reed homes of the time, were the basis of the writing of Inanna's name in later cuneiform script. Beyond these symbols are placed three animals, and storage jars for liquids and solid foods. Two small human figures, prob-ably statues, stand on pedestals. A female statue has the symbol of Inanna behind her, while a male statue holds in his hands a stack of bowls and something like a box, which together form the shape of the cuneiform sign for "lord," EN in Sumerian. That sign is the most common in the tablets from the period and seems to indicate a high temple official. While not inscribed with a text, the Uruk vase relief can be read as describing the human ruler offering the region's produce to the goddess.

Figure 2.2 The Uruk vase, partly reconstructed drawing of the relief, from Marc Van De Mieroop, *The Ancient Mesopotamian City*, p. 32

The temple's role in the collection and redistribution of goods created the need for an entirely new class of specialist – the administrator. The economy became so complex that accounting mechanisms were necessary to record goods coming into and going out of the central organization. This required the skills of people capable of working with the tools and techniques of a bureaucracy. Standard measures for amounts of dry and liquid goods, for land, for labor, and for time were in place, and writing, the technology to record them for future consultation, had originated. In considering changes in the society, it is important to realize that all this bureaucratic activity was the domain of a specialized group of people.

The specialization of labor that characterized the establishment of urban life in southern Mesopotamia caused a fundamental restructuring of society. The process of social differentiation culminated in the existence of a stratified society in which professional occupation primarily determined one's rank in the hierarchy. The large majority of people still were farmers, fishermen, herders, and so on, living in communities with little social differentiation beyond that within the individual family. These communities were probably in a tributary relationship with the city and provided part of their income to it, but they remained otherwise socially free and owned the land they worked. Many of the city-residents (we are unable to determine what percentage, however) were part of the temple organization, whose members were wholly dependent on the former for their survival. They were organized along strictly hierarchical lines. Most indicative of the urban hierarchy is a text called the "Standard List of Professions" (see document 2.1). It appeared first at the end of the Late Uruk period, thus amongst the first texts written, and was copied faithfully for some 1500 years, the later versions being clearer to us than the earlier ones. The list provides in several columns the titles of officials and names of professions, ordered in a hierarchy starting with the highest rank. While the first entry is not entirely comprehensible to us, later Mesopotamians equated it with the Akkadian word for king, which was probably an anachronistic way of indicating that the highest official of the land was meant. The following entries in the "Standard list of professions" contain a number with the element NAM$_2$, which we think represents "leader," and with the sign GAL, which means "great." The titles include such terms as "leader of the city," or "of the plow," and "great one of the cattle pen," or "of the lambs." The list contains terms for priests, gardeners, cooks, smiths, jewelers, potters, and others. While not fully understood, it is clear that it provides an inventory of specialist professions within the cities.

At the top of the Uruk society, then, stood a man whose powers derived from his role in the temple. Hence, scholars often call him a "priest-king." At the bottom of the social ladder of temple dependents were the people involved in production, both agricultural and otherwise. How extensive this group was remains impossible to determine, but through a projection from third-millennium conditions, we assume that the temple had a staff that could take care of all its own needs. In the third millennium, dependent laborers were given rations, fixed amounts of barley, oil, and cloth, as a reward for their services. It is likely that such a system already existed in the Late Uruk period. The Uruk IV tablets contain accounts of grain distributed to numbers of workmen, which seem to be precursors of later ration lists. The issuing of rations to numerous people may explain the abundance of the beveled-rim bowl in the archaeological record. These bowls, in a limited number of sizes, possibly functioned as containers for measuring out barley rations. The resemblance of the early cuneiform sign for ration (NINDA) and the beveled-rim bowl supports this suggestion. If correct, the first appearance of the beveled-rim bowl in the mid-fourth millennium would attest to a system of grain distribution already at that time. A fundamental opposition existed in this early period between the temple dependents, who were provided for yet unfree, and the inhabitants of the countryside, free but uninsured against disasters such as bad harvests. The temple, located in the city, was a focal point for all, however, and through its collection of tribute drew the entire region together. A state, albeit small, had developed by the late fourth millennium where the city held organizational controls.

2.2 The Development of Writing and Administration

Bureaucracy enabled control of the regional economy in the urban centers. By the end of the Uruk period, there existed a system of recordkeeping with texts, which lay at the basis of the subsequent history of the cuneiform writing system in ancient Mesopotamia. The Uruk system is traditionally called proto-cuneiform because the signs are drawn into the clay with thin lines rather than being impressed with wedges, as is the later cuneiform script. There is no need to see a conceptual difference between the earliest script and later developments, however. This is the first time in human history that writing was invented (although some scholars credit this to Egypt), and the first evidence for real script comes from the city of Uruk itself. The earliest tablets appear in the Uruk IVa and III archaeological layers of the Eanna precinct. These terms have become used to refer to stages in the development of the script itself, and as such applied to texts found outside Uruk.

Figure 2.3   Uruk IV tablet (W20907). Courtesy of Hans J. Nissen

Accounting provides two sets of data: a record of quantities, and an identification of the person or office involved in the transaction as a participant or supervisor. The second element can be indicated with techniques other than writing, such as the use of a seal. From the seventh millennium on, stamp seals were impressed on jars or on lumps of clay attached to containers, providing an identification of the authority that guaranteed the contents. In the middle of the Uruk period, the stamp was replaced by the cylinder seal, which enabled speedier coverage of large surfaces. Numerous seals are attested, especially known through their impression on clay lumps, with a large variety of pictorial imagery. Each seal belonged to an individual official or to an administrative office; their identity could be recognized through the design. The profusion of distinguishable seals demonstrates the presence of a class of officials in the city of Uruk who supervised transactions and guaranteed their legitimacy by attaching their mark of authority.

The seals do not disclose the quantity or actual contents involved in a transaction. Several techniques to record such information seem to have been tried out at the same time or in quick succession, and are documented in various sites throughout the Near East. At Uruk itself the archaeological stratigraphy is so confused that we cannot establish a sequence of techniques there. At the west Iranian site of Susa, however, we see, prior to the archaeological level corresponding to Uruk IV, a level where bullae first appeared, followed by one with numerical tablets. Bullae are hollow spheres of clay with seals rolled all over their surface, containing groups of small objects that we call tokens. The latter are stone and clay geometric objects, shaped as cones, spheres, disks, cylinders, and many other forms. These are thought to record the measure of a particular item (goods, animals, humans). The receipt of three units of barley, for example, could have been acknowledged by handing over three tokens representing one unit each. It is likely that larger tokens of the same form indicated a higher unit in a metrological system. They were kept together in the clay envelope, which was sealed to guarantee the contents through the authority of the sealer.

As consultation of such records was impossible without destroying them, the idea arose to impress marks on the exterior surface. Simultaneously there appear bullae onto which impressions were made, most likely by the tokens inserted inside, and solid tablets onto which sets of numerical signs were traced. The "numerical tablets" do not reveal to us what items are accounted for, but the metrological system and the shape of the numerals must have provided such information to the people using them. These recording devices were found at Uruk and other sites where Uruk influence extended. Only at Uruk itself and in Susiana in western Iran do records appear that remove this ambiguity: numbers were combined with one or two signs indicating what was involved, sheep, grain, textiles, etc. While the two regions shared the same system, immediately afterwards they developed distinct and independent systems of true writing. In the archaeological levels Uruk IVa and III, the proto-cuneiform script appeared; somewhat later the proto-Elamite appeared in Susiana.

Proto-Elamite remains undeciphered because subsequent scripts in the region are very different in character and do not show later forms of the signs used. The Uruk system is better understood because its practices were continued in later cuneiform script, which is well known. The script contained two types of signs to indicate numbers and words. The existence of a numerical sign system was fundamentally important, since 85 percent of the proto-cuneiform tablets were accounts. Numbers of goods, animals, humans, and time had to be recorded. The Uruk IV notations seem complicated to us because seven different systems were used, each of which varied the physical shape of the numeral according to what was measured. For example, a sexagesimal system, relying on units with increments of ten and six, was used to account for animals, humans, and dried fish, among other things. A bisexagesimal system, which diverges from the previous one as its units also show increments of two, was used for processed grain products, cheese, and fresh fish. Volumes of grain or surfaces of fields were measured differently. The basic sequence of units varied, then, from system to system (see chart 2.1). Although the shape of the number signs could differ between systems, the same shapes are found in various systems but sometimes with different values. For example, ● indicates 10 when counting discrete objects, but 18 when the surface of a field was measured. In total, there were sixty different number signs.

Chart 2.1 Examples of systems of weights and measures used in Uruk period accounts

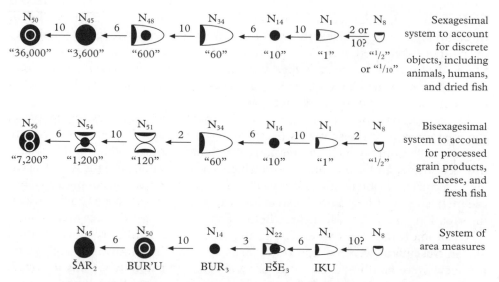

Based on Hans J. Nissen, Peter Damerow, and Robert K. Englund, *Archaic Bookkeeping: Early Writing and Techniques of Economic Administration in the Ancient Near East* (Chicago and London: University of Chicago Press, 1993), pp. 28–9.

A much larger group of signs, some 900, designated non-numerical concepts. Each sign stood for a word, a physical entity such as barley or cow, or an action such as distribution or receipt. The origin of the sign shapes is a matter of controversy. The ideas that they were based on drawings of the objects they signify or that they were two-dimensional renderings of the shapes of "tokens" do not by themselves explain the shapes of all signs. Various sources of inspiration were involved. Some of the shapes reflect the physical object represented or a part of it, such as an ox-head for an ox. Others are purely arbitrary in shape, such as a circle with a cross to indicate a sheep. New signs were created by combining several basic ones, slanting them, or cross-hatching parts of them. For example, the area of the mouth on a human head was marked with hatchings in order to indicate the word mouth, or the sign for water was added to that for head to indicate the verb "to drink." In order for the system to function, the meaning of these signs had to be known to all who used them, and conventions must have existed to enable someone to recognize the writer's intent and to guide the creation of new signs. These conventions are mostly unclear to us.

The word signs are crucial for the second group of tablets found at Uruk, the lexical texts, which make up 15 percent of the Uruk corpus. They are lists of words designating cities, officials, animals, plants, and manufactured goods, always in the same sequence. Their function was to show scribes how to write signs, and many exemplars are the work of students copying out parts of a list. Such texts remain part of the Mesopotamian corpus for the entirety of its history, later expanded to thousands of entries and giving translations of words in one or more languages, as well as an indication of how to pronounce them in Sumerian. Lexical texts are an integral part of the Mesopotamian cultural tradition, reflecting an organization of the vocabulary for practical purposes. Yet ideological concerns also informed the order given. First, the grouping of words in the same list indicates that a system of classification was used. Second, the ordering of words in a list may have been important: our interpretation of the "Standard List of Professions" as showing a social hierarchy suggests that the ranks of officials had been systematized and that their relative importance was established.

The proto-cuneiform signs show little connection to the spoken language, but there are indications that people speaking Sumerian developed them. They represented the Sumerian word for mother, AMA, for example, by the drawing a star into a box-shaped sign. As the star could be read AM, it intimated the pronunciation of the entire sign. There are other such examples that make clear that the inventors of the signs wanted to render their spoken language. The phonetic value of signs permitted their use to indicate terms beyond the names of concrete objects. The rebus principle was employed to extend their range. For example, the sign for "reed" was used to indicate the verb "to return," as both words sounded alike in Sumerian, GI. The majority of Sumerian words were monosyllabic. Consequently, the signs to write them could also be used to render syllabically a longer word or a grammatical element. A person's name

Document 2.1 *Lexical lists*

From the very beginning of writing in Mesopotamia the tablets included a genre we call lexical texts. They provided long lists of words of the same categories, such as designations of professions, animals, objects, and so on. The lists remained a central part of writing until the end of the use of the cuneiform script, and in the first millennium included many tablets with hundreds of entries each. They appeared not only in Babylonia but also in all other areas where cuneiform was written from the third millennium on. They were at first monolingual Sumerian, and later on included translations into other languages, especially Akkadian, and indications of how to pronounce the Sumerian terms. An important early example was a list of professional designations, *The Standard List of Professions*, which appeared from the Uruk IV period on and was faithfully copied until the Old Babylonian period, 1500 years later. It provides a sequence of some 120 terms, which we think were organized to reflect a hierarchy beginning with the most important official. Because of the list's antiquity we cannot translate most of the words, however. The popularity of the list was enormous, even though many of the terms found in it were not in use in contemporary documents. Manuscripts of it appeared in numerous Babylonian cities for the entire period from Uruk IV to the early second millennium. Outside Babylonia manuscripts appeared at Ebla in western Syria and at Susa in western Iran. In Ebla the list was used as the basis for another one that taught scribes how to pronounce Sumerian signs (the Ebla syllabary).

We read its first five lines as follows in Sumerian:

NAMEŠDA (written with the signs ŠITA.GIŠ.KU)
NÁM KAB
NÁM DI
NÁM NÁM
NÁM URU

The meanings of these terms are vague to us, as the words do not appear in context and no translation into another, better understood, language is provided in the list. Yet, although the list was no longer copied after the Old Babylonian period, terms from it appear in later lexical texts when the scribes included a guide to pronunciation and an Akkadian translation. They wrote, for example for line 1:

eš-da ŠITA.GIŠ.KU *šar-ru.*

The last word is the Akkadian term for "king," and strongly suggests that the first Sumerian entry in the Uruk *Standard List of Professions* referred to the highest official in the urban society.

could be spelled out with several syllables. Cuneiform writing was never used to give a full phonetic rendering of a text, however, even if it had the ability to do so. Throughout the history of its use, a single sign could be written to record a word, such as "king," irrespective of the language of the text or the grammatical form of the word. It was only in the mid-third millennium that elements of the conjugation of Sumerian verbs were written down. Only in the early second millennium, when Sumerian was probably a dead language, was a consistent effort made to record all grammatical elements in a sentence. It is important to keep in mind that cuneiform is a script, not a language. Just as the Latin alphabet has the potential to record any language, cuneiform script could do the same, and a large number of ancient Near Eastern languages were written in it (see box 2.2). We can only determine the identity of the language based on the syllabic writing of words, or on grammatical elements. The script invented in the Late Uruk period had all the elements of cuneiform writing. It developed further by reducing the number of signs, increasing the use of syllables, and changing the signs themselves, replacing curvy lines drawn into the clay by increasingly rectilinear ones impressed onto it. The triangular shape of a single line was the result of the impression of the head of the stylus into the clay and the pushing down of the side of the stylus underneath it. This shape led to our modern designation of the script as cuneiform, that is, wedge-shaped writing.

In order for accounting to function properly, a fully developed metrology had to exist as well. In the Late Uruk period, a complete system of weights and measures was used that lay at the basis of much of the later Mesopotamian system. The fundamental units were inspired by natural phenomena and ordered with a mixture of the sexagesimal and decimal systems that characterized the numerals. In the recording of time, a year consisted of twelve months of thirty days each, and an additional month was added intermittently to adjust the cycle to the solar year. In weights, the load a man could carry, a talent, was subdivided into sixty minas, each of which contained sixty shekels. Lengths used the forearm as the basic unit, subdivided into thirty fingers. Six forearms made up a reed. A set of equivalences may also have been established already at this time in order to facilitate the exchange of goods measured in different ways. These equivalences remained basically the same for the entirety of Mesopotamian history: one shekel of silver = one gur of grain = six minas of wool = twelve silas of sesame oil.

There was thus not an evolution of precursors to writing, from bullae with tokens to tablets with signs impressed on them, as is very often suggested. These so-called stages coincided and are to be seen as different and competing attempts at conceptualizing the surroundings. The most successful and consequential of these attempts ended up being the cuneiform writing system. It provided a new way to signify the physical world surrounding its users, and organized that world as a logical system that could be expressed through writing. The development of writing was thus a conceptual breakthrough, not merely an administrative one.

Box 2.2 *Languages of the ancient Near East*

The Near East always had people speaking various languages living side by side. Not every vernacular found its way into the written record, and oftentimes only the names of people give us an idea of what language they spoke. All languages could be written in cuneiform script, which was always the dominant writing system in the region until the last few centuries of the first millennium BC. In that millennium alphabetic scripts began to be used throughout the Near East and slowly supplanted cuneiform.

The most extensively written languages of Mesopotamia were Sumerian and Akkadian. The first was a language without any known cognates, and with a very distinct grammar and vocabulary. It was spoken throughout the third millennium in the south of Mesopotamia. By the early second millennium, it was only used by bureaucrats and cult personnel; the date of its disappearance as a spoken language remains uncertain. Akkadian was a Semitic language related to Hebrew, Arabic, and many other languages of the Near East, but of a somewhat different grammatical structure. Its verbal system classifies it as an "east Semitic" language, while the others are "west Semitic." Akkadian was written and spoken from the mid-third millennium to the late first over a wide geographical region. There were two main dialects: Assyrian in the north of Mesopotamia, Babylonian in the south. Both dialects show lexical and grammatical variations over time and according to the genre of the texts. We use the terms Old, Middle, and Neo-Babylonian and Assyrian for chronological phases, and Standard Babylonian to refer to a literary dialect found both in the south and the north. Earlier versions of Akkadian were used prior to the second millennium. We speak of Old Akkadian for the dialects found in texts from the Akkad and Ur III dynasties. The traces of the Semitic language found in texts predating these periods are more difficult to identify, and the term proto-Akkadian is used to refer to it. Babylonian was the language of culture and diplomacy throughout the Near East during the latter half of the second millennium. It was used in writing from Anatolia to Egypt, from the Levant to the Zagros Mountains, always written in cuneiform on clay tablets. It was used in addition to native languages and scripts, such as Ugaritic, a west Semitic language recorded in an alphabetic script in western Syria.

In the mid-third millennium, various other Semitic dialects were recorded in cuneiform script, the one from Ebla being the best known. The language shows grammatical affinities with later west Semitic languages, but also with what was spoken in Babylonia at the time. A commonly spoken west Semitic language in the early second millennium was Amorite, found from western Syria to southern Babylonia. No texts completely written in that language are preserved, however, and it is primarily known from the names of people. The same is true for the first-millennium west Semitic language Aramaic, which had a great vernacular spread. It was mainly recorded in an alphabetic script on perishable materials and relatively few remains are known. Only a couple of Aramaic texts in cuneiform are known.

During the second millennium, the Hittites of central Anatolia used a large variety of languages, several of which were written in cuneiform. Those included Hittite, an Indo-European language, and Hurrian, linguistically related only to Urartian, a language used in first-millennium eastern Anatolia. Hurrian was in use in northern Syria from the mid-third millennium on, and was very important in that area until the late second millennium, but few texts written in that language are preserved.

Finally, Elamite was written from the third through the first millennium in south-western Iran. It was linguistically distinct from the other Near Eastern languages and evolved over time. In certain periods it was supplanted by Akkadian as the language of administration in western Iran. It was still written by the Persians in the fifth century, but these rulers used numerous other languages across their vast empire, including Old Persian written in an alphabetic form of cuneiform.

The tools of bureaucracy, script, seals, measures, and weights, all continued to develop in later Near-Eastern history based on the foundation laid in the Uruk period. To a certain extent, these elements are what defines the ancient Near East: cuneiform writing on clay tablets, the cylinder seal, and the mixture of decimal and sexagesimal units in numerals. While there were local variations and changes over time, the continuation of the elements that we first observe in the Late Uruk period shows how important that period was for the formation of Near Eastern culture.

2.3   The "Uruk Expansion"

The aforementioned developments all occurred in the far south of Meso-potamia in the area around the city of Uruk. We are unable to determine whether similar processes took place independently in other parts of southern Mesopotamia because of an overall lack of excavation of Uruk period levels there. Nevertheless, the sheer size of Uruk, roughly 100 hectares, suggests that it was an unusual center whose complexity led to the use of writing and the organization of a city-state. Ironically, much more archaeological information for the Uruk period comes from regions outside southern Mesopotamia, especially western Iran, northern Syria, and southern Turkey. In the mid-fourth millennium, local developments there became fundamentally influenced by southern Mesopotamia. A variety of interactions between local populations and people from the Uruk region is attested, and some of the difficult questions are to determine why these interactions took place and to what extent local or foreign impulses caused change.

Just to the east of lower Mesopotamia is the area of south-west Iran, itself an alluvial plain below the Zagros Mountains, which is often called Susiana after the large site of Susa at its center. Although geographically similar to southern Mesopotamia and close in distance, travel between the two regions is difficult

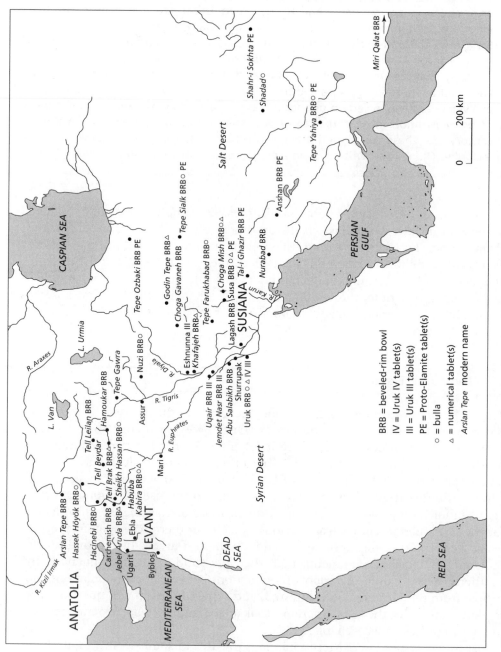

Map 2.2 The Uruk expansion (after Michael Roaf, *Cultural Atlas of Mesopotamia and the Ancient Near East* [Oxford: Equinox, 1990], pp. 64–5)

as they are separated by a string of large marshes. The nearest access route is in the foothills of the Zagros, going around the marshes. The difficulties of communication might explain why the cultures of the two areas remained distinct until the fourth millennium. As a result of indigenous processes, an initial centralization of power probably took place in the late fifth millennium at the site of Choga Mish. In the early fourth millennium, a new center emerged at Susa, which developed its own monumental architecture in the form of a massive platform atop which temples were built, although there are no archaeological remains to prove this. At the time of the Late Uruk period, Susa's material culture became entirely influenced by southern Mesopotamia. We find typical Late Uruk pottery in great quantity and the precursors of proto-cuneiform writing: bullae with tokens, numerical tablets, and tablets with numbers and one or two word signs. Susa had become a city in its own right, commanding resources from the entire Susiana region. Moreover, Susa extended its cultural influence over a wide geographical area in Iran. The beveled-rim bowl, which scholars consider to be inspired by the Uruk culture, appeared in sites all over the country. Examples have been excavated in the Zagros Mountains (e.g., Godin Tepe, Choga Gavaneh), in northern (e.g., Tepe Ozbaki, Tepe Sialk), central (e.g., Tepe Yahiya), and southern Iran (e.g., Nurabad). They were even found on the coast of modern Pakistan, near the Gulf of Oman (Miri Qalat). Some of these locations were more than a thousand kilometers from Susa, which we assume was the transit point for Uruk influences, as the contacts between these sites and Susa survived after the Uruk expansion had ceased. The situation in the north was different. In northern Iraq, Syria, and southern Turkey, elements of the Uruk culture appeared starting in the mid-fourth millennium, but the degree to which these affected local cultures varied. So far, no single site has been identified as the intermediary between Uruk and distant regions, as was the case with Susa in the east. In the early fourth millennium, the entire northern region was characterized by a low-level centralization of power in small centers. Southern influence had waned after the Ubaid period and the cultures attested are subsumed under the name Late Chalcolithic. In the mid-fourth millennium, Uruk influence spread throughout the region with different levels of intensity. In some places settlements of urban proportions were constructed on virgin soil. For example, Habuba Kabira on the Middle Euphrates became a densely inhabited and fortified city, with a cultural assemblage imported wholesale from southern Mesopotamia. Several other such settlements were built, and, because they display such a high degree of southern cultural influence, it is assumed that southern immigrants were the founders.

In other places Uruk people settled into existing settlements, creating enclaves for themselves. Their interaction with the local populations introduced innovations, such as monumental architecture, within the context of native traditions. For instance, at Tell Brak in north-east Syria a monumental temple was built showing a local cultic tradition in a southern-inspired architectural setting. The temple's plan, its location on a platform, its decoration with cone mosaics, and its contents were all ideas imported from the south. In still other places, the Uruk presence was restricted to a few buildings. But even there the influences on the local populations could be drastic. At Arslan Tepe in southern Turkey, for example, local elites seem to have been inspired to imitate southern practices and constructed a massive monumental building. Finally, there were ancient settlements, such as Tepe Gawra, where Uruk influence was completely absent.

The Uruk cultural elements that appeared in this region are building plans and decoration, pottery (especially the beveled-rim bowl), and precursors of writing, bullae with tokens and numerical tablets. Proto-cuneiform writing, found in Uruk IVa levels in the south, did not make its way into the north, so contacts must have ceased just before this development. These material elements are less important than the social change the Uruk expansion caused. Urban centers were suddenly established with the concomitant social hierarchy and economic organization. It remains unclear what was most important in this process, indigenous evolution or foreign influence. Local trends toward larger settlements and a hierarchy of settlements predated the Uruk expansion; certain places with predominantly local cultures, such as Hamoukar, attained urban proportions in the late fourth millennium. Uruk influence may thus have accelerated a process that had its roots in the local cultures. On the other hand, the massive foreign influence observed in a city like Habuba Kabira clearly shows a southern inspiration.

Aspects of Uruk culture are found beyond the spheres where influence was direct. The beveled-rim bowl is found at several sites near the north Syrian coast, for instance. Most intriguing is the possibility that Uruk influenced early Egypt, where in the late fourth millennium a number of cultural characteristics similar to those of southern Mesopotamia appeared: niched mudbrick architecture, decorative clay cones, some pottery styles, cylinder seals, and certain artistic motifs. The finds of some of these elements in central Egypt suggest that part of the contacts were made through travel via the Persian Gulf and the Red Sea rather than overland across Syria.

The most difficult challenge remains to explain why this expansion took place. For what reason did the young city-state or states of southern Mesopotamia decide to send out people to numerous distant places in order to settle there, bringing along their cultural baggage? The need to gain access to resources is most often thought to have inspired Uruk's expansion. What resources were sought is not obvious, however. Scholars often stress that southern Mesopotamia lacks wood, stone, and metals, and see the need to acquire these as the main reason for foreign contacts. That deficiency is exaggerated, however, and materials were locally available to compensate for it. It seems more appropriate to take the fundamental demographic and ideological changes that occurred in Uruk-times southern Mesopotamia into account. States had developed with a new type of ideology and a new social structure. Certain people held positions of importance never seen before and had influence over the lives of many. The newly emergent elites may have wished access to exotic materials, whose possession distinguished them from the rest of the people. Many luxury goods were only available outside Mesopotamia: semi-precious stones, gold, silver, and so on. The settlements to the east and north could be seen as colonies of southerners, assuring access to these resources through interaction with local populations. Moreover, the conviction that a god had influence beyond the city limits may have contributed to an expansionist ideology. Not only the immediate surroundings but also distant regions may have been considered as dependent on the city-god. Such ideological elements, while impossible to ascertain in the documentation, should not be entirely ignored in our interpretation of the Uruk expansion.

2.4   Uruk's Aftermath

The end of the Uruk period came with fundamental changes at home and abroad. Those outside southern Mesopotamia are the clearest to us, as we see a sudden discontinuation of contacts. Habuba Kabira, the fully southern installation in Syria, disappeared for unknown reasons. In places where local cultures had adopted Uruk practices, the older local traditions reemerged. Village life and social organization became the norm again in northern Mesopotamia and Syria. In the Susiana plain, the center at Susa seems to have been taken over by immigrants from the Zagros Mountains. Instead of political fragmentation, as in the north, the region became a state equivalent to what we find in southern Mesopotamia. We call it the proto-Elamite state because it seems to have been the precursor of later political entities in the area. Proto-Elamite culture maintained some Uruk traditions, but adapted them as local ones. It developed a distinct script, which differed from the contemporaneous Uruk script and was in use over a wide area of Iran. Tablets inscribed with the proto-Elamite script were excavated as far as 1200 kilometers from Susa. The Uruk-inspired centralization of power in the region of Susa led thus to a competing state there, which has been blamed for cutting off southern Mesopotamia's access to the Iranian plateau and areas further east. The timing of the collapse of the Uruk system is indicated by the discontinuation of accounting practices in the north and the independent development of a script in Susiana. The precursors of proto-cuneiform tablets are found everywhere, but not the Uruk IV-type tablets. The latter are found only at Uruk at the very end of the period (in archaeological level IVa), and it seems thus that contacts with outlying areas were cut off just before.

What happened in Uruk itself is hard to discern. The monumental buildings that dominated the Eanna complex were razed and the entire area was leveled. On top, in level III, a new set of buildings was constructed wherein were found numerous tablets, more elaborate than those in Uruk IV. Small finds of closely related tablets were found at Jemdet Nasr (ca. 150 tablets) and Uqair (ca. 35 tablets) in the north of Babylonia. Archaeologically, this period is called Jemdet Nasr after the site where its cultural assemblage was first found. The city of Uruk continued to be substantial in size, but other southern Mesopotamian centers developed as well, as the non-urban population moved into them, possibly as the result of social upheavals or invasions. The far-flung contacts of the earlier centuries ceased, but the Jemdet Nasr culture penetrated more profoundly into nearby regions, such as the Diyala River valley, which had been marginal before then. Moreover, direct contact with the Persian Gulf area is attested. There is thus a reorganization of society in southern Mesopotamia into more and similar-scale centers with more profound influence in areas nearby. The bases for further political development in the region were in place.

NOTE

1   Paul Bairoch, *De Jéricho à Mexico: Villes et économie dans l'histoire* (Paris: Gallimard, 1985), p. 107.

3
Competing City-States: The Early Dynastic Period

3000	2500	2000	1500	1000	500

ca. 2800	Archaic Ur
ca. 2500	Tablets from Fara and Abu Salabikh
ca. 2500–2350	Lagash-Umma border conflict
ca. 2400	Uru'inimgina of Lagash
ca. 2400–2350	Bau-temple archive at Girsu
ca. 2350	Ebla archives

At the end of the Uruk period, around the year 3100, the far-reaching cultural influence of Babylonia over the Near East waned. There was a reversion to local traditions throughout the region and certain skills, such as writing, became rare outside southern Mesopotamia. In the south itself, however, the written sources increased in number, enabling us to study political and cultural developments in much greater detail than before. The political situation there was characterized by the existence of city-states constantly interacting and competing with one another. After several centuries, cultural contacts between Babylonia and the rest of the Near East reemerged, which allows us to broaden the geographical focus of historical study once more and shows that elsewhere, too, small states formed the predominant political organization.

Babylonia thus becomes our focus of attention in the 550-year era that is usually referred to as the "Early Dynastic period." This period is often subdivided into Early Dynastic I (ca. 2900–2750), II (ca. 2750–2600), IIIa (ca. 2600–2450), and IIIb (ca. 2450–2350), but these are archaeological distinctions based on stylistic changes in the material remains that have little historical value. The period should be regarded as a unit in political terms, displaying the same basic characteristics for its entire duration.

3.1 The Written Sources and their Historical Uses

The written sources for the study of this period cover a variety of genres. Administrative documents continue to dominate in number, but we also have political narratives written for some rulers of the period, and later literary materials that relate stories about others. Administrative archives appear in different sites in increasingly large quantities. The information they contain becomes more extensive, and the texts themselves are more comprehensible to us, as they start to reflect more closely the spoken language through the expression of phonetic and grammatical elements. At Ur, some 280 tablets were excavated dating to around 2800. The tablets from Fara (ancient Shuruppak; ca. 1000 tablets) and Abu Salabikh (ancient name uncertain; ca. 500 tablets) date to around 2500 and were mixed together with lexical material (cf. chapter 2). The largest number of texts comes from the very end of the Early Dynastic period, with Lagash yielding some 1500 tablets. There are, furthermore, single finds from many sites during the entire period and from all over Babylonia. Late Early Dynastic texts were found outside Babylonia in Syria at Mari (ca. 40 tablets), at Nabada (modern Tell Beydar; ca. 150 tablets), and especially in the west at Ebla (ca. 3600 tablets).

For the study of political history, the most useful information is provided by a new type of text, royal inscriptions. They originated with the simple writing of a royal name and title on a votive object, indicating that it was dedicated by that individual. For instance, "Mebaragesi, king of Kish," was written on a stone vessel.[1] Soon they included short statements that rulers constructed buildings. Over time, inscriptions became lengthier through the inclusion of accounts of military feats associated with the event commemorated, culminating in the first millennium – with detailed year-by-year reports of campaigns and a description of the building raised. These records provide important data on the activities of the ruler both as builder and as warrior. From the Early Dynastic period, a handful of texts each were found in the Babylonian sites of Adab, Kish, Nippur, Umma, Ur, and Uruk. Mari on the Euphrates is the only Syrian city where royal inscriptions were excavated. The largest group of Early Dynastic inscriptions comes from the southern state of Lagash, where nine members of the local dynasty left a total of 120. A substantial number of these give an explicit description of a border conflict between that state and its neighbor, Umma, which will be discussed in detail below. Since the Lagashite side wrote the inscriptions, they present Umma as the illegal and sacrilegious aggressor in the conflict. This group of texts allows us for the first time in Near Eastern history to narrate an event based on contemporary sources.

Later Mesopotamian literature from the late third and early second millennia contains a number of compositions that relate to kings from the Early Dynastic period. They are often quite detailed and thus feature prominently in many modern historical reconstructions. Their reliability as historical sources is, however, suspect. Most influential among these has been the so-called Sumerian King List, which provides a detailed list of dynasties and kings of the Early Dynastic period (see box 3.1 and figure 3.1). Some parts – especially the earlier portions – are certainly unreliable, and for others we are unable to establish

---

Box 3.1   *The Sumerian King List*

Among the later Mesopotamian texts that deal with the Early Dynastic period, the Sumerian King List is perhaps the most important. The text is known only from manuscripts dating to the first centuries of the second millennium, almost 700 years after the Early Dynastic period. It depicts a world in which kingship "descended from heaven" and was passed on from city to city whose local dynasties held temporary hegemony over the entire region. A typical segment reads as follows:

> At Ur, Mesannepada was king; he ruled 80 years; Meski'agnuna, son of Mesannepada, was king; he ruled 36 years; Elulu ruled 25 years; Balulu ruled 36 years; four kings ruled 177 years. Ur was defeated in battle and its kingship was taken to Awan.[1]

Chronologically, the text addresses the period from the moment kingship first appeared, before the flood, to the dynasty of Isin (ca. 1900). In the segment that covers the Early Dynastic period, the city-states mentioned are primarily located in Babylonia, giving special prominence to the cities Ur, Uruk, and Kish. Also included are three non-Babylonian cities, Awan in the east, Hamazi in the north, and Mari in the west. From other evidence we know that some of the kings listed consecutively ruled concurrently. The text enumerates them sequentially because the main ideological elements expressed in this text are that there is only one divinely legitimized ruler at a time, and that hegemonic kingship circulated among a restricted number of cities. Incorporated in it were dynastic lists of kings from different cities and the number of years they ruled. The accuracy of the later parts can be checked against information from dated economic documents. The earlier parts of the Sumerian King List are legendary, however, assigning impossibly long reigns of 3600 years, for instance, to mythological figures such as Dumuzi, who was known as the husband of the goddess Inanna and was probably purely fictional. In its final version, it was used by the kings of the Isin dynasty to legitimize their claim to supreme power in Babylonia, even though they did not politically control the entire area covered by the King List.

[1] Translation after Jean-Jacques Glassner, *Mesopotamian Chronicles* (Atlanta: Society of Biblical Literature, 2004), pp. 120–1.

Figure 3.1 The Weld-Blundell prism inscribed with the Sumerian King List. Courtesy of the Visitors of the Ashmolean Museum, Oxford

historical accuracy. Consequently, the list loses much of its value as a historical source, although it remains our primary means of structuring Early Dynastic history. Other Sumerian literary texts, again known from manuscripts of the early second millennium only, tell stories about three kings of the city of Uruk (Enmerkar, Lugalbanda, and Gilgamesh), and involve far-flung military adventures and local conflicts. These texts are more important for the view they provide on the Sumerians' sense of the past than as sources on the Early Dynastic period.

A study of Early Dynastic Babylonia should be based first on the textual remains of the period itself, and by the early twenty-fourth century certain places provide us with a mixture of written sources that enable us to study questions from various angles simultaneously. From the state of Lagash, for instance, we have royal inscriptions relating military and political events, and a large number of administrative documents that record the activities of an important public institution. These allow us to reconstruct the activities of the royal administration and to compare the official rhetoric to records of actual day-to-day affairs. One vexing problem is that some of the words found in these sources are only understood because they appear in more extensive later documentation. We have to allow for the possibility that changes in their sense took place over time owing to new circumstances, and we cannot simply apply a meaning of the twenty-first century, for instance, to explain a term used in a record from the twenty-fifth. For example, the title énsi, well known later as a provincial governor in the service of the king, appears in the Early Dynastic period to refer to a ruler who is able to act independently. Changes in the political and other circumstances had an effect on the meaning of terms.

3.2   Political Developments in Southern Mesopotamia

The basic element of the political organization of Babylonia in the Early Dynastic period was the city-state: an urban center directly controlling a hinterland with a radius of some 15 kilometers, where people lived in villages. Owing to the agricultural regime of the region, which was wholly dependent on irrigation water for its crops, settlements had to be near rivers, primarily the Euphrates, or canals, which at this time were still relatively short. Throughout Babylonia about thirty-five city-states existed, more or less evenly divided over the region. The steppe lay between the cultivated and permanently inhabited zones and was used for seasonal animal herding and hunting. This area was only indirectly controlled by the urban centers.

In the early third millennium Babylonia saw a general population growth, possibly accelerated by immigration or the settling down of semi-nomadic groups. There was a regional trend toward urbanism: both the cities and the villages surrounding them became larger in size, whereas smaller hamlets seem to have disappeared. The city-states at first were located at sufficient distance from one another so as to be separated by steppe and land that was not part of their agricultural zones. But the continued increase in the population necessitated an extension of the cultivated areas, so the borders of the city-states, especially in the south, became contiguous to one another or even overlapped. This process may have been aggravated by a gradual drying of the climate, causing a lowering of the sea level and a retrenchment of the rivers into fewer branches. The disappearance of interstitial zones had important repercussions both within the states themselves and throughout the region. Among the changes were a secularization of power within the city-states and its centralization in regional terms.

A fundamental element in the Mesopotamian ideology regarding cities was the concept that each was the dwelling of a particular god or goddess. Cities were thought to have been constructed in primordial times for the gods, each of whom acted as their patron deities, e.g., Nanna for Ur, Inanna for Uruk, or Enlil for Nippur. This concept was linked to the role of the temple, or god's household (see below), in cities. The temple's function as collector and distributor of agricultural resources was founded in the ideology that the god received them as gifts and redistributed them to the people. Thus the head of

Map 3.1 The city-states of Babylonia in the Early Dynastic period (after Joan Oates, *Babylon* [London: Thames and Hudson, 1986], p. 13)

the temple administration served as leader in the city, and from the Uruk period on the primary ideological support for the city-ruler was his function in the temple household. The temple was, in fact, the dominant institution in the early city and the largest structure within its walls, sometimes built on an earthen platform towering over the other buildings. The gods were imagined as living in a world parallel to that of humans, so each god had a household, spouse, children, and servants. These dependent deities also had smaller temples and shrines in the cities, sized according to their status, and each city had a multitude of temples.

With the expansion of the city-states' zones of influence, competition for the remaining open areas developed and soon led to intercity wars over agricultural land. A leader's military rather than his cultic role became of primary importance in such situations. In the later Sumerian stories reflecting on this period, the people granted a war leader authority on a temporary basis only. In a moment of crisis, the popular assembly elected a physically strong man as war leader and that body controlled his movements. This system has been called "primitive democracy"[2] and was thought to have led to a dynastic system under which rule was passed on from father to son. The dynastic ideal of war leader was not compatible with that of chief temple administrator chosen by the gods for his managerial competence. They had different bases for their authority, one deriving from prominence in warfare, the other from a perception of divine favor. We associate the new military class with the palace and kingship. In the Early Dynastic period, we see the first appearance of a new type of monumental building in cities, the palace, identifiable as such by its residential plan. Moreover, documents of the time mention a new central institution, the é-gal, literally the "great house," which in later periods clearly refers to the royal household. This is distinct from the é, "house," of the city-god, the temple. These two sources of authority need not be regarded as inherently antagonistic to each other, but merging them into one was not a simple task.

A late episode in the history of Lagash during this period seems to document the attempt to harmonize the two bases of power. The last independent head of the state in the Early Dynastic period, around 2400, was a usurper, Uru'inimgina. Early in his reign he proclaimed a reorganization of the state, ostensibly removing control over the agricultural land from himself and his family and granting it to the city-god Ningirsu and his family. Moreover, certain duties and taxes imposed by officials on the population were lifted and certain obligations of indebted families canceled. At the same time, we see a fundamental change in the administration of the best-documented central institution in the state of Lagash. What had been called the é-mí, the household of the wife (of the city-ruler), was renamed é-Bau, the household of the goddess Bau, the wife of Ningirsu. The estate's holdings were identified as the property of Bau, but now Uru'inimgina himself and later his wife appeared as chief administrators. The name-change of the institution coincided with a substantial increase in its activities, doubling the number of its dependents and agricultural areas through the transfer of resources from other temples. These moves seem to indicate an attempt to merge the various households of the city under the ruler. As king and war leader, he ostensibly transferred the ownership of land and estates to the city-god and his family, while in practice he and his own family members were trying to dominate the gods' estates. The king ruled by divine favor, but he was totally in control of the gods' earthly possessions, so any prior distinction between secular and divine authority had disappeared. Uru'inimgina's measures turned out to be short-lived, but the merging of divine and earthly authority was not. Later kings all proclaimed that their powers derived from the gods, but they controlled temple property and the actual basis of their power was their military skill. The Sumerian King List could claim that kingship had descended from heaven, merging secular and religious powers.

The increased competition over land among city-states is most explicitly demonstrated in a series of inscriptions found in the southern state of Lagash (see document 3.1). Over a period of 150 years, from about 2500 to 2350, the kings of Lagash provided their accounts of a border conflict with their northern neighbor Umma. The war was described in terms of a dispute between Ningirsu, patron deity of Lagash, and Shara, god of Umma, over an area of fields called Gu'edena, "edge of the plain." The kings of Lagash portrayed themselves as deputies acting on behalf of the gods. One of them, Eannatum, even described himself as the giant son of Ningirsu, who engendered him to fight for his cause. According to the Lagash accounts, the chief god Enlil in the distant past had demarcated the border between the two states running through the Gu'edena. The inscriptions acknowledge that the act had historically been performed by a king of Kish called Mesalim, who would have lived around 2600. Thus at that early time the two city-states already had competing claims and recourse to outside arbitration. The sequence of events is difficult to establish, as only one point of view is documented. Whenever Lagash was strong, it tried to enforce its claims over the land, whether justified or not. Successive kings stated that Umma had illegally occupied the land and that its rulers had been defeated by the army of Lagash. Yet the conflict persisted over several centuries, which shows how inconclusive these battles were as well as the importance of the agricultural area to both states. We may assume that other states similarly attempted to extend their farming zones by annexing the fields of neighbors.

Not all interactions between states were hostile, however. The royal houses communicated with one another as equals and had diplomatic relations. The exchange of gifts strengthened these ties. In a cache of precious items found at Mari, there was a bead inscribed with the name of Mesannepada, king of Ur: the group of objects was likely given by one king to the other. The ruler's wife at Lagash, Baranamtara, is known to have exchanged presents with her counterpart at Adab, and this was probably a common practice.

Although the city-state characterized the political situation of the period, various processes of the centralization of power in larger territorial units were at work, due both to hostile and peaceful interactions between states. War between neighbors could lead to territorial occupations. Around 2400, for example, a king of Uruk, Lugalkiginedudu, claimed kingship over Ur, a city 50 kilometers to the south. The process of conquest and unification culminated at the end of the Early Dynastic period when the king of Umma, Lugalzagesi, conquered Ur and Uruk and then defeated Uru'inimgina of Lagash, thus taking control over the entire south of Babylonia. True, he may have overstated his accomplishment in his own inscriptions, in which he claimed control from the Upper to the Lower Sea, that is the Mediterranean to the Persian Gulf. But certainly the extent of his power reached beyond the traditional borders of a single city-state.

Political alliances whose participants agreed to accept the authority of an outsider are documented from ca. 2600 on. One example of such a regional coalition can be inferred from the title "King of Kish." When the god Enlil

Document 3.1 *The Umma–Lagash border conflict*

Excerpts of the account by King Enmetena

Enlil, king of the lands, father of the gods, upon his firm command drew the border between Ningirsu and Shara.[1] Mesalim, king of Kish, at the command of (the god) Ishtaran, measured the field and placed a stele. Ush, ruler of Umma, acted arrogantly. He ripped out the stele and marched unto the plain of Lagash. Ningirsu, the hero of Enlil, at the latter's command did battle with Umma. Upon Enlil's command he cast the great battle-net upon it. Its great burial mound was set up for him in the plain. Eannatum, ruler of Lagash, the uncle of Enmetena ruler of Lagash, with Enakale, ruler of Umma, drew the border. He extended the channel of the Inun-canal into the Gu'edena, giving up 2105 nindan (ca. 12,630 meters) of the field of Ningirsu to the side of Umma. As a field without an owner he established it. At the canal he inscribed a stele, and the stele of Mesalim he returned to its place. He did not cross into the steppe of Umma. On the levee of Ningirsu, named Namnundakigara, he built shrines for Enlil, Ninhursag, Ningirsu, and Utu. . . . At that time Il, who was the head of the temple of Zabalam, made a retreat from Girsu to Umma. Il received the rulership of Umma there. Into the boundary channel of Ningirsu and the boundary channel of Nanshe, the levee of Ningirsu – being at the edge of the Tigris and on the boundary of Girsu – the Namnundakigara of Enlil, Enki, and Ninhursag, its water was diverted. Of the barley of Lagash he repaid only 3600 gur_7. When Enmetena, ruler of Lagash, because of these channels sent men to Il, Il the ruler of Umma, the one who steals fields, said in a hostile way: "The boundary channel of Ningirsu and the boundary channel of Nanshe are mine. From the Antasura to the Edingalabzu I will shift the levee," he said. (But) Enlil and Ninhursag did not give (that) to him. Enmetena, ruler of Lagash, named by Ningirsu, at the just command of Enlil, at the just command of Ningirsu, at the just command of Nanshe, constructed that channel from the Tigris to the Inun-canal. He built the foundation of the Namnundakigara in stone. For the lord who loves him, Ningirsu, for the lady who loves him, Nanshe, he restored it. Enmetena, ruler of Lagash, given the scepter by Enlil, given wisdom by Enki, chosen in the heart of Nanshe, chief administrator of Ningirsu, the one who grasps the commands of the gods, may his personal god Shuturul stand before Ningirsu and Nanshe forever for the life of Enmetena. (If) the man of Umma, in order to carry off the fields crosses the boundary channel of Ningirsu and the boundary channel of Nanshe, be he a man from Umma or a foreigner, may Enlil destroy him, may Ningirsu after casting his great battle-net, place his hands and feet upon him. May the people of his own city, after rising up against him, kill him in the midst of his city!

Translation after Jerrold S. Cooper, *Sumerian and Akkadian Royal Inscriptions. Volume 1: Presargonic Inscriptions* (New Haven: American Oriental Society, 1986), pp. 54–7.

[1] i.e., between Lagash and Umma.

demarcated the border between Umma and Lagash, it was Mesalim, "King of Kish," who measured it out and set up a boundary marker. That Mesalim had some sort of power in Lagash is borne out by a ceremonial mace-head inscribed with his name found there; but the text ends by mentioning that Lugalsha'engur was the city-ruler (Sumerian énsi) of Lagash at the time. Similarly, an inscription of Mesalim from the central Babylonian city of Adab acknowledges the existence of its local ruler, one Ninkisalsi.[3] The title "King of Kish" appears repeatedly in the royal inscriptions of the late Early Dynastic period, and cannot be considered to indicate only kings who controlled the northern Babylonian city of Kish. Eannatum of Lagash, for instance, after defeating a number of southern cities was granted kingship of Kish by the goddess Inanna.[4] Why did the kingship of Kish carry this prestige? It is highly unlikely that it would confer full control over Babylonia and that the other city-rulers whose inscriptions we read were merely dependents of a dynasty in Kish. States like the well-documented Lagash do not seem to have been subject to any outsider. The king of Kish's power seems to have derived from some kind of coalition in the region. Backed by a certain military might (remember that Eannatum became king of Kish only after defeating several neighbors), the king of Kish had an authority that was regionally accepted.

Another such league is attested in the administrative texts from Shuruppak, dating to around 2500. Records of soldiers from Ur, Adab, Nippur, Lagash, and Umma were kept in this small city. Those men are said to be "stationed at KI.EN.GI,"[5] a term that a few centuries later came to mean Sumer, the southern half of Babylonia, but which at this time probably referred to a single locality. The same group of texts also makes reference to a coalition in a place called UNKEN, the Sumerian word for "assembly," made up of Lagash, Umma, and Adab. These mergers were ephemeral: the last two were upset by the border conflict between Umma and Lagash. The coalitions probably were a result of the urban competition characteristic of the Early Dynastic period: cities grouped themselves in various coalitions in order to stand up to one another.

There also existed, however, an overarching sense of religious unity that joined the cities of Babylonia together in war and peace. This is already attested around 3000, when multiple cities had just developed, and not surprisingly the oldest urban center, Uruk, played a prominent role in it. The existence of collective cult practices centered on Uruk is suggested by a group of seal impressions on tablets and lumps of clay, which display symbols that render the names of several other cities. Seal impressions on tablets from the Jemdet Nasr period (3100–2900) show a fixed sequence of city-symbols, including those of Ur, Larsa, Zabalam, Urum, Arina, and probably Kesh. It is likely that the tablets reported contributions made to the goddess Inanna of Uruk, and that the inhabitants of various cities supported her cult. In the slightly later Early Dynastic I levels at Ur, a large number of sealings were found, giving somewhat different combinations of city-symbols and often combined with the rosette symbol of Inanna. These had been mostly used to lock doors, indicating that a storeroom in Ur had been set aside to contain materials for her cult.

At some moment in the Early Dynastic period the focus of the unified cult shifted to the city of Nippur in the center of Babylonia. Each Babylonian city was the domain of a god, who resided there with his or her family of deities. These divine families were joined together in a common Babylonian pantheon that, by the late Early Dynastic period, was headed by Enlil, patron of the city Nippur. He had supreme power in the divine world, and demarcated, for example, the border between Umma and Lagash according to the descriptions of the war between the two cities. Enlil's city, Nippur, attained a unique status that was to last until the eighteenth century. In the late third millennium all Babylonian cities were to provide support for its cult, and in the early second millennium political control over it gave a king the right to claim sovereign rule. Somehow the priesthood of this militarily unimportant city had the authority to grant a special status to one of many competitors. They seem to have had this power already in Early Dynastic times, when kings of Adab, Kish, Lagash, Umma, and Uruk left short inscriptions at Nippur, suggesting that they sought to curry favor with its priesthood.

This sense of unity was not restricted to speakers of a single language. We can state with certainty that at least two languages were spoken in Babylonia during the Early Dynastic period: Sumerian and a Semitic language sometimes referred to as proto-Akkadian. These two languages were very different in character, but they shared some vocabulary, and Sumerian grammar influenced Akkadian, which indicates that the same groups of people used them simultaneously. It is not easy to determine someone's spoken language in a multilingual ancient society. All literate Mesopotamians in this period (or Near Easterners for that matter) shared the same scribal culture, which will be described below. Although they could, and did, write their own vernaculars, all were able to write Sumerian. A text written in Sumerian is thus not evidence that the writer's mother tongue was Sumerian. The scribes of Abu Salabikh, around the year 2500, bore Semitic names but wrote their texts almost exclusively in Sumerian. Indeed, the names of people are probably a better indicator of the language they spoke. In the ancient Near East, people's names were often short sentences with a recognizable meaning, and so give an indication of their family's familiarity with a language. For instance, the Sumerian name Aba-a'a-gin means "Who is like the father?" We tend to take the language of name-giving – Sumerian, Akkadian, and later Amorite, Aramaic, etc. – as evidence of the language spoken at home. So we see in Early Dynastic society a mixture of Sumerian and Semitic names, the former predominant in the south of Babylonia, the latter in the north. This distinction did not lead to ethnic conflict, as has sometimes been argued. Members of the two linguistic groups lived side by side. Politically, Early Dynastic Babylonia was divided; culturally it was not.

3.3 The Wider Near East

Early Dynastic Babylonia did not exist in a void. It was surrounded by regions that the Babylonians considered to be foreign and with which they had diverse

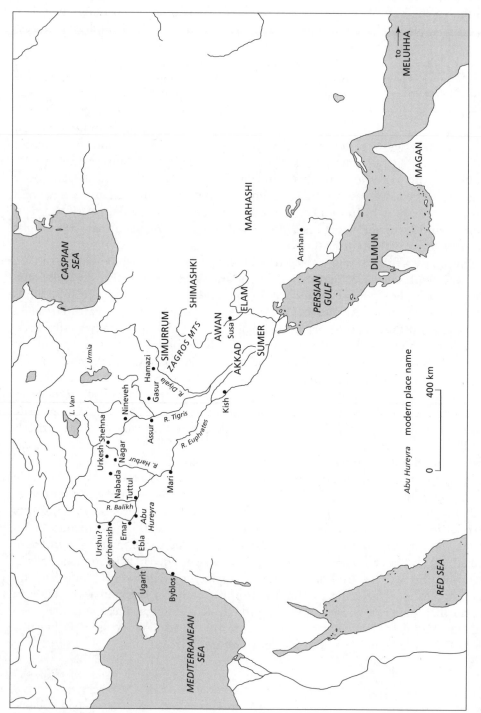

Map 3.2 The Near East ca. 2400

relations. The political situation in the rest of the Near East needs to be pieced together primarily from archaeological data. Only late in the Early Dynastic period do texts appear in a few Syrian sites, and by then Babylonian documents start to refer to the outside world. This is an unfortunate situation in that it leads to too great an emphasis on contacts with Babylonia and a focus on the south. With the end of the Uruk expansion in the late fourth millennium, contacts between Babylonia and the surrounding world changed radically. In the early third millennium, local traditions reemerged in full strength in the north and the east, and the Near East shows a great deal of cultural variety. Whatever southern influence there had been vanished. Simultaneously, certain nearby regions became more closely drawn into the Babylonian orbit, including one that had been outside the Uruk sphere, the Persian Gulf region.

The Gulf gave access to Omani copper mines, which were crucial to the newly developed bronze technology. Babylonian interest in the region was thus not unexpected. Texts start referring increasingly to a land of "Dilmun" as an important trading partner with southern Mesopotamia, a source for wood and copper. Dilmun had been attested only once in the texts from the Uruk IV period, but throughout the Early Dynastic period references to it became more numerous. Its location is uncertain: for this period north-east Arabia or the island of Bahrain are the most likely candidates. In either case, Dilmun itself was not the producer of timber and copper, but rather acted as a mercantile center, trading goods obtained further away. Archaeological material from eastern Arabia and Oman shows a great deal of contact with Babylonia. Many pottery vessels were Mesopotamian imports, but these were found within archaeological contexts that are not at all Mesopotamian in character. In Oman, for instance, numerous circular tombs with stones piled over them were constructed in this period, an entirely un-Mesopotamian practice. So we see here a kind of interaction different from that attested in the Uruk period: at that time the Babylonians seem to have traded through colonies, while in the Early Dynastic period they did so without a permanent presence in the region.

The regions to the east of Babylonia had been incorporated in the Uruk expansion. Susa, the main urban center there, had been heavily influenced by Uruk IV culture. This suddenly changed with the beginning of the third millennium, and a local culture we call proto-Elamite appeared, more closely related to eastern Iran. Some 400 kilometers to the south-east of Susa another center, Anshan in the modern province of Fars, became prominent and expanded substantially in size. Susa dominated the lowlands to the west of the Zagros Mountains, Anshan the highlands of the southern mountain range. It is unlikely that a regional state including both cities and the territories in between developed this early, yet mid-third-millennium texts from Babylonia start referring to a land of Elam. This was probably a loosely joined coalition of polities, which also appeared independently in Mesopotamian texts. Late Early Dynastic rulers from Lagash campaigned against what they called "Elam," probably for access to trade routes that reached places far afield. For instance, carnelian beads made in the Indus Valley and lapis lazuli from Afghanistan appear in archaeological contexts in Babylonia at this time. Babylonia seems to be on the receiving end, importing luxury goods demanded by its new elites. What was provided in return is not readily established, most likely textiles and other easily transportable manufactured goods. The material culture of Iran does not demonstrate strong Babylonian influence, which suggests that there was no permanent presence of Babylonian traders.

Throughout northern Iraq and Syria east of the Euphrates River, a new material culture appeared at the beginning of the third millennium which we term by its pottery style, "Ninevite 5." Its remains are usually found at sites on important overland routes, and it seems that the people with this culture were in control of trade. The regions further west show a variety of material cultures, suggesting the absence of any regional entity. These societies were not urbanized, at least in comparison with southern Mesopotamia. Several settlements that later developed into important centers originated at this time, but truly urban characteristics were absent until about 2600. Only then do walled cities and dense habitation reappear in such areas as the Habur Valley. While southern influence may have been a catalyst in this late urban development, it was an indigenous process and there are clear differences from the south.

The agricultural regime of northern Mesopotamia and Syria differs from that in the south in that it relies on rainfall rather than riverain irrigation for growing cereal crops. Yields per hectare are lower than when irrigation is used, however, so larger areas were cultivated to feed the same number of people, though with less intense labor. Consequently, cities in the north tended to be smaller than those in the south, and more of the population lived in outlying villages. Another difference lies in the role of the palace in northern society. Unlike in the south, where temples were the central and foremost institutions in early cities, secular authority was preeminent in northern economy and society and palaces usually dominated the cityscape.

These cities were the centers of small states incorporating the surrounding countryside where villagers farmed. Settlement in these states was more spread out than in the south and the hinterlands were larger. This was probably a result of different agricultural regimes, but with their focus on the central city these were still, in essence, city-states. Texts from Ebla in north-west Syria and from elsewhere in later periods allow us to identify several of these states by name: for example, Nagar, Shehna, and Urkesh in the Habur region, Mari, Tuttul, Emar, and Carchemish along the Euphrates, Assur and Hamazi in the east, and Ebla, Ugarit, and Byblos in the west. These states were in contact with one another through diplomatic and commercial means. The subject of trade dominates the palace documents found at Ebla, which seems reflective of widespread diplomatic contact. Kings and other foreign state representatives were commonly attested as visitors making offerings at Ebla sanctuaries; diplomatic marriages were concluded and gifts regularly exchanged. Warfare was also part of these contacts. Ebla had a long-lasting conflict with Mari on the Euphrates, probably for control over the trade route to Babylonia, and for some time had to pay a heavy tribute until Ebla's last ruler of the period,

Ish'ar-Damu, reversed the situation. Some of these centers – Mari, Nagar, and Ebla – seem to have become able to impose their will on surrounding states, but the details of their military actions are unknown. Besides the centralization of secular power, a certain sense of religious unity also developed, as rulers from various cities are attested as taking oaths in the temple of Dagan at Tuttul. The latter city may thus have had a regional prestige comparable to that of Nippur in Babylonia.

Another similarity between Babylonia and the region to its north is that both had multilingual societies. Most people spoke Semitic dialects, as attested in the texts from Mari and Ebla. But in northern Syria we also find evidence of Hurrian, a language that is neither Semitic nor related to Sumerian. Personal names again are the primary indicator of this linguistic multiplicity. Hurrians were probably predominant in the north of Syria, where a Hurrian state of Urkesh and Nawar later arose, but people with Hurrian names appear soon after the Early Dynastic period as far south as Nippur. People with Semitic names were present throughout Syria and northern Mesopotamia. This linguistic heterogeneity did not lie at the basis of any social or ethnic conflict to our knowledge.

The political organization of the north – a much larger area than Babylonia – was thus essentially similar to that in the south. Urban centers were the seats of power and dominated the surrounding countryside, even if the northern states were geographically larger. There was a difference in the ideological basis of power, however: in the north it was secular rather than religious. The city of Kish in the far north of Babylonia functioned as an intermediate point between these two worlds. It maintained close contacts with both the southern and the Syrian states and may have had a political organization that was based more on secular than on religious power. It is perhaps unsurprising, then, that a man from Kish, Sargon, was to upset the entire system.

3.4 Early Dynastic Society

For the study of Near Eastern social history in the Early Dynastic period, we rely on administrative documents. Characteristic for the period – and for the entire third millennium – is the organization of society into "households." These are social units larger than nuclear families whose members reside together. An important aspect of the household is the fact that it acted as a single unit of production and consumption: most goods needed for its survival were produced in the household itself. Households may have originated in economically autonomous kinship groups and eventually coalesced into institutions centered round a god or the king. Thus the Sumerian word for palace was é-gal, "great household," that for temple é and the name of a god, for instance "household of the god Ningirsu." The important tablet archives derive from these units and consequently portray a world with the household at its center. Activity outside the large palace and temple households remains undocumented.

Figure 3.2 Early Dynastic statuette. Photo © Trustees of the British Museum, London

   Each household can be regarded as an autonomous unit. It owned land, livestock, tools, and fishing boats, and included farmers, shepherds, fishermen, and people to produce and prepare food and to manufacture goods. Households were not specialized in their activities, and each had a high level of self-sufficiency. The larger incorporated several departments with distinct tasks, which were often themselves designated by the term é. In the late Early Dynastic period, individual members of the elites also had their own households. In Lagash, for instance, the queen had one, called the women's household, Sumerian é-mí, which she ran independently. Her property was smaller than that of the king, but it was self-sufficient and it seems that women administered the queen's household. We cannot document this for the Early Dynastic period, but in the later Ur III period its officials were mostly women.

   Internally, the personnel of each household was hierarchically organized. Male and female laborers (Sumerian gurush and géme) were at the bottom of this hierarchy and were by far the most numerous of its members. While they were not unfree, in the sense of slaves, they were dependent laborers. The workers could live with their families or in institutional lodgings provided by the organization for which they worked. They were rewarded for their work with rations: standard amounts of barley, accounted for on a monthly basis, and of oil and wool, accounted for annually (see document 3.2). The persons receiving these goods were mainly working men and women, but children and old people were also recipients. It is clear that these rations constituted the support given to the household's dependents, whether productive or not. The amounts were provided according to the sex and status of the worker: a male worker regularly received double the amount of grain given to a female worker, supervisors received more than their subordinates, specialized craftsmen more than unskilled laborers, and so on. This pattern whereby the household provided for its dependents by issuing them basic necessities of food and clothing remained a fundamental characteristic of Near Eastern society throughout the third millennium. Since the goods provided were insufficient for a complete diet, we have to conclude that these people had access to other foods through channels exterior to the household. Vegetables and fish were probably homegrown or caught by these dependents and family members; or perhaps part of the rations were exchanged for those goods.

Document 3.2 *Extract from a ration list*

Many administrative accounts list the rations issued to temple dependents in great detail. They provide the names of the recipients or identify them by gender and age, and list the amounts of barley issued to them. At the end of these texts totals are given and the official responsible for the disbursement is identified. For example:

In total: 1 man at 50 liters
1 man at 40 liters
5 men at 15 liters each
23 men at 10 liters each
They are males
56 female laborers at 20 liters each
72 female laborers at 15 liters each
34 women at 10 liters each
A grand total of 192 people, including young ones and adults, received barley.
The barley was 2935 liters. Barley rations. The female laborers and children are the property of the goddess Bau.
Shasha, the wife of Uru'inimgina, king of Lagash.
In the month of the eating of malt for Nanshe, did Eniggal, the inspector, distribute this from the granary of Bau. It is the ninth distribution of year 4.

Translation after Gebhard J. Selz, *Die altsumerischen Wirtschaftsurkunden der Ermitage zu Leningrad* (Wiesbaden: Steiner Verlag, 1989), pp. 93–4.

The majority of workers provided repetitive manual labor. Women were especially used as millers and weavers. Milling at this time was a backbreaking task which required that grain be rubbed back and forth over a stone slab with a smaller hand-held stone. The women were supposed to produce set quotas on a daily basis. The amounts produced depended on the quality of the final product, which varied enormously. From later Ur III period texts, we know that the quotas were high: one woman had to produce 10 liters of regular flour or 20 liters of coarse flour per day. Weaving quotas could easily be as high as 2 square meters a day. Those were heavy tasks, that could lead to physical injuries, as is shown by the skeletons of women excavated at the seventh-millennium Neolithic site of Abu Hureyra in Syria: their knees, wrists, and lower backs showed signs of arthritis while their toes were deformed from constantly tucking them under the foot.[6] While the Early Dynastic accounts are for women as groups, it is likely that they worked individually at home, simultaneously taking care of children. These tasks were primarily cottage industries.

Belonging to a great household also provided a means of survival to the weak in society. Widows and children unable to feed themselves entered temple households, where they received basic support in return for labor. The household was thus a fundamental building block of society, where both individuals and nuclear families found a place. Households existed both in the cities and in the countryside. In the latter there was probably a parallel continuation of rural communities existing outside institutional control, composed of large families that owned land in common. Their existence in the Early Dynastic period – but also the decline of their importance in that society – is clear from a group of about fifty land-sale documents. When a piece of agricultural land was sold, it usually went from multiple sellers to a single buyer. The sellers had unequal levels of claim to the land. Those most closely associated to it received the highest recompense, others somewhat less, and large groups of people were given symbolic gifts, such as meals, at the time of the transaction. The land was thus probably communally owned and could not be alienated by an individual. But all of the recorded buyers were single actors, probably members of the elite who were able to acquire individual ownership of rights, possibly at times by force. These elites were probably all members of the institutional households, who took advantage of their status to obtain personal property.

Several institutional households coexisted within each city-state: some belonged to gods, others to secular authorities. Among the temples there was a hierarchy reflecting that of the gods in the local pantheon. For instance, in Lagash the household of the city-god Ningirsu was larger than that of his divine wife Bau; and hers was in turn larger than those of their sons Shulshagana and Igalima. It is remarkable how encompassing the control of one of these institutions could be; the records from Shuruppak, for instance, show highly centralized control of the economy. Barley accounts register amounts that could provide a population of 20,000 with daily rations for six months, and grain silos excavated at the site show that these quantities could be stored together. The agricultural areas attached to institutional households were similarly enormous.

However, since all our textual documentation from southern Babylonia derives from temples, it used to be thought that temples were completely dominant in Early Dynastic society. Because the temple of the goddess Bau there is our primary source of texts, Lagash was once described as a temple-state, where all land and property was owned by the gods. Today, most scholars have rejected this idea, acknowledging the fact that other sectors of society were important participants in economic life but simply remain undocumented.

The far-reaching nature of central administration is even clearer in the case of Ebla in north-west Syria. All our documentation there was excavated in a palace archive and demonstrates how this institution controlled extensive economic activity. Eight administrative units are accounted for, four on the acropolis, which is called sa-za$_x^{ki}$ in the texts, four in the lower town, called eb-la^{ki}. The former includes the household of the king, é-en; the latter had four units referred to with the term é-duru$_5$, which in Babylonia meant "village." Whether the use of that term indicates that village communities coincided with administrative units, or were turned into administrative units with the advent of centralized power, is unclear. We can say, however, that agriculture in Ebla's territory remained the responsibility of villages under royal supervision, unlike in Babylonia where much of it was directly undertaken by institutional labor forces.

The ability of certain segments of society to draw unequal shares of resources to themselves is best shown in the archaeological record of the Early Dynastic period. The so-called Royal Cemetery at Ur clearly reveals the existence of a small group of people who could command great amounts of luxury items to be buried with them. Sixteen of the roughly two thousand graves excavated had elaborate chambers of stone and brick. Extremely valuable grave goods were placed in them: golden helmets, daggers, inlaid musical instruments, and so on. These were all the products of highly skilled craftsmen who learned their trade catering to the elites. Most telling of the power of the buried is the fact that some of them were accompanied by human attendants, killed or willing to die at their master's or mistress's burial. We do not know who exactly was honored with such elaborate burials, whether they were members of the palace or temple elites. This in itself demonstrates how power structures gaining legitimacy on various ideological bases coexisted in the late Early Dynastic period, and that the full definition of social and political hierarchies was still wanting then.

3.5 Scribal Culture

During the Early Dynastic period, the recently invented technology of writing evolved both in its ability to render spoken languages and in the extent of information it could provide. Writing is also the most eloquent indication at this time of the existence of a cultural unity in the Near East inspired by southern Mesopotamian traditions. Scribal techniques and text genres used throughout the region were all developed in Babylonia.

The writing system changed gradually in several ways during this period. First, the signs themselves became impressed using a bevel-tipped reed instead of being traced in the clay of the tablet. When the tip of the stylus was pushed into the clay, it formed a small triangle and a thin line, creating thus the wedge shape we now call cuneiform. The signs became increasingly schematic and standardized, and it was possible to impress them rapidly with a limited number of strokes. By the end of the Early Dynastic period, few of the signs any longer resembled the pictorial elements on which they were originally based.

The use of signs rendering syllables also expanded, indicating more and more elements of the spoken language. Nevertheless, signs representing words and requiring the reader to supply grammatical elements remained dominant. While indications of verbal conjugation, for instance, were absent in the proto-cuneiform texts from Uruk, the expression of such elements became increasingly explicit, although there was never an obligation in the cuneiform writing system to express them all. The growing use of syllabic signs made it possible to write languages other than Sumerian; personal names in Semitic dialects and Hurrian could be written out, Semitic prepositions were inserted in the text, and so on.

A script using word signs alone could theoretically render any language, but the increased use of syllabic signs facilitated the adaptation of the script for different language groups. Urbanization in Syria and northern Mesopotamia came with the adoption of scribal practices from the south. The scribes of Ebla, Mari, and Nabada, and probably at many other places where texts are still to be discovered, imported Babylonian tablet shapes, sign forms, and their readings. The continued predominance of word signs, originally developed for the Sumerian language, led scribes from Ebla to draw up lists of signs followed by a syllabic, phonetic, version of the term to show its pronunciation. More elaborate lexical lists included the translation of the terms in the local language and, sometimes, a pronunciation. The rarity of these texts strongly suggests that Syrian scribes were taught by Babylonians, especially since the ordering and format of these lists are identical to those found in the south.

The ordering of signs in texts also became more standardized. Tablets were divided into one or more vertical columns of boxes to be read from top to bottom, mostly containing one word only, with or without grammatical elements. The order of the signs became more reflective of the pronunciation of words, although even in the latest Early Dynastic texts they were sometimes still scrambled. These developments made the texts more comprehensible to their readers in antiquity, and to us today. Administrative texts became more explicit, indicating, for example, whether goods were issued or received by a specific person. Royal inscriptions expanded from simple marks of ownership to lengthy narratives. Writing thus acquired an expanded function and increased its ability to inform someone of new knowledge, while information could be preserved for future generations. A king who left a votive object in a temple could indicate on it who had given it, so that later visitors would acknowledge his act.

The archaic texts from Uruk already show that writing in Mesopotamia was not restricted to economic transactions, even though these texts continue to dominate the corpus numerically. Lexical lists, words in a set sequence, provide the earliest systematic evidence of Mesopotamian speculative and associative thought. They include lists of god-names, professions, animals, birds, metals, woods, city-names, and so on. In the Early Dynastic period this genre flourished and shows the acceptance of the same traditions over a wide geographical area. Most remarkable is the faithfulness with which these texts were copied in every city where they are found in the Early Dynastic period. Lists from Abu Salabikh are duplicated with only minor variants in Ebla, some 900 kilometers away. There are other literary texts from the Early Dynastic period, usually short compositions including incantations, hymns, and wisdom literature, that is, catalogs of proverbs or proverbs set in an artificial dialogue where a father gives advice to his son. These are difficult to understand owing to the still terse nature of the writing system. The same compositions are often found at different sites (those of Shuruppak and Abu Salabikh especially show much overlap), which demonstrates that a common source inspired the various scribal schools. While most of the material is in Sumerian, there is a proto-Akkadian hymn to Shamash which is found both at Ebla and Abu Salabikh.

In the middle of the third millennium, we thus see a cultural *koine* in the literate Near East. The intellectual center was southern Mesopotamia, where the scribal practices and most literary texts were first produced. The technique of writing was exported to Syria and northern Mesopotamia when urban cultures developed there, and certain cities probably acted as intermediaries in this process. Northern Babylonian Kish was very important, as was Mari on the Middle Euphrates. Some texts at Ebla state that "the young scribes came up from Mari,"[7] which suggests that the city provided training to Syrian scribes. People from western Syria read the same texts as those of southern Iraq. They employed the same scribal practices, shaping their clay tablets similarly, writing the same cuneiform signs, organizing them in the same way on the tablets, and so on. Politically they were separate, however, living in independent city-states. The states in the south were relatively small in territorial extent, while those in the north and in western Syria had a wider expanse. The states competed with one another through military means. Rulers routinely gained supremacy over their neighbors, or ephemeral alliances among city-states were concluded. These laid the groundwork for Sargon of Akkad, who initiated a new period in Near Eastern history by pursuing a policy of conquest to the extreme.

NOTES

1   Jerrold S. Cooper, *Sumerian and Akkadian Royal Inscriptions. Volume 1: Presargonic Inscriptions* (New Haven: American Oriental Society, 1986), p. 18.

2   It was first and most extensively argued by Thorkild Jacobsen, "Primitive Democracy in Ancient Mesopotamia," *Journal of Near Eastern Studies* 2 (1943), pp. 159–72.

3   Cooper, *Sumerian and Akkadian Royal Inscriptions. Volume 1: Presargonic Inscriptions*, p. 19.

4   Ibid., p. 42.

5   Francesco Pomponio and Giuseppe Visicato, *Early Dynastic Administrative Tablets of Shuruppak* (Naples: Istituto Universitario Orientale di Napoli, 1994), pp. 10–11. Capital letters are used to render the name KI.EN.GI as we are not certain about how to read it.

6   Theya Molleson, "The Eloquent Bones of Abu Hureyra," *Scientific American* 271/2 (August 1994), pp. 70–5.

7   Alfonso Archi, "Transmission of the Mesopotamian Lexical and Literary Texts from Ebla," in P. Fronzaroli, ed., *Literature and Literary Language at Ebla* (*Quaderni di Semitistica* 18; Florence: Dipartimento di Linguistica, 1992), p. 23.

4

Political Centralization in the Late Third Millennium

3000	2500	2000	1500	1000	500

2334	Accession of Sargon of Akkad
2254–18	Naram-Sin of Akkad
ca. 2100	Gudea of Lagash
2112	Beginning of the Ur III period
2004	Fall of Ur

The last centuries of the third millennium were characterized by successive periods of centralization of power under two city-dynasties: one from Akkad in northern Babylonia in the twenty-fourth and twenty-third centuries, the other from Ur in the far south in the twenty-first century. They not only exercised direct control over southern Mesopotamia, but through military means had great influence over large parts of the Near East. There is a substantial increase in the available sources, which are also better understood by the modern historian, thus enabling a more detailed reconstruction of these periods. The two states shared a number of characteristics: they were both founded through military means in Babylonia proper and in the surrounding regions; they pursued policies of centralization in political, administrative, and ideological terms; and they collapsed through a combination of internal opposition and external forces, especially from the east. Since they differed in the extent of their reach and their internal cohesion, however, they deserve separate treatment.

4.1 The Kings of Akkad

The dynasty of Akkad[1] was regarded in such later texts as the Sumerian King List as a family of city-rulers who held kingship over Sumer and Akkad in the same way as many other dynasties that came earlier (for a list of kings, see p. 302). The nature of its rule was very different from what preceded it, however, and temporarily it ended the system of city-states that had characterized Babylonia until then. The processes of political centralization in Babylonia and the spread of Babylonian influences throughout the Near East evident in the Early Dynastic period attained an unprecedented climax. Moreover, never before had Babylonian armies systematically campaigned that far, nor had the political dominance of one city been so great. The focal point of the developments was northern Babylonia. The creator of the dynasty, Sargon, seems to have been a commoner who rose to prominence in the city of Kish. He probably usurped power in that city, taking the programmatic throne-name Sharru-kin, "the king is legitimate." His two successors still bore the title "King of Kish," but Sargon moved the center of his rule to Akkad, either an entirely new city, as later sources state, or a place previously of little importance. Although its location is unknown, it certainly was in the very north of Babylonia, perhaps underneath modern Baghdad. This geographical position reflects the dual interests of the dynasty: full dominance of the Babylonian heartland and an extensive presence throughout the wider Near East.

Akkad's prominence was attained through its military might. It was written of Sargon that "daily 5400 men ate at his presence,"[2] which may refer to the existence of a standing army. Military activity is the sole subject of his own inscriptions. The south of Babylonia, where the city-states of the late Early Dynastic period had been partly united, was one area where he campaigned actively. Lugalzagesi, who controlled Uruk, Umma, and several other southern cities, acted as the focus of opposition to Sargon, and the latter claimed that he captured "fifty governors . . . and the king of Uruk,"[3] a victory that clinched his control over the entire region.

A new system of government had to be developed: the formerly independent city-states needed to be integrated within a larger structure in every respect, politically, economically, and ideologically. Politically, the original city-rulers mostly remained in place, only now acting as governors for the king of Akkad, despite Sargon's claim that these were Akkadian officials. Thus kings Meskigal of Adab, Lugalzagesi of Uruk, and perhaps Uru'inimgina of Lagash are still attested under the first Sargonic rulers. The term énsi, which in the Early Dynastic period designated independent rulers of certain cities, now became used throughout Babylonia to indicate governors. This system did not work, however. Sentiments of independence could be rallied around native governors, and over the entire period the Akkadian kings had to deal with a number of rebellions, as described later in this chapter.

Still, centralizing policies were actively pursued. A new system of taxation was developed, in which part of the income of each region was siphoned off and

---

Box 4.1 *The year name*

One aspect of the administrative centralization of the Akkad state was the introduction of an annual dating system that would be applied throughout Babylonia, although not at the expense of other systems used for local records. One of the earlier
existing systems was chosen, which we call the year name. Each year was indicated
with a name referring to a major event from the year prior or early in the year itself.
For instance, Sargon's destruction of Mari was used to name the following year. This
system remained in use in Babylonia until about 1500, and provides us with a list of
what the Babylonian rulers themselves saw as important events. The names usually
mention military campaigns, the building or restoration of temples or city-walls, the
digging of canals, the appointments of high priests or priestesses, or the donation of
cult objects. The dates appear primarily on economic records (not on letters). In order
to remember the proper order of years, official lists of year names were drawn up
from the Ur III period on. While the sequence of names for the entire period of the
usage of year names has not been fully recovered, we are certain about long stretches.
These provide an extremely useful insight into the chronological order of events, and
allow us to date the numerous accounts and administrative documents preserved.

  Under the Kassite dynasty in Babylonia in the second half of the second millennium, year names were replaced with a system numbered by the regnal year of each
king. The first official year started with the first New Year's day of his reign. The
period between the death of the former king and that day was indicated as the
accession year. This system stayed in use until the Seleucid period.

---

sent to the capital or used to support the local Akkadian administration. In the
reign of Naram-Sin, a standardization of accounting is visible in certain levels
of the administration in order to facilitate central control. For those aspects of
the economy that concerned the crown, scribes had to use a standard system
of measures and weights. Thus we see the introduction of the "Akkadian gur"
of ca. 300 liters to measure barley. The shape and layout of the accounting
tablets and the formation of the cuneiform signs were centrally prescribed. In
order to have a consistent method of dating in centrally controlled accounts,
year names (see box 4.1) were used throughout the state.

  The local scribes, who were forced to adopt new techniques of accounting, also
had to adjust to a new language. Akkad was a northern Babylonian city situated
in the region where people spoke a Semitic language rather than the Sumerian
of the south. The language of the region, in fact, came to be known as the
language of Akkad, hence our term "Akkadian." The existing cuneiform script,
however, had been developed as a vehicle for Sumerian, rooted in an entirely
different language family. Akkadian required more flexibility and accuracy
in the indication of grammatical forms, which could be obtained through the
increased use of syllabic signs. The royal inscriptions of the Sargonic kings were
mostly written in Akkadian, either by itself or, less often, with a Sumerian

translation. Few of these texts are known in a Sumerian version only. Sumerian remained commonly written in areas of the region with a long tradition of the language, however. The royal administration only demanded the use of Akkadian and of centralized accounting practices for the records it needed to consult. Those had to be uniform; local affairs were left to traditional ways.

The royal house drew many economic resources to itself. The Akkadian kings probably confiscated the estates previously owned by the city-rulers. Yet even this was seemingly insufficient for their needs. The Obelisk of King Manishtushu, one of the major monuments of the period, is a 1.5-meter-high diorite pillar onto which was carved a text recording his purchase of eight large fields in northern Babylonia, totaling almost 3.5 square kilometers. Although the price paid was not unusually low, it is almost certain that Manishtushu forced the sale on the owners in order to be able to parcel out the land to his own supporters. The creation of agricultural estates granted by the king to privileged people was a novelty introduced by the Sargonic kings. The land needed was taken from local owners, which certainly led to resentment and opposition to Akkadian rule.

In ideological terms also, the union of Babylonia was pursued, and Sargon sought to connect the cultic system of the region, with its shared pantheon, to his own family. For instance, he installed his daughter as high priestess of the moon god Nanna at Ur, where she was made the god's wife. For that function she received a purely Sumerian name, Enheduanna, "priestess, fitting for heaven." Thus an Akkadian princess was placed in one of the main Sumerian centers of the south and she actively participated in cultural life there. The authorship of several literary compositions in the Sumerian language is credited to her (making her the first identifiable author in world literature), including a set of hymns to temples located in thirty-five cities throughout Babylonia. The compilation of those hymns into one series shows how the various cults of the region were considered to belong to an integrated system. For some five centuries afterwards, the control of the high priesthood of Nanna at Ur remained an indication of political prominence in Babylonia. Any ruler who could claim authority in Ur installed his daughter there, giving her access to the temple's considerable economic assets. Naram-Sin expanded this policy by placing several of his daughters as high priestesses of prominent cults in other Babylonian cities, a clear attempt to gain a solid foothold throughout the region. He also explained his own deification (see below) as the result of a decision made by the gods of various cities all over his state.

The Akkadian kings did not exert power over Babylonia alone, however. Some Early Dynastic kings were known to have campaigned in different areas of the Near East, but none even remotely measured up to what the Sargonic kings accomplished. To determine the regional extent and nature of Akkad's influence, we have to turn to the royal inscriptions. These were inscribed on statues that the kings set up in the courtyard of the temple at Nippur, continuing the Early Dynastic tradition that gave this city regional prominence. Military matters dominate the contents of these inscriptions. We no longer have the statues themselves, but scribes in the early second millennium copied out the texts inscribed there, and some of these copies have been preserved. In these texts, the first five Akkadian kings make extensive boasts about their military exploits. The statements of Sargon and Naram-Sin stand out, however, because of their wide geographical range: these were certainly the greatest military men of the time. Yet, as Naram-Sin had to repeat many of his grandfather's campaigns, it seems these often amounted to no more than raids.

The Akkadian kings focused their military attention on the regions of western Iran and northern Syria (see map 3.2). In the east they encountered a number of states or cities, such as Elam, Parahshum, and Simurrum, whose location we cannot exactly pinpoint. In the north they entered the upper Euphrates area, reaching the city of Tuttul at the confluence with the Balikh River, the cult center of Dagan that acted as a central focus of northern and western Syria. Mari and Ebla, the most prominent political centers of the region up till then, were destroyed. These places, which had been so close to northern Babylonia in cultural terms during the Early Dynastic period, were now considered to be major enemies.

The accounts mention many places even more remote, such as the cedar forests in Lebanon, the headwaters of the Tigris and Euphrates rivers in central Turkey, Marhashi, east of Elam, and areas across the "Lower Sea," i.e., the Persian Gulf. These were reached in far-flung forays for the procurement of rare goods, hard stone, wood, or silver. Booty from these areas was brought to Babylonia. Several stone vessels excavated at Ur and Nippur were inscribed with the statement that they were booty from Magan (Oman), for instance. It seems unlikely, however, that these areas were subsequently controlled by Akkad. Rather, the raids aimed at monopolizing access to trade routes. Ships from overseas areas, such as Dilmun (Bahrain), Magan, and Meluhha (the Indus Valley) are said to have moored in Akkad's harbor. So when Naram-Sin claims that he conquered Magan, it seems more likely that he used his military might to guarantee access to its resources.

Local circumstances determined to a great extent how Akkadian presence was maintained in this wide region. We observe a variety of interactions. At Susa in western Iran, for instance, the language of bureaucracy became Akkadian and the local rulers were referred to with Sumerian titles, such as governor (énsi) or general (shagina), which imply a full dependence on the kings of Akkad. On the other hand, the rulers of Susa retained some degree of authority. Naram-Sin concluded a treaty with an unnamed ruler or high official of Susa, a document written in the Elamite language. The agreement specified no submission to Akkad, only a promise by the Elamite to regard Naram-Sin's enemies as his own. The autonomy of Elam should not be underestimated.

In Syria the Akkadians established footholds in certain existing centers, indicated by the presence of military garrisons or trade representatives there. At Nagar (modern Tell Brak), a monumental building was erected with bricks stamped with the name of Naram-Sin. Its character – military or administrative – cannot be established, however. At Nineveh, King Manishtushu is said to have built a temple devoted to the goddess Ishtar, which suggests that he wanted to promote the cult of a goddess who was considered of special importance to his dynasty.

The question remains how thorough Akkadian presence in the peripheral areas was. Throughout the Near East, documents in the Akkadian administrative style appear: in the Diyala region (probably part of the Akkadian core); at Susa in Elam; Gasur and Assur in Assyria; Mari on the Middle Euphrates; and in northern Syria at several sites, Nagar, Urkesh (modern Tell Mozan), Shehna (modern Tell Leilan), and Ashnakkum (modern Tell Chagar Bazar). The records using Akkadian style are not necessarily evidence of an Akkadian royal administration, however: just as in the late Early Dynastic period, this may merely show the spread of southern scribal practices. Widespread territorial control of the region seems unlikely. The Old Akkadian kings probably estab-lished points through which they could channel their commercial interests, possibly backed by the threat of military action.

More distant areas were tied to Akkad through diplomatic means, such as marriages. We find sealings of Naram-Sin's daughter, Taram-Agade, in the north Syrian city of Urkesh, and it is likely that she was living there as the wife of the local ruler. A princess of the eastern state of Marhashi was, conversely, married to Sharkalisharri or his son. Such marriages indicate that the Old Akkadian state did not exist in a political void, but was surrounded by states with which it had to negotiate on a level of equality. Unfortunately, the latter are only known to us through Akkadian eyes, so we cannot evaluate their extent or powers with any degree of certainty.

The far-reaching influence of the dynasty had a great effect on how the kings perceived themselves. Already under Sargon the traditional title "King of Kish" came to mean "king of the world," using the similarity of the name of the city of Kish and the Akkadian term for "the entire inhabited world," *kishshatum*. Naram-Sin took such self-glorification to an extreme. First, he intro-duced a new title, "king of the four corners (of the universe)." His military successes led him to proclaim an even more exalted status. After crushing a major rebellion in the entirety of Babylonia, he took the unprecedented step in Mesopotamian history of making himself a god. A unique inscription found in northern Iraq, but not necessarily put there in Naram-Sin's days, describes this act as requested by the citizens of the capital:

> Naram-Sin, the strong one, king of Akkad: when the four corners (of the universe) together were hostile to him, he remained victorious in nine battles in a single year because of the love Ishtar bore for him, and he took captive those kings who had risen against him. Because he had been able to preserve his city in the time of crisis, (the inhabitants of) his city asked from Ishtar in Eanna, from Enlil in Nippur, from Dagan in Tuttul, from Ninhursaga in Kesh, from Enki in Eridu, from Sin in Ur, from Shamash in Sippar, and from Nergal in Kutha, that he be the god of their city Akkad, and they built a temple for him in the midst of Akkad.[4]

Henceforth his name appeared in texts preceded by the cuneiform sign derived from the image of a star, which functioned as the indicator that what followed was the name of a god.

Conceptually, this placed him in a very different realm from previous rulers. Earlier kings had been offered a cult after death, but Naram-Sin received one while he was still alive. The court initiated a process of royal glorification through other means as well. Perhaps the most visible of these efforts was in the arts. Stylistic changes originating in the reign of Sargon culminated in amazing refinement, naturalism, and spontaneity during Naram-Sin's reign. Most impressive is his victory stele, a 2-meter-high stone carved in bas-relief depicting the king leading his troops in battle in the mountains. Naram-Sin dominates the composition in a pose of grandeur, and is much larger than those surrounding him. Wearing the insignia of royalty – bow, arrow, and battleaxe – he is also crowned with the symbol of divinity, the horned helmet (see figure 4.1). Court sponsorship led to technological and stylistic excellence in other areas of the arts as well. Sculpture in the round now showed enormous refinement. The copper Bassetki statue (bearing the text regarding Naram-Sin's deification), for example, shows great naturalism in the representation of the human body. It presents a technological breakthrough too, as it was made with the lost wax technique, a technique long credited to the classical Greeks. The stylistic elegance of these sculptures is also visible in the minor arts. Seals of royal family members and of many others in the Akkadian administration are remarkable works of artistry. Even the script of the time displays a high level of skill in the writing of cuneiform signs. The impression one obtains from the material remains of this period is one of skill, attention to detail, and artistic talent.

Old Akkadian hegemony was unstable, however. Both in Babylonia and in the wider Near East, Akkadian rule met resistance, a problem exacerbated by outside pressure on the state. Opposition to Akkad in Babylonia was a permanent feature of the period; it may have been the main cause of its failure. Rebellions were violently suppressed; in several of his inscriptions Rimush claimed to have killed or displaced tens of thousands of men from southern cities. Even allowing for exaggeration, these seem to have been drastic measures. The most elaborate description of an uprising derives from the reign of Naram-Sin. He was confronted by two coalitions of Babylonian cities: a northern one under Iphur-Kish, king of Kish, and a southern one under Amar-girid, king of Uruk. That even the region near the capital participated in the opposition to Akkad is a sign that the idea of centralized rule was intolerable everywhere. The number of rebel cities was great, not a single major city was absent. Iphur-Kish had armies from the northern cities Kish, Kutha, Tiwa, Sippar, Kazallu, Kiritab, Apiak, Eresh, Dilbat, and Borsippa. Amar-girid rallied the southern cities of Uruk, Ur, Lagash, Umma, Adab, Shuruppak, Isin, and Nippur, as well as settlements at the Persian Gulf coast. The battles are described as taking place in the open field and between two well-organized armies with numerous men. The ability of the cities to mount such military opposition indicates that local

Figure 4.1 The stele of Naram-Sin, Louvre Museum, Paris. Photo: akg-images/Erich Lessing

structures had continued to exist even after several decades of Akkadian rule. Naram-Sin claimed victory in a quick succession of battles, and it was probably after this that he proclaimed himself a god. The threat to his rule had been serious. It is probably not without irony that Naram-Sin stated that the gods of the very same rebellious cities were asked to grant him divine status.

These Babylonian problems were exacerbated by opposition to Akkad in other areas of the Near East. Since our knowledge of the Akkadian presence in different places is haphazard at best, and the nature of that presence varied in the first place, it is hard to determine when and how it was successfully rejected. At Susa in Elam, Epir-mupi, the man who may have been appointed governor by Naram-Sin or his son Sharkalisharri, was honored by his servants as "the strong one," an epithet usually reserved for kings. Ititi of Assur raided Gasur, an act that probably would have been impossible if the Akkadian ruler had truly been in firm control of both cities. Since we do not really know how direct dominion over these regions had been, we cannot determine whether this represents a serious weakening of Akkadian rule.

Akkad was frequently on the defensive, in fact, militarily threatened by groups within or adjacent to its zone of influence. Amorites, semi-nomadic groups from northern Syria, had to be kept in check, but there is no indication that they tried to move to the south at that time. Another major opponent of Akkad had always been the Iranian state of Marhashi, which lay to the east of Susa. In Sharkalisharri's reign it seems to have overrun Elam, and together the states fought a battle against Akkad near Akshak at the confluence of the Diyala and Tigris rivers, a site very close to the capital. The most severe threat, however, came from mountain people in the east, the Gutians, whose home-land most likely was in the Zagros. In Sharkalisharri's time they appeared in increasing numbers in Babylonia as settlers, necessitating the appointment of a Gutian interpreter in Adab. While they primarily seem to have entered Babylonia in the process of migration, their arrival there was not always peaceful. Sharkalisharri fought them in an unknown location, and we have at least one letter where they are accused of cattle-rustling.

The combination of internal and external pressures led to a rapid collapse of the Akkadian state during Sharkalisharri's reign. The entire Near East reverted to a system of independent states, some of them now governed by new populations. In Babylonia, the Gutians took over several city-states and may have been the strongest power in the region. Gutian rulers even presented themselves as heirs to the Akkad dynasty. One of them, Erridu-pizir, set up statues at Nippur in imitation of the Akkadian kings and claimed their title "king of the four corners (of the universe)," added to that of "King of Gutium." They did not supplant Akkad, however, as several independent city-rulers existed alongside them. Best known to us is the state of Lagash, where a local dynasty left numerous archaeological and textual remains. The statues and inscriptions of one of them, Gudea, rank among the masterpieces of third-millennium Mesopotamian art and literature. In the city of Akkad itself, a local dynasty continued to rule. The situation was so confused that the Sumerian King List exclaims: "Who was king? Who was not king?"

Outside Babylonia, the disappearance of Akkadian influence permitted the development of several new states. In the north of Syria, people speaking the Hurrian language created a small state named "Urkesh and Nawar" after two of its main cities. At Mari, a "dynasty of generals" (Akkadian *shakkanakku*) had perhaps already come into being in the reign of Manishtushu, ruling the city as an independent state for the next 350 years. Susa became part of the state of Awan. This political entity may already have existed in the Early Dynastic period, stretching from the central Zagros to the area south of Susa. At the end of the Old Akkadian period, however, it became more centralized. In the very beginning of the succeeding Ur III period, King Kutik-Inshushinak of Awan was portrayed as a major opponent to Babylonia by the kings of Ur. At that time, he was governor and general of Susa, as well as king of Awan, and controlled eighty-one cities and regions, including some in the central Tigris and Diyala areas. Western Iran, already a formidable adversary to Babylonian powers because of the state of Marhashi, thus became even more of a threat through a process of centralization. Such a development is often thought to have been a result of the earlier expansionist policies of Mesopotamian kings. The incessant campaigning by the Akkadians may have encouraged local rulers to join forces in a defensive reaction, and once stronger they turned against the Babylonian aggressors in their own land. Other examples of this process are visible in later Near Eastern history. Whatever the reason for the creation of these eastern states, the cities of Babylonia established trade contacts with them and others. Wood and hard stones were imported from northern Syria or obtained through military raids by rulers such as Gudea of Lagash. The latter kept trade routes with Magan in the Persian Gulf open. Throughout the Near East, there was thus a general return to the political situation that had preceded the Old Akkadian period. This indicates that Akkadian presence had not radically altered the fundamental political and economic organization of the region.

Still, the century of Akkadian rule and influence over the entire Near East was an important first in the region's history. Never before had armies campaigned so consistently across a wide area, and the Mesopotamians never forgot this. There was no doubt in the public imagination that Sargon and Naram-Sin had been the greatest kings who ever ruled. They became the paradigms of powerful rulers and were the subjects of numerous detailed stories, created and preserved for almost two millennia. Fact and fiction were combined in tales that accorded them increasingly greater achievements (see document 4.1). These literary creations, while providing us with an abundance of information, also pose great challenges to the modern historian. How do we identify historical facts in the accounts we have? How much did later Mesopotamians or other inhabitants of the Near East add to the images of these rulers for their own purposes? If we do not include information from the later stories in our historical reconstruction, although they are much more detailed and explicit than the texts produced during the actual reigns of these kings, we seem to ignore important data. Yet some of those very details may be entirely fabulous, or embroidered with anachronisms, and might produce only stories of how those early kings were perceived in later times. To keep fully separate the two types of sources is impossible; historians will always fill in gaps in the contemporary record based on an awareness of the later stories. But we can work to remain conscious of anachronisms and "improvements" these later stories include. And we can use them to study their creators, people as distant in time as the Assyrians of the seventh century, and try to understand why the Old Akkadian rulers left such a deep impression on them.

Not all later accounts presented the Akkad kings in a positive light. For a long time Sargon was seen only as a heroic warrior, until the mid-first

---

Document 4.1 *Later traditions about the kings of Akkad*

Especially Sargon and Naram-Sin were remembered throughout Mesopotamian history in numerous texts that granted them increasingly far-flung military successes until they ruled almost the entire world. These texts also included elements of criticism, however, from early on for Naram-Sin, only in the first millennium for Sargon. An example of a later tradition on Sargon is found in a chronicle of the first millennium that discusses several early kings:

Sargon, king of Akkad, rose to power in the era of Ishtar. He had no rival or equal, spread his splendor over all the lands, and crossed the sea in the east. In his eleventh year, he conquered the western land to its furthest point, and brought it under (his) sole authority. He set up his statues in the west, and he sent their booty across (the sea) by rafts. His courtiers he made reside at intervals of five double miles and he governed all lands at once. He went to Kazalla and reduced it to a ruin, destroying it to the last spot on which a bird could perch. Afterwards, in his old age, all the lands rebelled against him and laid siege to him in Akkad. But Sargon came out to fight, and defeated them, he overthrew them, and overpowered their large army. Later, Subartu rose up in full force and made him take up his arms. Sargon set out an ambush, defeated it, overthrew it, overpowered its large army, and sent its possessions to Akkad. He dug up earth from the clay-pit of Babylon, and made a counterpart of Babylon next to Akkad. Because of this transgression the great lord Marduk became angry and wiped out his people with a famine. From east to west they rebelled against him, and he (Marduk) afflicted him with insomnia.

Translation after Jean-Jacques Glassner, *Mesopotamian Chronicles* (Atlanta: Society of Biblical Literature, 2004), pp. 268–71.

---

millennium when accusations of arrogance appear. Naram-Sin had already been faulted for his insolence in the late third millennium. He was said to have destroyed the Enlil temple at Nippur, for which he was punished with the loss of his state. So the Mesopotamians also saw the negative aspects of these outbursts of military power and the self-aggrandizement these kings expressed in their texts and art.

4.2 The Third Dynasty of Ur

The period of fragmentation of power after Akkad's hegemony was short-lived. Although the chronology is confused owing to the Sumerian King List's practice of listing contemporaneous dynasties as successive, most likely only some forty years separated the death of King Sharkalisharri from the start of Babylonian

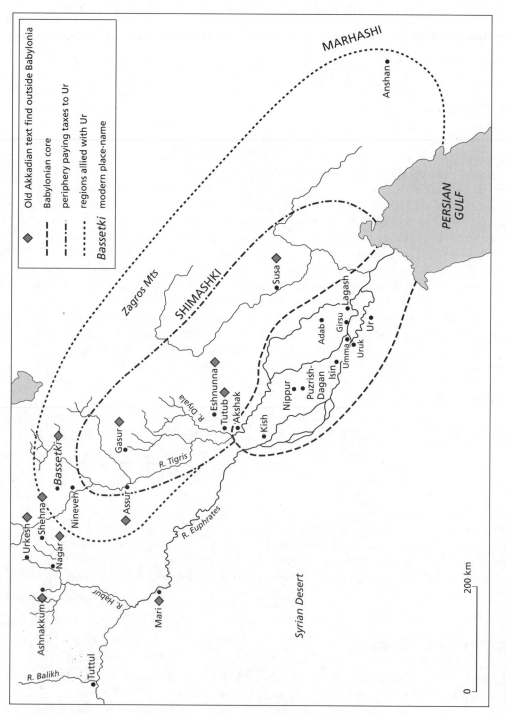

Map 4.1 The Old Akkadian and Ur III states (after Piotr Steinkeller, "The Administrative and Economic Organization of the Ur III State: The Core and the Periphery," in McGuire Gibson and Robert D. Biggs, eds., *The Organization of Power: Aspects of Bureaucracy in the Ancient Near East* [Chicago: The Oriental Institute, 1987], p. 28).

reunification. The return to centralized rule is portrayed in the sources as having begun with the expulsion of the Gutians. King Utu-hegal of Uruk relates how he chased them from southern Babylonia and returned kingship to Sumer. His brother, Ur-Namma, succeeded him and imposed the rule of a new dynasty over the entirety of Babylonia, using the city of Ur as his capital. Ur-Namma continued Utu-hegal's work: he forced into submission autonomous rulers and local rulers dependent on the Gutians, but the details are vague. Neither his inscriptions nor his year names devote attention to battles in Babylonia. Was there little opposition, or did he not want to describe how he won supremacy? In any event, he could claim by the end of his reign a new title, "King of Sumer and Akkad," referring to the entirety of Babylonia. The expulsion of the Gutians did not stop at the domestic borders, however. Ur-Namma campaigned in the Diyala region against them, and this brought him in conflict with Kutik-Inshushinak of Awan, who controlled a wide area of western Iran. Soon Susa was ruled by Ur.

Around 2100 Ur-Namma started the Third Dynasty of Ur (or Ur III dynasty), a succession of five generations of rulers from the same family (for a list of kings, see p. 303). According to the Sumerian King List, it was the third time that Ur held kingship, hence the modern designation. For about seventy years, this dynasty governed Babylonia and adjacent regions to the east, using an elaborate bureaucracy that produced an exorbitant number of written documents. Virtually no period of ancient Near Eastern history presents the historian with such an abundance and variety of documentation. Indeed, even in all of the ancient histories of Greece and Rome, there are few periods where a similar profusion of textual material is found. A basic sequence of the events of the Ur III period can be established through the year names, the succession of which is established from the start of Shulgi's reign to the end of Ibbi-Sin's, a period of ninety years. The royal court produced inscriptions commemorating military campaigns and building activity. Scribes also wrote a series of hymns honoring the kings, which refer to some of their important acts (see document 4.2).

Most plentiful are the archival texts from this period. Some 40,000 are now published and tens of thousands more are known to exist in museums and other collections. They range from the simple receipt of one sheep to the calculation of the harvest of 38 million liters of cereals. They document many aspects of economic life, including agriculture in all its aspects, manufacture, trade, taxation, and the sale of goods, and they derive from many cities in the state. The largest groups are from Ur, Umma, Girsu, Puzrish-Dagan, and Nippur, thus the southern half of Babylonia. But smaller finds were made throughout Sumer and Akkad. Ironically, this abundance presents a great challenge. Confronted with this mass of documents, scholars have to develop approaches that enable them to look at groups of texts rather than single documents. This task is made complicated by the fact that most of them were excavated by looters and dispersed into innumerable collections through the antiquities market. More serious is the impression that is created by the mass of texts,

Document 4.2 *Hymns to kings of the Ur III dynasty*

With the Ur III dynasty appeared a new form of royal celebration in literary form, the composition of hymns that praise the king for his accomplishments. Those were wide-ranging, including especially his skills in warfare, but also as an athlete, a virile sexual partner, a scholar, and a just ruler. The hymns connected the king to the pantheon, claiming that the gods protected and promoted him, and sometimes declared that he was related to mythical heroes of the past, such as Gilgamesh. The genre was popular until the late Old Babylonian dynasty, and used the Sumerian language. The compositions are mostly known from manuscripts written by schoolboys in the Old Babylonian schools. They formed an important part of scribal training. King Shulgi of the Ur III period had the largest number of such hymns devoted to him, possibly because of his long reign of 48 years. The extract here praises his skills as a schoolboy as well as a warrior, using metaphorical language.

> I am a king, offspring begotten by a king and born by a queen. I, Shulgi the noble, have been blessed with a favorable destiny right from the womb. When I was small, I was at the academy, where I learned the scribal art from the tablets of Sumer and Akkad. None of the nobles could write on clay as I could. There where people regularly went for tutelage in the scribal art, I qualified fully in subtraction, addition, reckoning and accounting. The fair goddess Nanibgal, the goddess Nisaba, provided me amply with knowledge and comprehension. I am an experienced scribe who does not neglect a thing.
>
> When I sprang up, muscular as a cheetah, galloping like a thoroughbred ass at full gallop, the favor of the god An brought me joy; to my delight the god Enlil spoke favorably about me, and they gave me the scepter because of my righteousness. I place my foot on the neck of the foreign lands; the fame of my weapons is established as far as the south, and my victory is established in the highlands. When I set off for battle and strife to a place that the god Enlil has commanded me, I go ahead of the main body of my troops and I clear the terrain for my scouts. I have a positive passion for weapons. Not only do I carry lance and spear, I also know how to handle slingstones with a sling. The clay bullets, the treacherous pellets that I shoot, fly around like a violent rainstorm. In my rage I do not let them miss.

Translation: Jeremy Black et al., www-etcsl.orient.ox.ac.uk/c.2.4.2.02

namely, that it is complete in its coverage of economic activity. That is not the case. The record is extremely biased, produced almost exclusively by the state, and it illuminates that area of society, leaving other aspects, such as private economic activity, nearly in the dark.

 Remarkable is the lack of interest in this period by later Mesopotamians when compared to how the Akkadian kings were remembered. In the first centuries of the second millennium, Ur III rulers were known primarily through the school curriculum. Students at that time copied out hymns, royal correspondence, and some inscriptions, but few new compositions were created around the Ur III kings. The failure of Ur, rather than its success, was the focus of these new literary texts. Soon after its collapse several laments were composed describing the destructions of Ur, Nippur, and other southern cities. These did not narrate the destruction of the Ur III state for its historical interest, but were probably intended more to justify the presence of new dynasties, which could claim to have restored order after great calamities. In later centuries, only a handful of references to the Ur III kings are found. Those are almost totally restricted to omens giving vague remarks about kings' deaths, like one that states that Amar-Suen died from "a bite of his shoe," a reference we fail to understand. These kings did not leave the impression on the Mesopotamian consciousness that the Akkadian ones did.

The Ur III state was indeed of a different character than its predecessor: geographically more restricted in size, but internally more centrally organized. The state itself had two distinct parts: the heartland of Sumer and Akkad, and a militarily controlled zone to the east in between the Tigris and the Zagros Mountains. Outside lay the rest of the Near East with which diplomatic contacts were maintained, or where the armies of Ur raided. The system was developed primarily during the forty-eight-year reign of King Shulgi, who restructured the heartland of the state and conquered the adjacent zones to the east starting in his twentieth regnal year. It was not put in place overnight – nor did it stay unchanged over time – but in its general outlines it worked as follows.

The heartland was the traditional area of Babylonia including the lower Diyala Valley. It was divided up into about twenty provinces, in essence the territories of the formerly independent city-states. These were administered on the king's behalf by governors, indicated by the Sumerian term énsi, which in Early Dynastic days had designated the sovereign ruler of the city-state. These men often were from prominent local families, and the office of governor regularly passed from father to son. Other family members held high positions in the province. Part of the king's strategy was thus to keep these families on his side, something he may have pursued through marriage. Shulgi, for instance, is known to have married at least nine women, each of whom may have been members of the various important local families. The governors primarily controlled the temple estates, which were especially extensive in the south. They were responsible for the maintenance of the canal system and acted as the highest judges in the province. While representing the king, a wide range of powers was concentrated in their hands.

The civil administration of governors was paralleled by a military one, headed by generals (Sumerian shagina), although zones of authority did not always fully coincide with the provinces. The province of Umma, for instance, had one governor and several generals, each with a separate district. The generals were not native to the region where they were stationed, nor descendants of prominent old families, but were chosen by the king from groups of men who had made their careers in royal service. Many of them had Akkadian or foreign (Hurrian, Elamite, Amorite) names, the latter seemingly recent arrivals in

Babylonia. They were personally tied to the king, often marrying women of the royal family, and they received their income from royal agricultural estates and other properties.

The central administration established a system of taxation that collected a substantial part of the provinces' resources. This system was given the Sumerian name bala, which basically meant "exchange." It was a massive fund to which all provinces had to contribute and from which they could withdraw goods, enabling the state to use resources from all over its territory. The amount and composition of each province's contributions depended on its economic potential and the nature of its productive sector. For instance, Girsu provided grain, which it grew in abundance, while its neighbor Umma also contributed manufactured goods in wood, reeds, and leather. Many of the taxes were consumed locally by crown dependents, but some were sent to specialized collection points from which they were distributed when and wherever the goods were needed. Each province's contribution was calculated in advance on the basis of its agricultural and manufacturing potential. In the case of cereals, for example, officials measured the size of the agricultural area, and estimated the potential harvest. On the basis of that figure, the amount to be contributed to the state was determined. At the end of the year, the actual contributions were compared to what had been demanded and often a positive or negative balance was carried over to the next year. Also, contributions of the periphery, especially in the form of livestock, were added to the bala-fund (see below). Provinces were able to withdraw from the fund for their needs, thereby getting access to their neighbors' resources. All of the movements of goods were carefully accounted for by state administrators.

Under the Ur III dynasty, Sumer and Akkad flourished economically, partly as the result of royal works. The archaeological record shows that there was a high level of urbanization at this time and the population density was higher than ever before. The degree to which wealth was available is also indicated by the extensive building activities of kings throughout the state. In their year names the kings often commemorated the digging of irrigation canals increasing the available agricultural zones. For these works a great labor force had to be available, and the organization of this labor perhaps best shows how far-reaching was the influence of the crown in economic life. Hundreds of able-bodied men and many women (called gurush and géme respectively in Sumerian) were conscripted to provide labor to the state, and that labor was also part of the bala-fund. Two classes of workers can be distinguished: those who provided labor year-round, and those who were only forced to do so half of the year. Service was predominantly paid for in rations – barley, oil, and wool – the amounts of which depended on the laborer's status. They were usually assigned specific tasks, such as weaving or the cutting of reed, but when needed in the times of high demand they could be transferred to agricultural duties, for harvesting or canal maintenance. It seems that the people whose labor was only requisitioned part-time hired themselves out to the state at other times. Since the state's assets were so enormous, including fields, fishing grounds, manufacturing workshops, and so on, the demand for manpower was very high. The Ur III state was not a totalitarian regime whose inhabitants were fully subjected to the bureaucracy, so labor had to be recruited by offering sufficient compensation. Many of the texts we have record the issuing of rations, which had to be taken from the state's central resources.

This depth of organization was applied throughout the heartland of the Ur III state, the geographical extent of which was well defined. It incorporated the region in the Mesopotamian alluvium where irrigation agriculture was practiced. Its northern border was delineated by a wall erected by Shulgi, and strengthened by Shu-Sin, in the area where the Tigris and Euphrates rivers are nearest to each other. The wall is usually seen as intending to keep Amorites out of Babylonia, but can also be interpreted as a clear demarcation of a northern boundary.

Ur ruled the territories to its east through means different than those employed in the heartland. Already Ur-Namma had campaigned in the area between the Tigris River and the Zagros Mountains, and by the end of Shulgi's reign Ur fully controlled the area from Susa in the south to the Mosul plain in the north. The Ur III kings imposed a military government over this region. They put in place a system of direct exploitation that was headed by generals (shagina), who could be moved at will from one center to another. The royal chancellor (sukkal-mah), representing the interests of the crown, supervised the system from the capital out. He charged the generals with collecting tribute calculated in exact numbers of cattle, sheep, and goats to be procured by different levels of the military establishment. How the soldiers acquired the animals is not stated, but most likely they gathered them from the local populations. Large numbers of animals were taken to Babylonia where they were assembled in a place near Nippur called Puzrish-Dagan, especially created for this purpose by Shulgi in his thirty-eighth year. There they entered the bala taxation system and could be issued for food for the court or for offerings in the numerous temples. Many animals were kept for their wool. The numbers of animals involved, both from the eastern territories and from Babylonia proper, were staggering: records demonstrate that up to 200 sheep and goats and fifteen head of cattle could pass through Puzrish-Dagan on a single day. The eastern periphery was thus exploited for its resources of animals, which entered the economy of the heartland.

Beyond these eastern dominions were large regions considered to be hostile and frequently the targets of military campaigns. Royal inscriptions mention a variety of peoples and places raided for booty and captives. Some of the states encountered there had already existed in the time of Akkad and remained formidable opponents. The Ur III kings used diplomacy to appease their rulers: three of the five kings of Ur sent their daughters to marry Iranian princes. In the end the policy failed: eastern states such as Shimashki remained perpetually hostile, and eventually played an important role in the overthrow of the Ur III state. In the Persian Gulf, Ur maintained the trade contacts that had existed since the Old Akkadian period. Already Ur-Namma claimed to have restored trade with Magan, and throughout the Ur III period we find administrative documents that mention that region. Merchants' records indicate that wool and textiles, abundantly produced in Babylonia, were sent there to be exchanged for copper and stones, such as diorite. Ur's contacts with the east and south were thus for the purpose of obtaining mineral resources, through trade, diplomacy, and military raids.

The Ur III kings approached the regions to the north and west differently. Diplomatic relations with the states there were established, with no attempts toward military control. Ur-Namma arranged for the marriage of a Mari princess to his son Shulgi, perhaps in the hope that this state on the Middle Euphrates would act as a buffer and intermediary with regions further north. Syrian states maintained friendly relations with Ur, but contacts were rare. The archaeological record shows a reduction in the number and sizes of settlements in northern Syria, for reasons unknown. Possibly the region went through an economic downturn, and only those cities that controlled trade routes were in contact with Babylonia. In the Ur III sources from Babylonia we find references to people from the Syrian cities Tuttul, Ebla, and Urshu, and messengers from the Mediterranean harbor of Byblos also appear. There is no indication of any single city dominating Syria politically or militarily. The Syrian force that did play a crucial role in political events was made up of Amorites, predominantly semi-nomadic people who are depicted in the Babylonian record as hostile invaders. Their pressure would substantially contribute to the end of the Ur III state.

Akkad's military interactions with Syria had thus been replaced by diplomacy under Ur. Even if the Ur III rulers proclaimed themselves "kings of the four corners (of the universe)," their military reach was geographically smaller than that of the Old Akkadian rulers. Yet the Ur III state's internal coherence was greater. Several reforms were instituted in Babylonia in order to facilitate the functioning of the state. The bala taxation system was a major organization that enabled the collection and distribution of resources throughout Sumer and Akkad. The state's involvement in the local economies was enormous, and its employment of men and women extensive. In order to account for all movements of its assets, an elaborate bureaucracy was needed, hence the profusion of texts. These had to be written by scribes trained to use proper accounting techniques and formulae. We see a uniformity of the writing system in official documents throughout the Ur III state, and it is likely that schools were established to teach this. The system of weights and measures was simplified, and Shulgi may have attempted to introduce a standard calendar throughout the land. While each city continued to use its own sequence of month names, a calendar appeared in his reign that was used at Puzrish-Dagan and in places like Umma, Girsu, and Eshnunna for royal business. It was never imposed on the entire region, however, not even for central accounts, which shows that local practices had great resilience. Only in the next century, when the region was once more politically fragmented, one calendar, that of Nippur, became used throughout Babylonia.

Figure 4.2 Dish inscribed with the name of the high priestess of the god Nanna, Enmahgalanna, daughter of King Amar-Suen. Photo © Trustees of the British Museum, London

The kings did pursue an active policy to unify the land under them in ideological terms as well. They placed their children as high priests and priestesses in the major cults, and they built and restored temples all over the kingdom (see figure 4.2). Before his twentieth year of rule, Shulgi was deified and his successors assumed this status when they came to the throne. They were regarded as gods of the entire land, rather than of individual cities, and cults were established for them throughout the state. Temples and statues of the kings as gods were built in various cities, thus providing a focus of centralization through the cult as well. Many officials used cylinder seals to certify the business they undertook, and those usually contained an inscription providing the owner's name and his or her title (see figure 4.3). It is important that they always referred to their status as "servant of the king," indicating that their authority ultimately derived from him. Moreover, people gave their children names referring to the king as god, and officials were encouraged to change their names to include a reference to the king. Names such as "Shulgi is my god" were common. The ideology of the centralized state thus permeated down to the level of the entire citizenry.

One can doubt, however, that in practice this royal ideal was achieved. The local economies and hierarchies survived quite independently, even if they had to pay taxes and homage to the king at Ur. This is most clearly demonstrated

Figure 4.3 Impression of the cylinder seal used by King Ibbi-Sin's official, Ilum-bani. The Metropolitan Museum of Art, Gift of Martin and Sarah Cherkasky, 1988 (1988.380.2). Photograph, all rights reserved, The Metropolitan Museum of Art

by the aftermath of the Ur III state's collapse. Babylonia did not experience a period of decline at that time, but regions that had been part of the unified state reverted to their local habits without evidence of disruption. This would not have been possible had their economies become specialized and inter-dependent components of a single system. We have to keep in mind the bias of the documentation used in our historical reconstructions: almost all our texts derive from the state bureaucracy and describe the state's activities. It would thus be easy to see the Ur III state as a highly authoritarian one, documenting and directing all the movements of its dependents. But within this abundance of state records we see traces of economic activity that was not controlled by it. People often simultaneously provided services to the state and interacted economically with others on their own behalf. We also see that regional variations in many respects had survived: in the south the state administered its extensive holdings through the temple-estates that had existed for many centuries, while in the north it relied more on individual agents who may have contracted other business on the side. Other traditions survived through this period, and the multiplicity of local systems must not be forgotten.

The end of Ur's hegemony was sudden and (as usual) we do not fully understand what happened or what the main causes were. Both internal and external factors played a role. Within Babylonia itself, the former city-states and their local governors had always nursed a sense of local independence. Early in Ibbi-Sin's reign, some provinces stopped contributing their taxes, and by his ninth year the whole bala system had disappeared. Scribes stopped dating tablets with Ur III year names in Puzrish-Dagan at the end of Ibbi-Sin's year 2, at Umma in year 4, at Girsu in year 5, and at Nippur in year 8. An independent dynasty came to the throne in Isin in Ibbi-Sin's eighth year, headed by one of his former generals, Ishbi-Erra. The new dynasty soon took control over Nippur, the religious center of the entire region. Simultaneously, a famine may have struck the area of Ur. Some of the king's correspondence, known only from later copies, shows that Ibbi-Sin implored Ishbi-Erra, when still his general, to acquire grain in the north at whatever price was necessary. At Ur grain seems to have risen fifteen times in price and it could no longer be used as animal fodder. How much of that was due to the lack of good harvests and how much to the refusal of the provinces to pay their taxes is unclear. Certain spheres of the economy seem in fact to have performed well at this time. Ur had a workshop that produced precious goods for the temples and palace, and records from Ibbi-Sin's fifteenth year indicate that some 18 kilograms of gold and 75 kilograms of silver were used that year. The state's coffers were still well stocked.

The literary tradition of the early second millennium placed great emphasis on external forces in explaining the fall of Ur. Two groups of attackers were mentioned: Amorites from the west and Elamites from the east. The Amorites were semi-nomadic groups from northern Syria, whom Babylonian literature described in extremely negative terms:

> (The Amorite,) he is dressed in sheep's skins;
> He lives in tents in wind and rain;
> He doesn't offer sacrifices.
> Armed [vagabond] in the steppe,
> he digs up truffles and is restless.
> He eats raw meat,
> lives his life without a home,
> and, when he dies, he is not buried according to proper rituals.[5]

When Shu-Sin fortified the northern wall, he named it "a wall to keep the Amorites out," and royal officials frequently complained about attacks on it. Similarly, Ishbi-Erra used the Amorites as an excuse for not being able to deliver grain to Ur. The official portrayal of the Amorites as hostile invaders was not fully accurate, however. Already in the early Ur III period, many people with Amorite names resided in Babylonia, both in the cities and the countryside. They were already integrated in all levels of society. The image that they were aggressive invaders probably derived to a great extent from the common prejudice of settled populations against semi-nomadic people, which led to the literary trope of such people as barbarians. The exact role of the Amorites in the overthrow of the Ur III state is thus difficult to discern from such writings, but we can see a parallelism with the Gutians' role in the end of the Akkadian state. Both groups came from outside the region, acquired political importance, and were later regarded as crucial in the overthrow of the existing political situation.

The final blow to Ur came from the east, however. The ruler of Shimashki, which had been Ur's major opponent in the east, seized Elam and surrounding territories when Ur's power waned. Late in Ibbi-Sin's reign he turned against

Babylonia itself and raided it. He captured the capital Ur and deported King Ibbi-Sin to Susa. For some seven years the Elamites occupied the city, until Ishbi-Erra of Isin chased them out. He and his successors claimed to be the heirs of the kings of Ur, but they could not control the same geographical area. More and more independent city-states emerged throughout Babylonia, a situation that will be discussed in the next chapter.

The spotlight on Babylonia in the twenty-first century is so bright that the rest of the Near East is often ignored in historical reconstructions. Regions often can be studied only when they were in Ur's orbit. But states in the east, primarily Shimashki, and the semi-nomadic Amorites in the west escaped the control of Ur and developed into formidable opponents. These external forces were presented as the catalysts of change in later traditions, but the role of internal opposition to centralized rule should not be underestimated.

NOTES

1 There are various designations for the state, most commonly Old Akkadian or Sargonic. The name of the dynastic seat, Akkad, is sometimes anglicized as Agade or even Accad.
2 Douglas R. Frayne, *Sargonic and Gutian Period (2334–2113 BC)* (*The Royal Inscriptions of Mesopotamia. Early Periods*, volume 2) (Toronto, Buffalo, and New York: University of Toronto Press, 1993), p. 31.
3 Ibid., p. 16.
4 Translation after Walter Farber, "Die Vergöttlichung Naram-Sîns," *Orientalia* 52 (1983), pp. 67–72.
5 Marriage of Martu, lines 132–8; translation after Jean Bottéro and Samuel Noah Kramer, *Lorsque les dieux faisaient l'homme* (Paris: Gallimard, 1989), p. 434.

5

The Near East in the Early Second Millennium

3000	2500	2000	1500	1000	500

2017	Ishbi-Erra founds dynasty at Isin
ca. 1910–1830	*Karum*-Kanesh level II
1897	Beginning of open warfare between Isin and Larsa
1834	Kudur-Mabuk dynasty established at Larsa
ca. 1810–1740	*Karum*-Kanesh level Ib
ca. 1800–1762	Mari archives
1793	Rim-Sin of Larsa conquers Isin
1763	Hammurabi of Babylon conquers southern Babylonia
1762	Eshnunna sacked by Hammurabi
1761	Mari conquered by Hammurabi

Throughout the period from ca. 2000 to ca. 1600 the political and social structures of the Near East show the same basic characteristics: numerous states were spread over the landscape from western Iran to the Mediterranean coast. Their rulers, all military men, vied for power, joined in ever-shifting alliances, and turned against one another. A passage from a letter excavated at Mari and written in the early eighteenth century sums up the situation aptly:

> No king is truly powerful on his own. Ten to fifteen kings follow Hammurabi of Babylon, Rim-Sin of Larsa, Ibal-pi-El of Eshnunna or Amut-pi-El of Qatna; but twenty kings follow Yarim-Lim of Yamkhad.[1]

A handful of powerful rulers from southern Babylonia to western Syria had carved up the Near East by forcing smaller kings to be their vassals. In the second half of the period, some succeeded in establishing dominance over larger territories, albeit only for a short while. There is no clear chronological division between the moments of political fragmentation and those of centralization. Here we will explore the former, which still exemplifies the basic political structure of the Near East in its early history, the prevalent city-state. In the next chapter the moments of centralization will be examined. A purely chronological sequence of the narrative is not possible by this arrangement.

Our grasp on Near Eastern history becomes very wide-ranging in geographical terms with the start of the second millennium. Writing in cuneiform became a common skill known from southwestern Iran to central Anatolia and western Syria, with a great number of practices shared throughout that region. Babylonia clearly continued to be the source of most of the scribal traditions. Its language, which can now be identified as a separate dialect of Akkadian, was used almost everywhere by native speakers of other languages (Amorite, Hurrian, Elamite), who also adopted the southern writing style and spellings. The most prominent exception to this is found in a central Anatolian colony of merchants from Assur, who wrote a different dialect of Akkadian, Old Assyrian. They used different forms of the cuneiform signs, and read them often unconventionally. This is all the more remarkable since the official texts found in their hometown are Babylonian in character. Sumerian flourished as a language of culture, but almost exclusively in Babylonia.

There is a great variety in the origin of the texts available to us, as they derive both from institutional and private contexts. The primary source varies regionally, however. In Babylonia the recovered cuneiform records are predominantly from private contexts, in great contrast to the Ur III period, when they had almost all come from central archives. Also in the Assyrian colonies in Anatolia we find only private records, but elsewhere in the Near East it is the palaces and other royal institutions that provide almost all the texts in the early second millennium (see box 5.1). Especially in northern Syria, royal chancelleries trained in Babylonian practices left the writings we have. One genre of writing that flourished in these centuries is that of the letter, and we have the correspondence of private businessmen in Babylonia and Assur, members of royal courts, officials, generals, ambassadors, and so on. Mostly they wrote to one another about official business, but once in a while we get a glimpse of other concerns – health, love, rivalries . . . The letters provide us with a more intimate view of the people we study, a perspective not available before this period.

5.1 Nomads and Sedentary People

All our texts and archaeological remains derive from cities. Throughout the Near East, cities flourished, and areas such as northern Syria, which had experienced a drop in permanent occupation in the late third millennium, became fully

Box 5.1 *The Mari letters*

French excavations since the 1930s at the Middle Euphrates site of Mari in Syria have unearthed a large royal palace of the nineteenth and eighteenth centuries. In it, some 20,000 tablets were found, a number that increases with continuing excavations. Many of these are letters written between the palace and its court representatives, both domestic and foreign. Because of Mari's location between Babylonia and Syria, and between the agricultural areas of the Euphrates Valley and the steppe used by semi-nomadic tribes, these letters inform us about a vast array of political and military affairs throughout the Near East, and about the interactions between settled and nomadic people. The letters were carefully drafted documents in which the scribes often summarized the original queries or orders before a reply was given. They were composed in full Babylonian manner: the language, writing style, and tablet shapes were of southern derivation although the majority of people at Mari, and at other courts with which Mari was in contact, spoke a west Semitic language rather than Akkadian. Influences from the vernaculars can be identified in the letters from various regions. When Hammurabi conquered Mari in 1761, his scribes made inventories of the palace archives, and identified and removed letters involving Babylonian affairs, which were probably taken off to the capital. This indicates how important these diplomatic archives were considered to be.

The court at Mari was not the only one to have such archives. Palaces excavated at Qattara (Tell Rimah), Shushara (Shemshara), Shubat-Enlil (Tell Leilan), and others have yielded smaller, yet similar, diplomatic archives. They show how the entire region made up a system of kingdoms whose rulers had to remain informed in order to survive.

urbanized by the nineteenth century. Very important in the political and social life of the Near East, however, were people whose livelihood was not tied to the agriculture that supported the urban centers. These were semi-nomadic pastoralists who spent part of the year moving around with their flocks in search of pasture in the steppe, the other part in villages near the rivers. Such people were a permanent feature of the Near East, but in certain periods they became more visible in the urban record because they interacted more closely with city residents, competing for political power. Different designations were given to them, always from the point of view of the people in the cities who wrote the texts. In the late third and early second millennia they were grouped together under the term Amorites, which coincided with the term for the "west," Akkadian Amurru. Whether the geographical designator gave its name to the people living in the west, or the people's name led to the compass direction, is unclear. The term Amorite did not refer to a well-defined ethnic or tribal group, but its use was flexible and referred primarily to people who were considered to have a semi-nomadic background and roots in the west.

The life of pastoralists revolved around their flocks. Throughout the Near East millions of sheep and goats were herded for what is called their renewable resources: especially wool and hair, and when dead, skins, bones, horns, and tendons. Meat consumption was limited, so relatively few animals were slaughtered. The natural environment with its dry summers necessitated the moving around of the flocks to different pastures. In the summer, they were kept near the river valleys, close to cities and villages, while in the winter, the steppe had sufficient vegetation to graze the animals there. The patterns of movement were well planned with groups using the same winter pastures year after year. Pastoralists thus led a hybrid life – sedentary in villages in the summer, nomadic in the steppe in the winter – and modern scholarship uses the term semi-nomadic to refer to them.

The interactions between nomads and sedentary people took place on several levels. The two groups were economically complementary, one producing animal products, the other agricultural and crafts goods, and exchange was to the benefit of both. Arrangements had to be made to insure that the animals did not destroy cereal crops by grazing or trampling. Fallow fields were made available for grazing which encouraged plant growth and provided natural fertilization. Because of this interaction, cities and states could enforce some type of control over the pastoralists. Depending on the proximity of the pastoralists' villages and grazing grounds to the centers of power, they were more or less subjected to political control, military and labor levies, and taxation.

Whenever pastoralists moved into the orbit of settled societies, they entered the realm of the written documentation that we study. In the early second millennium, we are provided with a uniquely informative record from the palace archives of the city Mari on the Middle Euphrates. That city controlled a long stretch of the Euphrates Valley, which incorporated villages of pastoralists who used the Syrian steppe for winter pasture. The social organization of the semi-nomadic pastoralists was tribal. People claimed descent from a common ancestor, real or fictional, but those affiliations were loose: some tribes were absorbed by others, and some people changed tribes. The tribes that lived around Mari were divided into two major branches: those "of the left," i.e., the north when facing the rising sun, the Sim'alites, and those "of the right," i.e., the south, the Yaminites. The latter lived the closest to the city and their subdivisions are better known. They included, for example, Amnanu and Yakhruru, groups that were attested in Babylonia as well. So these designators had a long history by the early second millennium, and tribes over a wide geographical area could claim common descent. Tribal names were given to settled and non-settled people alike, which shows the hybridity of the pastoralist lifestyle.

In the interactions between Mari and the pastoral groups, the palace had the most control over those whose villages were nearby. Inhabitants were subjected to a census, they had to provide labor and military service, and headmen were appointed to take responsibility for the group's interactions with the palace. More distant groups, such as the Sutians, escaped this control and often Mari's relationship with them is portrayed in very negative terms. They were constantly accused of being robbers and murderers, an image that derives partly from the prejudices settled people had against non-settled ones. On the other hand, we should not fully dismiss the accounts as prejudiced: competition over scarce resources between farmers and pastoralists could be fierce and violent.

Ethnographic research shows that sedentarization by pastoral nomads usually took place among the richest and poorest of the group. Very successful herders could not continue to expand the size of their herds as they would become unmanageable, so they started to invest some of their wealth in land, and settled down to take care of it. The poorest had too few animals to support themselves and tried to gain employment among settled people, including as mercenaries to states. At the turn of the third to the second millennium, we see a major increase in the presence of Amorites in cities throughout the Near East, and during the first four centuries of the second millennium many people made explicit references to their tribal origins. This probably resulted from the political situation in Babylonia at the end of the third millennium. Amorites were present in the Near East from the mid-third millennium on, as is documented in texts from Shuruppak and Ebla. In the Ur III state they appeared in increasing numbers in the texts: we can recognize them either because they are explicitly identified as Amorite, or because their names are in the Amorite language, a Semitic idiom distinct from Akkadian. While they were active in all levels of Ur III society, including as generals in the army, official texts emphasized hostile relationships between the Amorites and the state. Shulgi and Shu-Sin's year names commemorated the building of a wall to keep Amorites out of the land, and Ibbi-Sin claimed to have defeated them in his seventeenth year. Later literary tradition placed a lot of blame for the collapse of the Ur III state on the Amorites.

Upon the disappearance of the Ur III state and the political fragmentation that ensued in Babylonia, many of the new dynasties claimed Amorite ancestry, something that was mentioned with pride. In the eighteenth century, Hammurabi of Babylon, who came to rule a large urbanized territory, still referred to himself as "king of the Amorites." Under his fourth successor, Ammisaduqa, a list of ancestors of the dynasty explicitly recognized that they were Amorite. A list of ancestors of Shamshi-Adad found in Assur contained the same Amorite names as those given by Ammisaduqa. There was thus perhaps a set of common ancestors that was acknowledged by all Amorites. There was no stigma attached to being Amorite, even if the literature composed and copied in Babylonia at the time constantly depicted them as hostile and uncivilized.

The process we observe was one in which semi-nomadic groups, primarily of Syrian origin, spread out throughout the Near East. Some members rose in the political hierarchies of the existing city-states, often through a military career. When the central power of Ur in Babylonia fell apart at the end of the third millennium, some men of Amorite descent were able to seize the throne in several city-states. Possibly because of the competition between old and new lineages of power, between urban Sumerians and Akkadians and non-urban Amorites, these backgrounds were emphasized. The clear acknowledgment of dynastic roots outside the cities in ancestral lists may indicate that the concept of the city-state as the center of all power was waning, and the idea of a larger territory as a political unit started to develop. The presence of Amorites throughout the Near East, however, did not translate into the creation of a new cultural ideal. In Babylonia, Amorites fully adopted the existing culture, including the use of Sumerian and Akkadian for their literature; nowhere did the Amorite language become the official language in the written record. In cities like Mari, their vernacular influenced the written language to a great extent, but the latter remained Akkadian.

5.2 Babylonia

The end of Ur's hegemony over Sumer and Akkad did not lead to an immediate fragmentation of political power. Early in the reign of Ibbi-Sin, the last king of Ur, Ishbi-Erra, a general under his authority, had established a dynasty in Isin, and took over control of much of the region. When Ur was captured by the Elamites, it was Ishbi-Erra who freed the city, and his successors usurped the title "king of Ur." Even so, decentralizing forces were strong, and an increasing number of local dynasties arose in the twentieth and nineteenth centuries. Most prominent were the royal families at Isin and Larsa in the south, and Babylon in the north, but cities such as Uruk, Kish, and Sippar at times had their own kings. In the region to the east of the Tigris, independent dynasties established themselves at Eshnunna and Assur, while Elam remained outside the Babylonian political orbit. Rulers claimed the right to issue year names, and the presence of tablets dated with the names of particular city-dynasties allows us to identify what areas they controlled and when. By the early nineteenth century, competition escalated into open conflict between these states, resulting in what seems to us incessant warfare. Nevertheless, the states of Babylonia acknowledged that they were part of a common system, one that centered round Nippur as a religious capital. Political control over that city, which shifted several times, gave a king the right to the title of "king of Sumer and Akkad." A calendar of month names from Nippur was used as the official one throughout the region, and the blessing of Nippur's priesthood provided a king with a special status. Another tradition that survived and shows that the cities regarded themselves as partners in a common system was the appointment of the high priestess at Ur. From the time of Sargon of Akkad, the daughter of the dominant ruler of the region had held that position. In the early second millennium, high priestesses were installed by the city-dynasty that ruled at Ur, but the incumbent was not immediately replaced when that political control changed. For instance, the daughter of the Isin king Ishme-Dagan remained in office after Gungunum of Larsa had conquered Ur, and cults of the deceased priestesses survived long after the authority of their hometown dynasties. The conviction that the Babylonian city-states were part of a single system enabled the local rulers to adhere to an ideology that there was only one kingship in Babylonia, which passed from one city to

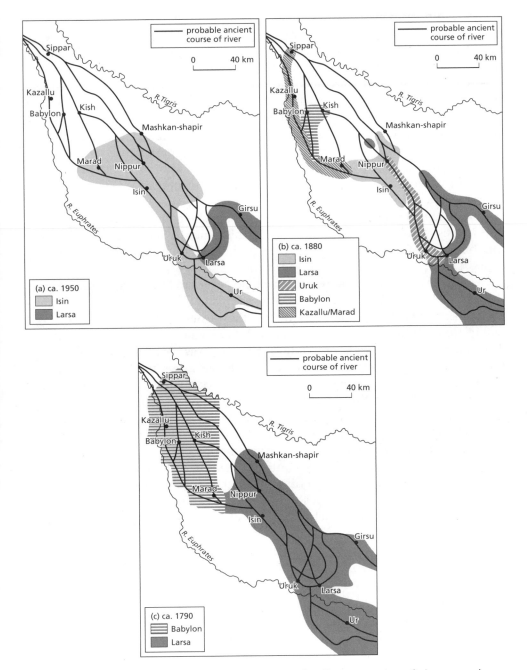

Map 5.1 The political division of Babylonia in the first centuries of the second millennium (after Michael Roaf, *Cultural Atlas of Mesopotamia and the Ancient Near East* [Oxford: Equinox, 1990], p. 109)

another. Whoever was acknowledged by the Nippur priesthood was king of Sumer and Akkad, even if in reality his powers were limited. It is in this context that we have to see the creation of the Sumerian King List, a document that insisted on the idea that there was only one king at a time.

Isin and Larsa were the main actors on the political scene in southern Babylonia. At first the Isin dynasty was heir to the much-reduced Ur III state (for a list of kings, see p. 303). The Nippur priesthood acknowledged its kings, who maintained control over most southern cities, including Ur, and undertook public works in several of them. For a century the region was at peace. Later in the twentieth century, however, a rival dynasty established itself at Larsa (for a list of kings, see p. 304), soon taking full control over the south and east of Babylonia, while Isin's power was reduced to central Babylonia. In 1897 Abi-sare, king of Larsa, openly attacked his Isin colleague, which enabled other cities to reject Isin's supremacy. At this time the region had the greatest number of rival dynasties in the period, several of which could claim the support of the Nippur priesthood in turn.

Centralizing forces were at work as well, however, and the initiative came from the city of Larsa. After a period of internal instability, with a series of short-lived rulers often from different families, the throne of Larsa was seized by a family from the area east of the Tigris, the so-called Kudur-Mabuk dynasty. The father, Kudur-Mabuk, probably an Elamite, was based in Mashkan-shapir, the easternmost city of central Babylonia. He placed his son Warad-Sin (ruled 1834–23) on Larsa's throne, but meddled in local affairs. When Warad-Sin died, his brother Rim-Sin replaced him and had the longest reign recorded in Mesopotamian history, sixty years (1822–1763). His life vividly illustrates the political and military vicissitudes of the time, which we can reconstruct from varied sources including year names, economic records, and letters. Upon his accession the territory his family controlled was a 230-kilometer-long stretch of eastern Babylonia from Nippur and Mashkan-shapir in the north to the head of the Persian Gulf in the south, where it extended westward to include Larsa and Ur. The states of Babylon, Isin, and Uruk bordered it from north to south. The death of Kudur-Mabuk shortly before Rim-Sin's eighth year may have placed the entire area in his charge, and soon he asserted himself militarily. In his thirteenth year (1810), he defeated a coalition of forces led by Uruk, Isin, and Babylon, capturing some villages near Uruk. After further military successes near Larsa and a recapture of Nippur, which had been lost to Isin in his ninth year, he destroyed Uruk in 1800.

When Rim-Sin captured Isin in 1793, his thirtieth year, Larsa's only remaining rival in Babylonia was the state of Babylon, where Hammurabi inherited the throne in 1792. Rim-Sin spent the next thirty years consolidating his grasp over the south by concentrating administrative functions in the capital, and he seems to have reduced the economic independence of the earlier city-states. Hammurabi waited until Rim-Sin was an old man to initiate his swift conquest of all his neighbors, including Larsa, which he conquered in 1763. He left Rim-Sin's organization in place, however, continuing to rely on men from Larsa to supervise the administration of southern Babylonia. Rim-Sin thus laid the groundwork for Hammurabi's centralized state, to be discussed in the next chapter.

Despite political fragmentation and extensive conflict, there are no indications of an economic decline of Babylonia in the first three centuries of the second millennium. Urbanization remained dense, and documents from an increasingly large number of cities show high levels of economic activity. Even the city of Ur flourished, despite being deprived of the regional system that had supported it. Fundamental changes in the administration of the economy took place, however. In the twenty-first century, the Ur III state bureaucracy had supervised virtually everything and had employed large segments of the population as a labor force, which it supported with rations. In the early second millennium there occurred what we could call a partial "privatization" of the economy through a gradual and probably unintentional process. The large institutions, palaces and temples, still held very extensive resources. They owned large tracts of land and other properties and were great consumers of goods and services. At the start of the second millennium, there was a continuation of Ur III practices, albeit on a local scale as political power had fragmented. For example, we have an archive from a craft workshop attached to the palace at Isin that was responsible for the manufacture of a wide array of goods in wood, reed, leather, and wool for the royal household. The workshop was supervised by the royal administration, but craftsmen who spent part of their time working for others as well performed the labor. Other institutions likewise started to contract out work and services. Instead of having their lands farmed by dependent staff, they gave the use of fields to tenant farmers who were expected to hand in a share of the harvest and keep the rest for their own needs. Herds of sheep and goats were assigned to shepherds, who were obliged to deliver set amounts of wool and hair and to increase the herd by a fixed number of animals. Excess production was to the producers' benefit, but a deficit had to be made up from their own share. When the institutions required labor they hired people, paying them a salary for the time of employment only, rather than year-round rations. Gradually, more tasks were undertaken by people outside the institutions, and earlier offices, such as that of the temple brewer, became sinecures broken down into parts as small as half a day a year. These were traded as they guaranteed a small percentage of the institution's income for the period the office was held.

Administrative tasks were also assigned to independent contractors. Instead of employing and supporting large bureaucratic staffs, the institutions asked private entrepreneurs to act as intermediaries between themselves and the citizenry, collecting dues, issuing payments, and organizing the collection and distribution of resources. In addition, they converted those collections, paid in perishable produce and of limited use to the pared-down institutions, into easily storable silver. How they did so is not recorded in our sources, but most likely they sold them to organizations and individuals for silver. The entrepreneurs were rewarded for their services with a share of the assets transferred.

This privatization of the administration was well suited to the new political circumstances. In Ur III times, bureaucrats had owed their appointment to the king, and a change in dynasty would lead to a disruption of administrative practices. The private businessmen who were contracted for their services did not owe political allegiance to any dynasty, and were left alone to function in politically uncertain times.

This system of economic organization and management was a hallmark of the entire period from 2000 to 1600. Ultimately its effects on Babylonian society were disastrous. The contributions required from producers seem to have been high and, in a region like Babylonia where sequences of bad harvests were not uncommon, people were often unable to meet them. They could only ask for credit from the businessmen who collected their dues. Moreover, when they could not even survive until the next harvest on the amounts set aside for their own needs, they turned to these men for emergency loans. These were high-interest loans: tradition and royal proclamations allowed for a 20 percent interest on silver loans and a 33 percent rate on grain loans. These were collected whatever the duration of the loan. Since emergency loans were usually short-term, their repayment with the full rate of interest after only a month or so presented an enormous burden to the debtors. The records found in the houses of businessmen include a great number of loan contracts, which show that the level of indebtedness was high. That there was a debt crisis is clear from edicts in which kings claimed to restore order by annulling outstanding consumer loans. References to such acts are especially clear in the official statements of the kings of Isin, Larsa, and Babylon. Only one of the original edicts, issued by Ammisaduqa of Babylon (ruled 1646–26), is sufficiently well preserved for us to understand its detail. In it he abolished all debts contracted by producers for their survival or to pay for outstanding dues, but not those of businessmen who sought capital for commercial enterprises (document 5.1). It was the palace that absorbed the loss, but it did so because of the tradition that a king needed to maintain order and justice in the land – and because, after all, a large indebted population would no longer form a stable tax base, but would exist only to enrich a competing class of private businessmen.

5.3 Assyria and the East

Babylonia's political situation at this time was paralleled throughout the Near East. From western Iran to the Mediterranean coast small states led by local dynasties existed, often competing for power. The study of their history is much facilitated by the fact that many places have yielded their own textual record. This evidence is still very partial and its focus of attention varies from place to place. In the early second millennium, the material from Assyria stands out for its total emphasis on international trade, conducted by merchants from the city of Assur. Located on the Tigris in the very south of Assyria, Assur was the central point of a network that traded tin from the east, textiles from

---

Document 5.1 *Extract from the edict of*
King Ammisaduqa of Babylon

§ 1: The tablet [of the decree that the land was ordered] to hear when the king established justice for the land.

§ 2: The debts of farming agents, shepherds, knackers of the provinces, and other crown tributaries – the . . . of their firm agreements and the promissory notes . . . of their payments are herewith remitted. The collecting officer may not sue the crown tributary's household for payment.

§ 4: Whoever has given barley or silver to an Akkadian or an Amorite as an interest bearing loan or as fees, and had a document drawn up – because the king has established justice in the land, his document is voided; he may not collect the barley or silver on the basis of his document.

§ 8: An Akkadian or an Amorite who has received barley, silver, or (other) goods, either as merchandise for a commercial journey, or as a joint enterprise for the production of profit, his document is not voided; he must repay in accordance with the stipulations of his document.

Translation after Jacob Finkelstein, "The Edict of Ammisaduqa," in J. B. Pritchard, ed., *Ancient Near Eastern Texts Relating to the Old Testament*, third edition (Princeton: Princeton University Press, 1969), pp. 526–7.

Babylonia, and silver and gold from Anatolia. The system is known to us from the discovery of more than 20,000 tablets left by Assyrian merchants in a colony at the edge of the central Anatolian city Kanesh, some 1000 kilometers from Assur (see figure 5.1). The colony, while under the control of the local ruler, functioned as a separate entity, and in Assyrian texts it was referred to as *Karum*-Kanesh, the port of Kanesh.

The colony's fortunes depended on local events in Anatolia, very poorly known to us. Archaeology has distinguished several periods of occupation. Almost all of the tablets come from houses in level II, dated between 1910 and 1830, followed by a hiatus in settlement. When reoccupied in level Ib, ca. 1810 to 1740, substantially fewer tablets were left behind. It seems that the number of Assyrians had diminished and that representatives from other regions in Syria and Anatolia were now the principal agents at Kanesh.

Assur acted almost solely as a transit point in this trade. It imported tin from unknown sources in Iran or beyond and textiles from Babylonia. This part of the trade is not directly documented, and we do not know what was given in exchange. The connections with Anatolia, however, are very well known. Donkey caravans were organized in Assur, each animal loaded with 150 pounds of tin and thirty textiles, some locally produced but mostly from Babylonia. All expenses were shared by groups of traders, who invested their own resources

(a)　　　　　　　　　　　　　　　　　　　(b)

Figure 5.1 Old Assyrian cuneiform tablet and its envelope, recording a trial. The Metropolitan Museum of Art. Gift of Mr. and Mrs. J. J. Klejman, 1966 (66.245.5a and b). Photograph, all rights reserved, The Metropolitan Museum of Art

or those assigned to them by others: they paid for the animals, the merchandise, the personnel to accompany the caravan, and the various taxes and expenses incurred during the trip. The voyage to Kanesh easily lasted fifty days, and was impossible for four months during the winter when weather prevented passage through the Taurus Mountains. When the caravan arrived in Kanesh, most of the donkeys were sold and the merchandise was exchanged for silver and gold, which was then taken back to Assur. Assyrian merchants, who were usually brothers or sons of those in Assur and permanent residents of Anatolia, distributed the imported goods throughout Anatolia using a network of smaller trade settlements. They also collected the bullion to be readied for the next caravan. Although firm estimates of the volume of trade are difficult to make, on the basis of extant evidence it has been suggested that in forty to fifty years 100,000 textiles and 100 tons of tin were imported in Kanesh. Private entrepreneurs were at the heart of all this activity, and the palace was not directly concerned. Since families undertook the trade, women also were actively involved in it. They often remained home in Assur while their husbands, fathers, or brothers went off to Anatolia, and were in constant contact by letter about the business. The women were responsible for the textiles that were used in the exchange and had to arrange for their weaving, if they did not do it themselves. The men often criticized the quality of the products sent to them, and, conversely, women complained about the lack of resources given to them or even that they did not have enough to eat. The domestic situation sometimes led to difficulties in the marriage. Men often stayed away for many years and married local Anatolian women while their wives in Assur felt abandoned (see document 5.2).

Document 5.2   *Old Assyrian correspondence: examples of letters written by and to women*

Tell Pushuken; Lamassi[1] says:
Kulumaya is bringing nine textiles to you, Iddin-Sin three. Ela has refused to take care of textiles, while Iddin-Sin has refused to take care of five (more).

Why do you keep on writing to me: "The textiles that you send me are always of bad quality!" Who is the man who lives in your house and criticizes the textiles that are brought to him? I, on the other hand, keep on striving to produce and send you textiles so that on every trip your business gains ten shekels of silver.

Translation after Cécile Michel, *Correspondance des marchands de Kanish* (Paris: Les Editions du Cerf, 2001), p. 430.

Tell Innaya; Taram-Kubi[2] says:
You wrote to me as follows: "Keep the bracelets and rings that you have; they will be needed to buy you food." It is true that you send me half a pound of gold through Ili-bani, but where are the bracelets that you have left behind? When you left, you didn't leave me one shekel of silver. You cleaned out the house and took everything with you.

Since you left, a [terrible] famine has hit the city (of Assur). You did not leave me one liter of barley. I need to keep on buying barley for our food. [several unclear lines] Where is the extravagance that you keep on writing about? We have nothing to eat. (Do you think) we can afford indulgence? Everything I had available I scraped together and sent to you. Now I live in an empty house and the seasons are changing. Make sure that you send me the value of my textiles in silver, so that I can at least buy ten measures of barley.

With respect to the tablet with the witness list that Assur-imitti, son of Kura, obtained: he has caused a lot of trouble to the business and has seized servants as guarantee. Then your representatives have settled the affair. I have had to pay two-thirds of a pound of silver so that he will not lodge a complaint until you arrive. Why do you keep on listening to slander, and write me irritating letters?

Translation after Cécile Michel, *Correspondance des marchands de Kanish* (Paris: Les Editions du Cerf, 2001), p. 466.

Puzur-Assur says; Tell Nuhshatum:
Your father has written to me about you so that I would marry you. I have sent my servants and a letter to your father about you so that he would let you come. I am asking you, the moment you read my letter, ask your father (for permission) and come here with my servants. I am alone, I have no one who serves me or who sets my table. If you would not come with my servants I would marry a young girl from Wahshushana. Pay attention. You and my servants, don't delay and come!

Translation after Cécile Michel, *Correspondance des marchands de Kanish* (Paris: Les Editions du Cerf, 2001), p. 508.

¹ Wife of Pushuken.
² Wife of Innaya.

The profit margins in this trade were high, however: tin cost at least double in Anatolia what it cost in Assur, and textiles tripled their value. A merchant could easily make a 50 to 100 percent profit in a year. That was the reward for a high-risk enterprise. The trade functioned within a political setting where it could not rely on one power alone for its protection and support. The caravans to Anatolia, Babylonia, and Iran traveled through territories of many independent, and sometimes hostile, rulers. Assur was no more powerful than its neighbors, but it could negotiate trade arrangements. Although no actual treaties are preserved, we can reconstruct from references to them that the kings of the cities on the trade routes demanded taxes and the rights to collect certain goods. In return, the Assyrian traders were given access to the local merchant districts and provided with protection. King Ilushuma in the nineteenth century proclaimed that he established freedom for the Akkadians from the Persian Gulf to Assur, which must indicate that Babylonian merchants were free to travel on the route connecting the areas. Although we hear a lot about war generally at this time, it seems that commercial concerns kept states from blocking traders.

The two most powerful states to the south-east of Assur were Eshnunna in the Diyala region and Elam. Their histories can be pieced together only in the barest outlines because of our lack of chronological data on the lengths of reigns and sometimes even the correct sequence of kings. These states did follow similar patterns of behavior on the international scene, however. Eshnunna (present-day Tell Asmar) had become independent from Ur early in Ibbi-Sin's reign. The local governor proclaimed himself ruler, but kingship of the state was said to belong to the city-god, Tishpak. After the first independent ruler, Shu-ilija, who alone deified himself and took the title king (Sumerian lugal), the rulers of the state merely used the title "governor (Sumerian énsi) of the god Tishpak" for more than a century. It was only in the early nineteenth century that the rulers took on the title king and occasionally deified themselves. Similar behavior is visible in other places where Ur had politically dominated. At Assur, the local independent rulers became "governors (Sumerian énsi) of the god Assur," and at Elam the highest title was "grand regent" (Sumerian sukkal-mah), the title that had previously been held by the region's foremost Ur III official. Eshnunna's final acceptance of the title king may have been the result of Isin's loss of control over Nippur. If in Babylonia itself the certainty of who was the true king had waned, perhaps its neighbors felt more at ease in claiming the title themselves. It is at this time that Eshnunna expanded its control over the Diyala Valley as far as its confluence with the Tigris, incorporating such previously independent cities as Nerebtum (modern Ishcali), Shaduppum (modern Tell Harmal), and Dur-Rimush (location unknown). Ipiq-Adad's sons Naram-Sin and Dadusha continued his expansionist policy, which brought Eshnunna into the maelstrom that characterized Mesopotamia in the early eighteenth century, becoming one of the most powerful players in the region (for a list of kings of Eshnunna, see p. 304).

Eshnunna competed with the other states in its surroundings and mixed war and diplomacy to gain its prominence. For example, Dadusha joined forces with Shamshi-Adad of the kingdom of Upper Mesopotamia in 1781 in order to conquer the region between the two Zab Rivers, and commemorated the campaign in a victory stele, where he stated that he handed the lands over to Shamshi-Adad (see figure 5.2). Somewhat later the latter turned against his ally and took some of Eshnunna's cities, including Shaduppum and Nerebtum. But when Shamshi-Adad died the roles were reversed, with Eshnunna capturing cities close to Assur. By then it was the strongest state of the region.

Crossing along the northern border of the still-isolationist state of Babylon, Eshnunna entered the Euphrates Valley and reached Mari. When Shamshi-Adad's son Yasmah-Addu had governed there, relations had been hostile. With the establishment of a new king at Mari, Zimri-Lim, Ibal-pi'el II of Eshnunna sought to conclude an alliance, which Zimri-Lim rejected. In a letter to his envoy to Aleppo he stated:

Figure 5.2 Stele of Dadusha, from Mark W. Chavalas (ed.), *The Ancient Near East*, Blackwell 2006, p. 99. Drawing by Frans van Koppen

When you find yourself in the presence of Yarim-Lim (king of Aleppo) speak to him as follows about Eshnunna: "(The king of) Eshnunna keeps on sending me messages with respect to an alliance. A first time he sent me a messenger and I sent him back at the border. A second time he sent me a messenger and I sent him back at the border. Then a high official came and I sent him back at the border, stating: 'How could I conclude an alliance with Eshnunna without the consent of Yarim-Lim?'"[2]

A war between the two states ensued, which forced Mari to accept Eshnunna's peace offer. Three years later, however, Elam's ruler, denied direct access to Mesopotamia by the border kingdom of Eshnunna, allied himself with Babylon, Mari, and probably Larsa, and attacked and pillaged the city in 1766. A puppet ruler was appointed by Elam, soon replaced by a native Eshnunnan king named Silli-Sin. He helped Hammurabi of Babylon in his destruction of the

Elamite state, but in 1762 that savvy ruler turned against his former ally and sacked Eshnunna. The region was not incorporated in Hammurabi's state, but the latter prevented it from having a strong ruler. In later year names of Hammurabi and his successor Samsuiluna, references are made to Eshnunna, but we know very little about it.

The state of Elam was a crucial player in all of the events described above. These centuries show it to have been more closely involved in Mesopotamia than at any other time of its history. The state incorporated both the lowlands surrounding Susa and the Zagros highlands around Anshan (present Tal-i Malyan), a bipolarity reflected in the ruler's title "king of Anshan and Susa." The political organization was headed by the sukkal-mah, "grand regent," using a title from the Ur III period but now as an independent ruler. Next to him functioned officials with such titles as sukkal of Susa and of Elam, often the son of the sister of the ruling sukkal-mah. When the latter died, he was at times succeeded by his nephew, but we are uncertain that this was the normal rule of succession.

Soon after Elam had gained independence from Ur, it turned against its former master and its troops aided in the defeat of that state, seizing the capital and taking its ruler prisoner. The armies of Isin shortly thereafter terminated the Elamite occupation of Ur, and subsequently prevented Elam from having much influence in Babylonia. A century later, when other Babylonian cities asserted their independence at the expense of Isin, however, they often sought foreign aid, and Elam was drawn into their shifting alliances and conflicts. Several kings of Larsa conquered Elamite cities, and Elam allied itself with Uruk, Isin, and others in the local Babylonian wars. It is possible that the last two Larsa rulers, Warad-Sin and Rim-Sin, were of Elamite descent: they were sons of Kudur-Mabuk, son of Simti-Silhak, tribal rulers of an area east of the Tigris, who in the late nineteenth century took over several Babylonian cities. Their relationship to the state of Elam is unknown, but it is possible that they may have acted on its behalf in Babylonian conflicts, and the already complicated political and military picture would become even more complex with the involvement of tribal groups.

Until the disappearance of Eshnunna as a major power, Elam remained at a distance from affairs in the north of Babylonia and Mesopotamia in general, even if its importance was acknowledged by all. The removal of Eshnunna by a coalition of Babylon, Mari, and Elam brought the latter in direct contact with the region's states. Now its influence was remarkable and very wide-ranging. The ruler of Qatna in western Syria, for example, is known to have offered his territory to Elam in order to gain support in his conflict with Aleppo. The sukkal-mah received correspondence from Hammurabi of Babylon, Zimri-Lim of Mari, and others. They declared themselves to be his "sons" rather than his "brothers," the usual term when they corresponded with one another. To them he was "the great king of Elam." His armies placed rulers on thrones as far away as Shubat-Enlil in northern Syria. Elam's strength derived from the size of its state and the manpower it could summon. Contributing to its

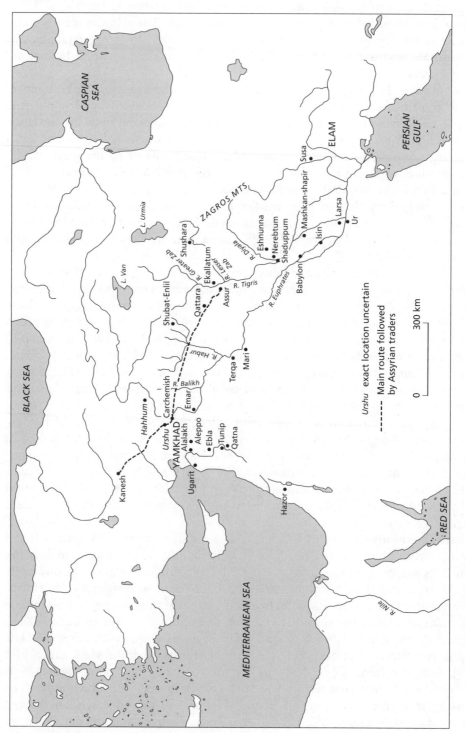

Map 5.2 The Near East in the early second millennium

prominence was the fact that it controlled the flow of Iranian tin to the west after the end of *Karum*-Kanesh. This crucial ingredient for bronze production reached the Mediterranean from Elam via Mari. Elam was also in close contact with Dilmun in the Persian Gulf, so it may have monopolized access to other foreign resources and routes as well. Its success was ephemeral, however. Hammurabi of Babylon concluded an alliance with Mari and Aleppo against Elam, and in his twenty-ninth year (1764) that state was defeated. While Elam was not incorporated into the Babylonian state, its influence ended and our knowledge of it ceases.

5.4 Mari and the West

Ambassadors to the king at Mari submitted reports on the final days of Larsa, Eshnunna, and Elam to their master which enable us to study these events. Because of this city's location and its ancient role as intermediary between southern Mesopotamia and Syria, its archives also shed abundant light on affairs in the west. A vast area in modern-day Syria and its surroundings with numerous states fell into the orbit of Mari's representatives. Cities as distant as Hazor in modern Israel are mentioned. The western area of the Near East made up a single, politically integrated system of small states. The royal houses of its petty kingdoms were often related by blood and intermarriage, and the king of Mari, for example, traveled as far as Ugarit on the Mediterranean coast. The histories of a few cities will serve to demonstrate that the pattern of competition, coalition, and hegemony described for the eastern part of the Near East could also be found in the west. Here I will describe the histories of Mari and Yamkhad, the two most powerful states in the region, but half a dozen others could be written just as well.

Mari had been independent from the Ur III state, albeit in close diplomatic contact with it. Nevertheless, the collapse of Ur coincided with a downward turn in Mari's fortunes: although its dynasty of rulers who held the title "general" (Akkadian *shakkanakku*) remained in power for another century, the city's importance was greatly reduced. Finally the dynasty ended, for reasons unknown, and the city may even have been abandoned. By the mid-nineteenth century, however, a new dynasty was in place, and Mari began its most prosperous century (for a list of kings, see p. 305). The new dynasty had its origin in northwestern Syria among the Sim'alite branch of the Amorites, who had conquered various cities in the Middle Euphrates Valley before settling at Mari. The first ruler we can study was Yahdun-Lim who, despite his western roots, introduced Babylonian language and writing style as a chancellery standard, including the practice of using year names. He started to rebuild a royal palace that later became famed throughout the Near East for its scale and opulence. He established Mari as the dominant state on the Middle Euphrates, stretching as far north as the Balikh confluence, and pursued the Yaminites as far west as the Lebanon Mountains. Development works in the region, such as the building

of irrigation systems and fortresses, consolidated his grasp. The expansion into
the Habur region brought him into conflict with the newly emergent Kingdom
of Upper Mesopotamia, however, and he fought several battles against Shamshi-
Adad. Yahdun-Lim was assassinated in a palace conspiracy, and his son,
Sumu-Yaman, did not survive long thereafter. Two or three years later in 1795,
Mari was conquered by Shamshi-Adad and integrated into his large state, to
be discussed in the next chapter. Shamshi-Adad placed his younger son Yasmah-
Addu on Mari's throne in order to keep an eye on the western states and on
the Amorite tribes.

The rule of Yasmah-Addu lasted some twenty years and ended suddenly when
his father died around 1776. Shamshi-Adad's kingdom fell apart, the pieces
picked over by ambitious men. At Mari that man was Zimri-Lim. Although he
often declared himself to be the son of Yahdun-Lim, it is clear that he was not,
and may at best have been his grandson or nephew. When he took power, Mari
once again acted fully in its own interests. Zimri-Lim reestablished strong ties
with Babylon and with Aleppo, confirmed through his marriage to the princess
Shiptu. His state encompassed the Euphrates Valley from just south of Mari to
the border with Aleppo and the lower Habur Valley. Further north he exercised
control through vassals and he made sure that independent rulers were on his
side. Mari flourished, and Zimri-Lim's palace is one of the greatest architectural
monuments of the early second millennium known to us. The kingdom was
respected by its competitors in the region and kept the nomadic tribes at bay.
While Zimri-Lim was a faithful ally of Hammurabi of Babylon, his prestige
and wealth must ultimately have pushed the latter to turn against him. In his
thirty-second year (1761), Hammurabi defeated Zimri-Lim and conquered Mari.
Two years later, his anger incited by unknown causes, Hammurabi razed the
palace and the city-walls and incorporated the Euphrates Valley up to Mari
into his state. Mari lost its preeminent status and the center of power for the
Middle Euphrates shifted some 100 kilometers north to Terqa.

The city of Aleppo was the capital of the state of Yamkhad (for a list of
rulers, see p. 305). Strategically located on the trade route from the Euphrates
Valley to the Mediterranean Sea, it seems to have come to prominence only
after the beginning of the second millennium, perhaps after Ebla's loss of
power. Since Aleppo has been continuously occupied from that time until
today, excavations there are impossible and we have to write its early history
based entirely on outside sources. These derive first from Mari, which shared
dynastic lineage with the Yamkhad kings. The Mari letters reveal that Yamkhad's
most stubborn opponent in the west was Qatna, a city of central Syria located
to its south, which received support from Shamshi-Adad of the Kingdom of
Upper Mesopotamia. The first two known rulers of Yamkhad, Sumu'epuh
and Yarim-Lim, became involved in wars with Shamshi-Adad, which sucked
them and their successors into the volatile politics of the south. The death of
Shamshi-Adad created the space for Yarim-Lim of Yamkhad to expand down
the Euphrates Valley, as far as the Mari kingdom. As Zimri-Lim of Mari was
Yarim-Lim's son-in-law, contacts between the two were friendly. Yarim-Lim's

prominence in the west is clear from the Mari letter quoted in the beginning of this chapter in which twenty kings are said to follow him, more than any other ruler at the time.

When Hammurabi of Babylon picked off his neighbors one by one, Yamkhad, like Mari, at first provided him with support. But then Babylon turned against its old allies and conquered Mari. Yamkhad remained simply too far for Babylonian troops to reach, so the two major states were not in direct conflict. Subsequently, southern sources stop dealing with matters concerning Yamkhad. Around this time, however, texts from the smaller city of Alalakh to the west of Yamkhad indicate that its local ruler had been placed on the throne there by Abba'el of Aleppo, his brother. Yamkhad remained the dominant force of north-west Syria, controlling a large number of vassals and allies in cities like Carchemish, Urshu, Hashshu, Ugarit, Emar, Ebla, and Tunip. It presented thus the main obstacle to Hittite military expansion from Anatolia into Syria during the second half of the seventeenth century. The Hittite king Hattusili I reports in his annals how he attacked and destroyed several vassals of Yamkhad over several years, such as Alalakh, Carchemish, and Hashshu. He did not seem to engage Yamkhad itself, however. That task was left to his son, Mursili I, who captured and destroyed the city on his way to Babylon in 1595, thereby ending the political situation that had characterized the Near East for four centuries.

NOTES

1 Translation from J. Sasson, "King Hammurabi of Babylon," in J. Sasson, ed., *Civilizations of the Ancient Near East* (New York: Charles Scribner's Sons, 1995), volume 2, p. 906.
2 Translation after Jean-Marie Durand, *Les Documents épistolaires du palais de Mari* (Paris: Les Editions du Cerf, 1997), volume 1, pp. 441–2.

6

The Growth of Territorial States in the Early Second Millennium

3000	2500	2000	1500	1000	500

1808	Shamshi-Adad seizes throne of Assur
ca. 1795	Mari placed under Yasmah-Addu's rule
1792	Hammurabi inherits throne of Babylon
1776	Death of Shamshi-Adad
ca. 1740	Samsuiluna loses control over southern Babylonia
ca. 1650	Creation of the Old Hittite state
1595	Hittite King Mursili sacks Babylon

Within the hurly-burly of competing dynasties that characterized the first half of the second millennium, a small number of highly accomplished rulers stand out. For short periods of time, these men were able to extend their political control over a wide geographical area, creating short-lived territorial states. These states were not radically different in nature from others of the period, only more successful in competing with their neighbors. They appeared in various regions of the Near East as the result of an individual's military successes and disintegrated soon after their founders' deaths. First, Shamshi-Adad unified Northern Mesopotamia, then Hammurabi Babylonia, and later Hattusili I Central Anatolia (see map 6.1). Despite the ephemeral nature of their states, the changes these men initiated laid the foundations for the system of territorial states in later centuries.

Since these events overlapped with the developments discussed in the previous chapter, the available historical sources are largely the same. In Babylonia
and Upper Mesopotamia, the most explicit records do not derive from the
capitals but from other cities conquered and controlled by the territorial rulers.
Conversely, in the case of the Old Hittite state, almost all our information
comes from the capital Hattusa, but the texts are dated centuries later and can
only claim to be copies of the original royal annals. Their information thus has
to be checked carefully against sources contemporary to the events they describe.

6.1 Shamshi-Adad and the Kingdom of Upper Mesopotamia

The early history of King Shamshi-Adad is vague to us. We cannot even establish when and where he first ascended any particular Mesopotamian throne.
Most likely around 1833 he inherited rule from his father, Ila-kabkabu, in
Ekallatum, a city still unlocated but certainly in the vicinity of Assur. There
he governed about ten years, until he had to flee to Babylon when Naram-Sin
of Eshnunna conquered Ekallatum. When Naram-Sin died seven years later,
Shamshi-Adad took the opportunity to return from exile and three years
later conquered Assur as well. There he integrated his ancestors into the list
of city-rulers, and is said to have ruled for thirty-three years (for a list of early
Assyrian rulers, see p. 315). This allows us to date his accession to Assur's
throne to 1808.

At that time he was still only the ruler of a minor power in the region. Soon,
however, he extended his influence westward into northern Syria, where he
clashed with Yahdun-Lim of Mari. Shamshi-Adad took control over the northern
Habur Valley, annexing kingdoms such as the land of Apum whose capital,
Shehna, he turned into his own royal seat and renamed Shubat-Enlil. The
mighty kingdom of Mari to his south became easy prey when Yahdun-Lim was
assassinated, and, probably in 1792, its capital was captured. Shamshi-Adad
ruled now an area from Assur on the Tigris in the east to Tuttul on the Balikh
in the west. The entire region to the north of Babylonia was incorporated in
his state, which we will here call the "Kingdom of Upper Mesopotamia."

Shamshi-Adad was very tolerant of existing practices in the various states he
had united. At Assur he took on the title "governor of Assur," and in Nineveh
he restored the Ishtar temple, said to have been built by Manishtushu five
centuries before. Certain cities, such as Qattara, retained their former rulers,
who now became his vassals. Local administrative procedures continued to be
used, although we observe that officials used seals that indicated that they were
in the service of Shamshi-Adad. Perhaps one crucial change was imposed, the
dating of documents with the Assyrian eponym system to indicate the years
(see box 6.1). Under Shamshi-Adad's rule it became used in such varied places
as Mari, Tuttul (present Tell Bi'a), Shubat-Enlil, and Terqa. This "Assyrian"
system of dating thus became the official system for the Kingdom of Upper
Mesopotamia.

Box 6.1 *The eponym dating system*

Unlike Babylonia, where years were indicated with names based on important events of the previous years, in northern Mesopotamia a dating system existed where each year was named after an individual holding office. The Akkadian term used to refer to such an individual was *limmu*, meaning something like rotation, which we translate with the Greek term indicating a rotating office, "eponym." The dating system probably originated in the city of Assur, and it remained the official system in Assyria to the end of the Assyrian empire in the seventh century (see document 12.2). The names of the officials who became the eponyms were originally chosen by lot, but in the first millennium a fixed rotation of officers headed by the king constituted the *limmu*. The office in the first millennium was of a cultic nature.

In the early second millennium, the office of eponym in Assur had an administrative character, and seemingly was more involved with trade than was the king. The earliest known attestations of year eponyms are at *Karum*-Kanesh. They became used in other Assyrian colonies in Anatolia corresponding in time to the later occupation of that site. The dating practice is attested throughout northern Mesopotamian cities,[1] and its spread was undoubtedly due to Shamshi-Adad's unification of the north: we see that in some places like Mari, year names were replaced by eponyms under his occupation alone. When his state fell apart, several cities, while politically independent, continued to use eponyms, but we do not know whether or not the names they used were chosen in Assur.

In order to keep track of the sequence of years, eponym lists were established, sometimes also adding succinct statements about events. These are fully reconstructed from the tenth through seventh centuries. In earlier periods the sequence is uncertain, owing to the absence of complete lists. At Mari an eponym chronicle was found covering a period from before Shamshi-Adad to when his son sat on the throne there. Unfortunately, it is not fully preserved, and the sequence of eponyms in the nineteenth to eighteenth centuries remains a matter of scholarly debate.

Having to control this large kingdom, Shamshi-Adad, who resided in Shubat-Enlil, placed his two sons in strategic locations. The eldest, Ishme-Dagan, ascended the throne at Ekallatum, the ancestral home, while the younger, Yasmah-Addu, was instated at Mari. The southeastern and southwestern frontiers were thus given direct attention. In the east the Kingdom of Upper Mesopotamia bordered on Eshnunna and states at the foothills of the Zagros, in the west it bordered Yamkhad and the Syrian steppe controlled by semi-nomadic groups. Babylonia to the south may also have been subject to Shamshi-Adad: a contract drawn up at Sippar in 1782 contains oaths to both Hammurabi and Shamshi-Adad, which seems to indicate the latter's authority there as well for some brief time. The two sons in turn were given supervision of a number of districts in which governors were placed: Ishme-Dagan looked after those between the Tigris and the Zagros, Yasmah-Addu those along the Euphrates, lower Balikh, and Habur rivers. Shamshi-Adad directly governed the region of Shubat-Enlil, while military governors were in charge of cities to its south. Ishme-Dagan clearly had more authority than his younger brother, and often scolded Yasmah-Addu for his inaction. The father kept ultimate authority, however, sending numerous letters to his sons. Those to Mari accused Yasmah-Addu of being a lazy weakling. He stated repeatedly:

> How long do we have to guide you in every matter? Are you a child, and not an adult? Don't you have a beard on your chin? When are you going to take charge of your house? Don't you see that your brother is leading vast armies? So, you too, take charge of your palace, your house![2]

The meddling in local affairs by the great leaders was not unusual, and this micromanaging was part of the ideal of kingship of the time, as I will show in the discussion of Hammurabi of Babylon. That it was not always appreciated by their subjects is clear from an episode in which Shamshi-Adad arranged for the marriage of Yasmah-Addu to Beltum, the princess of Qatna, a crucial ally in his conflict with Yamkhad. The king of Qatna wanted his daughter to have a prominent role in the Mari palace, but Yasmah-Addu already had a leading wife, the daughter of Yahdun-Lim. So Yasmah-Addu preferred to keep Beltum in a secondary position outside of his palace, among the group of lower-ranking women. Shamshi-Adad sternly reprimanded him and forced his son to keep her at his side in the palace. The hierarchy of power in the kingdom was clear.

Shamshi-Adad's state disappeared suddenly and under unclear circumstances. When he was old he was attacked simultaneously by Yamkhad and Eshnunna, his two major neighbors, and he died in battle or of natural causes in 1776. Local powers quickly reasserted themselves. Zimri-Lim, an Amorite upstart, chased Yasmah-Addu from Mari, while Ishme-Dagan lost control over all of his father's kingdom except Ekallatum and Assur. Northern Syria became a patchwork of small independent states, while in the south Eshnunna picked up the pieces nearby. Some of the histories of the new states can still be written because Mari kept a close watch on developments, but also because some of the local kings maintained court bureaucracies and actively communicated with one another by letter. The politically divided region was open to attacks from Eshnunna, Elam, and Babylonia, whose kings could make or break local rulers. Political intrigues and military conflicts were numerous and complicated. Zimri-Lim of Mari was the most powerful ruler of the area but too geographically marginal to control everything that happened. While local dynasties existed throughout Upper Mesopotamia, some kings, such as the ruler of Andariq, exercised strong influence over their neighbors, sometimes imposing rulers on their thrones. The crucial role of the palaces in these cities continued earlier practices. They seem to have been the dominant force in the economy and to have maintained a centralized administration. By 1720, northern Mesopotamia became unable to sustain this lifestyle, however. Many cities were abandoned

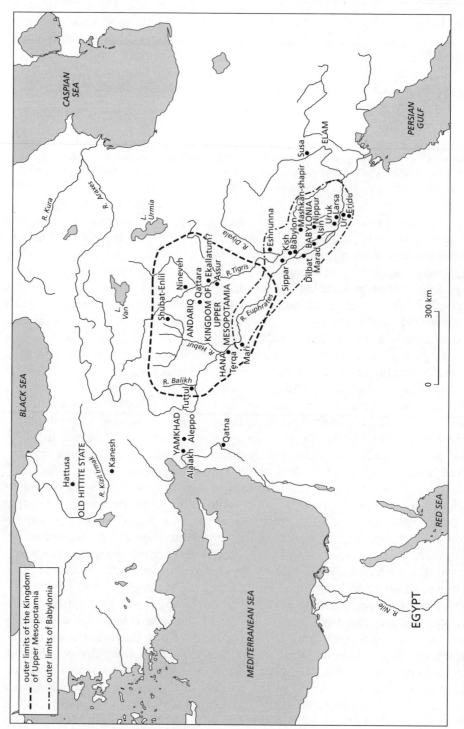

Map 6.1 Territorial states of the early second millennium

Legend:
- - - - outer limits of the Kingdom of Upper Mesopotamia
- · - · - outer limits of Babylonia

CASPIAN SEA

PERSIAN GULF

ELAM

Susa

Mashkan-shapir

Babylon

Kish

BABYLONIA

Marad Isin Nippur

Dilbat

Uruk

Ur Larsa

Eridu

Sippar

Eshnunna

R. Diyala

R. Tigris

Assur

Ekallatum?

UPPER MESOPOTAMIA

KINGDOM OF

ANDARIQ

Qattara

Nineveh

Shubat-Enlil

L. Urmia

L. Van

R. Kura

R. Araxes

R. Euphrates

R. Habur

HANA

Terqa

Mari

R. Balikh

Tuttul

YAMKHAD

Aleppo

Alalakh

Qatna

BLACK SEA

Hattusa

OLD HITTITE STATE

Kanesh

R. Kizil Irmak

MEDITERRANEAN SEA

RED SEA

R. Nile

EGYPT

0   300 km

for reasons we can only suspect. Possibly a mixture of popular opposition to the court's domination and changes in the rainfall patterns led to a shift to a semi-nomadic life in villages and in the steppe. With the end of the palaces, the historical record disappeared.

6.2 Hammurabi's Babylon

During the last decades of Shamshi-Adad's life, the throne at Babylon was held by a man who would become one of the most famous kings of Mesopotamian history: Hammurabi. Babylon had existed for several centuries, known from the Old Akkadian period on, and Hammurabi's predecessors had managed gradually to create a state incorporating previously independent northern cities, such as Sippar, Kish, Dilbat, and Marad. Babylonia was hemmed in by the more prominent states of Eshnunna, Larsa, and the Kingdom of Upper Mesopotamia. When Hammurabi became king in 1792, Rim-Sin had just unified the entirety of southern Babylonia while Shamshi-Adad reigned supreme in the north. Hammurabi may at first have even owed allegiance to Shamshi-Adad. Hammurabi ushered in what we now call the "Old Babylonian period," the beginning of Babylon's political dominance over southern Mesopotamia for the next 1500 years (for a list of Old Babylonian kings, see p. 306).

In these extremely volatile times, the young king could not avoid being drawn into regional conflicts. His early year names mention campaigns against all of his powerful neighbors, but the results of those are ambiguous. Most of Hammurabi's attention seems to have been devoted to the internal development of his state, mainly digging canals and fortifying cities. When he decided to act on a wide scale, his military activity was short but devastating, and he used his considerable diplomatic skills. At first using troops from states such as Mari, he turned against those who earlier helped him once he was strong enough. The diplomatic correspondence from Mari shows how he first used diplomacy, then military action, to reach his goals (see document 6.1). In just five years, from 1766 to 1761, Hammurabi established his full dominance over southern Mesopotamia, after the death of Shamshi-Adad and when Rim-Sin was an old man. He defeated Elam, Larsa, Eshnunna, and Mari in quick succession, and incorporated Larsa and the Middle Euphrates area up to Mari into the Babylonian state. Eshnunna he left without a leader, while he blocked Elam's ability to exercise any influence over Mesopotamia. The only area of concern remained northern Mesopotamia, where Hammurabi campaigned twice in later years without fully controlling the region. There is no doubt, however, that he was the strongest king in Mesopotamia. After these events, he could proclaim himself "the king who made the four quarters of the earth obedient."[3]

His inscriptions make clear, however, that the core of his state was Babylonia. Many of the earlier city-states there and their cults received the benefit of Hammurabi's rule. It is indeed in this region that we can study his style of government: as ruler he concerned himself with the smallest detail. Due to

Document 6.1 *Letters to Zimri-Lim of Mari regarding Hammurabi and Eshnunna*

Tell my Lord (Zimri-Lim); Yarim-Addu, your servant, says:
I have written to my Lord about the instructions regarding the man of Eshnunna that Hammurabi issued to [ ]. When Hammurabi was in Borsippa messengers of the man of Eshnunna came to him, but he did not see them. Only on the second day they met with him. After having them wait a night, he gave an answer to their news. He gave instructions to [Sin-], son of Kakkaruqqum and Mar[duk-mushallim, son of], and he sent them along. They took with them the small tablet (i.e., draft treaty), and they will make the man of Eshnunna accept it. [ ] will go and Hammurabi will accept it. After they will have accepted the small tablet, Hammurabi will send a large tablet, that is a treaty tablet, to the man of Eshnunna, and he will make him swear to it. The man of Eshnunna will send the large tablet, the treaty tablet, back to Hammurabi and they will establish an alliance. The alliance between Hammurabi and the man of Eshnunna is concluded or will be so very soon, that is certain. At this moment the answer to the diplomatic mission of Sin-[ ] and Marduk-mushallim has not yet arrived from Eshnunna. I cannot report on it for my lord. After this letter I will write to my lord all the news that reaches me from Eshnunna.

The letter continues with news about Larsa and Andariq.

Translation after Dominique Charpin, *Archives épistolaires de Mari* (Paris: Editions Recherche sur les Civilisations, 1988), volume 1, part 2, pp. 179–82.

Tell my Lord (Zimri-Lim); Yarim-Addu, your servant, says:
I have written earlier to my Lord that the words of Hammurabi were secret. Hammurabi has renewed frank conversations with the ruler of Elam as he did before. Elamite messengers who have come from the ruler of Elam to Hammurabi are staying at the entrance of his palace right now. After the ruler of Elam had given them his instructions they were escorted from Susa to Der of the god Ishtaran. The man of Der received them and has sent them under escort to Malgium, and the man of Malgium was supposed to give them an escort to Babylon. But the army of Eshnunna barred their way and they were unable to enter (the territory). Hammurabi heard that the army of Eshnunna blocked the roads. He no longer sends regular missions to Elam via Malgium and Der, as he did before. But there are open areas in the land Eshnunna and his couriers go to the ruler of Elam through these areas. The message from the ruler of Elam has not yet reached him.

The letter continues with news about Malgium and about Ishme-Dagan of the Kingdom of Upper Mesopotamia.

Finally, regarding the small treaty tablet that Hammurabi previously sent to the king of Eshnunna, Silli-Sin. Silli-Sin continues to answer with a refusal and he has not concluded a treaty with Hammurabi.

Translation after Dominique Charpin, *Archives épistolaires de Mari* (Paris: Editions Recherche sur les Civilisations, 1988), volume 1, part 2, pp. 182–4.

extensive later rebuilding and the recent rise of the water table, the city of Babylon itself is virtually unknown archaeologically for this period, and only a handful of tablets from it have survived. Our information derives primarily from other cities, where royal agents represented Babylon's interests. In Larsa, for instance, these men were Sin-iddinam and Shamash-hazir, and some two hundred letters the king wrote to them are preserved. These involve themselves with matters of seemingly little importance. For example:

> To Shamash-hazir say, thus speaks Hammurabi: "From the fields that belong to the palace give one of one hectare near the gate of Larsa, a fallow field that is of good quality and lies near the water, to Sin-imguranni the seal-cutter."[4]

This concern perhaps does not fit our image of a great ruler, but well reflects the ideology of kingship at the time. The king was a shepherd and a farmer. He had to take care of his people, providing them with fields for their sustenance and making these fields fertile through irrigation projects. The people expected such a level of concern from him.

The same ideology was expressed repeatedly in the introduction and conclusion of his most famous monument, Hammurabi's law code. He stated there:

> I am indeed the shepherd who brings peace, whose scepter is just. My benevolent shade was spread over my city, I held the people of the lands of Sumer and Akkad safely on my lap.

The function of the law code itself has been much debated, but consensus is growing that the modern designation of it is wrong: it is not a code of law but a monument presenting Hammurabi as an exemplary king of justice. The text is best known to us from a 2-meter-high black diorite stele almost fully covered with an inscription (see figure 6.1). Framed between a prologue and epilogue are listed some three hundred statements, all structured on the same pattern: "if . . . , then . . ." For example, "If a man commits a robbery and is caught, that man will be killed" (§ 22). While dealing with many areas of life, the entries do not, by far, cover all possible crimes, and there are even some contradictions. Moreover, the many legal documents of the period, including records of law cases, never make reference to the code. Instead of a list of legal precepts, the entire monument is a vivid expression of Hammurabi as a king who provides justice in his land. He said himself:

> May any wronged man who has a case come before my statue as king of justice, and may he have my inscribed stele read aloud to him. May he hear my precious words and may my stele clarify his case for him. May he examine his lawsuit and may he calm his (troubled) heart. May he say: "Hammurabi . . . provided just ways for the land."[5]

To prove his ability to guarantee justice, Hammurabi listed these three hundred-some cases, and thus urged future kings to study and follow his example.

Figure 6.1 The stele of Hammurabi. Photo: Hevre Lewandowski. Courtesy of Réunion des Musées Nationaux/Art Resource, NY

Notwithstanding this, the code's contents provide insights into Babylonian society at the time. It demonstrates a social hierarchy with a tripartite structure of free man (Akkadian *awilum*), dependent (*mushkenum*), and slave (*wardum*). Punishments varied according to the status of the victim or the perpetrator of a crime: injuring a free man led to a harsher penalty than injuring a dependent. But these terms were not absolute, often defining someone's position in relationship to another. A high court official was still a "slave" to the king. The status of the intermediate group of dependents is most difficult to define. The term could indicate a relationship to the palace or to another person, but we do not understand exactly what was the basis or degree of dependence. The structure of society had changed from the third millennium, partly through the process of "privatization" described in the previous chapter. Full-time palace dependents were rare and contract labor provided most services. Hence the dependent class of Hammurabi's code was often in a situation where it owed obligations to private citizens. The use of entrepreneurs to take care of palace business was a

characteristic of the period, and their credit transactions led to the social disturbances described in the last chapter. Loan contracts continue to be numerous
in private archives. Hammurabi and several of his successors are known to
have decreed the annulment of debts several times, but the need to repeat such
acts indicates their failure to rectify the situation.

By the end of his reign, Hammurabi had fundamentally altered the political layout of Mesopotamia. Babylonia was the single great power, surrounded
by weak remnants of formerly great rivals: Elam, Eshnunna, and Assur. Only
in western Syria were states such as Yamkhad unaffected by his actions. His
unification of Babylonia was short-lived, however. Only ten years after his
death his son, Samsuiluna, faced a major rebellion in the south led by a
man calling himself Rim-Sin after Larsa's last ruler. Samsuiluna was militarily
successful, but his grasp on the region gradually slipped away. Texts dated
with his year names disappeared from southern cities by his tenth or eleventh
year. By Samsuiluna's thirtieth year, Nippur and other middle Babylonian
cities ceased to be under Babylon's control. The problems were not purely
political, however. Archaeology shows that previously flourishing cities like
Ur and Nippur were mostly abandoned. Segments of the population, such as
the priesthood of Uruk, migrated to northern Babylonian cities. It is difficult
to determine exactly what happened. Babylon's response to rebellions may
have been so ferocious that the southern urban infrastructure was irreparably
damaged, watercourses perhaps deflected, and agricultural fields turned into
steppe. It is also possible that the policies of Hammurabi and his predecessor
in the region, Rim-Sin, ultimately had a negative result. They had integrated
the local economies of southern Babylonia into a system under which districts
became interdependent. When the center required to coordinate production
weakened, the exchange system may have collapsed, leading to an economic
decline of all the regions.

Northern Babylonia continued to flourish, however. Hammurabi had five
successors who ruled uncontested for 155 years over the area that he had
originally inherited as a young king, in addition to the Euphrates River valley
up to the vicinity of Mari. Samsuiluna campaigned even further upstream,
attacking and perhaps annexing the new northern state of Hana around Terqa
and reaching the Upper Habur. New opponents appeared on the scene, which
indicates that the political situation there was unsettled. A previously unattested
group of people called Kassites became a target of Babylon's military activity.
In the sixteenth century, they would become rulers of Babylon.

The rapid abandonment of southern and central Babylonian cities under
Samsuiluna in the mid-eighteenth century had as an unintended side-effect the
preservation of most of the manuscripts of Sumerian literary texts now known
to us. These were copied out or excerpted by young men who were schooled
as scribes in private houses, and in Ur and Nippur the remnants of their work
have been excavated. Normally the tablets containing their exercises would
have been recycled and their clay reused, but when scribal activity stopped, the
last works were left behind. We can study the school curriculum on the basis

of these exercises, including mathematics, surveying, and music. Most elaborate was the training of cuneiform writing and the Sumerian language. Rote learning was the norm. At first the students had to practice making single strokes with the stylus. This led to learning signs and their readings. Cuneiform signs were memorized by shape or by the sound of their pronunciation, and the order of learning was based on their increasing complexity. They were mastered by repeated copying. Then the students moved on to copying lists of Sumerian words with their Akkadian translations. The lexical corpus, already known from the late Uruk period tablets, was thus a central part of the curriculum. It is in this period that the first Akkadian translations of the Sumerian words started to appear. Grammar was taught similarly by repeating the paradigms of nouns and verbs in different forms.

The students learned syntax by writing out actual Sumerian compositions, chosen for their grammatical complexity. Thus the study of certain Ur III royal hymns was introduced at this time. Finally, the training culminated with the copying out of passages from the classics of Sumerian literature. A wide variety of literary genres were represented: myths, hymns, proverbs, literary letters, and others. The student exercises are often the only manuscripts we have of these texts, whose original date of composition is unknown. The court's patronage is clear: many of the compositions were intended to glorify the living king or his distant ancestors. That message is most obvious in the royal hymns and the accounts of legendary rulers. The courts of the early second millennium continued the Ur III tradition of glorifying the king with hymnic songs. They portrayed him in superhuman terms and thus perpetuated the ideology that saw him as a divinity. Similar ideas were expressed in a cycle of stories concerning the legendary rulers of Uruk, Enmerkar, Lugalbanda, and Gilgamesh. Part-human, part-divine, they were considered to be the ancestors of the Ur III kings and the creation of the tales in that court seems likely. Their popularity in the early second millennium suggests that the ideals of kingship displayed there were still alive.

Royal hymns dedicated to early second-millennium kings demonstrate the ability of some scribes to compose intricate texts in the Sumerian language, which probably was no longer spoken at the time. It is likely that other genres of literature were also composed during these centuries, while earlier compositions were recorded in a fixed form. The intensity of scribal activity in the Sumerian language may have resulted from the fact that the language was under threat: oral preservation was no longer guaranteed, so written versions with explicit indication of all the grammatical elements were needed. The primary writers of the extant manuscripts were boys trained to compose contracts and administrative accounts made up almost entirely of stock phrases. Their education went beyond the skills they would need on a daily basis. They were trained in the private houses of learned men, who each worked with a group of boys assisted by a student helper. The teachers were probably affiliated with the temples and, when Sumerian texts needed to be composed for such occasions as a royal visit, they most likely were the authors.

In northern Babylonia, Sumerian literature was also studied. The majority of compositions found there are of a liturgical nature and often written out more syllabically than in the south. Scribal skills were not necessarily inferior, however. The numerous letters found throughout the courts of the Near East were inspired by models from Babylonia. Scribes at Mari, for example, were probably trained in the south or by Babylonian men engaged by the local kings. The courts were important patrons of scribes, and schooling may have been centralized in the palaces rather than in private houses of temple affiliates. The situation in Babylon itself is unknown as we do not have access to archaeological remains of the period. Nevertheless, literature in the Babylonian language, as well as in Sumerian, continued to be composed. Some of the royal inscriptions of Samsuiluna, including bilingual Sumerian–Akkadian examples, are of a high literary quality. This was also the first significant period of literary composition in the Akkadian language. Certain texts that have a long history in Mesopotamia, such as the Epic of Gilgamesh or the Flood story, are first attested in Old Babylonian times, and many Akkadian hymns and incantations of this period are known. Their mood reflected the political situation of the times: uncertainty and violence are dominant themes. The writers of these texts were not spared the difficulties that confronted the inhabitants of the Old Babylonian state.

At this time we see the first extensive written documentation of a science for which Babylonia was famous in the ancient world: mathematics. From the beginning of writing the administrators of Babylonia showed their mathematical abilities when measuring fields, harvests, numbers of bricks, volumes of earth, and many other things that were of importance to bureaucrats. The tools to calculate these had to be taught but, as with literature, the skills displayed in the school texts show a much higher level than needed in daily practice. At first the students repeatedly copied out standard lists of capacity, weight, area and length, division and multiplication. Their most challenging tasks were formulated as word problems, but these were not really of great practical value even if their wording related to actual accounting tasks. For instance, the size of a grain pile was given, and it was asked how one could calculate the contents, or the circumference and slope of a heap of grain were provided in order to calculate the height:

> A heap. The circumference is 30. In 1 cubit the slope is 0;15. What is the height? You: Double 0;15, the slope. You will see 0;30. Take the reciprocal of 0;30. You will see 2. Multiply 0;30 the circumference, by 2. You will see 1, : the height. <This is> the method.[6]

The knowledge of mathematics displayed in such texts is very sophisticated, and based on an algebraic logic. For example, the Babylonians had calculated the square root of 2 accurately, and applied it in geometric calculations (see figure 6.2). They were aware of the Pythagorean theorem that in a right-angled triangle, the square of the hypotenuse is equal to the sums of the squares of the other sides. The basis of most of these calculations was information provided

cm
0   1   2   3

Figure 6.2 Old Babylonian mathematical tablet. Courtesy of The Yale Babylonian Collection (YBC 7289)

in tables, listing numbers in their sexagesimal notation and their reciprocals (that is, 60 divided by that number), and their creation is one of the many accomplishments of the Babylonian schools.

The political supremacy of Babylon shifted the religious focus of the region to that city. The city-god Marduk was favored by kings Hammurabi and Samsuiluna. He was integrated in the Sumerian pantheon of Nippur by making him the son of Ea, himself the god of Eridu in the extreme south. While Marduk's cult predominated only in the region surrounding Babylon at that time, a few centuries later it would become the primary cult of Babylonia. The popularity of northern Babylonian deities increased and people throughout Babylonia adopted them as their personal gods. Thus in the centuries of the Old Babylonian dynasty, many of the cultural elements characteristic of the Near East in the second half of the second millennium were developed, and the political, religious, and cultural focus of Babylonia shifted permanently to its northern part.

The end of this period is something of a mystery. Each one of Hammurabi's successors ruled for more than two decades, a situation that is usually indicative of political stability. They kept northern Babylonia unified for 155 years, longer than the entire Ur III period, for example. The written evidence from the region shows a continuation of administrative and economic practices, and there are no indications of a weakening of the Old Babylonian state. Yet it existed in a void, surrounded by sparsely inhabited regions. The only political powers equal to it were located at a great distance in northwestern Syria and in Anatolia. Conflict between those states ultimately affected Babylon. In 1595, King Mursili of the Hittites, after a campaign in northern Syria, led his troops down the Euphrates River, seemingly without much resistance. He sacked the city of Babylon, ending its famous dynasty, and left the region leaderless.

6.3 The Old Hittite Kingdom

Central Anatolia became a pivotal player in the history of the Near East at this time. The appearance of the Hittites in the heartland of Mesopotamia was the result of a relatively short process of centralization of power and the creation of an entity we now call the Old Hittite state or kingdom. Anatolia's earlier history is mostly shrouded in mystery: there are no written sources until the Old Kingdom period, and our information for those early centuries of the second millennium derives solely from the colonies of Assyrian merchants in the region. These sources depict a network of small kingdoms, often in conflict with one another, and with populations that used varied languages. Many of the languages survived into later centuries: Hattic, Luwian, Palaic, Hurrian, and what is now called Hittite. In the native tradition the latter was called Nesili, the language of Nesa, which was the indigenous name for Kanesh, where the main Assyrian merchant colony was located. Nesili became the official written language of the Hittite state, even if it may not have been spoken by most of its subjects. Several of the Anatolian languages in the second millennium, most notably Hittite, were Indo-European. Under the influence of an outdated nineteenth-century idea that there was an Indo-European homeland somewhere north of India, much attention in scholarship has been devoted to finding out when and where the Indo-Europeans entered Anatolia and to finding evidence for an invasion. This search is futile, however. There is no reason to assume that speakers of Indo-European languages were not always present in Anatolia, nor can we say that they would have been a clearly identifiable group by the second millennium. We can only observe that when the textual sources inform us of the languages used in Anatolia, some people spoke Indo-European ones, others not.

The fact that Hittite was considered to be the language of Nesa, i.e., Kanesh, provides a connection between the period of the Old Assyrian colonies and later Hittite history. Another link is the find of a dagger on the citadel of that city, inscribed with the name Anitta, who is identified as the ruler. The inscription was written in the Old Assyrian script and language, which seems to indicate that the Assyrian merchants imported the technology of writing at that time. Anitta was the central character of one of the earliest records of the Hittites, the so-called "Anitta text." It described how he and his father, Pitkhana, kings of the unlocated city of Kussara, conquered various central Anatolian cities, including Nesa, which may then have become their new capital. They unified the entire valley of the Kizil Irmak River up to its mouth on the Black Sea. Such military operations may have caused the end of the Assyrian trade network. While the kingdom of Anitta collapsed soon after his death, the preservation of his memory in later records may indicate that he was regarded as the ancestor of the later Hittite royal house.

The history of the Old Hittite kingdom is written using sources that are very different from those available in the rest of the Near East. The palace archives of the later Hittite state contained a set of texts relating military campaigns of these early rulers or dealing with succession problems (see document 6.2). For example, King Hattusili's campaigns are described in annalistic texts, which, if indeed from his reign, would be the oldest such texts from the Near East. But the manuscripts we have were mostly written in the fourteenth and thirteenth centuries, and it is unclear whether they are actual copies of older texts or later compositions set in ancient times for current political purposes. They often provide vivid descriptions of events, but their historical accuracy is hard to establish. The records relating to succession problems are to be seen as very biased as they were intended to portray the ruler under whom they were written as the legitimate successor. The Hittite habit of providing surveys

---

Document 6.2 *An account of early Hittite history: extract from the Edict of Telepinu*

Afterwards Hattusili was king, and his sons, brothers, in-laws, family members, and troops were all united. Wherever he went on campaign he controlled the enemy land with force. He destroyed the lands one after the other, took away their power, and made them the borders of the sea. When he came back from campaign, however, each of his sons went somewhere to a country, and in his hand the great cities prospered. But, when later the princes' servants became corrupt, they began to devour the properties, conspired constantly against their masters, and began to shed their blood.

When Mursili was king in Hattusa, his sons, brothers, in-laws, family members, and troops were all united. He controlled the enemy land with force, took away their power, and made them the borders of the sea. He went to the city Aleppo, destroyed Aleppo, and took the deportees from Aleppo and its goods to Hattusa. Afterwards he went to Babylon and destroyed Babylon. He also fought the Hurrian [troops]. He took the deportees from Babylon and its goods to Hattusa. Hantili was cupbearer and he had Harapshili, Mursili's sister, as wife. Zidanta stole up to Hantili and they committed an evil deed: they killed Mursili and shed his blood.

Translation after Inge Hoffmann, *Der Erlaß Telepinus* (Heidelberg: Carl Winter-Universitätsverlag, 1984), pp. 14–19 and Th. P. J. van den Hout, "The Proclamation of Telepinu," in W. W. Hallo, ed., *The Context of Scripture* vol. 1, (Leiden: Brill, 1997), pp. 194–5.

of earlier reigns may seem a boon to the historian, but can be a trap where we repeat fully fictional accounts.

Based on these suspect sources, the following reconstruction of Old Hittite history can be made. A ruler called Hattusili created the Hittite state in the early or mid-seventeenth century (for a list of kings, see p. 306). Heir to the throne of Kussara, he rapidly defeated his competitors in central Anatolia. Among his conquests was the city of Hattusa, located in the center of the region in a strategic and well-protected site thanks to its position on a hilltop. He made Hattusa his capital, and possibly changed his name to coincide with that of the city. The city was in the center of Anatolia, but not at the heart of the Hittite state, which primarily extended south into Syria. Its northern location exposed it to attacks from groups from the Black Sea shores, especially a people called Gasga, who at times completely sacked it. Although some later rulers temporarily established capitals further south, Hattusa remained the political and religious center of the Hittite state until the very end of that state's existence.

Hattusili initiated a pattern of southward expansion. As Anatolia is divided into river valleys with a limited agricultural area, the search for control over north Syria may have been driven by the need to obtain access to large cereal fields. Hattusili invaded the kingdom of Yamkhad, which by the mid-seventeenth century controlled north-west Syria. The Hittite king sacked several of its cities, including Alalakh. Aleppo, the capital of Yamkhad, remained uncaptured, however, despite several campaigns in the region. Hattusili also campaigned in southwestern Anatolia and had, by the end of his reign, created a large state. Internally, however, that state was in disarray. Hattusili's sons rebelled late in his life, and even the nephew he had chosen as his successor turned against him. Thus, on his deathbed, Hattusili appointed his grandson, Mursili, as his heir. The new king's reign is poorly known, but the laconic sources mention two extremely important acts: the destructions of Aleppo and of Babylon. His military operations were not followed by an occupation, however. By annihilating Aleppo, Mursili upset the balance of power in north-west Syria and created space for other entities to develop. The conquest of Babylon is only mentioned in later Hittite and Babylonian sources, and nothing is known about it except that it took place. We can only speculate how and why Mursili led his troops so far south in what is sure to have been merely a raid. The result was a power vacuum in Babylonia as well.

The situation that had characterized Mesopotamia and Syria for two centuries was thus totally reversed. No longer did a set of strong rulers dominate the scene, and the entire region was reduced to political fragmentation. Neither did the Hittites themselves benefit from this situation: upon his return home, Mursili was assassinated by his brother-in-law, Hantili, who seized the throne. When Hantili in turn was murdered, various parties contested the succession to the Hittite throne, and internal instability prevented the Hittites from maintaining control over anything beyond the heartland of their state. The Hittite state would not reemerge as a significant player on the international scene until the fourteenth century.

The Hittite scribal tradition was not an offspring of the Old Assyrian one, despite the fact that this was the earliest in Anatolia, but was fully inspired by Babylonian practices. Many of the early texts were bilingual, using Hittite and Akkadian. The Hittite language was written in cuneiform script inspired by the Babylonian forms and readings of signs, and the penetration of these practices into Anatolia has to be seen as an extension of their influence throughout the Near East. Babylonia was thus the center of literate culture for all courts of the Near East, even if they spoke different languages.

The nature of the Hittite sources leads to an almost total ignorance about the workings of the Old Hittite state. No administrative archives from this period are known, so the organization of the economy, for instance, is a mystery. Much has been made in scholarship of the references to a gathering of warriors and officials in Hattusili's succession edict. This is thought to refer to an assembly of noblemen, who elected one from amongst themselves as king. Sometimes Indo-European practices are assumed here, since they are considered to be more democratic than those of others in the Near East. But such conclusions are not founded in evidence, and most likely the Old Hittite court functioned in ways similar to the others of the time. The Hittite state is thus very poorly known beyond its military successes. On that front it had a radical impact on the Near East by its removal of Aleppo and Babylon. But neither the Hittites nor any other older powers immediately filled the void that was left behind.

6.4 The "Dark Age"

By 1590 the Near East looked very different from what it had been four generations earlier. A system of flourishing states, ruled by courts in close contact with one another, spreading from the Mediterranean coast to the Persian Gulf, had been fully wiped out. Some royal houses still existed in cities such as Babylon, Terqa, and Hattusa, but they were pale reflections of the past and most often had no connection to their famous predecessors. Throughout the Near East, urbanism was at an all-time low since the year 3000. Many cities, such as Mari, had been destroyed as a result of the earlier military competition. Some others were abandoned for reasons unknown: changes in the river courses or rainfall patterns, social and political upheavals may all have played a role. The situation had the usual consequence for the historian: a lack of centralized power led to a discontinuation of administrative and scribal practices as the levels of economic and cultural activities decreased. Texts were only sparingly written and we have thus no data with which to work. We enter into a "Dark Age."

The length of this age is much debated. Depending on whether scholars see continuity or discontinuity between the first and the second halves of the second millennium, their perception of the timespan of historical silence will be shorter or longer. Some crucial changes took place in this hiatus, which would lead to a very different situation in later centuries. My opinion is somewhere in the middle of current theories. When roughly one century of full darkness lifted in the early fifteenth century, the state of Mittani appears in the record of northern Mesopotamia.

The political ascendancy of new population groups, the Kassites in the south and the Hurrians in the north, seems to have been the most important development in the sixteenth century. Both groups had been present in the Near East before, but only in this "Dark Age" were they able to begin asserting clear political control. Kassites had lived in the north of Babylonia from the eighteenth century on, recognizable by their names, which reveal a clearly distinct language from the other inhabitants in the region. There are many indicators that they had a tribal social organization, and they were most closely associated with the area where steppe and agricultural zones border one another. But as with earlier nomadic groups, Gutians and Amorites, some Kassites were fully integrated social members of the agricultural and urban economy from the moment we encounter them. The Hana dynasty, which had emerged at Terqa upstream from Mari, included a ruler with a Kassite name. The Middle Euphrates region may thus have been the first area where the Kassites gained political control over cities. When Babylon was sacked in 1595, it was left leaderless, but within the next decades a Kassite dynasty had taken over control there. By 1475 it had incorporated southern Babylonia. It is only in the fourteenth century, however, that we can really study its history.

In northern Syria and Mesopotamia, there is evidence that people with Hurrian names had been present since the mid-third millennium. States with Hurrian rulers are attested from the end of the Old Akkadian period on. In the late third millennium, there was a nebulous state called "Urkesh and Nawar," after two cities in the northern Habur basin, ruled by a man named Atal-shen. Several of the early second-millennium states known to us had Hurrian rulers, and at certain places a substantial percentage of the population bore Hurrian names. They were spread out over an extremely wide zone, from the Zagros Mountains to the Mediterranean. When the Kingdom of Upper Mesopotamia fell apart, waves of Hurrian speakers may have entered its territory from the mountains to its east. These immigrants probably brought some cultural elements we usually associate with Indo-Europeans, even if Hurrian itself is not an Indo-European language. Later Hurrians honored the Indian gods Mitra, Varuna, and the divine pair Nasatya. There has been much speculation as to whether the Hurrians themselves were subjected to an Indo-European military upper class: later rulers of Mittani, the Hurrian state in northern Syria, bore Indo-European names and their charioteers were designated with the word *mariyannu*, a term that might include the Vedic word for "young man." The evidence is inconclusive as to the character of the military class, however, and it seems best to regard its members as men with a special training for warfare. In that aspect the Hurrians were very successful. They became a formidable opponent, invading the Old Hittite kingdom several times. Their moves southward may have pushed people from Syria-Palestine into Egypt, where they formed the so-called Hyksos dynasties of the early sixteenth century. The Hurrians certainly became the most prominent population group in a vast area

by the time the historical sources resume. Not only did they have their own
territorial state by the early fifteenth century, called Mittani, but they were also
dominant among the Hittites and in Kizzuwatna (south-west Anatolia), while
several rulers of the Syro-Palestinian city-states had Hurrian names.

While Kassites and Hurrians became politically dominant during the "Dark
Age," culturally they barely made an impression across the Near Eastern scene.
Although many personal names were Kassite, and Babylonian texts indicate the
existence of a Kassite vocabulary, no single text or sentence is known in the
Kassite language. Some twenty Kassite names of gods are attested, but only
for the divine couple that guarded the dynastic family do we know anything
concerning a cult and the building of a special temple. The speakers of Kassite
were fully assimilated into Babylonian culture.

The Hurrian tradition was older as far as we know and interacted with a
variety of cultures that were not as dominant as that of Babylonia. We do have
a number of Hurrian language texts, a few from the Mittani state itself, and a
few from the Hittite state. The latter's multicultural environment permitted the
survival of Hurrian myths and rituals. Still, in comparison with their political
importance, the cultural impact Hurrians made in Near Eastern history was
not that significant.

The Hurrians may have been responsible, however, for a major technological innovation that took place during the "Dark Age": the use of the horse
and chariot. In the second half of the second millennium, all Near Eastern
armies fielded chariotries while previously only infantries had fought, with asses
or donkeys as draft-animals. A long Hittite manual for the training of horses,
found in later centuries, starts with the statement, "Thus speaks Kikkuli, the
horse-trainer, from the land of Mittani," and the text contains a lot of Hurrian
vocabulary. It is thus possible that the Hurrians were responsible for the spread
of horsemanship throughout the Near East.

Another technological change that may have taken place at this time related
to seafaring. After 1500 we observe a shift of attention of the people of the
Near East from east to west: islands and countries across the Mediterranean
Sea became included in the Near Eastern world-view. Cyprus and the Aegean
became regular trading partners, while trade contacts with Egypt intensified. A
maritime trading system developed by which the countries along the eastern
Mediterranean shores were tied together, visited by ships that circled the sea
in a counterclockwise direction picking up items at all stops and exchanging
them for others. Although the lands of Mesopotamia were too distant from
the sea to participate directly in this system, they benefited from it. Tin, for
example, which had been imported from the east until this time, now probably
came from western sources. While contacts with Aegean islands such as Crete
were already attested in the Mari archives, the mass of goods that entered the
Near East from the west was much greater in the second half of the second
millennium than ever before. It seems likely that innovations in boat construction and navigational techniques had something to do with this, but the details
of those changes or who initiated them are unclear.

Our uncertainties about the events and historical developments of the sixteenth and early fifteenth centuries are great. That some radical changes took place is undeniable, however. The Near Eastern world that arose out of the "Dark Age" was in many respects a totally new one.

NOTES

1 Shubat-Enlil, Qattara, Ashnakkum (present Chagar Bazar), Tuttul, Mari, Terqa, and Qala'at al-Hadi and Tell Taya (ancient names unknown).
2 Jean-Marie Durand, *Documents épistolaires du palais de Mari* (Paris: Les Editions du Cerf, 1997), volume 1, p. 138.
3 Douglas R. Frayne, *Old Babylonian Period (2003–1595 BC) (The Royal Inscriptions of Mesopotamia. Early Periods*, volume 4) (Toronto: University of Toronto Press, 1990), p. 341.
4 Translation after F. R. Kraus, *Briefe aus dem Archive des Shamash-hazir* (Leiden: E. J. Brill, 1968), no. 1.
5 For a recent translation of Hammurabi's law code, see Martha T. Roth, *Law Collections from Mesopotamia and Asia Minor*, second edition (Atlanta: Scholars Press, 1997), pp. 71–142.
6 Translation from Eleanor Robson, *Mesopotamian Mathematics, 2100–1600 BC* (Oxford: Clarendon Press, 1999), p. 224.

Part II
Territorial States

7
The Club of the Great Powers

3000	2500	2000	1500	1000	500

ca. 1365–1335	Amarna archive
1274	Battle of Qadesh

During the centuries from 1500 to 1200 the Near East became fully integrated in an international system that involved the entire region from western Iran to the Aegean Sea, from Anatolia to Nubia. A number of large territorial states interacted with one another as equals and rivals. Located between them, especially in the Syro-Palestinian area, was a set of smaller states that owed allegiance to their more powerful neighbors, and which were often used as proxies in their competition. The system spanned beyond the confines of the Near East as defined in this book: it incorporated the Aegean world and Egypt, which at this time had its largest territorial expansion and was actively involved in the Near East to its north and Nubia to its south. Over these three hundred years the major polities involved changed in some places, but there was a remarkable consistency in the division of power over the entire area. The great states were Kassite Babylonia, Hittite Anatolia, Egypt, and, in northern Mesopotamia and Syria, first the Mittani state followed in the mid-fourteenth century by Assyria. On their eastern fringe was located the powerful kingdom of Elam, to the west the state of Mycenae, whose political organization is difficult to describe. In their midst were the states of Syria and Palestine, mostly city-states in extent and organization, and always dependent on one of the great powers. The histories of all of these great and small states can be written separately, and I will do so for those of the Near East in subsequent chapters. But the fact that they all participated in a common system without one of them dominating all the others makes this an unusual period of ancient history. It is this system that I will explore first.

The historian's task is greatly facilitated by the abundance of sources available for all but a few of the states involved. Except for the Aegean and some Syro-Palestinian states, all have yielded a wide variety of textual data. Royal inscriptions, legal and administrative documents, and literary texts are found almost everywhere. Moreover, since the courts were in contact with one another, their chancelleries contained diplomatic correspondence and international treaties. The centralized character of each of the states led to a high level of scribal production. Also the archaeological information is very rich, as building activity and artistic creation were prolific as a result of the wealth of the states. We are presented with a multitude of sources, both in number and variety, which derive not from a single participant in the system but from many of them simultaneously. Our view on the period is thus not filtered through the eyes of only one of the actors.

The greatest difficulty confronting us is the uncertainty about chronology. While we may feel cautiously confident about the sequence of rulers and lengths of reigns in certain states, information about other kings and kingships remains very vague. Thus, even writing the history of the Mittani state, for example, poses great difficulties, as we cannot date events based on evidence from the state itself. We have to rely on synchronisms with Egypt and Hatti to find out approximately when and how long a Mittani king ruled. When his name appears in a text of one of those states, we have some idea when he was active. Yet the chronologies of all states of the time are not as firm as one would wish, and even when contacts are attested, we are sometimes at a loss to fit events together, despite the close interactions between kings. Consequently, the dates assigned here are often tentative (see chart 7.1).

7.1 The Political System

From 1500 to 1200 all the regions of the Near East went through a cycle of creation, florescence, and fall of centralized states. There were at least five zones where political unification and centralization of power took place, followed by a period of prosperity that ended in a rather sudden collapse. In four of those zones the entire period can be studied as the history of one state: the Middle Elamite Kingdom in western Iran, Kassite Babylonia in southern Mesopotamia, the Hittite New Kingdom in Anatolia (a state called Hatti by its contemporaries), and New Kingdom Egypt in north Africa. In northern Mesopotamia two distinct states dominated in succession, Mittani and Assyria. The latter was originally a province of the Mittani state, gained independence, and then replaced its original master as the regional power. A similar cycle of political unification and disintegration may have taken place in western Anatolia and the Aegean, but the situation is murkier there, owing to the absence of textual sources.

Chart 7.1 Comparative chronology of the major states of the second half of the second millennium

Date	Mittani	Babylonia	Assyria	Hatti	Egypt
1500	Parrattarna				Amenhotep I
1450					Tuthmose III
1400	Artatama I				Amenhotep III
		Kadashman-Enlil I			
1350	Tushratta		Assur-ubalilt I		Akhenaten
		Burnaburiash II			
	Shattiwaza			Suppiluliuma I	
		Kurigalzu II			
				Mursili II	
1300					
			Adad-nirari I		
	Elam			Muwatalli II	
1250	Untash-Napirisha	Kadashman-Enlil II	Shalmanseser I		Ramesses II
				Hattusili III	
		Kashtiliashu IV	Tukulti-Ninurta I	Tudhaliya IV	
1200				Suppiluliuma II	Merneptah
	Shutruk-Nahhunte				
1150	Kutir-Nahhunte				Ramesses III
	Shilhak-Inshushinak				
			Assur-resha-ishi I		
		Nebuchadnezzar I			
1100			Tiglath-pileser I		
1050					

The simultaneity of these cycles in the various states of the eastern Mediterranean cannot be pure coincidence. The proximity of the states and the close interactions between them, as attested in numerous sources, force us to look beyond their individual histories to explain the waxing and waning of their fortunes. The end of this period has been intensively investigated and its causes much debated, especially for the Aegean, Anatolian, and Syro-Palestinian regions. The beginning, however, has mostly been portrayed as the accidental coalescence of individual histories into a regional system as a result of inter-actions between courts that had established themselves independently. Local circumstances certainly were to a great extent responsible for what happened in the different areas, but also the rise of the individual states may be better understood when seen in a regional context. Just as the end of these states was precipitated by the disappearance of the system that tied them together, their rise was conditioned by the growth of the system. Since much of this took place in the so-called Dark Age, the development of the regional system is hard to study in detail. But by placing local histories within a wider context, we can account better for the developments in individual states than by looking at the internal circumstances alone.

In that sixteenth-century Dark Age, the entire Near East was politically fragmented: nowhere do we see strong states, and as a result the textual documentation is extremely scarce. Only in Egypt do we have a grasp on the situation, but even there our understanding is limited. From the mid-seventeenth century

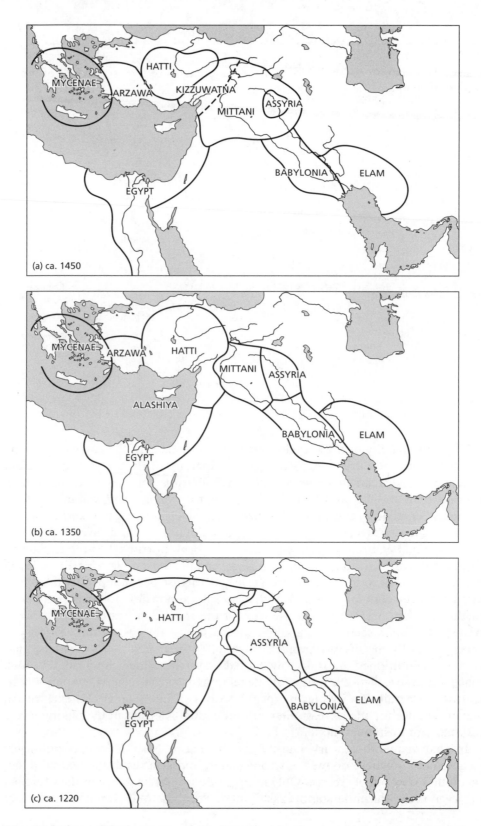

Map 7.1 The political systems of the Near East in the second half of the second millennium (after Mario Liverani, *Prestige and Interest* [Padua: Sargon, 1990], pp. 299–300)

on, the country had been divided into a number of principalities, several of which were ruled by foreigners called "Hyksos." In the Near East, the great states had disappeared and competing dynasties ruled everywhere. The near-total absence of textual remains suggests that their economies were underdeveloped and their political control weak. Mesopotamia, Anatolia, and Syria-Palestine saw a sharp reduction of inhabited zones and an increase of semi-nomadic groups. The urban centers had become fewer in number, and were isolated in a surrounding with little permanent settlement.

The situation of political and economic decline was gradually reversed starting in the late sixteenth and the fifteenth centuries: out of the landscape of small and weak states developed an unprecedented system of territorial states with more or less equivalent power. Many, if not all, of the states involved attained a size and cohesion never known before in their histories. The best-known examples are Egypt, and Babylonia and Assyria in Mesopotamia. The Mesopotamian states became truly territorial. Babylonia and Assyria in the second half of the second millennium were regional entities, ruled from one political center by dynasties that considered themselves to govern a country, not one or more cities. The territories included several cities and their hinterlands, knit together by a degree of economic integration unseen before. Ideologically, the idea that the city was at the heart of cultural and political life still survived, but the political autonomy and economic autarky of cities had disappeared. Egypt, which had been a territorial state from its inception in the early third millennium, at this time developed into a large empire extending into foreign lands, stretching from Nubia in modern-day Sudan to northern Syria.

Also in the other regions of the Near East, territorial states developed where there had been a multitude of small states before the mid-second millennium. Northern Syria in the early second millennium had been politically divided between states such as Qatna, Yamkhad, Tuttul, Apum, and so on. All those had suffered decline in the sixteenth century, and when the new state of Mittani arose in the fifteenth century, it was a territorial one unifying the entire region. New Kingdom Hatti similarly instituted a political integration of Central Anatolia and north-west Syria. The cohesion of the Middle Elamite state and the differences from what preceded it are difficult to evaluate, as is true for the Aegean world. In the latter case, the mention of western states in the Hittite texts (Arzawa and Ahhiyawa), and the homogeneity of material culture in the centuries after 1500, suggest a substantive political change compared to earlier times.

The only exception to this general trend toward larger regional political units was the Syro-Palestinian area: here the basic system of small states centered round a single city continued to exist. Numerous examples are known, such as Jerusalem, Byblos, Damascus, Ugarit, and Aleppo. Qualitatively, we see no difference from the situation in the first part of the second millennium, even if the earlier picture is much less clear. Perhaps this exception to the rule underlines how fundamental the changes elsewhere were. The Syro-Palestinian region was sandwiched between competing territorial states: first Egypt and Mittani, later Egypt and Hatti, with Assyria lurking in the background. It acted as a buffer between these states and as a place where they could interact competitively, both directly and by proxy. The region was not permitted to unify and to develop into a territorial state itself, nor did it become firmly integrated within the territories of one of its powerful neighbors. The surrounding great states were strong enough to prevent that from happening. The difference between themselves and the Syro-Palestinian rulers was acknowledged in their formal interactions. Only the rulers of the territorial states regarded themselves as equals and addressed each other as "brothers," while those of the Syro-Palestinian states were of a lower rank and were "servants." Thus these small states were forced to pledge allegiance to one of the neighboring overlords, switching that allegiance to the stronger power as needed. The level of integration within these larger state-systems depended on the proximity to the political center and on the policies of the sovereigns. Egypt's control of Syria, for example, was a lot more hands-off than Hatti's. But also the latter used a flexible approach: it administered the important region of Carchemish through a viceroy, while in Amurru, for instance, it permitted a local king to govern as a vassal. We cannot say, however, that any of the Syro-Palestinian states ever became fully integrated in the territories of their dominant neighbors. They continued to exist as separate political entities, distinct from the suzerains in the great states, which at the same time prevented them from uniting with their neighbors.

We can seek explanations for these sociopolitical developments within the histories of the individual states, and indeed the growth of territorial states during the first half of the second millennium has been studied in the previous chapter. But the presence of an overarching system in which all consciously participated must have reinforced the local processes toward greater political centralization. This becomes more likely if we consider how closely these states interacted with one another, both in friendly and hostile ways, and how they shared a social and ideological structure.

7.2   Political Interactions: Diplomacy and Trade

All participants in this system knew what their place was in the political hierarchy and how to interact with others. They behaved as if they lived in a large village where communications were close and people were related to each other. In order to maintain the system, they were in constant contact with one another, sending envoys back and forth with oral and written messages. All courts had a chancellery where scribes worked, writing in Babylonian, the international language of diplomacy. By far our best evidence for this practice comes from Egypt, where in the fourteenth century King Akhenaten moved the capital to the new city of Akhetaten (modern Amarna), where his and his father's international correspondence was kept. These clay tablets are usually referred to as the Amarna letters (see box 7.1). The group of 350 letters was primarily written to the Egyptian king by his vassals in Syria-Palestine, but around forty of them were from or to the kings he considered to be his equals, the "Great

Box 7.1 *The Amarna letters*

In the late nineteenth century AD, local peasants found a group of cuneiform tablets at the modern-day site of Amarna, where in the fourteenth century BC King Akhenaten had built the new capital of Egypt, Akhetaten. These contained the diplomatic correspondence between two kings of Egypt, Akhenaten and his predecessor Amenhotep III, and their equals and vassals in the Near East, a total of 350 letters. Most of them were addressed to the king or high court officials by rulers of small states in the Syro-Palestinian area, and detailed their interactions with their overlord. They called themselves servants of the king of Egypt, and sought to ingratiate themselves by making their neighbors look like untrustworthy vassals. The letters show that Egypt had divided the region into three administrative districts and ruled it with a relatively small military presence. The region controlled stretched from the south of Palestine to central Syria, with the state of Amurru as the northernmost Egyptian dependency. The language of the letters is Babylonian, but influences of the local Semitic languages are visible in the vocabulary and grammar.

A group of about forty of these letters had been written to the Egyptian king by his colleagues in the other great states of the time: Babylonia, Assyria, Mittani, Hatti, Alashiya, and Arzawa. The kings saw themselves as equals and addressed each other as brothers. They discussed diplomatic matters, especially the exchange of precious goods and of royal women, which reinforced the ties between them. While most of the letters were written in Babylonian, there were two in Hittite and one each in Hurrian and Assyrian.

These Amarna letters cover a short period of at most thirty years from ca. 1365 to 1335, but it is certain that this type of correspondence was maintained throughout the period at several locations. The state archives of the Hittite capital, Hattusa, have revealed similar letters, and other courts must have had the same type of international exchanges. The use of the Babylonian language and writing material shows how the culture from that region continued to dominate in the Near East.

Kings." Those were the rulers of Babylonia, Assyria, Mittani, Hatti, Alashiya (on Cyprus), and Arzawa (in south-west Anatolia). The last two were probably included because of their control of resources needed by all kings – in the case of Alashiya, copper. The letters from Arzawa were written in the Hittite language rather than Babylonian, which shows that its court was not yet fully integrated in the system. That the Egyptian archive was not unique is clear from small finds in Syro-Palestinian cities of similar diplomatic letters contemporaneous to the Amarna ones, and from the thirteenth century international correspondence of the kings of Hatti, Assyria, and Babylonia has also been found, albeit in smaller numbers. The palace at Ugarit, one of the states subject to Hatti, had such texts as well. Isolated finds from other palaces throughout the Near East show that all courts were involved in this diplomacy.

They portrayed the world they lived in as an extended family household: kings of equal status called one another brother; those of lower rank called themselves servants (see document 7.1). Each state's status was demarcated, but, since the political situation sometimes changed quickly, frictions arose. When Assyria gained political and military prominence, King Assur-uballit sent two letters to the king of Egypt as if he were an equal. This enraged Burnaburiash, king of Babylon, who complained to his Egyptian colleague: "With regard to my Assyrian vassals, it was not I who sent them to you. Why did they go to your country without proper authority? If you are loyal to me, they will not negotiate any business. Send them to me empty-handed!"[1] Such quarrels were unavoidable as status was very important and the political reality changed faster than the willingness to acknowledge newcomers.

In one sense we see here a continuation of early second-millennium practices in which the royal houses of the Near East corresponded with each other. A major difference, however, is that political issues were never now directly discussed by the Great Kings. Some allusions to them appear, but these men were primarily interested in the diplomatic exchange of messengers, goods, and women. The opposite was true in the letters of vassals to their overlords. They focused on the everyday political situation in their surroundings, and often accused others of being unreliable vassals to the king. These accusations were technical maneuvers in the competition over land and the control of routes. Their declarations of loyalty and the denunciations of their neighbors have to be regarded as hyperbole and rhetoric. They tried to avoid or delay the payment of taxes and tribute, and drew attention away from that topic by pointing out their neighbor's disloyalty. In contrast they claimed to be politically loyal, even if they did not obey all of the pharaoh's orders. In the period of the Amarna letters, Egypt's widespread influence over the Syro-Palestinian area indeed was threatened by Hatti, which sought to pick off its northern vassals one by one. This activity was often carried out by proxy via client kings, and what appear as petty local squabbles were, in fact, contests between the great states. Bickering is characteristic even of many letters between equals: the Great Kings complained about the lack of respect others had for them. The Hittite King Hattusili, for example, wondered aloud why his Babylonian "brother" no longer sent messengers. Was he so weak that he could not force safe passage through the lands in between? Did evil tongues in his court set him up against Hattusili? Since the exchange of gifts was a major aspect of maintaining good relations, their quality and quantity were often discussed. The kings were not shy about complaining and expressing their displeasure.

Relations between states had to be codified, especially when they involved one of the great kingdoms and their vassals. This was accomplished through treaties between their rulers. They were always agreements between two men, not between the states, and had to be renewed when a change of ruler occurred. The treaties that have been preserved all involve the Hittite state or Alalakh, but references in other texts suggest that they were common throughout the Near East. Two types existed: between equal powers, and between a Great King and his vassal. The first was probably only drawn up after a serious conflict or

Document 7.1   *Examples of Amarna letters*

1 Between equals: letter from Tushratta of Mittani to Amenhotep III of Egypt

Tell Nimmureya, king of Egypt, my brother, my son-in-law, whom I love and
who loves me; Tushratta, king of Mittani, who loves you, your father-in-law, says:
All is well with me. May all be well with you. May all be well with your house,
with my daughter Tadu-Heba, and with your wife, whom you love. May all be very,
very well with your wives, your sons, your leading men, your chariots, your horses,
your troops, your country, and whatever else belongs to you.

   Shaushga of Nineveh, lady of all lands, said: "I wish to go to Egypt, the land that
I love, and then come back." Now I send her and she is on the way.

   Now, in the time of my father, she went . . . to this country. And as she stayed
there and they honored her earlier, may my brother now honor her ten times more
than before. May my brother honor her and let her come back at his pleasure.

   May Shaushga, the lady of heaven, protect my brother and me for 100,000 years,
and may our lady give us great joy. Let us act as friends.

   Is Shaushga not my goddess and my brother's goddess?

Translation after William L. Moran, *The Amarna Letters* (Baltimore: Johns Hopkins University
Press, 1992), pp. 61–2.

2 From a vassal: letter from Rib-Adda, king of Byblos, to the king of Egypt

Tell the king, my lord, my Sun; Rib-Adda, your servant, says: I fall at the feet of
my lord seven and seven times. Let the king, my lord, know that Pu-bahla, the son
of Abdi-Ashirta, has taken the city Ullassa by force. Ardata, Wahliya, Ampi, Shigata,
all these cities are theirs. Let the king thus send help to Sumur, until he gives
thought to his land. Who are the sons of Abdi-Ashirta, the servant and the dog?
Are they the king of the Kassites or the king of Mittani, so that they can take the
king's land for themselves? In the past they would take cities of your mayors,
and you did nothing. Now they have driven out your governor and have taken
his cities for themselves. They have seized Ullassa. If you will do nothing under
these circumstances, they will certainly seize Sumur and kill the governor and the
garrison. What can I do? I cannot go to Sumur. The cities Ampi, Shigata, Ullassa,
and Erwada are hostile. Should they know that I am in Sumur, there would be these
cities with ships, and the sons of Abdi-Ashirta in the countryside. They would attack
me and I could not get out. Byblos would be joined to the *habiru*.[1] They have gone
to Ibirta and an agreement has been made with the *habiru*.

Translation after William L. Moran, *The Amarna Letters* (Baltimore: Johns Hopkins University
Press, 1992), p. 177.

[1] Semi-nomadic social outcasts; see chapter 8.

for a specific purpose. The examples are thus few. The most famous one was concluded between Hattusili III of Hatti and Ramesses II of Egypt in 1259, fifteen years after their two states had clashed in a major battle near the Syrian city of Qadesh.[2] The agreement strove for full equality and brotherhood between the two, reflecting the idea of family found in the diplomatic correspondence. They promised not to attack each other, to help the other when attacked, and to extradite people who fled their respective territories. The only divergence between the two versions of the treaty we have, one for the Hittites, the other for the Egyptians, related to the question of succession to the throne. Since Hattusili had himself usurped kingship in Hatti, he was worried that his son would not be accepted, and he inserted in the treaty that the Egyptian king would guarantee his succession. The extradition of people fleeing states was one of the main concerns of all these agreements. Three of the treaties between equal partners were entirely devoted to this subject,[3] a reflection of the social situation of the time, to be discussed below.

The treaties of subservience known from this period were all concluded with the Hittite king. The details of the arrangements varied, but all contained some basic elements: the vassals in Anatolia and northern Syria had to contribute taxes and military contingents, and they had to yield their right to independent foreign relations. They could not engage in war with other Hittite vassals, nor contact other great rulers. They had to return fugitives. Loyalty to the Hittite king was principal obligation and this was sworn before numerous gods, from both the Hittite and vassal states. These treaties legitimized the relations between the rulers of the region, which were maintained through the exchange of messengers.

Diplomatic marriages further confirmed these close treaty relations and were often the concern of the letters sent by the Great Kings. Much of the Amarna correspondence between Babylon and Egypt dealt with this subject. The kings of Egypt were very eager to bring foreign women into their palace and demanded women of royal blood. They had a rule, however, that no Egyptian princess could marry a foreigner, leading to a great deal of frustration among the other kings. The latter usually did send their daughters to Egypt, however, as the bride price included the much-desired gold in which Egypt held a monopoly. Non-Egyptian kings used princesses extensively to strengthen political alliances. The kings of Hatti, for example, often gave their daughters in marriage to vassals after a treaty had been signed.

These marriages could seriously affect the internal histories of states. The Babylonian King Burnaburiash II (ruled 1359–33) had married Muballitat-Sherua, the daughter of the Assyrian Assur-uballit I (ruled 1363–28). When their son and successor, Kara-hardash, was murdered in a native Babylonian uprising, Assur-uballit intervened militarily, deposed the rebel king, and replaced him with Kurigalzu II. The bizarre episode of the recently widowed queen of Egypt, probably the young wife of Tuthankhamun, shows a similar unhappiness with the idea that the offspring of a foreign king would rule. The Egyptian queen asked the Hittite King Suppiluliuma for one of his sons to become her husband. After verification of the request, which he originally received with great skepticism, Suppiluliuma sent out one of his younger sons from Hatti to Egypt, but he was murdered during the voyage. The alliance between Hatti and Egypt was clearly not in the interest of some factions at the Egyptian court, who subsequently placed one of their own on the throne. The peculiarity of this episode in Hittite–Egyptian relations cannot be underestimated. First, the Egyptians were always eager to marry foreign princesses, but never allowed one of their own royal women to marry a foreigner. Second, in this instance the male traveled to the foreign court, not the other way around, as was customary. This situation presents a complete gender reversal: a female ruler invited a male prince to become her spouse at her palace, instead of the usual request for a foreign princess to become the spouse of the Egyptian king.

Naturally, these marriages strengthened the idea that the rulers of the Near East all belonged to the same community, as if they lived in a village. This concept was crucial in the way they perceived their interactions, but all knew that in reality it was merely a fiction, as circumstances were very different from those in a village. For example, when Kadashman-Enlil of Babylon wrote to Amenhotep III of Egypt to invite him to the opening of his new palace as if he were a close neighbor, the latter could not attend. The voyage would have required several months' travel each way! But the invitation had to be proffered as one would invite a neighbor in the village. The distances between the courts were very great, and often led to questions about the fate of messengers and royal wives. When Babylon's king protested to Egypt that he did not know whether or not his sister was still alive, the Egyptian pointed out that he should not complain. No messenger qualified to ascertain who among his consorts was the Babylonian princess had ever been sent: "The men whom you sent are nobodies. . . . There has been no one among them who knows her, who was an intimate of your father, and who could identify her."[4] So, the idea that they all lived in a village was a deliberate fiction.

The most frequent topic of discussion in the letters among equals was the exchange of gifts, another way in which the cohesion between these states was maintained. These transactions had a dual function. On the one hand, they enabled rulers to obtain luxury goods not locally available; on the other hand, they reinforced a system of mutual respect, prestige, and brotherhood. The two functions cannot be separated. The exchanges operated according to a set of (unwritten) rules, known by all. The idea of reciprocity dominated: someone's gift should be repaid with one of almost equal value, although the return did not have to be immediate. On certain occasions, such as on the accession of a new king to the throne, gifts were expected. Hattusili III of Hatti complained, for instance, to the king of Assyria: "When I assumed kingship, you did not send a messenger to me. It is the custom that when kings assume kingship, the kings, his equals in rank, send him appropriate gifts of greeting, clothing befitting kingship, and fine oil for his anointing. But you did not do this today."[5] Gifts were also sent when treaties were concluded or when a military victory was celebrated. These exchanges tied the rulers together in a common system.

On the other hand, the system created a circulation of precious and highly desired goods throughout the region. In a non-commercial way, the courts could obtain products that were absent at home. Gold was of special interest to all as a rare and exotic luxury. Only the king of Egypt could send it, as only he had goldmines in his territory. The others sent Egypt horses, copper, craft goods, and so on, with the understanding that they would receive gold in return. Between other rulers similar exchanges took place. For example, Alashiya had great amounts of copper and Babylonia was the source for lapis lazuli. Manufactured objects, fancy textiles, or fine oils were often included in the gifts. The fiction that these were presents was carefully maintained, although everyone knew that access to rare goods was the intent. Thus some seemingly irrational practices can be observed: the king of Alashiya, for instance, sent a small amount of ivory along with a large shipment of copper and wood to Egypt – the land where ivory was abundant. He did so in order to indicate clearly to his colleague that he hoped to be repaid in ivory. In general the rulers often had no qualms about discussing the quality and quantity of these goods. This was frankly mentioned in the Amarna letters, and complaints about the stinginess of the Egyptian king, for instance, were common. Thus the king of Babylon wrote: "You have sent me as my greeting gift, the only thing in six years, thirty pounds of gold that looked like silver,"[6] while the Mittani ruler whined: "In my brother's country, gold is as plentiful as dirt."[7] Not only were the kings themselves involved in this exchange system of precious goods, but their wives also kept similar contacts with women of equal status in other courts.

The royal gift exchange focused on luxury items for a tiny elite. It was a small part of an extensive trade network that enabled the spread of materials and manufactured goods throughout the Near East. This activity is not well documented in the textual record, but archaeological finds show its extent, demonstrating that it tied distant regions together. For example, cylinder seals carved in Babylonia have been found in the mainland Greek city of Thebes. Seaborne trade in the eastern Mediterranean was very active and integrated the islands and coastal regions into a coherent system. Ships traveled in a counterclockwise direction, hugging the coastline as much as possible. From western Syria they went to Cyprus and southern Anatolia, then to the Aegean islands and mainland Greece. The sea was crossed from Crete to the Libyan coast in north Africa, and then ships worked their way eastward back to Syria. From the Egyptian Nile Delta to Lebanon, no good sea harbors existed, and it is possible that the ships entered the Nile itself to find anchorage.

The merchants picked up new cargo in every harbor in exchange for some of their stock on board. The ships were loaded with a mixture of goods and products from the entire region. This is best shown in a shipwreck found off the coast of southern Anatolia at Uluburun and dating to the late fourteenth century (see figure 7.1). Its main cargo was ten tons of Cypriot copper and one ton of tin of unknown origin, both poured into easily transportable ingots. The amounts found reflect the proper ratio of ten to one required for bronze production. These metals were most likely picked up in Cyprus, southern

Figure 7.1 Excavation of copper ingots from the Uluburun shipwreck. Courtesy of Don A. Frey and the Institute of Nautical Archaeology

Anatolia, and western Syria and intended for the various harbors along the sea route. There, local goods were acquired: the ship contained logs of ebony, which the Egyptians must have obtained in tropical Africa, and cedar logs from Lebanon. Ivory tusks and hippopotamus teeth also came from Egypt, while murex shells, prized for their dye, could have been obtained in various locations in north Africa and on the Syrian and Lebanese coast. In addition to these raw materials, the ship contained manufactured goods, such as Canaanite jewelry, Cypriot pottery, beads of gold, faience, agate, glass, and so on, all from different sources. There was even a jeweler's hoard on board with scraps of gold, silver, and electrum, a scarab with the name of the Egyptian Queen Nefertiti, and cylinder seals from Babylonia, Assyria, and Syria. The mixture of goods was so heterogeneous that it is impossible to identify the origin of the ship. Its cargo was truly international.

The trade also included goods that have not survived in the archaeological record. Wine and oil from the Aegean and Syria were exported to Egypt, as we can determine from the jars in which they were shipped. Drugs, perfumes, and incense were transported over great distances, often in vessels and jars with distinctive shapes to identify their contents. The maritime system was connected as well to the riverain and overland trade routes. Moreover, sailors from the Mycenaean world probably ventured as far west as Spain to obtain goods such as silver and tin. The eastern Mediterranean seaborne cycle must be seen as the nexus of a network that extended far beyond its shores.

Certain places acted as hubs in this system. Ugarit is a prime example, a city on the Syrian coast, which had its own dynasty but was vassal first to Egypt, then to Hatti. It was located on the crossroad of routes from Mesopotamia, Central Anatolia, and Egypt, and it had a good sea harbor. Trade at Ugarit was most likely undertaken by private entrepreneurs, both from the city itself and from other states. Traders from Cyprus, Egypt, Anatolia, and northern Syria resided there, and texts in a multitude of languages (Ugaritic, Babylonian, Hittite, Hurrian, Cypro-Minoan) were found in the city's houses. They document contacts with other Syrian harbors, with Cyprus and Crete, as well as with inland cities such as Carchemish and Emar. Its archaeological record also contained many foreign goods. Not only did the city act as a transit point, it was also the site of manufacturing. A workshop for the production of bronze was found in its harbor district, and Ugarit was the source of purple textiles famed throughout the region. The states tried to regulate trade to a certain extent and to use it in their rivalries. For example, in his treaty with Shaushga-muwa of the northern Syrian state Amurru, Tudhaliya IV of Hatti (ruled 1237–09) stated: "Your merchant shall not go to Assyria, and you shall not allow his merchant into your land. He shall not pass through your land. But if he comes into your land, seize him and send him off to My Majesty."[8] It seems unlikely, however, that trade embargoes were extensively used in this period, since all states of the region depended on this exchange for access to the foreign goods their elites desired.

Trade and diplomacy were thus intrinsically tied in this era: the relations between the kings of the great states were cemented by the trade of highly valued goods and materials. This was portrayed as an exchange of gifts between friends, but was also the only means accessible to the kings to obtain prestige items they lacked at home. Royal gift exchange was only part of a much wider system of trade interactions between the different regions. Merchants traveled by land and by sea to circulate goods from all parts of this world across political boundaries. While this exchange still pertained to the elites of these societies, the awareness that other people and cultures existed was raised by the presence of foreign goods everywhere.

7.3 Regional Competition: Warfare

At the same time that the great states of the region traded and exchanged diplomatic messages with each other, they were in a constant situation of rivalry, and sought to extend their territorial influences at their neighbors' expense. The official rhetoric of both Egyptians and Hittites in royal inscriptions and annals was very much focused on warfare, and the careers of many of their kings can be sketched as a list of military campaigns. Elsewhere the focus on warfare developed later: in Assyria the practice of detailing campaigns started only around 1300, while in Babylonia it never replaced attention to building activity. That military conflicts also took place there can be gathered from other sources, however. These wars were fought in two ways: either by picking off the other's vassals, or by direct confrontation. The former was the preferred way for many years in the Syro-Palestinian area. At first Egypt and Mittani competed over the region; after 1340, it was Egypt and Hatti. Although the Egyptian pharaohs claimed to have campaigned far and wide in the Levant, even up to the Euphrates River, they mostly confronted only the armies of small states. This is how, by 1400, they were able to extend control as far north as the city of Ugarit, whose king became an Egyptian vassal. The Amarna letters show how the Hittites tried to draw some of these vassals to their side. Syrian rulers incessantly complained to the pharaoh that neighboring kings acted as Hittite agents and urged them to turn against their Egyptian overlord. Even if much of this may have been to excuse themselves for non-payment of taxes, the gradual expansion of the Hittite sphere of influence in northwestern Syria without major battles cannot be denied. By 1300, the Hittites had extended their system of vassal states as far south as Qadesh, making cities like Ugarit fully dependent on them.

In other regions of the Near East, a lack of large buffer zones between the great states led to more direct conflicts. Assyria and Babylonia had several border wars, but there was no attempt at annexation or annihilation of either one. The only great state that lost its independence in this period was that of Mittani. At first preeminent in northern Syria, it was greatly reduced in size and power by the Hittites under Suppiluliuma I (ruled 1344–22), who turned its king into a vassal but left the state in existence. In the early thirteenth century, the Hittite–Egyptian rules of competition-by-proxy were broken when their armies clashed directly, most famously at Qadesh in 1274. The Egyptians presented this battle as a major confrontation between two enormous armies. Ramesses II claimed that Muwatalli fielded some 47,500 men against him, and that both kings personally led their troops. The direct war resulted from Hatti's successful encroachment on Egyptian-controlled territory, which could only be confronted by the royal army itself. Egypt lost the engagement, and subsequently Ramesses II limited his control to southern Palestine, where he drew a firm and fortified boundary. It seems thus that warfare, while sustained but low-level, was not intended to destroy the system that characterized the region, but rather to readjust the power relations between the various states that continued to tolerate and respect each other's existence. It was not until late in the period, in the late thirteenth century, that this system started to fall apart and the rules of competition, and aims of warfare, were changed. That will be discussed in a later chapter.

The "small kings" of the Syro-Palestinian area were as actively involved in warfare as their superiors. At first they resisted the raids and annexation by their mighty neighbors, but once defeated they fought one another over local disputes when the sovereign powers' attention was engaged elsewhere, as is illustrated by the Amarna letters. The constant skirmishes required all states to devote substantial resources to their military, and the army consequently took on a greater role in these societies. The technology of warfare had fundamentally changed since the early second millennium. All the armies now had fast horse-drawn chariots that enabled warriors to advance rapidly against the enemy and shoot arrows. The equipment was expensive, but clearly so effective that everyone adopted it soon after the Hurrians had introduced it in the region. Charioteers and fighters had to be trained and acquired a special status. They became the military elites, and in Mittani society, for example, they were like an aristocracy. In all states men who had made their careers in the military became politically prominent. While we cannot say that the preceding or succeeding phases in the history of the region were actually more peaceful, the second half of the second millennium does stand out because of the great geographical distances regularly covered by the armies, and because no single power dominated the rest. Militarism was the order of the day.

7.4 Shared Ideologies and Social Organizations

The rulers of the Near Eastern states were fully aware that they all belonged to a common system that encompassed the entire region. This is clear from the way they interacted with each other in diplomatic and military terms. They also shared an ideology about the social structures within their states and the role of the majority of the people living in them. While the political organization of the states varied, they were all characterized by an enormous discrepancy in access to wealth and power between the numerically small elites and the mass of the populations. An international elite class emerged, whose participants had more in common with their colleagues in the other states than with the lower classes at home. The elites engaged in an unprecedented accumulation and display of wealth, and simultaneously distanced themselves from the rest of the people by living in separate cities or city-quarters. Everywhere in the region this was a period of great building activity and artistic production, an era that produced some of the most impressive monuments of ancient history. Egypt presents perhaps the most telling example of this. With the exception of the great pyramids, virtually every one of Egypt's most famous tombs and temples dates to this time. Its royal tombs were filled with gigantic treasures: the funerary

Figure 7.2 View of the Büyükale citadel at Bogazköy. Courtesy of Paul Zimansky

goods from the tomb of Tuthankhamun were, after all, only for a minor king. Elsewhere in the region the same was true. The remains of Mycenaean Greece show monumental fortresses and lavish burials. The city-states of Syria-Palestine built elaborate palaces, sometimes more than one in a city. The capital of the Hittites, Hattusa, had numerous temples and a massive palace.

A common characteristic throughout the region is that these public buildings were often situated in clearly delineated and protected areas of the cities, or even that entire cities served as royal residences. Hattusa was perched on a well-defended rock and its palace on a high citadel within it (see figure 7.2). The palaces of Mycenaean kings, such as those at Mycenae and Tiryns, stood on hilltops reinforced by cyclopean walls. In Assur the walled inner city, where all palaces and temples were located, was clearly distinct from the residential area. The desire of the ruling elites to separate themselves from the rest of the population was taken to its logical conclusion by building new capital cities. We see the construction of entirely new cities in almost every state now: Al-Untash-Napirisha in Elam, Dur-Kurigalzu in Babylonia, Kar-Tukulti-Ninurta in Assyria, Per-Ramesse and Akhetaten in Egypt. The names of these cities themselves show how they were connected to the person: except for the last, all incorporate a specific ruler's name. The name Akhetaten referred to the god Aten, who was the king's personal deity. These were not cities for the people, but residences for the king. The ability to construct them, all of them substantial if not gigantic in size, demonstrates the wealth of resources that were available to kings. Psychologically, it points toward a desire to distance the ruling elites from the people. These cities also reflect the power struggles that went on among and between the elites. It is likely that in these places a new bureaucracy was created, one of men who were fully dependent on the king rather than on their familial ties for their social status. But the old families could fight back: Akhetaten was abandoned upon the death of its founder. Al-Untash-Napirisha and Kar-Tukulti-Ninurta lost their primacy when their founders died, but lingered on for centuries.

These cities, palaces, and temples were all extensively decorated. The requests for gold so often made in the Amarna letters were inspired by the need for conspicuous display. In that sense the rulers may have tried to outdo one another, attempting to impress the emissaries and visitors from other countries. What has sometimes been called an "international" style developed in several of the arts of the time. The high culture in the different states was a hybrid of local traditions mixed with foreign influences. Perhaps the elites strove for a fashionable lifestyle that was shared amongst themselves, and distinguished them more from the people in their own states than from their counterparts elsewhere. These cultural borrowings were certainly not limited to materials we can recognize in the archaeological record today, but must have included ephemeral things such as clothing, foods, perfumes, drugs, and so on. Could they have included language? Just as the European elites in the eighteenth century AD conversed exclusively in French, the Near Eastern elites of the fourteenth century may have shown off their knowledge of Babylonian, not because they were erudite but to demonstrate their social identity. We know well that the scribes attached to the palaces used the language for international correspondence with various levels of competence, but we may be looking at their skill too much in a purely utilitarian way. Amongst the tablets excavated at Hattusa, Emar, Ugarit, and Akhetaten were several examples of Akkadian literature. A fragment of the Epic of Gilgamesh was found at Megiddo in Palestine, and it seems certain that the numerous palaces of the region will yield further evidence that the Akkadian language was not just used for wholly practical purposes. We cannot determine who enjoyed reading or listening to these texts; their presence suggests, however, that a certain class in these societies thought it useful to use a foreign language and its literature (see document 7.2).

The textual documentation shows the existence of a strict social hierarchy, one that involved two sectors of the society: the palace dependents and the free population in village communities. We cannot talk, then, of a single hierarchy based solely on wealth or access to the means of production. The palace dependents were not "free," they did not own their own land, but if we take wealth as an indicator of social status, they were often much better off than the free people. It is in the palace sector that we see the greatest degree of social stratification. On the bottom of the palace hierarchy were serfs working the agricultural estates. Since status depended on the services one provided for the palace, the more specialized skills bestowed a higher status. Thus specialist craftsmen, scribes, cult personnel, and administrators all had their particular positions.

Document 7.2 *Babylonian literature in the Greater Near East*

The elites of the Near East in the late second millennium shared a literary tradition that was fundamentally inspired by Babylonia. Throughout the palaces of the time were kept cuneiform tablets with compositions in the Babylonian language. The content was sometimes adapted to local tastes, however. The following example derives from a collection of counsels given by a man with a Babylonian name, Shupe-Ameli, to his son. The composition was found in variant versions in Emar and Ugarit in Syria, and in Hattusa, the Hittite capital, where a partial Hittite translation had been added. No version of it is known from Babylonia proper, but the text fully fits within the cultural tradition of the region, where this genre of literature originated in the third millennium.

Do not open your heart to a woman you care for,
Seal it up, even if she wrestles or attacks.
Keep your present in a strong room,
let your wife not know what's in your purse.
Those who came before us established this,
our fathers only divided income with the gods.
They drove in a peg, made firm a ring and attached clay (i.e., they sealed off the door).
Keep your seal on a ring.
Surround the ring, and guard your house.
May your seal be the only access to your assets.
Whatever you see, leave it.
Only when you need it, spend it.

Translation after St. Seminara, "Le Istruzioni di Shupê-ameli," *Ugarit Forschungen* 32 (2000), pp. 503–5, and Benjamin R. Foster, *Before the Muses*, third edition (Bethesda: CDL Press, 2005), p. 418.

For a long time, military elites topped this hierarchy: specialist charioteers in these societies were highly prized and well rewarded for their services. In the Syro-Palestinian area they were designated with the term *mariyannu*, which became a generic term for an elite social status in certain societies. The rewards given to palace dependents were issued in various forms: rations for the lower levels, payments and the usufruct of fields for the higher ones. As service was expected in return, the use of these fields was granted on an individual basis, not to families. Later in the period, military elites tried to make tenancies heritable and paid for this in silver rather than with services.

The free people, however, were not entirely outside government control: they were also obliged to pay taxes or provide corvée labor when requested. But they owned their fields, often as a community rather than as individuals, where they scratched a poor living from the soil. The palace provided them with some support: in the irrigation societies of Mesopotamia and Egypt, they maintained the canal system, while other infrastructures were probably maintained elsewhere. The extent of the free sectors of the various societies is hard to establish and varied from state to state. In terms of social stratification, its members, together with the agricultural palace serfs, were at the bottom. Much of their labor and the harvests they produced were usurped by those higher up, as the elites' wealth had to be created somewhere. To a certain extent the wealth came from foreign conquests – in the case of Egypt, especially from Nubia with its goldmines – but the mass of producers in each of these states must have carried a heavy burden. The rulers no longer felt the obligation to restore social balances wholesale, as they had done in the early part of the millennium, and the level of indebted servitude increased substantially. Individuals and families had little respite from this system, and consequently many fled their communities and sought refuge outside the grasp of the states. They joined groups in inaccessible regions, such as mountains or deserts, and crossed political boundaries to escape their former masters. This development explains why the return of refugees was so important in the international treaties of the period, as states could not afford to lose the manpower. In the end, this social erosion may have been one of the main causes the entire system collapsed, as will be discussed in a later chapter.

NOTES

1   William L. Moran, *The Amarna Letters* (Baltimore: Johns Hopkins University Press, 1992), no. 9.
2   Gary Beckman, *Hittite Diplomatic Texts*, second edition (Atlanta: Scholars Press, 1999), no. 15.
3   Ibid., no. 1; Erica Reiner, "Akkadian Treaties from Syria and Assyria," in *Ancient Near Eastern Texts Relating to the Old Testament*, third edition (Princeton: Princeton University Press, 1969), pp. 531–2.
4   Moran, *The Amarna Letters*, no. 1.
5   Beckman, *Hittite Diplomatic Texts*, p. 149.
6   Moran, *The Amarna Letters*, no. 3.
7   Ibid., no. 19.
8   Beckman, *Hittite Diplomatic Texts*, p. 106.

8

The Western States of the Late Second Millennium

3000	2500	2000	1500	1000	500

ca. 1500	Parrattarna of Mittani rules northern Syria and northern Mesopotamia
1344–22	Reign of Suppiluliuma of Hatti
ca. 1325	Aziru of Amurru switches allegiance from Egypt to Hatti
1267	Hattusili III usurps Hittite throne
1259	Peace treaty between Hattusili III and Ramesses II of Egypt

The states that made up the international system of the Near East in the second half of the second millennium all had their own histories, which can be written to a large extent on the basis of their own sources. One of the remarkable aspects of this period is the fact that our information derives from so many places at the same time. The local histories were in significant ways determined by the interaction with others, especially since militarism was a major characteristic of the period. But internal factors were also of great importance, and we have to remember that each was located in a distinctive ecological environment and was made up of different populations, who spoke, for instance, a multitude of languages, and had diverse cultures and religious opinions. In this chapter the histories of some of the states in the western part of the Near East will be described, while the next will deal with those in the east.

8.1 Mittani

The political history of Mittani is much more difficult to write than that of its great neighbors owing to the absence of official texts from the state itself. Egyptian, Hittite, and Assyrian sources are our primary guide, which we can complement with texts from Mittani, mostly legal and administrative records from vassal territories. The state was known under various designations: the native term was Maittani, later Mittani, a term we also find in texts from Palestinian cities and the Hittites. Simultaneously, the term Hanigalbat was in use in Mittanian texts themselves, and in texts from Assyria, Babylonia, and Hatti. The state was also referred to as the "land of the Hurrians" in Hittite texts, while the Egyptians also used Nahrina. This variation in terminology seems to depend on whether one referred to the state as a polity (Mittani, Hanigalbat), to the perceived ethnicity of its inhabitants (Hurrians), or to its location on the Euphrates River (Nahrina).

The center of the Mittani state was the north Syrian area between the Euphrates bend and the Tigris. At the height of its power it incorporated territories to the east of the Tigris and on the south coast of Anatolia. In the south it had influence along the Middle Euphrates Valley and perhaps bordered Babylonia directly. How far north it reached cannot be determined at present. Its capital was Washukanni, but that city has not yet been identified archaeologically. Most likely it was located somewhere in northern Syria near the headwaters of the Habur River.

A further difficulty in the study of the early history of Mittani is the uncertainty about chronology. The exact lengths of the reigns of all Mittanian rulers are unknown owing to the absence of king lists (for a list of kings, see p. 307). We also cannot establish when exactly we first encounter the state. The earliest references to it are in the accounts of eighteenth-dynasty Egyptian rulers, but their campaigns can be associated with various Mittanian kings. So there is no firm chronological point that anchors Mittani history into that of Egypt. The early history of the state is especially a mystery. We know that northern Syria in the eighteenth century was made up of small kingdoms with numerous Hurrian inhabitants. We also know that by the early fifteenth century there was a Mittanian ruler with extensive regional power. How and exactly when this state developed is uncertain. The power vacuum left by the Hittite destruction of Aleppo may have enabled a new state to develop. It is clear that by the first half of the fifteenth century the Mittanian king, Parrattarna, had control as suzerain over an area including Kizzuwatna in the west, Nuzi in the east, and Terqa in the south. His state was the most powerful in western Asia, and the only obstacle to early eighteenth-dynasty Egyptian expansion there. The state was made up of several vassal areas under local rulers who owed obedience to the Mittanian king. This is most clearly visible in an autobiographical inscription carved on a statue found at Alalakh in southwestern Anatolia (figure 8.1).

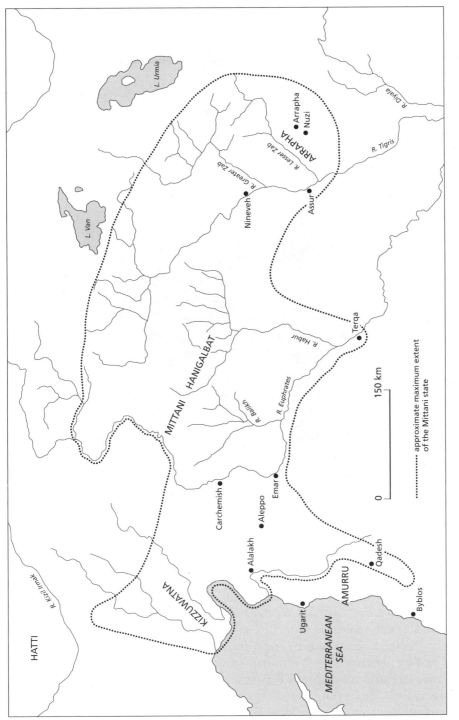

Map 8.1 The Mittani state (after Volkert Haas, ed. *Hurriter und Hurritisch* [Konstanz: Universitätverlag, 1988], p. 295)

Figure 8.1 Statue of King Idrimi. Photo © Trustees of the British Museum, London

In it the local king, Idrimi, relates how he acquired power in that city. For some unknown reason, he and his brothers fled their hometown Aleppo for the city of Emar on the Euphrates. Unhappy at remaining an underling there, Idrimi decided to leave the city and to roam the countryside of Canaan, where he became a leading *habiru* warrior, i.e., a leader of semi-nomadic social outcasts. With this power behind him he captured the city of Alalakh and its surroundings. Then he contacted the Mittanian king, Parrattarna, who endorsed Idrimi's rule of the city and made him his vassal. The text shows thus how the king of Mittani was the main power in this area of south-west Anatolia, and how he exercised his control through local rulers who were made vassals.

The dominance of Mittani in northern Syria continued until the mid-fourteenth century. The Egyptian rulers of the early eighteenth dynasty who campaigned repeatedly in the region mention the state as a significant opponent. Egypt tried to control the coastal region through a system of vassals, and the Mittanians backed rebellions there. The conflict between the two major states was thus not direct. After initial hostile relations, starting with Amenhotep II (ruled 1426–00), Egypt began to treat Mittani and its king, Saustatar, as an ally. Soon afterwards, over the relatively short period of the Amarna archive, from about 1365 to 1335, the Mittani state suffered a number of internal and external difficulties. Internally, two branches of the royal family competed for the throne, each seeking support for their respective claims from outside powers. Tushratta, who corresponded with the Egyptian King Amenhotep III (ruled 1390–53), had been placed on the throne by the murderer of his older brother. Initially Egypt had resented this state of affairs, and only after Tushratta executed his brother's murderer did its king reestablish diplomatic relations. The two discussed the conclusion of a marriage between Tushratta's daughter and Amenhotep III. But during Tushratta's reign, another brother, Artatama, established a rival kingship, receiving initial support from the Hittites. Artatama's son, Shuttarna III, may have been responsible for the murder of Tushratta, and he shifted his allegiance from Hatti to the newly ascendant state of Assyria. This roused the ire of the Hittite King Suppiluliuma, who for many years had raided the land of Mittani and picked off most of its west Syrian allies. He thus took the side of an exiled son of Tushratta, Kili-Teshub, and helped him by providing troops under his son's command. Together they defeated Shuttarna and his Assyrian supporters. Suppiluliuma placed Kili-Teshub on the throne of what remained of the Mittani state under the name of Shattiwaza, married him off to one of his daughters, and made him his vassal. A treaty outlined his duties to the king of Hatti. The west of the state was thus under Hittite control, while in the east Assyria continued to dominate regions that previously had been Mittanian domain.

The Hittites allowed the rump of the Mittani state to survive, and several of Shattiwaza's descendants occupied the throne. The Assyrians took advantage of a weakening of Hittite power after the death of Suppiluliuma to maintain pressure on the region. The core of the state was gradually turned into Assyrian territory under Adad-nirari I (ruled 1305–1274) and Shalmaneser I (ruled 1273–44). They left a native dynasty in place, but forced its rulers to become vassals. The remnants of the Mittani state, which the Assyrians always referred to as Hanigalbat, regularly resisted the Assyrians, seeking help from Hittites and Arameans, a new people in northern Syria who would become very important later on. They were not successful, however. The Assyrians established administrative centers throughout the region as far west as the east bank of the Euphrates River, where they faced Hittite fortresses on the west bank. The centers were placed in strategic locations to control trade and military movements. The death of the last strong Assyrian king, Tukulti-Ninurta (ruled 1243–07), coincided with the upheavals that characterized the western Near East around 1200. The disappearance of political centralization in the Mittani region can thus be related to those events.

The study of society in the Mittani state has to be based on documents found in cities outside its core: Alalakh in the extreme west and Nuzi in the extreme east. In the early part of the state's history, the fifteenth century, these were governed by native dynasties whose rulers were under the control of the Mittani king. Alalakh had a series of kings who were the descendants of Idrimi. Nuzi had a "mayor" who was dependent on the king of Arrapha, himself a vassal of the Mittani ruler. Yet, the city had a large central building and its texts referred to a "palace." The Mittani state seems to have been a loose political structure held together by the king in person, who regularly concluded treaties with his vassals. There was thus probably little influence on the local affairs, and the Nuzi and Alalakh situations should not be regarded as typical for the entire Mittani territory. But some common characteristics can be defined. The entire state was located in the region where agriculture depended on rainfall and village communities were strong. The urban centers where the palaces were located relied on these villages for their support, and, as stated before, the relationship between the two was exploitative. The local palaces held censuses in order to calculate exactly how much taxation and corvée labor they could impose. In their records they divided the population into groups whose meanings are not fully clear to us, but they make a distinction between palace dependents and free villagers. Men indicated by the term *mariyannu* dominated the first group. Their role initially had been in the military as charioteers, but they started to gain control over agricultural resources by circumventing some of the customary laws. At Nuzi much of the land was family owned and by law could not be sold to individuals; it could only be passed on from father to son. To get around this, certain urban residents had themselves adopted numerous times. They drew up contracts, called *mārūtu*, "sale-adoptions," where in return for a "gift" they acquired the use of the land, which they would later inherit. A man named Tehip-tilla, for example, had himself adopted some fifty times, by people who became his *de facto* tenant farmers. Likewise he acquired indentured labor by paying off the debts of men who henceforth had to take care of his fields or orchards. These practices were possible because of the high level of debt that was carried by the peasants. When they had to take out loans, interest rates were usually 50 percent. Unlike in earlier periods, the palace did not help these people out by annulling outstanding debts. The king of Arrapha himself is known to have taken advantage of such practices to obtain access to labor and land. The peasantry was at the mercy of the urban moneylenders, who could set any terms they wanted and acquire control over their resources.

The Hittites referred to the Mittani state as the "land of the Hurrians," and indeed one of the official languages of the state was Hurrian. Spoken in northern Syria and Mesopotamia for a millennium before, it never managed to become one of the commonly written languages. Babylonian always dominated, including in the second half of the second millennium, when the administrative and legal texts from the entire Mittani state were written in the Babylonian dialect derived from the south of Mesopotamia. The rarity of Hurrian texts may be due to a large extent to the fact that the Mittani capital, Washukanni, has not been identified and excavated. A lengthy letter by Tushratta fully written in Hurrian, found in the Amarna archive, demonstrates that the Mittani court did have a chancellery with scribes who could write the language. In content the letter parallels those written in Babylonian, so we do not know why it was composed in that language and who in Egypt could read it. Other texts or passages in the Hurrian language, appear in the archives of such cities as Ugarit and Hattusa, while people with Hurrian names lived all over Anatolia, Syria-Palestine, and eastern Mesopotamia (see document 8.1). This reveals how widely the language was spoken outside the Mittani state.

Document 8.1 *Hurrian writings*

Relatively few texts that are written entirely in the Hurrian language exist, mainly from the cities of Ugarit, Emar, and Hattusa. This scarcity does not give an accurate reflection of the use of the language in the Near East of the second millennium, however. Many personal names over a wide area of Anatolia, Northern Syria and Mesopotamia, and the Syro-Palestinian area, including the names of kings, were Hurrian. The common use of the language in speech is also clear from passages in Hittite texts, which regularly include Hurrian phrases or terms. This occurs often in descriptions of rituals where the cult official is quoted as speaking in Hurrian. The following passage appears in a Hittite tablet describing rituals of a priest identified as AZU:

Now the AZU-priest takes a goose with the left hand, and with the right hand he lifts the cedar wood from the incense-burner. Then he drips oil in a cup of water and performs the *katkiša* (Hurrian term) of the goddess Hepat. He puts the cedar in the cup of water, lifts the cup of water up, and pours the water towards the goddess. He says the following in Hurrian: "*ašseš Hepat šuunip šiaai ahraai unamaa kešhepwe kelteieni ambaššini kelu.*" Then he pours water towards the one who commissioned the offering and sets the cup of water down on the table of woven reed.
Then the AZU-priest takes the cedar wood from the incense-burner and throws it in the *huprušhi*-vessel (Hurrian term) on the hearth, and says in Hurrian: "*aharreš laplihhineš* etc." And he holds the goose out to the one who commissioned the offering and puts his hand on it. The AZU-priest takes a piece out of its breast, dips it in oil from the incense-burner, throws it in the *huprušhi*-vessel on the hearth, and says in Hurrian: "*anahiteneš tatuššeneš kelu.*"

Translation after Mirjo Salvini and Ilse Wegner, *Die Rituale des AZU-Priesters* (Rome: Multigrafici Editrice, 1986), pp. 40–2.

8.2 The Hittite New Kingdom

The central area of Anatolia in the second millennium was the core region of the kingdom of the Hittites, called Hatti in native, Assyrian, Babylonian, and Egyptian texts. Its capital city, Hattusa, is our predominant source of texts, which contain a great deal of information on political history (see box 8.1). The treaties that the Hittite kings regularly concluded usually had an introduction in which the past relations between the two states were outlined, and these provide some of our best evidence, albeit very biased, on their political histories. Yet, the writing of Hittite history is faced with many chronological difficulties. Several of the Hittite kings bore the same names, for example, Tudhaliya or Arnuwanda, and while today we number them I, II, etc., this was not done in the native sources. Thus, often we cannot determine the ruler to which a text relates. The absolute chronology is problematic as well. The Hittites did not leave us king lists with the lengths of reigns, thus even for the creator of the New Kingdom state, Suppiluliuma I, we have different suggestions for his years of rule, varying from twenty-two to forty years. Not a single moment of Hittite history can be dated without synchronisms to Egypt, Assyria, or Babylonia, and the points of contact we have are few and mostly from the later part of Hittite history. While in practice we assign absolute dates to the individual rulers, these are always approximate and may need to be shifted, especially according to changes in our understanding of Egyptian chronology.

Geographically, the Hittite state's borders shifted constantly. The capital city was in central Anatolia in the basin of the Kizil Irmak River, and military expansion efforts focused especially toward the south, where in its heyday Hatti controlled western Syria. It is unclear whether its borders in the north and west extended as far as the shores of the Black and Aegean seas, which were closer to Hattusa than was Syria (see map 8.2). As the state's organization was not by direct territorial control but by domination over vassals, the borders were determined more by the relative dependence of states within the Hittite sphere of influence than by actual hegemony. Throughout the period discussed here, there was clearly a greater interest in Syria than in the peripheral areas of Anatolia. The political center of the state lay at its northern fringe.

The Hittite state existed for a relatively short time, from about 1800 to 1200. It knew two periods of great strength, one in the seventeenth century referred to as the Old Kingdom, the other from about 1400 to 1200, the New Kingdom period (for a list of kings, see p. 307). Sometimes the term Middle Kingdom is used to refer to the period in between, but as Hatti was in decline, the historian's grasp of what happened then is very weak. The road to recovery was led by a number of rulers whose histories are still vague, including two with the name of Tudhaliya. They reaffirmed Hittite dominance over central and southern Anatolia, including the area of Kizzuwatna on the south-east coast, which had been ruled by Mittani before. Moreover, Aleppo, the foremost city in northwestern Syria that was vital for access to regions farther south, had to

Box 8.1 *Hittite historiography*

The reconstruction of Hittite history is to a great extent based on accounts the Hittites themselves wrote, covering events in a chronological sequence over several reigns or in successive years of a single reign. These are found as freestanding texts or included in edicts and international treaties. Among the first group are annals, year-by-year accounts primarily of military campaigns. These appear already in the Old Kingdom when Hattusili I left a bilingual Hittite-Akkadian account of his military accomplishments. This type of text became very widely written in Assyria after the disappearance of the Hittite state in the twelfth century. It is likely that the Assyrian genre, one of our main sources for the reconstruction of first-millennium history, was inspired by the Hittite practice.

From the Old Kingdom on, the Hittites also summarized, mainly military, events over several reigns. The sixteenth-century edict of Telipinu, for example, recounts the campaigns of preceding kings as far back as the founder of the dynasty (see document 6.2), Labarna. Also in international affairs they kept track of former relations between Hatti and other states. When a treaty was concluded, the previous hostile and friendly interactions over several generations were mentioned. In this sense they were not followed by the Assyrians, who both in their annalistic accounts and in their, admittedly few, treaties focused on the present ruler.

Not only did the Hittites record annals, but they also preserved these texts in later centuries. Much of the Hittite textual record available to us comes from the last century of Hattusa's existence, the thirteenth century, and it includes newly made copies of historical records from many centuries earlier. While we cannot always determine when they were composed, some fragmentary older manuscripts show that the Annals of Hattusili, for example, were composed in or close to his reign.

Why the Hittites had this concern with past events in previous reigns is difficult to determine. While they saw some causal relations between the past and the present (in prayers to the gods, King Mursili II asked what deeds in the past had caused a plague), they did not seek explanations beyond the fact that it was the wish of the gods. In that sense, they shared the ideas of their contemporaries. Hittite historical records are very detailed and structured in such a way that historians are tempted to use them as a template for their reconstructions of Hittite political history, but they have to be treated with great caution. They often portray the idea that the present king's actions led to a good situation, while those of his predecessors caused aberrations and misery. Our accounts of Hittite history are mostly based on this heavily biased evidence, as we often lack external data to verify statements. We have to remain alert then to the aims of the authors.

shift allegiance from Mittani to Hatti. The Hittites' competitors in the region were Egypt and Mittani, two states that had fought each other before, but in the early fourteenth century they may have joined forces in reaction to the Hittite advances. The diplomatic marriages and letter exchanges between the

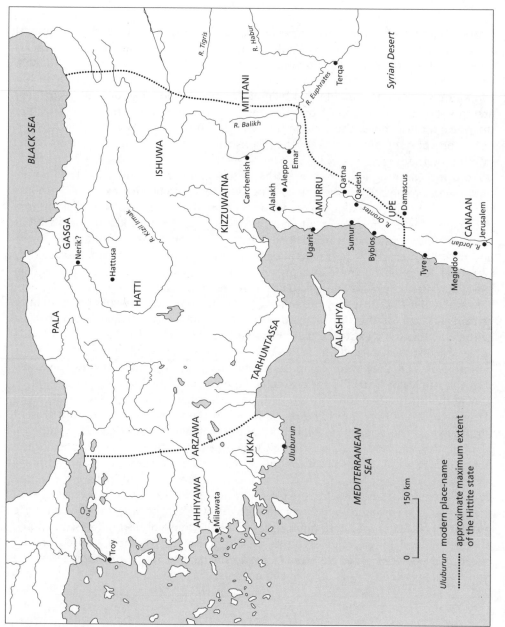

Map 8.2 The Hittite state during the New Kingdom (after Michael Roaf, *Cultural Atlas of Mesopotamia and the Ancient Near East* [Oxford: Equinox, 1990], p. 139)

two show the changed attitudes. Egypt also tried to establish good relations with Arzawa to the west of Hatti, including the proposal of a diplomatic marriage, in order to weaken the emerging power. And indeed, the west and north presented great difficulties to Hatti: the Gasga, a people from the south coast of the Black Sea, attacked and perhaps even destroyed Hattusa, and a vassal of the west, Madduwatta, conquered south-west Anatolia and Cyprus in the mid-fourteenth century.

These setbacks were reversed, however, by Suppiluliuma I (ruled 1344–22), who already under his father Tudhaliya III proved to be one of the Hittites' ablest military leaders. After solidifying his control over Anatolian regions to the south and east of the Hittite heartland, he invaded the Mittani state from the north, occupying the capital city. Western Mittani became his vassal. To the west of the Euphrates he extended Hittite control as far south as Damascus. Rulers from numerous states, including Ugarit, Qadesh, and Amurru, concluded treaties of vassalage with him. His main competitor in the region, Egypt, was at the time less attentive to its Asiatic territories, and no direct clash between the two powers ensued. Indeed, Hatti and Egypt saw each other as equals, a sentiment that may have led to the highly unusual request by the recently widowed queen of Egypt for a son of Suppiluliuma to become her husband, as mentioned in the last chapter.

At the end of Suppiluliuma's reign, Hatti was in firm control of much of northern Syria, with two princes as viceroys in the strategic cities of Carchemish and Aleppo, and vassals in Mittani and the areas as far south as Damascus. The reign ended in disaster, however. Probably the king himself and his first successor both died of a plague that had been brought home by soldiers from Syria. Another son, Mursili II (ruled 1321–1295), was able to maintain control over Syria, however, and also devoted attention to the Anatolian areas ignored by his father. Arzawa in the west, which had been courted by Egypt early in Suppiluliuma's reign, was defeated and the Gasga people in the north were attacked. The latter continued to present a threat, however, even taking the capital city Hattusa in the reign of Muwatalli II (ruled 1295–72). This shows how Hatti's involvement in Syria led to loss of control over its Anatolian hinterland by leaving its northern flank ill-guarded. And Muwatalli was very much preoccupied with Syria, to the extent that he moved his capital to a previously obscure city in a southern region of Anatolia, Tarhuntassa (exact location unknown). Whether this move was necessitated by the sack of Hattusa by the Gasga or led to that event is unclear. The reemergence of Egypt under the nineteenth dynasty and its incessant campaigning in Syria culminated in the battle of Qadesh between Ramesses II and Muwatalli in 1274. This event was given enormous attention by the Egyptian in numerous inscriptions and representations, despite the fact that he lost the battle, something he himself failed to acknowledge but which is evident from the subsequent expansion of Hittite control over southern Syria. It presents the climax of the centuries-long struggle between Egypt and Hatti over Syria, one in which the Hittites typically had the upper hand.

Muwatalli left his brother, the future King Hattusili III, in charge of the northern areas, and the latter reconquered Hattusa as well as the cult center of Nerik, which had been lost to the Gasga many years before. When Muwatalli's son, Urhi-Teshub, came to power under the throne-name Mursili III (ruled 1272–67), Hattusili III used the north as a power base from which to undermine the young king. Although Urhi-Teshub as legitimate heir may have had the support of Egypt and Babylonia, Hattusili III finally succeeded in removing him and remained king for another thirty years (1267–37). The peace treaty with Egypt was the major accomplishment of his reign. In 1259, fifteen years after the battle of Qadesh, the two states concluded a detailed arrangement to end hostilities, establish a defensive alliance, and exchange political refugees. Ramesses II also promised to support Hattusili's choice of successor, a promise not reciprocated by the latter. The threat of Assyria, now in full control over much of the Mittani area, may have inspired this agreement, although some scholars suggest that it was more important for the legitimization of Hattusili's rule. The concern for Hattusili's succession, of which he was all too aware as a usurper, also seems to have been important, and future events show how well founded his fears were. While the relations between the two powers may not have been as cordial as was hoped, the struggle over Syria had ended.

Hatti declined rapidly, however. Internally, the designated heir to the throne, Tudhaliya IV (ruled 1237–09), had to deal with a powerful claim by a son of Muwatalli, Kurunta, who had been made "king of Tarhuntassa" by Hattusili III. Kurunta may have temporarily deposed Tudhaliya IV in 1228–7, when he appeared as "Great King" on sealings found at Hattusa. In any case, Tudhaliya regained the throne. External pressures were great as well. Tukulti-Ninurta I of Assyria (ruled 1243–07) attacked the Hittite state from the east, and vassals in the west and south-west of Anatolia rebelled. Trouble in the regions adjoining the Aegean Sea may have been inspired by an elusive "king of Ahhiyawa," certainly a major player in the area, but hard to pinpoint in space and time. Tudhaliya IV was able to take Milawata, classical Miletus, from them, but in the end Hatti's grasp over the west of Anatolia seems to have slipped.

When Suppiluliuma II came to the throne in 1207, the fall of Hatti was imminent. The causes of its collapse as a territorial state are not fully clear to us. Hattusa was sacked, and no more royal records were produced. Other important cities under Hittite control, such as Ugarit, disappeared as well, and Egyptian sources suggest a general devastation of the entire Anatolian and west Syrian region. But certain Hittite cities survived, most prominently Carchemish, where members of a branch of the Hittite royal family continued to refer to themselves as "Great Kings." These events need to be seen in the context of the collapse of the entire regional system around 1200, which will be discussed in a later chapter, but in contrast to other areas, no Hittite state would ever reappear in central Anatolia.

Hittite history was to a great extent determined by events in the west and north of Anatolia. It is clear that states existed there, some of which were considered of equal political importance to the great powers of the Near East. Some of those were important actors in the international system of the time: the king of Arzawa corresponded with Egypt, as did the western vassal states with the Hittite king. In the south, the king of Alashiya was an active correspondent with the Egyptian court in the Amarna period. But no sites to the west of Hattusa have yielded texts so far, and we have to piece together the histories of these states primarily from information in Hittite texts.

The states of importance in western Anatolia seemed to have changed over time. At first Kizzuwatna in the south was preeminent. It became the battleground between Hatti and Mittani because of its location, which gave access to northern Syria. With King Tudhaliya II in the early fourteenth century, Kizzuwatna firmly moved into the Hittite camp. Simultaneously, Alashiya, a kingdom that controlled the entirety or part of the island of Cyprus, was one of the great states of the period, as attested in the Amarna letters. Its prominence derived from its access to copper mines. Later Hittite kings invaded it and established pro-Hittite rulers, but never fully controlled it. During the period of the Amarna letters, Arzawa, located in the southwestern part of Anatolia, was also one of the great states in correspondence with the king of Egypt, who requested the ruler's daughter as a wife. The fact that the letters were written in Hittite rather than Akkadian demonstrates that Arzawa was not fully integrated in the international system and had a secondary status to its neighbor Hatti. It seems to have kept a special status as a Hittite subject until the end of its existence around 1200.

The most important kingdom of the west in the later part of the period was that of Ahhiyawa. The writing of its history is complicated by the question of whether or not it had anything to do with the Mycenaean Greeks, who certainly established commercial outposts on the Anatolian coast. The similarity between the names Ahhiyawa and Achaians, the Homeric term for the Greeks, has suggested this equation from the first discovery of the name, but the issue remains hotly debated. The evidence remains inconclusive, but it is possible that we find here textual evidence of Mycenaean political and military presence in western Anatolia. The Ahhiyawa were mentioned in Hittite texts from the fifteenth century on, but remained of minor importance until two centuries later. Hattusili III, attempting to restore order to rebellious western districts, wrote to the Ahhiyawa king, addressing him as brother, in order to convince him to control rebels active in his territory. His successor, Tudhaliya IV, campaigned in the west and invaded the territory of Ahhiyawa. The fact that Ahhiyawa was regarded as an important state is clear from that king's treaty with Shaushgamuwa of Amurru. In it he pointed out those kings whom he considered to be his equals: Egypt, Babylonia, and Assyria. The king of Ahhiyawa completed that list, but after writing it the scribe erased the words. Whatever the meaning of that erasure, it is evident that the latter's status around that time had been regarded as that of a Great King. The demand in the treaty that Amurru prevent seaborne trade between Assyria and Ahhiyawa indicates that the Ahhiyawans were sailors and providers of certain important goods. After Tudhaliya IV, the textual information regarding the Ahhiyawans disappears, unless they can be equated with the Ekwesh, part of the Sea Peoples according to Egyptian accounts. If so, they contributed to the general upheaval in the eastern Mediterranean in the early twelfth century. Their hostility toward the Hittites would have led to their participation in the destruction of that state.

To the north of Hattusa was not a centralized state but an area that was dominated by people called Gasga in the Hittite texts. These were always portrayed as aggressive and wild tribesmen who raided Hittite cities, at times taking them out of government control. One of Hattusili III's duties under his brother had been to regain territory occupied by the Gasga and to free the northern cult center of Nerik from them. The pressure of the Gasga may have contributed to the troubles that ended Hittite history, but we are mainly uninformed about the details. The west and north of Anatolia were thus never part of the Hittite state, although they were the targets of many military campaigns. Nevertheless, their interactions with Hatti tied them into the political system of the Near East.

The political structure of the Hittite state is often compared to that of medieval western European vassalage. The Great King of Hatti directly governed the core area, but had vassals in most regions under his control: western and southern Anatolia and Syria. The vassals were locals who swore allegiance to him, but who could switch it to other powers, such as Egypt or Assyria. Although Hittite princes governed certain key places such as Carchemish and Aleppo, others regions remained under the rule of their own royal house while under Hittite supremacy. Two such centers are well known through their own sources, Ugarit on the Syrian coast and Emar of the kingdom of Astata on the Euphrates. The traditions of the various regions seemingly continued to be respected by the Hittite overlords, and there was no attempt to integrate the entire region in political or cultural terms. In this sense, the organization of the Hittite state seems to parallel that of Mittani, and the people of northern Syria were thus able to maintain their local cultures and political hierarchies.

The king's supreme status was beyond doubt, however. He bore a set of titles that clearly identified him as such, including that of "Great King" and of "the Sun." An old Hattic title was given to him, Labarna or Tabarna, which may refer to the name of the first ruler of the dynasty. His wife was given the title Tawananna, probably alluding to the first queen, and held a lot of power, which she exercised even upon her husband's death. There were repeated problems with royal succession; oftentimes the father–son sequence was not respected and a brother became king. This led to one of the best-documented struggles for kingship in Near Eastern history between the son and the brother of Muwatalli. Urhi-Teshub, the latter's son with a concubine, came to the throne under the name Mursili III, but Hattusili III, Muwatalli's brother, rebelled and overthrew his nephew after five years. The usurpation of power was a sufficient breach of the law for Hattusili to compose a long document, his Apology, in which he explained his acts. In it he describes how he was put in charge of the northern territories while his brother had moved the capital to the southern region of Tarhuntassa, and how he successfully conquered peripheral areas for his brother. When Muwatalli's son came to the throne, Hattusili initially supported him but became increasingly frustrated with his nephew. In order to preserve his power and that of his friends, Hattusili went to war. Having captured the young king, he sent him into exile in an outlying part of the state. In order to justify this act, Hattusili made accusations that Urhi-Teshub had used magic, which shows the weakness of the legality of his claim to kingship.

The titulary and names of the rulers of Hatti demonstrate the multicultural character of the state. The title Tabarna and the royal throne names were Hattic, i.e., of a group of Anatolian people who had perhaps dominated the area of Hattusa many centuries earlier. But the birth-names of the kings were of different origin: Urhi-Teshub, for example, was clearly a Hurrian name. Yet the official language of the chancellery at Hattusa was Hittite. Moreover, the archives excavated there also reveal texts in other Anatolian languages, such as Luwian and Palaic, while scribes who could write in the Mesopotamian languages Akkadian and Sumerian also worked there. All of these texts were written in cuneiform. Simultaneously, a Hittite hieroglyphic script was in use on official monuments and personal seals, which rendered the Luwian language, related to Hittite, and survived the end of the Hittite state.

The literature recorded at Hattusa also derived from a great variety of sources. Hurrian traditions are represented in a number of myths translated into Hittite. Hattic elements are often found in shorter stories, while original Hittite material seems to have been rare. Certain literary texts from Mesopotamia were imported wholesale, translated into Hittite, or somewhat adapted to local tastes by changing the leading deities to reflect Hittite preferences. The scribes of Hattusa copied lexical lists from Mesopotamia, adding a Hittite translation column to them. Many Anatolian myths seem to have had a ritual function and the prescriptive rituals show a great variety of languages, including Hattic and Hurrian. Also Canaanite mythology was imported from the Syro-Palestinian areas the Hittites had conquered.

Hatti was thus certainly one of the most important states of the Near East in the second half of the second millennium, and an active participant in the international culture of the time. Its location at the edges of the Near Eastern world exposed it more to outside pressures than its colleagues and its internal political structure was relatively loose. Consequently, its collapse was sudden and almost total. Central Anatolia in the first millennium would be very different from what we observe in the New Kingdom period.

8.3 Syria-Palestine

The Syro-Palestinian area in the second half of the second millennium was politically characterized by myriad small states whose control was fought over by the powerful neighbors to the north, east, and south: Hatti, Mittani, and Egypt. The region stretches from the south of Anatolia, between the Mediterranean

Figure 8.2 Hittite vessel terminating in the form of a stag. The Metropolitan Museum of Art, Gift of Norbert Schimmel Trust, 1989 (1989.281.10). Photograph, all rights reserved, The Metropolitan Museum of Art

and the Euphrates, to southern Palestine, where it borders the Sinai Desert. It runs along the coast in a band that becomes increasingly narrow the further south one goes, from some 200 kilometers in the north to some 70 kilometers in the south, west of the Dead Sea. The eastern border is set by the Syrian Desert and the Jordanian mountains, regions where urban settlement is impossible.

The history of this area is reconstructed through documents from the nearby great powers, and from texts found in an increasing number of cities in the region itself. The palaces there had scribes for their own bookkeeping and for international contacts. Most of the text finds are of limited extent so far, except for those in three northern cities, Ugarit, Alalakh, and Emar, where relatively large palace, temple, and/or private archives have been excavated. The international correspondence found at Amarna in Egypt demonstrates how widespread writing was in the area, however, and it is certain that further archaeological work will uncover more archives. The language of most of the texts is Babylonian, heavily influenced by local west Semitic languages, and the script is syllabic cuneiform, also borrowed from the east. Simultaneously, local languages and alphabetic scripts were in use, very poorly attested except in the city of Ugarit, where a cuneiform alphabetic script written on clay tablets was in use.

The political fragmentation of the region made it an easy area for expansion by the great powers surrounding it, and its wealth and technological expertise made it an appealing prey. Throughout the period under consideration, almost the entire area was constantly controlled by several of the great powers. A political history is thus most often written from their point of view. When the obscure centuries of the mid-second millennium ended, northern Syria was dominated by Mittani, which governed the region west of the Euphrates through a system of vassals. Mittanian control extended as far south as Qadesh and as far west as Kizzuwatna in southern Anatolia. But with the rise of the eighteenth dynasty, Egypt expanded rapidly into the region. After conquering Palestine, sometimes inflicting severe destruction on cities there, Egypt picked off Mittanian vassals further north, reaching Ugarit on the coast and Qadesh inland. The two powers fought over the states bordering on Mittani. Egypt's army raided as far as the Euphrates Valley, while Mittani supported local resistance to those raids. The Egyptian annals, especially those of Tuthmose III, provide great detail on this military activity.

Egypt's control over the regions it had conquered was more direct than that of Mittani. Three provinces were established, Amurru, Upe, and Canaan, each with an administrative center governed by an Egyptian official. These were responsible for collecting critical resources directly. Native dynasts were allowed to continue their rule over the small states, but had to provide annual tribute to Egyptian emissaries. This system of control is well documented in the Amarna letters. The local vassals wrote many letters to the king, asking for help against troublesome neighbors, pledging obedience, promising payments, and so on. Egypt remained aloof to most local problems and focused its attention on the collection of tribute, which could be done without a substantial military presence. During this period, we find little evidence of Egyptian campaigning in Asia, probably because its grasp on the region was firm and because Egypt and Mittani had become allies rather than enemies.

The threat to this arrangement came from Hatti in the north, whose king, Suppiluliuma, had subdued Mittani shortly after 1340, and then expanded into territory Egypt saw as its own. Ugarit, Qadesh, Amurru, as well as all northern Syrian states previously dependent on Mittani, became Hittite vassals. The Hittite king placed his sons as viceroys in the key cities of Carchemish and Aleppo, and kept the Mittanian system of vassalage for other states. The governmental arrangements are well documented at Ugarit on the coast, and Emar on the Euphrates River. Both continued to be ruled by native dynasties that took care of most local affairs. The viceroy at Carchemish settled conflicts between vassals, while the king of Hatti received tribute and made arrangements of political and economic importance to the entire state. The treaties between the Hittite overlord and the vassals were expressed as personal agreements between two men, and were renewed when a new king ascended the throne. From such information we can recover the names of the local rulers, but we know little else about their political careers.

The division of Syria-Palestine between Hatti and Egypt remained stable until the beginning of the nineteenth dynasty in Egypt, when kings Sety I and Ramesses II tried to extend their control further north. Muwatalli of Hatti thwarted this attempt at the battle of Qadesh (1274), and fifteen years later the two states concluded a peace treaty, probably under the pressure of Assyrian expansion into northern Syria. Egypt's control over southern Syria and northern Palestine seems to have slipped, and Ramesses II built a number of fortresses close to the Egyptian border. The Hittite administration over the north continued according to the earlier pattern.

The situation of the states of Syria-Palestine can be exemplified by the history of Amurru, a kingdom extending from the Mediterranean coast in northern modern-day Lebanon to the plain of Homs in Syria inland (for a list of kings, see p. 308). Its history is known only from texts found outside the state, in the records of Hatti, Egypt, and Ugarit. Initially Amurru belonged to the Egyptian sphere of influence, probably conquered by Tuthmose III, and figured prominently in the Amarna correspondence. In the early years of that archive, the ruler, Aziru, seems to have been engaged in establishing himself as king of the region, including by conquering Sumur, a city where the Egyptian representative had his residence. After Aziru succeeded in taking the city, the Egyptians demanded that he restore it, and only then was he accepted as king by the pharaoh. Amurru was located at the northern edge of Egypt's area of control, and when Hatti became more powerful, Aziru tried to keep that state happy as well. His relations with Egypt were soured by the constant complaints by the ruler of Byblos, Rib-Adda, who accused Aziru of trying to overthrow him and forcing others to join the pro-Hittite camp. Aziru was asked, and reluctantly agreed, to visit the Egyptian court to defend himself against these charges, something he managed to do successfully. It is clear, however, that he did extend his territory at the expense of his neighbors and that he kept good relations with Hatti. When Suppiluliuma wiped out Mittani influence in north-west Syria, Aziru concluded a treaty with him and accepted Hatti as his overlord. He promised tribute, military assistance, and the extradition of refugees, and that he would not seek Mittanian or Egyptian support.

The future relations between Amurru and Hatti were founded on this agreement. Aziru's second successor, Tuppi-Teshub, renewed it with Mursili II, who was especially worried about the vigorous Egyptian expansion into Syria under the early nineteenth-dynasty rulers. The next ruler of Amurru, Benteshina, seems to have thought that he could take advantage of Egypt's military successes, precipitating a retaliatory campaign by Muwatalli II. Benteshina was defeated and deported to Hatti, where he was placed in the care of the man who later ruled as Hattusili III. At home he was replaced by one Shapili, who remained a loyal vassal to Muwatalli for some fifteen years. But the political changes in Hatti had repercussions in Amurru politics as well: when Hattusili III grabbed power, seemingly with Benteshina's help, he rewarded the latter by reinstating him as king of Amurru. A treaty was concluded between the two men, and their alliance was confirmed by the marriages of Benteshina with Hattusili's daughter and of his daughter with Hattusili's son. Benteshina remained loyal and was succeeded by his son Shaushga-muwa, who concluded a treaty with Tudhaliya IV, his brother-in-law and uncle (see document 8.2). The treaty stipulated that Amurru had to follow Hatti's lead in international relations.

Document 8.2 *Excerpts from the treaty between Tudhaliya IV of Hatti and Shaushga-muwa of Amurru*

[Thus says Tabarna, Tudhaliya], Great King, [King of] Hatti, hero, beloved of the Sun-goddess of Arinna, [son of Hattusili, Great King, King of] Hatti, hero, [grandson of] Mursili, Great [King], King of Hatti, hero, [descendant of] Tudhaliya, [Great King, King of] Hatti, hero:

I, my Sun, [have taken you] Shaushga-muwa [by the hand], and have made you my brother-in-law. And you [shall not change the words] of this treaty tablet.

. . .

When [the king] of Egypt is my Sun's [friend], he will also be your friend. [But] when he is my Sun's enemy, he shall also be [your enemy]. And the kings who are equal to me in rank are the King of Egypt, the King of Babylonia, the King of Assyria, and the King of Ahhiyawa.[1] When the King of Egypt is my Sun's friend, he shall also be your friend. But when he is my Sun's enemy, he shall also be your enemy. When the King of Babylonia is my Sun's friend, he shall also be your friend. But when he is my Sun's enemy, he shall also be your enemy. Since the King of Assyria is my Sun's enemy, he shall also be your enemy. Your merchant shall not go to Assyria, and you shall not let his merchant into your country. He shall not pass through your country. If he would enter your country, take him and send him to my Sun. This matter [is placed] under an oath for you.

Since I, my Sun, am at war with the King of Assyria, gather together an army and a chariotry unit, as my Sun has done. Just as it is for my Sun an issue of urgency and . . . , it shall be for you an issue of urgency and . . . Gather together an army and a chariotry unit. This matter is placed under an oath for you.

No ship of Ahhiyawa shall go to him (the King of Assyria).

Translation after Gary Beckman, *Hittite Diplomatic Texts*, second edition (Atlanta: Scholars Press, 1999), pp. 103–8.

[1] The words "King of Ahhiyawa" were erased from the tablet.

Its attitude toward Egypt and Babylonia should depend on that of Hatti, while relations with Assyria had to be hostile. Shaushga-muwa had to contribute troops to Hatti, which was involved in a war against Assyria. Moreover, he was barred from sending his merchants to Assyria and had to arrest and extradite Assyrian merchants. He also had to intercept traders moving between Assyria and Ahhiyawa. The last information about Amurru derives from Ugarit and relates to the divorce of its ruler Ammistamru II from Benteshina's daughter. The affair was of sufficient concern to the king of Hatti that he personally intervened. Further information is unavailable.

This history demonstrates how dependent the Syro-Palestinian states were on their powerful neighbors. They had to yield to the political and military realities of the times, and switch allegiance between Mittani, Hatti, and Egypt when these powers' fortunes in the region changed. The relations between the kings of Hatti and the local rulers were expressed in personal terms, reaffirmed by new treaties when one of the rulers changed. The supremacy of Hatti was evident, however. Locally these states may have been allowed to lobby for more power against their neighbors, which was tolerated as long as they did not upset the overlord's interests.

This entire system collapsed soon after 1200. The destruction of Hattusa was paralleled by the ruin of Ugarit and Emar among others. The end of Emar can be dated to or soon after 1185. The last years of Ugarit seem to have been characterized by trouble, including attacks by seaborne raiders, and the invasion of the Sea Peoples of Egyptian sources were certainly partly responsible for the widespread upheavals in the Syro-Palestinian area in the twelfth century. Certain cities were left intact, however, but survived only at a much poorer level. The entire area soon fell into historical obscurity lasting several centuries.

The Syro-Palestinian region illustrates most clearly the tension that existed between the lavish lifestyle of a small elite and the impoverished situation of the mass of the population. There were fewer cities in the region than in the preceding period, but those remaining were richer than before. A city like Ugarit had several palaces, large residences, and temples. The region was famed for its crafts: Egyptian tomb paintings showing tribute bearers from foreign dominions often portray Syrians as carrying elaborately manufactured furniture, vessels, ornaments, and so on. Artistic production was of a high quality, as is documented by archaeological finds: works in gold, silver, and ivory are found throughout the region. Texts record the existence of "guilds" of craftsmen, such as jewelers, scribes, housebuilders, etc., which shows a high level of labor specialization in the cities.

Especially trained men were also responsible for the composition and pre-servation of the literature of the region. These works are the only extensive remnants of literature from the Syro-Palestinian area in ancient Near Eastern history, except for the later Hebrew Bible, and they, together with some material remains, give an insight into the religious ideologies of the time (see figure 8.3). Ugarit provides the largest selection of texts, but cities such as Emar have yielded literary material as well. At Ugarit the scribal "guild" wrote down, if not com-posed, a set of religious texts involving the native pantheon. The stormgod Ba'al, a very important deity in Syria, was the main character of a cycle of myths that describe the defeat of the forces of chaos and his rise to kingship of the gods. Human actors were also important, less as great warriors than as the ancestors to the living kings. Tales of the mythical kings Aqhat and Keret relate their difficulties in having children, and the gods' intervention in this matter. The texts deal not only with the creation of a dynasty, but also with the cult of ancestors, which was of great concern in the ritual texts as well. The Ugaritic accounts provide the most extensive record of what is often called Canaanite

Figure 8.3 Statuette of Syrian deity. The Metropolitan Museum of Art, Gift of George D. Pratt, 1932 (32.161.45).

culture, the literary and religious traditions of western Syria and Palestine in the second millennium. These texts were recorded in the Ugaritic language and the cuneiform alphabet of that city, one that was relatively easy to learn with its reduced set of characters. But the scribes there also knew how to write and compose in the Akkadian, Hurrian, and Hittite languages, using the Babylonian syllabic cuneiform. They were trained to do so in the same way as the Old Babylonian students in Mesopotamia, using a series of increasingly difficult tools: sign lists and lexical texts, which sometimes have added to them Ugaritic and Hurrian translation columns. They completed the training by copying literary texts. This instruction took place in the houses of trained scribes, and often the work was signed, so we know the name of the writer. Whereas the literature shows strong Babylonian influences, it is clear that also the Egyptian presence in the region had its cultural effects. Representations of local gods appear with Egyptian crowns, for example.

The Syro-Palestinian cities were supported by relatively small hinterlands where the population was sparse. Estimates of their numbers are difficult, but records from Ugarit, for example, suggest that a rural population of 20,000 to 25,000 living in some 150 villages had to support an urban population of 6,000 to 8,000 people. Labor was thus in short supply, a situation exacerbated by the behavior of the palaces. A distinction was made between those people employed by the palace, the "people of the king," and those who were not, "the sons of Ugarit." The former included the urban elites, who in return for their specialized labor were fully supported by the palace, with a mixture of payments and agricultural land, sometimes even entire villages. Although their estates were originally held only as long as they provided service, some were able to pass them on to their children and run them virtually as private property. While land was perhaps sufficiently available among the palace dependents, labor was not, and the independent villagers became drawn into the labor pool by making them indebted to the urban residents. The villagers were obliged to contribute taxes and corvée labor, but because of their restricted numbers these demands were often excessive. In order to meet taxes, they had to take out loans, and contracts from the period often include a statement that they had to provide labor in return. This reduced their ability to work their own fields and led to an increased dependence on urban residents. Even the kings recruited labor in this way, and they did not abolish debts as had been customary in the early second millennium. Debt-slavery flourished at this time.

The only way out for the laborers was to fully abandon their communities, and this they seem to have done in great numbers. Throughout the Syro-Palestinian area there was an increased presence of men and women who had cut ties with their political and social communities and joined groups of outcasts beyond the reach of the states. They became semi-nomadic and lived in inaccessible areas in the steppe and the mountains. The urban residents whose texts we read regarded them with great disdain and fear, and grouped them under the derogatory term *habiru*, which can be translated as "robber" or "vagabond." All states of the Near East of this period refer to them. They are to be seen not as an ethnic or tribal group but as a social one, made up of people who had fled their states and communities. The attitude toward them was hostile, and in the Amarna letters, for example, they were constantly depicted as presenting a threat to the stability of the region. Although there is a degree of urban prejudice here, these descriptions were not pure rhetoric. Relations between *habiru* and the states were probably extremely antagonistic and raids of villages and cities frequently took place. On the other hand, the states had to turn to them for manpower, and *habiru* turn up in their records as laborers and mercenaries, now possibly being able to set their own terms. The diplomatic exchange between states was often involved with this issue: refugees had to be returned, and Hattusili III, for instance, declared that he would not accept any person from Ugarit as a *habiru* in Hatti. The discrepancy between the high demands of urban elites and the limited supply of labor was so great, however, that the resulting tensions probably caused the collapse of the palatial system that characterized the Syro-Palestinian region in the second half of the second millennium.

9

Kassites, Assyrians, and Elamites

3000	2500	2000	1500	1000	500

1595	End of the Old Babylonian dynasty
ca. 1475	Kassite control over the entirety of Babylonia
ca. 1400	Unification of Susiana lowlands and highlands of Anshan in western Iran
ca. 1350	Assyria emerges as a major state under Assur-uballit
1305–1207	Sustained Assyrian military expansion
1225	Tukulti-Ninurta I of Assyria sacks Babylon
1155	Shutruk-Nahhunte of Elam invades Babylonia. End of the Kassite dynasty
ca. 1110	Nebuchadnezzar I of Babylon sacks Susa

The eastern part of the Near East, especially southern Mesopotamia, had been the focus of political and cultural developments for the centuries of history before 1500, and provided the historian with the most detailed sources for study. In the second half of the second millennium, in political terms the states there became integrated in the greater Near Eastern system as the equals of those in the west. At first, they were perhaps less powerful than their western neighbors (Hatti, Mittani, and Egypt), but after 1400 they developed into substantial territorial powers, closely interacting with one another. Babylonia was the earliest to gain the status of a great kingdom, followed by Assyria to

Map 9.1 The Middle Assyrian, Kassite, and Middle Elamite states

its north. Elam in the east became a crucial player on the international scene only after 1200, the time of the major disruptions in the west. The eastern states suffered from the collapse of the regional system, and by 1100 they became isolated and weak kingdoms.

9.1 Babylonia

A power vacuum probably emerged after Mursili I sacked Babylon in 1595. The ancient social and political structures vanished and much of the population of Babylonia no longer lived in cities. A people using the name Kassites took advantage of this situation and seized the throne of Babylon at some undetermined date. The first-millennium Babylonian King List A places its rulers among the dynasties that governed Babylon in succession from Hammurabi's to the beginning of the Neo-Babylonian dynasty (in 626 BC), and assigns the Kassite dynasty the longest rule of all: thirty-six kings who ruled for 576 years and nine months. We can date the dynasty's end to 1155. Adding the years given by the King List to that date would place its beginning in the eighteenth century, when Old Babylonian rulers held Babylon. It is thus clear that ancestors of the Kassite kings appear in the king list and the date of accession to the throne is unknown to us. When outside forces terminated Kassite rule over Babylon in 1155, a dynasty said by the Babylonian King List to be from Isin took control over the land (for a list of rulers, see pp. 309–10). Its rulers saw the country slide into a general decline that would last for more than four hundred years. The Kassites were recent immigrants in Babylonia, clearly distinct from the older populations, and they spoke a language without a linguistic relationship to any other language we know. Until the thirteenth century, all their kings had Kassite names, and subsequently only a few took Akkadian ones. Despite the official adherence to Kassite, this language did not have much influence on Babylonian culture. No complete texts written in it have been found, and only a few words in Kassite appear in other texts. There exist two Akkadian–Kassite vocabulary lists that include nouns, verbs, and adjectives. The lists indicate that the Kassite language was of interest at least to scholarly circles, but these scholars did not compose Kassite works. Similarly, the Kassites had their own pantheon, known to us primarily from people's names. Their gods did not become prominent in the cult of Babylonia, however. The only gods for whom shrines were built were the patron deities of the king, Shuqamuna and Shumaliya. They were important in coronation rites and had a chapel in the palace. But otherwise, Kassite kings honored the ancient Babylonian gods as their own (figure 9.1). As was the case with the Amorites earlier, the Kassites acquired political power but did not have a cultural impact.

They may have fundamentally affected the social structure of Babylonia, however. As semi-nomadic groups before they settled, they were organized in family and tribal units. They continued to refer to such units after they had taken control over cities, and distinguished people as belonging to the "House of so-and-so" (Akkadian *Bit* + name of a person), named after an ancestor, who may have been fictitious or not. The males of the unit were the "sons" of that ancestor. In a sedentary setting these houses could incorporate several villages and areas of agricultural land and became administrative entities. Each house had a leader who could act as the chief administrator. After the Kassites lost political control, they stayed in Babylonia and the neighboring areas and maintained their organization in houses with ancestral Kassite names. These remained the administrative units of some areas after the disappearance of the dynasty, so the Kassite influence on Babylonian social structure was lasting.

We do not know how these units related to the royal power in the capital. The Kassite kings were referred to by their colleagues in other Near Eastern states as "kings of the land Karduniash," the latter being a term for Babylonia that may have been Kassite in origin. In some Assyrian sources the Babylonian

Figure 9.1 Kassite stele of the Babylonian goddess Lama. The Metropolitan Museum of Art, Gift of Elias S. David, 1961 (61.12). Photograph, all rights reserved, The Metropolitan Museum of Art

ruler is called "king of the Kassites." This duality probably reflects the political reality. The Kassites held political power, but they remained sufficiently distinct from the rest of the population to be regarded as a separate group. Their lack of roots in a single city facilitated the development of an ideology that they ruled a territorial state. In the Kassite period, the idea of the land of Babylon, that is Babylonia, was firmly established.

The creation of that state took place in the sixteenth and fifteenth centuries, which are extremely poorly known. In 1475 a Kassite named Ulamburiash became lord of the "Sealand," replacing a dynasty that had ruled southern Babylonia perhaps since the disappearance of Babylon's control in the eighteenth century. Subsequently, he may have succeeded his brother Kashtiliashu as king of Babylon, hence uniting the entire area, but the evidence for this is much later and very vague. By the fourteenth century, however, the Kassites were in control of the whole of Babylonia and areas beyond. The Diyala region east of the Tigris was in their hands and a Kassite governor was present on the island of Dilmun (modern Bahrain) in the Persian Gulf. Thus Babylonia rightfully belonged to the great powers of the time, and indeed was acknowledged as such by its neighbors. The Amarna correspondence of the kings of Egypt contains fourteen letters to and from Babylon. Two successive kings there were the correspondents: Kadashman-Enlil I (ruled 1374?–60) and Burnaburiash II (ruled 1359–33). Their letters are almost wholly concerned with diplomatic marriages and the exchange of substantial bridal gifts and dowries. Some political problems arose, however, and demonstrate the change in power relations in Mesopotamia. Assur-uballit of Assyria had contacted Egypt, which caused Burnaburiash to claim angrily that he was a Babylonian vassal and could not act independently in such affairs (see chapter 7).

Babylon's claim to supremacy over Assyria was certainly unrealistic by then, if it had ever existed. Assur-uballit (ruled 1363–28) had made Assyria sufficiently powerful for Burnaburiash to have married his daughter as his main wife. When the Babylonian king died, his son Kara-hardash took over, but was assassinated in a rebellion. Assur-uballit did not appreciate his grandson's murder, and invaded Babylonia to place Kurigalzu II (ruled 1332–08) on the throne. Assyria's importance could no longer be doubted. Babylonia did not live under Assyrian domination, however. It remained one of the great states of the time and, as such, its kings were courted by others who needed legitimation of their own rule. Thus we see that Hattusili III of Hatti contacted Kadashman-Enlil II (ruled 1263–55) when the latter ascended the throne, in order to plead for a continuation of good relations.

This period is documented by a very substantial administrative archive that was excavated in Nippur and is principally concentrated in the reigns of Burnaburiash II to Kashtiliashu IV (ca. 1360–1225). Of the 12,000 or so tablets found, only one-eighth has been published so far, and those are poorly studied. They show a highly centralized administration under a governor, who was in charge of the province of Nippur. He headed an agricultural organization that collected harvests and animal products, often in huge amounts. These were redistributed to institutional dependents as rations, the quantities of which were set by the recipient's rank in the hierarchy. Recipients included administrators, cult officials, military personnel, and laborers. While the governor's office was secular, he could also hold the high priesthood of Nippur's god, Enlil. The Enlil temple seems to have been one of the most important institutions in the land at the time, and control over its assets made the governor of Nippur second in rank only to the king. The temple organization provided people with loans and advances, possibly in return for labor, which may have led to a situation of indebtedness found elsewhere in the Near East at this time. There are very few

Figure 9.2   Remains of the ziggurat at Dur-Kurigalzu. Photograph by the author

texts from other parts of the Kassite state, and the study of its economy and society is difficult. While the level of urbanization in the region was lower than that in the early second millennium, there was a great deal of reconstruction of old cities. The Kassite kings patronized building activity all over Babylonia. Among these projects was the construction of a new capital city, named Dur-Kurigalzu, "fortress of Kurigalzu," in the far north of Babylonia. It extended over some 5 kilometers and included a vast palace and temple, including a high tower made up of a set of mudbrick platforms (figure 9.2). Such a tower is called ziggurat in modern scholarship after the Akkadian word *ziqqurratu*. The city was built in the fifteenth century by the barely known Kurigalzu I, which shows that the court at that time already had the ability to command large resources for itself.

The end of the dynasty was the result of the combined pressures of Assyria and Elam. Tukulti-Ninurta I (ruled 1243–07), continuing a gradual expansion of Assyria that had started in the early thirteenth century, invaded Babylonia and deposed Kashtiliashu IV (ruled 1232–25), whom he took in chains to Assur. The end of the Nippur archive at this time is probably not coincidental. After assuming kingship of Babylon for a short time, Tukulti-Ninurta appointed a series of puppet rulers, who represented Assyrian interests for a decade. Elamite pressure and a successful Babylonian rebellion returned Babylon to Kassite control, but Elam's raids eventually led to the collapse of the Kassite dynasty in 1155. The reaction against the Elamite forces was led by a non-Kassite dynasty, referred to as the second Isin dynasty. Its most forceful and famous ruler was Nebuchadnezzar I (ruled 1125–04), whose conquest of Susa may have led to the collapse of that state. But his own success was short-lived, and soon after his rule Babylonia drifted into historical obscurity. The decline of the region is usually blamed on invasions by the Arameans, but has to be considered within the larger context of the end of the general Near Eastern system at the time.

One practice of the Kassite dynasty that was continued under the second Isin period was the king's granting of substantial areas of land to members of his family, officials, priests, and military personnel. These grants were recorded on stone stelae, decorated with symbols representing gods and inscribed with a declaration in which the king stated in detail what area was given to whom. The stones themselves were referred to by the Akkadian term *kudurru*, which also means "boundary". The reasons for such grants are rarely given, but they seem to have been rewards for special services or offered in support of a cult. The areas involved could be extensive, on average sufficient to feed two hundred people. Sometimes the labor of villagers was included in the donations, or the estates were exempt from taxes. These estates were granted in perpetuity to select members of the elites, but for special purposes only, and it seems doubtful that the stelae document the regular practices of land tenure at the time.

While the Kassite rulers were originally foreign to Babylonia and maintained their own language, at least in their names, they did not impede the development of Babylonian culture. On the contrary, these centuries were crucial for the creation of a Babylonian literary corpus in the Akkadian language. As the palace supported the scribes and authors involved in the process, the Kassites have to be credited with patronizing this activity. Even the Sumerian language was not abandoned as a language of culture and the cult. A part of the literary corpus from the Old Babylonian period in that language was preserved. Several of the texts were provided with an Akkadian translation, recorded in a format where each Sumerian line was immediately followed by its Akkadian counterpart. Moreover, a quite artificial form of Sumerian was used to compose some literary and religious texts and royal inscriptions, and many cylinder seals of the time were inscribed with prayers in the Sumerian language. It is clear that this activity was undertaken by a literate elite that preserved Sumerian as an esoteric language.

It is in the Akkadian literary production that we see a great deal of creativity in this period. A literary dialect developed, called Standard Babylonian by modern scholars, and heavily inspired by the literary Akkadian of the Old Babylonian period. Standard Babylonian remained the literary dialect for the rest of Mesopotamian history, both in Babylonia and in Assyria, and while it was influenced by the vernaculars, it preserved its distinct grammar and lexicon. As a literary language, it was also used in the royal inscriptions of the first millennium.

Much of the literature from this period is known only from first-millennium manuscripts or from late second-millennium manuscripts found outside Babylonia. It is evident, however, that these were composed in second-millennium Babylonia, and in the first millennium the importance of writers from this period was acknowledged. First-millennium Babylonian scribes were grouped into "families," whose eponymous ancestors had the names Sin-leqe-unninni, Hunzu'u, Ekur-zakir, and Ahhutu, and it was suggested that these families dated back to the Kassite period. Sin-leqe-unninni was also credited with having composed the version of the Epic of Gilgamesh that became the standard in the first millennium. These finds suggest the importance of Kassite period literary production, which was also extremely varied in nature. They reflect the palace culture of the time, and several kings are praised in hymns for their military and cultic acts. During the second Isin dynasty, there is a sense that the individual is less secure than in the Old Babylonian period. Man is portrayed as victim to the whims of the gods, for example, in the poem of "the righteous sufferer."[1] It is a monologue in which the speaker describes how he fell from fame and fortune to disgrace, destitution, and disease. There is no explanation for this suffering, except that the god Marduk imposed it for unknown reasons.

The composition of some literary texts was inspired by military and cultic events. In this period, the importance of the god Marduk in the cult increased over the entirety of Babylonia. During the New Year's festival, a ritual of renewal and regeneration, his statue had to be reintroduced into the city of Babylon. The absence of that statue thus had a disastrous effect on the cult, and its recovery was a significant feat. Several texts deal with this issue. In one, the so-called Marduk prophecy,[2] the god narrates how he left Babylon three times in this period, to go to Hatti, Assur, and Elam. These seem to be references to the sacking of Babylon by Mursili I, Tukulti-Ninurta I, and Kutir-Nahhunte. The first recovery is credited in another literary text to an otherwise unknown Kassite king, Agum, who may have lived in the sixteenth century, if indeed he is a historical figure. Nebuchadnezzar I recovered the statue from Elam, a feat that was acclaimed repeatedly in literature. The act probably led to the composition of one of the most famous pieces of Babylonian literature, the so-called Creation myth.[3] It describes how the god Marduk rose to kingship among the gods by defeating the forces of chaos, personified by the sea, Tiamat. Subsequently, he organized the universe and built the city of Babylon as the earthly residence for the gods. The myth thus reflects an ideology that the city held a position of universal importance.

And indeed, Babylon's culture had an impact on the entire Near Eastern world. In all the courts of the second half of the second millennium, manuscripts of Babylonian literary and scholarly texts were kept, copied out, and imitated. Thus at Hattusa, for example, lexical texts, hymns, incantations, and medical texts were found, some of which were bilingual Sumerian and Akkadian. Moreover, several versions of the Gilgamesh Epic were preserved: a Babylonian version and translations into Hittite and Hurrian. Tales about the Old Akkadian kings Sargon and Naram-Sin were preserved in Babylonian. In smaller courts the same situation was found. At Emar in Syria, the corpus of Babylonian texts included omens and incantations, many lexical lists, and fragments of the Epic of Gilgamesh and other Sumerian and Akkadian literature. Even at Amarna in Egypt, with its very distinct literary tradition, manuscripts of literary and lexical texts were found. These include the myths of Adapa and of Nergal and Ereshkigal, and an account of Sargon of Akkad. They are the products of the palace scribes trained to maintain the Babylonian-language correspondence between the courts. While these men may originally have come from Babylonia itself, at least in the larger courts, locals learned how to read and write Babylonian and passed their skills on to their sons. The literary remains had a utilitarian purpose in the training of scribes, but it is highly possible that familiarity with them was part of the elites' way of distinguishing themselves from the general populations.

It is at this time that Assyrian literature became fully inspired by Babylonia, and from this period on there is no clear distinction between the two traditions. This influence was partly a result of the general Near Eastern admiration for Babylonian literature. But political acts sometimes speeded up the process of adoption. Tukulti-Ninurta I, for example, after sacking Babylon, took home literary tablets as booty. He may thus have laid the foundation of a royal library in Assyria filled with Babylonian manuscripts. These influenced local authors. Assyrian literary compositions of the time include genres unknown in Babylonia, such as the royal epic, but their style and language were Standard Babylonian, albeit terser than what we find in the south. Local imitations of Babylonian texts were not always successful. For example, in Elam, cylinder seals in the Kassite style were carved with lengthy inscriptions in Sumerian or Akkadian. The carver's ignorance of those languages sometimes led to incomplete lines being written. While Babylonian influence was strong everywhere, it did not replace local cultural and literary traditions. In most places it became part of a multiplicity of cultural heritages. Thus in Ugarit, for instance, literatures in Ugaritic and in Hurrian coexisted with Babylonian. The patronage of literary culture came from the palace. The fact that Babylonian literature was known everywhere in the region indicates the strength of the palace culture in this period. In the cultural heartland, Babylonia, this creativity was supported by a foreign dynasty, the Kassite, which may be credited with providing that region with its longest era of stability.

9.2 Assyria

The Assyrians themselves presented their history as a long succession of kings, from a distant pre-sedentary past to the mid-eighth century, who ruled the city of Assur. Royal power passed from one family to another many times, but we are unable to subdivide the history on that basis as a sequence of dynasties. Instead, modern historians use a vaguely defined tripartite division of Old, Middle, and Neo-Assyrian periods, which correspond to three periods with relative textual riches, each reflecting a stage of the Assyrian language. The middle to late second millennium is often called the Middle Assyrian period.

The history of these centuries is usually written with a particular focus on individual kings who were militarily very active and successful. From the fourteenth to eleventh centuries Assyria was able to turn itself from a small state around the city Assur to a substantial territorial state and leading player in regional affairs. Our sources, mostly royal annals (see box 9.1), present this feat as the result of the incessant campaigning by certain kings. This bias is reflected in our modern histories, but we should not ignore the diplomatic means by which Assyria gained its status on the international scene, surely backed by military might.

Box 9.1 *Assyrian royal annals*

In the late Middle Assyrian period, in the reign of Tiglath-pileser I (1114–1076), there appeared a new genre of royal inscription that provides the most detailed chronologically organized account of military events: the royal annals. Accounts of this type became increasingly numerous and extensive, and by the late Assyrian period the corpus left by individual rulers is enormous. Annals describe year by year where the king campaigned, what places he conquered, and what booty he brought back with him. While there are some annalistic texts that describe one year only, the majority involves several years up to the moment the text was composed. Each year became identified with a campaign. Versions of the same campaign written at different times often provide various accounts of the events. This could be an abbreviation of the original report, as more emphasis and detail were given to the events immediately preceding the composition. But there could also be a rewriting of events to reflect changes in the political situation. For example, King Sennacherib (ruled 704–681) had great difficulties with Babylonia and campaigned there repeatedly in order to establish a government loyal to him. One solution he tried out was to place a local man, Bel-ibni, on the throne, and in the earliest annalistic accounts he stated so. But this solution did not work out, and after three years Bel-ibni had to be replaced by the Assyrian prince. Annals written after that date did not mention Bel-ibni, even when talking about rule in Babylon, as that man no longer had any relevance to Assyria. While annals may seem to us to be factual, albeit heavily biased, they have to be used critically as historical sources.

Many of the annalistic texts were part of building inscriptions and were structured in three main sections: the epithets of the king, a year-by-year narrative of his military acts up to the moment of composition, and a description of the building project undertaken at that time. As a result, they provide a chronological framework for building activity. They were written on clay tablets, barrels, and cylinders, often buried in foundation deposits, or carved on stone wall reliefs and stelae. Their military focus and the abundance of details about military campaigns have led to the situation that modern reconstructions of Assyrian history are primarily military. We should not conclude from them that the Assyrians were more militaristic in their behavior than were their neighbors, whose inscriptions do not have this focus.

The first ruler of importance in this period was Assur-uballit I (1363–28); he was able to establish firm control over the heartland of Assyria, i.e., the Tigris Valley and plains to the east, from the city of Assur to the Taurus Mountains in the north. Previously, Assyria had probably never been more than a city-state, Assur, controlling its hinterland, and in the fifteenth century it may even have been fully dominated by the Mittani of northern Syria. Nuzi, to the east of Assur, was certainly under Mittani rule, and possibly the king of Assur was a vassal as well. When the Hittites attacked the Mittani kingdom from the west, Assur-uballit was able to annex its eastern territories. He established himself as a figure of international importance. Two letters by him to the king of Egypt were found at Amarna, in which he tried to claim a status at least equal to that of the king of Mittani. The diplomatic opening to Egypt prompted a reaction by Burnaburiash II, king of Babylon, who urged his Egyptian counterpart to ignore Assyria and regard it as his vassal. Yet, the importance of Assyria could not be denied, and the Babylonian king himself married an Assyrian princess, Muballitat-sherua. When their son, Kara-hardash, was murdered in an uprising, Assur-uballit intervened, deposed the Kassite claimant to the throne, and replaced him with Kurigalzu II.

With Assur-uballit's death, Assyria's power was temporarily in decline and his immediate successors were unable to exert influence internationally. Babylonia was certainly independent from Assyria, if not a serious military rival. This trend was reversed by a series of three long-lived kings, whose rule spanned almost the entire thirteenth century: Adad-nirari I (1305–1274), Shalmaneser I (1273–44), and Tukulti-Ninurta I (1243–07). The primary focus of their military activity was the west, where they gradually turned the area of the former Mittani state east of the Euphrates into directly controlled Assyrian territory. At first the king of what the Assyrians called Hanigalbat became a vassal. But when he rebelled, Shalmaneser I occupied the southern and eastern parts of his state and established fortresses and administrative centers. A later rebellion by northern and western areas led Tukulti-Ninurta I to annex the entirety of northern Syria east of the Euphrates. He faced the Hittites, who remained in control of western Syria, and although the two states fought each other, there were no significant battles.

The diplomatic acceptance of Assyria in the league of great states was slow. After Adad-nirari had established *de facto* control over the Mittani area, he wrote to the king of Hatti and called him brother. The Hittite ruler replied rudely: "On what account should I write to you about brotherhood? Were you and I born from one mother?"[4] Soon afterwards the reality that the Assyrian kings were among the great rulers could no longer be denied. Successive Hittite kings engaged in diplomatic exchanges with Adad-nirari I and Shalmaneser I. Both threats and friendly approaches were used, probably in order to avoid a direct conflict. When Tudhaliya IV in the late thirteenth century concluded a treaty with Shaushga-muwa of Amurru, he listed Assyria among the great states. That treaty sought to restrict Assyria's commercial access to the Mediterranean, denying Amurru the right to deal with Assyrian merchants.

The administration of western territories by Assyria was centered round settlements placed in strategic locations and connected by canals and roads. The latter sometimes ran through the steppe and were provided with wells at regular intervals. The Assyrian centers were probably situated in places where they protected trade routes and controlled the districts surrounding them. The records found in these settlements document that officials from Assyria were settled there by the king and ran affairs without much input from the local populations. There was thus no attempt to turn the Syrian people into Assyrians, or any adaptation of local practices. The main concern of the records is agricultural production. Areas around the settlements were cultivated by groups of laborers directly dependent on the Assyrian administration and supported by it through rations. With Shalmaneser I a new method of control of the local people was introduced: entire groups were displaced within Hanigalbat itself, with their families and properties. Under Tukulti-Ninurta I this practice was extended by deporting north Syrian people to Assyria, where they were set to work on public projects and agriculture. Northern Syria thus became a source of agricultural produce and laborers for Assyria.

Assyrian expansion in the thirteenth century was not limited to the west. The campaigns extended into territories to the north of Syria, in eastern Anatolia. The Assyrians encountered peoples there who may have been pushed into forming states or federations. The accounts start referring to regions such as Nairi and Uruatri, where in the early first millennium the important state of Urartu developed. Mountain tribes to the east of Assyria with antiquated names, such as Gutians and Subarians, were also the targets of campaigns. Babylonia once more came under Assyrian control when Tukulti-Ninurta I defeated Kashtiliashu IV, an event described in a long epic poem. He took the titles "King of Assyria and king of Karduniash, king of Sumer and Akkad, king of Sippar and Babylon, king of Dilmun and Meluhha, king of the Upper and Lower Seas, king of the extensive mountains and plains, king of the lands of the Subarians (and) Gutians, and king of all the lands of Nairi,"[5] thereby claiming control over a wide expanse. But this period of strength was abruptly terminated by his assassination and the subsequent confusion in Assyria, which allowed the infiltration of new, non-sedentary, people into eastern Anatolia and northern Syria. The latter area became increasingly occupied by Arameans, who had been kept at bay by Shalmaneser I. Two kings temporarily halted the decline of Assyria: Assur-resha-ishi I (ruled 1132–15) stabilized the region internally, and Tiglath-pileser I (ruled 1114–1076) campaigned aggressively in all directions. In the west, he fought against Arameans and Mushku and reached the Mediterranean Sea. In the south, he raided Babylonia, which was, however, also able to respond and captured Ekallatum, near Assur. In the north, Tiglath-pileser reached the shores of Lake Van. These successes were ephemeral, however, and by 1050 Assyria was reduced to its heartland, with Arameans in control of most of northern Syria and large parts of Mesopotamia. A one-hundred-year period of total obscurity ensued.

The military successes provided the economic resources for great building activity in Assyria itself. The greatest project was the construction of a new capital city by Tukulti-Ninurta, named Kar-Tukulti-Ninurta, opposite Assur on the Tigris River. It was built after he had defeated Babylon, and the spoils of that campaign may have helped provide the means. The city was founded on virgin soil and covered an enormous area, some 240 hectares, if not more. In its center a massive inner city was laid out, with a temple to the god Assur and two large palaces. Documents reveal that Syrian deportees provided the labor. The city's life as a capital was short, however. After Tukulti-Ninurta was assassinated, it became a place of secondary status.

Middle Assyrian society was very much influenced by the militarism of the state. In the heartland of Assyria, much of the agricultural land was held by the crown and given as concessions to men and their families in return for service. When someone was called up for service, he was said to join the "army," although not all duties were purely military. For instance, participation in the building projects was also required. In return, the state gave fields that could be treated almost like private property, as long as the tenant provided service. The lots were passed on from father to son, and could be sold to someone else without palace interference. But when the holder defaulted on his duties or had no heirs, the land reverted to the palace, even if it had been sold. To fulfill the service requirements people could substitute another person, who was usually indebted to them. As in other Near Eastern societies of the period, in Assyria the level of indebtedness was high and many of the contracts preserved are loans backed up by the debtor's labor.

Among the official records of the period are a set of tablets we call the Middle Assyrian Laws and the Palace Decrees (see document 9.1). These indicate that social rules were very strictly regulated and austere, especially for women. The latter were wholly dependent on their husbands and fathers for support and were severely punished for any transgression. A wife whose husband had been captured by an enemy had to wait two years before she could remarry. Meanwhile, she was supported by her father or sons, or if they were not present, by the community. If her first husband returned after two years, he had to take her back, although her children by the second husband would remain with the latter.[6] Punishment for crimes was often bodily mutilation. A woman who was caught stealing from an individual would have her ears cut off by her husband, or her nose by the victim. Public behavior was rigidly controlled. Although married women were allowed to go outside the house on their own, they had to cover their heads. Unmarried women, slaves, and prostitutes were forbidden to cover their head. A prostitute who covered herself would be punished by being given fifty lashes and having her clothes taken away and hot pitch poured over her head. Anyone who did not report such a transgression would be penalized equally severely. The so-called Middle Assyrian Palace Decrees regulated behavior within the court. They also dealt primarily with women. Access to women was monitored and outsiders had to be checked, possibly to see whether they were castrated. If a palace woman met with a man

Document 9.1   *Excerpts from the Middle Assyrian laws*

Tablet A, Paragraph 45

If a woman is married and the enemy seizes her husband, and she has no father-in-law or son, she shall wait for two years for her husband. If she has nothing to eat during these two years, she shall come forward and say so. If she belongs to a community dependent on the palace, her [father?] shall feed her, and she shall work for him. If she is the wife of a low-ranking soldier, [ ] shall feed her, [and she shall work for him]. [If she is the wife of a man whose] field and [house cannot support her?], she shall come forward and say to the judges, "If I have [nothing to] eat." The judges shall question the major and city-leaders, and according to the going rate of fields there, they shall assign a field and house to her for her support for two years and give it. She shall live there and they shall write a tablet to that account. She shall let two years pass, and then she can go and live with the husband of her choice. They shall write a tablet for her as if she is a widow. If later on her missing husband returns to the country, he shall take back his wife who had married outside the family. He will have no claim over the sons she had with her new husband. Her new husband shall take them. As for the field and house that she had sold at full price outside the family to support herself, if it has not become a royal holding, he shall pay as much as was given and take it back. If he does not return and dies abroad, the king shall give his field and house wherever he wants.

Tablet A, Paragraph 47

If either a man or a woman should be caught practicing sorcery, and should they establish and prove the charges, they shall kill the one who had practiced sorcery. A man who heard from the mouth of someone who observed sorcery: "I saw it myself," shall go and tell it to the king. Should the eyewitness deny what was told the king, the hearsay-witness shall say in front of the divine Ox, son of the Sungod: "He did indeed tell me," and he shall be clear. As for the eyewitness, who (first) spoke but then denied, the king shall question him as he likes and investigate him. An exorcist shall make the man speak when they purify and he himself shall say: "No one shall release you from the oath that you swore to the king and his son. According to the tablet you swore to the king and his son."

Translation after Martha T. Roth, *Law Collections from Mesopotamia and Asia Minor*, second edition (Atlanta: Scholars Press, 1997), pp. 170–3.

without an attendant, both would be killed. If a servant spoke to a palace woman with bare shoulders, he would be given one hundred lashes.[7] The sense we get of Assyrian society at this time is that it was dominated by a court that imposed very strict rules of conduct on its subjects.

9.3 The Middle Elamite Kingdom

On the eastern border of the Near Eastern world of the late second millennium, the state of Elam developed along the lines of its great neighbors, although its role in the international system remained of secondary importance (for a list of kings, see pp. 310–11). After Hammurabi of Babylon had defeated Elam in the eighteenth century, the earlier political unity probably shattered. This situation was reversed only around 1400, but from 1500 on rulers in Susa referred to themselves as "Kings of Susa and Anshan" in Akkadian, or as "Kings of Anshan and Susa" in Elamite. After 1400 the lowlands of Susiana in the west were unified with the highlands of Anshan, in the modern province of Fars some 500 kilometers to the south-east, and the shore of the Persian Gulf, some 400 kilometers to the south. The Elamite state was a large geographical entity, uniting people from various cultural backgrounds. The western lowlands had been much influenced by Mesopotamia, while the highlands preserved local traditions. This distinction is clear in the usage of languages and religious practices. The Akkadian of Mesopotamia had been used in earlier periods of Elamite history, and in this era was at first the official language. After 1400, Elamite took over that role. In the early part of the period, Mesopotamian deities were popular in Susa, even though Elamite gods were worshiped there as well. After 1400, Elamite gods came to dominate the official cult.

To write the history of this period, we rely primarily on building inscriptions. The attestation of a king's name in several places allows us to determine the extent of his state. Moreover, genealogical information is often provided, so we can reconstruct the sequence of kings with some certainty, although there is still disagreement among scholars. To date any of these rulers, we have to rely on synchronisms with Mesopotamia. Babylonian sources sometimes relate military clashes with Elam, and there are some letters that deal with dynastic marriages. In general, however, our knowledge of events is vague.

Three dynasties in succession ruled Elam in the centuries between 1500 and 1100. We are the least informed about the first, which governed until around 1400. All we have is a list of the names of five rulers, without their affiliation, so we are not even certain that they formed a dynasty. Almost all of them held the title "King of Susa and Anshan." This may have been a fiction, however, as we have no evidence of control outside the Susiana plain. It is even possible that the ruler's power there was also limited. The best-attested act of one of the rulers, Tepti-ahar, was the building of a new settlement, Kabnak (modern Haft tepe), some 20 kilometers from Susa. It has been suggested that this construction was necessitated by his loss of control over Susa, but there is no clear evidence for this. In any case, if the early Middle Elamite rulers had a wide geographical reach, they did not have the ability to leave a mark on more than the western lowlands.

The formation of the Middle Elamite state was the work of the second dynasty of the period, whose founder was Igi-halki. It held sway for some two centuries. The succession of kings was unusual for the period in that the throne moved back and forth between the descendants of two sons of Igi-halki. The first successor, Pahir-ishshan, was followed by his brother Attar-kittah, whose son and grandson succeeded him. Then the throne reverted to two sons of Pahir-ishshan in succession, and they were followed by descendants of Attar-kittah. There may have been friction between the two branches of the family, but we have no firm data. The dynasty's control over the lowlands is well attested by its building inscriptions. The work included activity in Liyan, a harbor on the Persian Gulf. The largest project by far was the construction in the late fourteenth century of a new city 40 kilometers from Susa, Al-Untash-Napirisha, named after its founder, Untash-Napirisha. Its center was a massive ziggurat surrounded by an inner enclosure with numerous temples. Inside a second enclosure, more secular buildings were located. The ziggurat was devoted to Napirisha, the great god of Elam, and Inshushinak, the patron deity of Susa. The construction was truly monumental: it contained millions of bricks, a substantial part of which was baked at great expense of fuel. The inner core of sun-dried brick was encased in a 2-meter-thick layer of baked brick. Every tenth layer of the outer casing had a row of bricks inscribed with a dedication from Untash-Napirisha to Inshushinak. Because of the solidity of its construction, this is the best-preserved ziggurat in the Near East. Many of the temples in the inner enclosure were devoted to purely Elamite deities, while some of the others honored Mesopotamian gods popular in Susa. There was thus an increased attention to Elamite traditions. Another move away from Mesopotamian influences was the shift to the Elamite language in the official records of the state. With few exceptions, building inscriptions were no longer written in Akkadian. Al-Untash-Napirisha, like many other new foundations of the time, did not survive its creator as a capital. While not abandoned, it had secondary status to Susa soon after the death of Untash-Napirisha. The last rulers of this dynasty became militarily involved in Babylonia. When that state was under the control of Tukulti-Ninurta I of Assyria, who appointed a string of puppet rulers, Kidin-Hutran III attacked the eastern Tigris region. Twice he entered Babylonia, the first time taking Nippur, the second attacking Isin. Soon after the Kassites regained control of the Babylonian throne on Tukulti-Ninurta's death in 1207, Kidin-Hutran also died and a change of dynasty took place in Elam.

The details of this change are unknown to us. The building inscriptions at Susa of the early twelfth century report the activities of a Shutruk-Nahhunte, son of Hallutush-Inshushinak, and we can document that his descendants ruled Elam for the rest of the century. Shutruk-Nahhunte was married to the eldest daughter of the Kassite Meli-Shipak (ruled 1186–72), but relations with Babylonia became extremely strained at the time, perhaps because the Elamite felt that he should have become king of Babylon as well. There is a royal letter from this period, where both the names of the Elamite sender and the Babylonian recipient are lost. Most likely the writer was Shutruk-Nahhunte. He complained: "I am king, son of a king, seed of a king, and born from a king. I am ruler of the lands of Babylonia and of Elam. I am the offspring of

Figure 9.3 Statue of Queen Napir-asu, wife of Untash-Napirisha, Louvre Museum, Paris. Photo: D. Chenot. Courtesy of Réunion des Musées Nationaux/Art Resource, NY

the eldest daughter of the great king Kurigalzu. Why do I not sit on the throne of Babylonia?"[8] As revenge he threatened an invasion of Babylonia. Surprisingly, this letter is preserved only in a copy made in the sixth century and found in Babylon. It remains a mystery why someone at that time would have found its contents of interest, so we may have a fictitious account here, which would undermine much of our reconstruction of the period!

It is certain, however, that Shutruk-Nahhunte invaded Babylonia around 1155 and terminated the reign of the last Kassite king. He brought back an enormous quantity of spoils from all the important cities there, including some of the most famous early Babylonian monuments, such as the stele of Naram-Sin and the law code of Hammurabi. Many of these monuments were inscribed with an Elamite text commemorating their capture, identifying where they were taken and that they had been presented to the god Inshushinak by Shutruk-Nahhunte (document 9.2). This explains why so many Babylonian monuments were excavated in Susa. The king also collected objects from Elamite cities, including Al-Untash-Napirisha, and rededicated them in Susa.

Document 9.2　*Middle Elamite inscriptions*

After his raid in Babylonia around 1155, Shutruk-Nahhunte took a large number of monuments from several cities as loot back home to Susa. He inscribed several of those with a text in the Elamite language, identifying the original patron of the monument and where he captured it. Those inscriptions were carved in prominent locations to celebrate the king's victory. Three of them are translated here.

1. On the stelé of Naram-Sin, captured in Sippar (see figure 4.1)
I am Shutruk-Nahhunte, son of Hallutush-Inshushinak, the beloved servant of the god Inshushinak, king of Anshan and Susa, who has enlarged the kingdom, who takes care of the land of Elam, the lord of the land of Elam. When the god Inshushinak gave me the order, I defeated Sippar. I took the stele of Naram-Sin and carried it off, bringing it to the land of Elam. For Inshushinak, my god, I set it up as an offering.

2. On a statue of Manishtushu, captured in Akkad[1]
I am Shutruk-Nahhunte, son of Hallutush-Inshushinak, the beloved servant of the god Inshushinak, king of Anshan and Susa, who has enlarged the kingdom, who takes care of the land of Elam, the lord of the land of Elam. When the god Inshushinak gave me the order, I defeated Akkad. I took the statue of Manishtushu and carried it off to the land of Elam.

3. On a statue of Manishtushu, captured in Eshnunna[2]
I am Shutruk-Nahhunte, son of Hallutush-Inshushinak, king of Anshan and Susa. When the god Inshushinak gave me the order, I defeated Eshnunna. I took the statue of Manishtushu and carried it off to the land of Elam.

Translation after Friedrich W. König, *Die elamischen Königsinschriften* (Graz, 1965), pp. 76–7.

[1] Pierre Amiet, *L'art d'Agadé au Musée du Louvre* (Paris: Éditions des Musées Nationaux, 1976), no. 13.
[2] Ibid. no. 11.

　　　Shutruk-Nahhunte handed kingship over to his son Kutir-Nahhunte, who in somewhat later Babylonian sources is accused of plundering that country and stealing the statue of Marduk. His brother and successor, Shilhak-Inshushinak, claimed to have raided Babylonia and Assyria repeatedly and to control the area east of the Tigris as far north as Nuzi. The collapse of Kassite authority and the weakening of Assyria must have made that region an easy target. Elam flourished economically at this time and the eastern part of the state was developed. Babylonian resurgence under Nebuchadnezzar I put an end to this prosperity, however. The Babylonian king recovered Marduk's statue from Susa and the Elamite state disappeared from our records for three centuries.

Despite the fact that the Middle Elamite period is the best documented for the entire history of the region, our grasp on it remains limited. We can see the state as a late arrival on the scene whose international influence was restricted to Babylonia and Assyria. It cannot be ignored as a significant force, however. The fact that Elam does not figure in international correspondence probably results from its rise after the Amarna archive and its distance from Syria. Contacts with the Kassites in Babylonia were close, but we lack the Babylonian royal archives from this period, so we have no letters from Elam, except in late copies, which may be fictional. Elam shows a strong Babylonian cultural influence, but also a resistance against it. The Akkadian language was used, but after 1400 played only a minor role when compared to Elamite. On the other hand, the visual arts of the period imitate Babylonian practices and styles. This mixed behavior may be a result of the heterogeneity of cultural traditions in Elam itself, with neither the Mesopotamian-influenced lowlands nor the Elamite highlands fully dominant.

NOTES

1   Benjamin R. Foster, *Before the Muses: An Anthology of Akkadian Literature*, third edition (Bethesda: CDL Press, 2005), pp. 392–409. See also, Benjamin R. Foster, *From Distant Days: Myths, Tales, and Poetry of Ancient Mesopotamia* (Bethesda: CDL Press, 1995), pp. 298–313.
2   Foster, *Muses*, pp. 388–91; *Distant Days*, pp. 215–17.
3   Foster, *Muses*, pp. 436–86; *Distant Days*, pp. 9–51.
4   Gary Beckman, *Hittite Diplomatic Texts*, second edition (Atlanta: Scholars Press, 1999), p. 147. The name of the Hittite king is lost. Scholars have suggested Muwatalli II, Mursili III, and Hattusili III.
5   A. K. Grayson, *Assyrian Rulers of the Third and Second Millennia BC* (*The Royal Inscriptions of Mesopotamia. Assyrian Periods*, volume 1) (Toronto: University of Toronto Press, 1987), p. 275.
6   Middle Assyrian Laws, Martha T. Roth, *Law Collections from Mesopotamia and Asia Minor*, second edition (Atlanta: Scholars Press, 1997), pp. 153–94.
7   Middle Assyrian Palace Decrees, Roth, *Law Collections*, pp. 195–209.
8   Jan Van Dijk, "Die dynastischen Heiraten zwischen Kassiten und Elamern: eine verhängnissvolle Politik," *Orientalia* 55 (1986), p. 162, lines 37–40. The author of this article assigns the letter to Kutir-Nahhunte.

10

The Collapse of the Regional System and its Aftermath

3000	2500	2000	1500	1000	500

1209	Merneptah of Egypt fights "Sea People"
ca. 1200	End of Mycenaean culture
	Fall of Hatti
	Sack of Ugarit
1185	Sack of the city Emar on the Euphrates
1180	Ramesses III of Egypt fights "Sea People"
1155	End of Kassite dynasty in Babylonia
ca. 1120	End of the Middle Elamite period
ca. 935	Reemergence of the textual record in Assyria

The twelfth century was extremely eventful, and radical changes took place in all societies of the Near East and its surroundings during this period. Several factors were involved, including a great amount of military activity and destruction. Yet, elements of continuity are also visible and certain regions were less affected by the events than others. Because of the disruption of standard bureaucratic and other recording practices, it is difficult to ascertain what exactly happened in various places, and the dating of observed changes is often doubtful. Even more difficult is the interpretation of events: no single cause can explain what happened in all regions and states. Local circumstances modified the impact of wide regional changes. The end result was the total disappearance of the system that had characterized the Near East in the

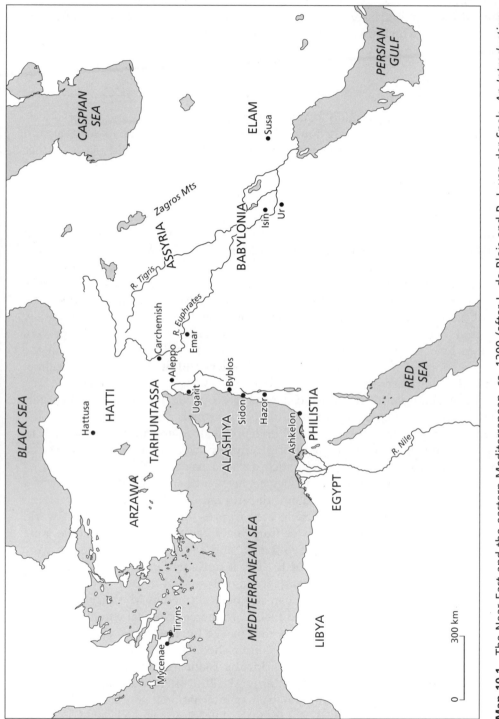

Map 10.1 The Near East and the eastern Mediterranean, ca. 1200 (after L. de Blois and R. J. van der Spek, *An Introduction to the Ancient World* [London and New York: Routledge, 1997], p. 21)

preceding centuries. The unraveling of that system certainly exacerbated the difficulties that individual localities experienced and ultimately becomes the framework in which this period has to be explained.

10.1 The Events

The available documentation focuses especially on disruptions and disturbances. Archaeologically, the burning down of a city is more visible than its survival, and royal inscriptions, with their concentration on warfare, highlight battles rather than peaceful conditions. The story of the twelfth century is therefore primarily one of upheaval, but there were also strong elements of continuity and of gradual change. The latter are harder to examine, but should not be forgotten. There is great scholarly debate about the relative importance of the forces of continuity and change. All scholars agree, however, that the Near Eastern world in 1050 was very different from what it had been in 1250. What happened, why, and exactly when, is more controversial.

We can observe that the forces of disruption were the strongest in the area of the eastern Mediterranean, that is, the Aegean and Anatolia, and extended eastward with less force. Coastal Syria and the Levant were more fundamentally affected than the inland areas. The great states of Mesopotamia and Egypt were able to hold out against the major destructive forces, but did suffer from the repercussions of what happened on their borders and finally went into decline. The following description will thus move from west to east (see map 10.1).

The Aegean world of the Mycenaeans was outside the Near East but part of the system that characterized the fifteenth through thirteenth centuries. The precise nature of Mycenaean social and political organization is still unclear, but the primary evidence for a strong central power in various regions is the massive fortresses built in places such as Mycenae and Tiryns, inhabited by elites with access to great wealth. Mycenaean influence had extended over a large part of the Greek mainland and the Aegean islands, including Crete, and there had been a great deal of trade with Cyprus and the Levant. That world disappeared in the early twelfth century: overseas trade ceased, people were no longer buried with lavish grave-goods, and several of the fortresses were destroyed or substantially reduced in size, if not abandoned. The destruction did not happen all at once, but was spread over several decades. Although the subsequent archaeological culture can still be described as Mycenaean in character, it was impoverished and had lost its wide geographical extent. Linear B writing disappeared, which indicates that palace bureaucracies were no longer needed as centralized economic activity diminished. While decline and disruption are visible in most of the Aegean world, the island of Cyprus seems to have developed in the opposite direction: around 1200, there was increased urban expansion and metal production, as well as international contacts with Egypt, the Levant, and the central Mediterranean. The disappearance of Mycenaean power may thus have enabled the Cypriots to fill a void.

Anatolia underwent fundamental political changes around 1200: the state of Hatti that had dominated the region for centuries collapsed, but again the circumstances are mysterious. Several elements played a role. Already in the late thirteenth century the king in Hattusa had to deal with a competing royal house in the south of Anatolia, in the region of Tarhuntassa. The kings there also claimed descent from the earlier great rulers of Hatti, and carved out an almost independent state of their own. Simultaneously, western Anatolia needed to be brought under military control, and the last king of Hatti, Suppiluliuma II, was engaged in sea battles for the control of the kingdom of Alashiya on Cyprus. Some scholars have suggested that a famine struck the region, based on references to grain deliveries in Egyptian and Ugaritic texts. The unstable agricultural base of Anatolia with its many poor harvests may explain these isolated references better than a sustained famine, however. The end of Hatti was due to violence, but the destruction was far from uniform over the region. In the capital city Hattusa, the royal fortress was burned down as well as some individual public buildings in the lower town, though private residences were untouched. Throughout Anatolia a similar pattern is visible: on those sites where destruction took place, it was not complete. Many settlements were left unscathed, but were nevertheless abandoned. As a result, Hatti disappeared as a political power. In the south, the previously dependent Hittite viceroy of Carchemish survived, however, and claimed to be the descendant of earlier Great Kings, prolonging the history of the Hittite royal house. The succession of rulers there could not keep the region unified, and an increasing number of small states developed by 1100.

With the end of Hittite dominance the Syrian cities became independent, but several were destroyed, especially those in the coastal area. The events are best documented in the city of Ugarit. Its last king, Ammurapi, was a faithful vassal to the king of Hatti and was in direct contact with the viceroy at Carchemish. As such, he supported Hatti with a number of grain deliveries. He was also in correspondence with several rulers of the region, who warned about the imminent danger of raiders on the sea. The Hittite king identified one of the groups involved as "Shikalayu who live on boats,"[1] and he instructed Ugarit to send him a man they had captured so that he could be questioned about these people. The king of Alashiya advised Ammurapi to fortify his towns and gather his warriors and chariots. But the reply presented a distressing picture: several villages had already been sacked, and most of Ugarit's troops were in Hatti, while its ships were on the south coast of Anatolia (see document 10.1). The excavator of Ugarit, Claude Schaeffer, claimed that these letters were found in an oven, where they would have been baked before their dispatch, and that the city had been sacked before they were ready. This gave a dramatic context to these texts, as if they were written as enemy troops were advancing and were never sent because Ugarit was sacked first. Now, it seems that this was an archaeological phantom. The enemy was not at the gate when the letters were written, and we have here an accidental grouping of texts written on different dates. In any case, we know what happened. Ugarit was destroyed and was not

Document 10.1   *Letters from Ugarit*

Letter from the king (of Alashiya) to Ammurapi of Ugarit

Thus says the king, tell Ammurapi, king of Ugarit: May you be well and may the gods guard your well-being.

Regarding what you wrote me before: "Enemy ships were observed at sea!" If it is true that ships were observed, reinforce yourself. Where are your troops and chariots? Are they not with you? If not, who will deliver you from the enemy? Surround your cities with walls and bring your troops and chariots into them. Watch out for the enemy and reinforce yourself well!

Letter from the king of Ugarit to the king of Alashiya

Tell the king of Alashiya, my father; the king of Ugarit your son says: I fall at the feet of my father. May my father be well. May your houses, your wives, your troops, and everything that belongs to the king of Alashiya, my father, be very, very well.

Father, the ships of the enemy have been coming. They have been burning down my villages and have done evil things to the country. Does my father not know that all my troops [and chariots] are in Hatti and that all my ships are in Lukka? They have not yet reached me, so the country is undefended. May my father be informed of this. Now the seven ships of the enemy that came have done evil things. If other enemy ships appear, send me a message so that I know.

Letter from the senior governor of Alashiya to the king of Ugarit

Thus says Eshuwara, senior governor of Alashiya. Tell the king of Ugarit: May you and your land be well.

Regarding the things that the enemies have done to the people of your country and your ships, they have done these transgressions against the people of the country. Thus, do not be angry with me.

Now, the twenty ships that the enemies earlier left in the mountainous areas, have not stayed behind. They left suddenly and we do not know where they are. I write to you to inform you so that you can guard yourself. Be informed!

Translations after Gary Beckman, in A. B. Knapp, ed., *Sources for the History of Cyprus.* *Volume 2: Near Eastern and Aegean Texts from the Third to the First Millennia* BC (Greece and Cyprus Research Center, 1996), p. 27.

to be resettled for a thousand years. Its harbor, Ras Ibn Hani, was also sacked but was soon resettled, perhaps by the people who had attacked it.

Further south in the Syro-Palestinian area, the pattern of selective destruction continued. Prominent harbors like Byblos and Sidon survived unscathed, but cities like Ashkelon and Hazor were destroyed. The destruction was not simultaneous and a timespan of several decades was involved. In Palestine, the urban culture that had characterized the region was gradually replaced by one of villages. New people settled in the region, such as the Philistines, who took over control of the southern coastal area up to the Egyptian border.

Reports from Egypt are the most detailed available, but their point of view was self-centered and biased. Two Egyptian kings described in narrative and pictorial accounts what happened in the eastern Mediterranean. They set the events in the context of a war with outside invaders who always included Libyans, coming from the west. Although the accounts are separated by twenty-five years, they narrate very similar things. King Merneptah (ruled 1213–04) claimed that he successfully repelled an attack by Libyans and an assortment of people from the north, whom he called "of the countries of the sea." Although they tried to enter Egypt using military force, they brought their families and cattle, which indicated their intention to settle there. Ramesses III (ruled 1187–56) provided much more detail. After mentioning attacks by people from the north in his fifth year, his account of the eighth year purports to provide an overview of what happened throughout the eastern Mediterranean:

> The foreign countries made a conspiracy in their islands. All at once the lands were removed and scattered in the fray. No land could stand before their arms, from Hatti, Kode (= Tarhuntassa), Carchemish, Arzawa, and Alashiya on, being cut off at [one time]. A camp [was set up] in one place in Amurru. They desolated its people, and its land was like that which had never come into being. They were coming forward toward Egypt, while the flame was prepared for them. Their confederation was the Peleset, Tjeker, Shekelesh, Denyen, and Weshesh, lands united.[2]

This account presents a clear image of an invasion by island people into the states of Hatti, Tarhuntassa, and others, and these states supposedly collapsed at once. The invaders gathered forces in northern Syria and marched on toward Egypt, to be defeated by Ramesses III both on land and at sea (see figure 10.1). He identified certain groups explicitly, including Peleset and Shekelesh, who must be the same as the Shikalayu mentioned before in the letter found at Ugarit. Upon closer examination, Ramesses' detailed reconstruction becomes doubtful, however. Carchemish, for example, was not destroyed. More importantly, the names of the "Sea People" who were portrayed as swooping down the Syrian coast from distant islands were already attested several decades earlier as present in the region, including as mercenaries in the Egyptian and Hittite armies. In other words, Ramesses III turned what may have been clashes with groups in Syria into a major battle between Egypt and an invading foreign army

Figure 10.1   Ramesses III's battle against Sea People, relief from Medinet Habu.
Courtesy of the Oriental Institute of the University of Chicago

that had destroyed everything in its path. The interpretation of this data is very complicated. Some scholars have even suggested that Ramesses III merely repeated battle accounts by his predecessor Merneptah and claimed earlier victories for himself, something not unusual in Egypt. We have no way to confirm or deny this idea. Whatever the details of events, it is clear that Egypt lost most of its direct control over territories in Asia, although it still had access to mines in the Sinai. It survived as a territorial state, but the century after Ramesses III shows internal disorder and social upheaval, a reduction of contacts with regions beyond its borders, and ultimately, around 1100, a political fragmentation of the country.

Similar processes were visible in the eastern states of the region, which became cut off from western Syria and the Mediterranean. Assyria, Babylonia, and Elam continued to interact with one another, often through military clashes. Each remained a territorial state, but had internal problems and little permanent influence beyond its borders. After the militarily successful thirteenth century, Assyria abandoned its policy of constant campaigning for some ninety years. Internal problems after the assassination of Tukulti-Ninurta I in 1207 may have been responsible, and the military disturbances in western Syria were probably also a factor in this change of policy. These disturbances did not spill over into the region east of the Euphrates, however. The easternmost city destroyed was Emar, a Hittite dependency, where two texts mention "the year that the hordes(?) afflicted the city," and the latest dated text is from 1185. East of Emar, Assyrian outposts in Syria did not disappear, but they were reduced in size and scribal activity stopped. The countryside was controlled by the semi-nomadic Arameans, who became prominent in military and political terms. The level of urbanization in the region declined. For three centuries Assyria was reduced to its heartland, perhaps with some outposts in the region to its west.

Scholars often regard the change of dynasty from the Kassites to the so-called second dynasty of Isin in twelfth-century Babylonia as a relatively unimportant shift in power from one royal house to another. But it demonstrates how in political terms the centralized power held by the Kassites for four hundred years had disintegrated. The existence of a competing dynasty in central Babylonia, which captured Babylon's throne by 1150, shows that the strength of the state had dissipated. Moreover, the archaeological record indicates that urbanism was in sharp decline, although this has to be seen as part of a long process that had started in the early second millennium. The number of true urban centers became very small, perhaps only Babylon, Isin, and Ur, and the large majority of the settled people lived in villages. Nippur, for example, had lost its urban characteristics by 1200 and by 1000 it had perhaps nothing more than a small population around its ancient ziggurat. The size of the sedentary population had dwindled to 25 percent of the level of the late third millennium. There were regional variations, with for instance a much steeper decline in the Diyala Valley than in the region of Ur. But there is no doubt that the urban organization and its infrastructure of irrigation canals had collapsed by the end of the second millennium. Many of the occupants of the region reverted to a semi-nomadic lifestyle. The primary causes for this development may have been non-political. The bulk of the Euphrates water flow seems to have shifted toward western branches of the river, which deprived some major urban centers of earlier days of sufficient irrigation to support a large population. Moreover, overuse of the soil leading to salinization probably reduced yields. Certainly, a complex interaction between political and ecological factors was at work. The organization of large irrigation projects to counter these natural changes was made impossible by the weakening of central power. That process may have been precipitated by the outside military interference from Elam and Assyria, and the Babylonian state lost control over its countryside.

Since we do not know the organization of the state of Elam in the preceding era, it is impossible to determine how it changed in the twelfth century. The military action by Nebuchadnezzar I (ruled 1125–04) that triggered the end of the Middle Elamite period may have been facilitated by earlier internal decline. In any event, the result was similar to what happened throughout the Near East: a centralized state was terminated and the region was infiltrated by new population groups, in this case seemingly coming from the east.

10.2 Interpretation

Many explanations of these events have been proposed in scholarship, mostly focused on one state or on the eastern Mediterranean by itself. Invasions and migrations, social revolutions, and ecological disasters have all been suggested as the main causes for the collapse of the states. On the other hand, some scholars have stressed the visible continuities, disputing the idea that the twelfth century was one of radical change. An explanation to account for the differences between the late second millennium and the early first would then have to be sought in subsequent centuries, where our data are almost completely lacking.

It seems clear, however, that the changes that started around 1200 precipitated the end of the Near Eastern world of the fifteenth to thirteenth centuries, and that the causes for this end have to be sought in the twelfth century. Moreover, it cannot have been accidental that all societies experienced drastic change at this time. Since they were tied together in a common system for centuries, the end of that system must have had wide-ranging repercussions. No single cause can explain this comprehensive change.

When referring to the Aegean, Anatolia, and Syria-Palestine, the ancient sources stress invasions by outsiders as a significant cause of disruption. Most prominent are the contemporary Egyptian sources. But later Greek accounts of the rise of the classical world, and the Biblical depiction of the creation of the ancient state of Israel, also describe invasions in this period, whereas Babylonian sources describe a period of great upheaval (see document 10.2). This general image has inspired scholars to interpret other data in that light. The appearance of a new type of pottery in the Zagros Mountains, for example, has been seen as the result of the invasion by people from the east. References to Arameans in Assyrian texts have been considered to demonstrate these people's attempts to infiltrate that state. An analysis of the textual records of invasion shows that they draw too simplistic a picture. They contain internal contradictions and other references provide a different image. For example, Ramesses III's statement that the Sea People came down from their islands and destroyed the states of Anatolia and Syria-Palestine in one fell swoop, only to be stopped by him at the Egyptian border, is contradicted by the fact that people with their names appeared decades earlier in the region. The archaeological record does not show a sequence of destruction in one short period of time but a prolonged period in which individual sites were destroyed, while others survived yet declined in size. Military confrontations with unconventional troops, including people who originated outside the Near East, most probably took place, but they were not the result of a widespread invasion. In the eastern part of the Near East, interstate warfare is often seen as a major cause of disruption and decline. But this was not a novelty of the twelfth century. Throughout the second half of the second millennium states had clashed. So the effects of these wars by themselves do not provide sufficient explanation for the widespread collapse.

Other scholars have looked more at internal developments to explain change. An important characteristic of the system of great states was the existence of a palace elite that exploited the agricultural communities under its control. There was a huge discrepancy in wealth and lifestyle between the two groups. The lavish grave-goods and architectural remains we admire were produced from the income of impoverished farmers and herdsmen. A situation of rural indebtedness led to many seeking refuge outside the structures of the state. The period's records are filled with references to people identified as *habiru*. That term was used in records from almost all great states, Mittani, Hatti, Egypt, and Babylonia, and in those of the Syro-Palestinian area. It does not refer to an ethnic group but to a social one. *Habiru* were outcasts from society

---

Document 10.2 *Later reflections on the Dark Age*

During the centuries after the disturbances that engulfed the Near East in the twelfth century virtually no texts were written, or at least extremely few are preserved today. Several people from the first millennium reflected back on this period, however, and described conditions of great disorder. The classical Greeks depicted the period after the Mycenaean civilization disappeared as one of invasions of people such as the Dorians. The Bible places the Israelite conquest of Canaan in this period as well. In Babylonia, a possible literary reflection on this period is a long poem probably written in the seventh century. Scholars often refer to it as the Erra Epic. The author identified himself at the end of the text as Kabti-ilani-Marduk of the Dabibi-family, and he claimed that the work was revealed to him in a dream. The epic relates how Erra, the god of plagues, became enraged because he felt snubbed by the other gods, and rampaged throughout Babylonia, leaving death and destruction in his wake. In Babylon the citizens rallied around him and burned down temples, until they were massacred by royal troops. Nomads, identified with an anachronistic tribal designation as Sutians, overran Uruk and molested Ishtar's cult personnel. Sippar's wall was torn down and Der was destroyed. The gods of those cities were horrified, and only then did Erra calm down and give Babylon his blessing to rule the whole land. The text was considered to have an apotropaic value and parts of it were copied out on amulets that protected houses. The following excerpt is just a short part of a long litany of chaos and violence.

He who did not die in battle, will die in the epidemic;
He who did not die in the epidemic, the enemy will rob him;
He whom the enemy has not robbed, the thief will thrash him;
He whom the thief did not thrash, the king's weapon will overcome him;
He whom the king's weapon did not overcome, the prince will kill him;
He whom the prince did not kill, the stormgod will wash him away;
He whom the stormgod did not wash away, the sungod will carry him away;
He who has left for the countryside, the wind will sweep him away;
He who has entered his own house, a demon will strike him;
He who climbed up a high place, will die of thirst;
He who went down to a low place, will die in the waters;
You have destroyed high and low place alike!

Translation after Luigi Cagni, *L'epopea di Erra* (Rome: Istituto di studi del Vicino Oriente, 1969), pp. 112–13 and Benjamin R. Foster, *Before the Muses*, third edition (Bethesda: CDL Press, 2005), p. 905.

---

who sought refuge in territories that were difficult to control and who lived outside the structures of the states. Idrimi, for example, reported how he became a *habiru* after fleeing his hometown Aleppo. The references to these people are almost consistently hostile. They were portrayed as robbers and murderers, but they were also used as mercenaries. Thus there was a contradiction in attitudes toward them: while supposedly completely hostile, they could be employed in the service of the states. The problem of palace dependents leaving the countryside was considered a serious threat to the palace system: labor was scarce, and when more people fled palace control, it was harder to find workers. Hence the frequent references in treaties to the extradition of refugees. A shortage of laborers reduced the agricultural productivity of the states and threatened palace revenue. To compensate for the loss of labor, palaces may have increased demands on the remaining dependents, consequently exacerbating the problem. The laborers may have turned against their masters and joined any hostile forces that challenged them, including such groups as the Sea People. The selective destruction we observe is in that case no surprise. People around Hattusa, for instance, turned against the symbols of their exploitation, the royal fortress and public buildings. Not all cities were destroyed, but the rural infrastructure of most disappeared, which led to their reduction in size or total abandonment.

Some scholars have looked at natural causes for the collapse observed. Certain archaeological sites show evidence of earthquakes, but this could not explain the regional disintegration. Lack of food is attested in some textual sources, and scholars have used this to suggest that famines were a great problem. Either a general desiccation of the climate in the north or a shift of river courses in southern Mesopotamia has been proposed as an explanation for agricultural decline. The evidence remains ambiguous, however. There was always an unstable agricultural base throughout the Near East, and the textual references to difficulties with food supplies may simply refer to isolated instances rather than a long-lasting famine. If a drying of the climate had indeed taken place, it would certainly have exacerbated the already severe problems of insufficient support for the lavish lifestyles of the elites. Nevertheless, environmental stress by itself does not seem adequate to explain all the changes that we see in the Near East.

Since all these explanations have some foundation in the historical record, we may conclude that a variety of causes was probably at the root of the changes we observe. Military clashes and social rebellions may have been the main reason for the destruction of individual sites. What made each separate cause more important was that it contributed to the unraveling of an entire system that had characterized the region and had provided its stability from 1500 to 1200. The states had not existed in isolation, but had been closely tied to one another. The contacts between them had been vital for maintaining their internal organizations. The interruption of those contacts had a fundamental impact on all of them. When the Hittite state disappeared and Syria-Palestine underwent turmoil, Egypt was cut off from Asia. It had no other equals with whom to interact, as Babylonia and Assyria were out of reach. Trade and diplomatic exchange ceased, leaving Egypt blind to events in the north. The country had substantial resources of its own, so it could survive, but the international system that had supported its palace elites was gone. Similarly, the eastern states of Assyria, Babylonia, and Elam were reduced to a small international system with only the three of them as participants. The Mediterranean Sea or Egypt were no longer accessible, and trade routes were cut. The absence of this wide geographical infrastructure led to their own disintegration, which allowed new people, especially the Arameans, to control the areas between them and further isolate them from one another. No one power filled the vacuum created by the decline of these states, enabling new groups and lower social strata to acquire control. When we talk about collapse of the states, we should not imagine that everyone suffered. There was a rearrangement of power, and large parts of the populations of the Near Eastern states may have benefited from the newfound freedom.

10.3 The Aftermath

As can be expected, the crisis of the palace system led to a sharp reduction in the number of sources available to the historian. Bureaucracies ceased to function and building activity was minimal. Textual and archaeological data are lacking, and the history of the Near East entered another "Dark Age." The length of this period varied from region to region. The first to come out of it was Assyria, where textual records were extremely rare from ca. 1050 BC to 935 BC. Afterwards its expansionist policy drew many surrounding regions into its orbit and its increasingly detailed records document some of the circumstances there. But often the use of writing in these areas was limited until much later. Even in Babylonia, the region with the oldest and strongest literary tradition, we have to wait until the mid-eighth century to see a level of scribal activity beyond the isolated document.

Very little is known about the centuries from 1100 to 900. We can determine, however, that in that time important technological and social changes occurred, largely due to the disappearance of earlier structures. Social and economic life reformed itself to adapt to the new circumstances. Technological practices had been maintained by the palaces, and when the latter ceased to exist, the infrastructure collapsed, leading to a need for change. We can see that the regions where the palaces remained stronger in this period, Assyria, Babylonia, and Egypt, became technologically backward as they carried on older methods. This situation is well demonstrated by changes in writing practices. Throughout the Near East, the palaces of the second millennium had supported chancelleries where scribes read and wrote Akkadian. This was a foreign language for most of them, and it was recorded in a script, cuneiform, that was relatively difficult to master. Training and support of these skilled people was possible in an institution that had sufficient wealth. With the end of the palaces, the infrastructure for these specialists disappeared, as did the rationale for their existence. No longer were letters written to other courts requiring knowledge of the diplomatic language. Moreover, the disruption of economic practices led to a reduced need for bureaucracies. Trade was interrupted, fields and labor were no longer centrally administered, and private economic activity declined. In the states where the palaces retained some prominence, bureaucracies were preserved to some extent. This explains the continuation of cuneiform writing practices in Assyria and Babylonia. But in other regions, that particular recording system was no longer in use and people reverted to local practices. Egypt, with its still relatively strong palace, used only its own hieroglyphic script and its derivatives to write the Egyptian language.

Elsewhere very few texts were written. In southern Anatolia and northern Syria, the successors of the Hittites expanded the use of what we call the Hittite hieroglyphic script, with which they rendered the Luwian language. Previously the script had been reserved for short seal inscriptions and marks of ownership, but in the twelfth to tenth centuries it was used for longer royal inscriptions and for some economic records on strips of lead. In the Syro-Palestinian area the script of choice was the linear alphabet. Developed many centuries before, it had only a limited use among a variety of scripts and languages (see box 10.1). In the eleventh and tenth centuries, it became the sole system of writing in the region. Most inscriptions known to us were from the Phoenician harbor cities that had not been destroyed during the disturbances around 1200. The alphabet used only twenty-two letters, and the direction of the script was fixed from right to left. In the ninth century, Hebrew and Aramaic were also recorded in it, and an increasing number of mostly short inscriptions were written. With the spread of Aramaic as a spoken language throughout the Near East, the script spread as well. As a simpler system that rendered the language locally spoken, it was much easier to learn and the scribes did not have to be as extensively trained as those who wrote cuneiform. Thus there was no need for a palace organization to support them.

A fundamental technological change also took place in metallurgy. The most commonly used metal up to 1200 had been bronze, an alloy of copper and tin. In most countries of the Near East, both metals had to be imported from different sources. No one had access to both locally. The international trade system of the second half of the second millennium had greatly facilitated the acquisition of these metals. This is well illustrated by one of the shipwrecks of the period (Uluburun), which contained ingots of copper and tin in the correct ratio of ten to one (see figure 7.1). The palace workshops housed and supported the craftsmen needed for bronze production. Around 1200 several places, especially in the eastern Mediterranean, were cut off from new metal supplies and their bronze workshops were destroyed. People turned to another metal as a substitute: iron. Iron ore was available almost everywhere, so it did not need to be imported. Although it had been in use since the third millennium, it may have been only a by-product of bronze manufacture and was certainly only reserved for special objects. In the twelfth and eleventh centuries, the technology was discovered to alloy iron with the charcoal of the furnace during the smelting process, and so steel was produced, much harder than bronze. This invention seems to have taken place in the eastern Mediterranean (Anatolia and the Levant) and suited the new social conditions perfectly. A cheap metal, superior in strength

Box 10.1 *Alphabetic scripts*

In the Syro-Palestinian area of the second millennium, the first evidence of what can be called alphabetic scripts appeared. Instead of indicating word signs and syllables with one, two, or three consonants, these scripts used one sign for each consonant of the language, and this required fewer than thirty characters. The idea may have been inspired by the Egyptian writing system, which includes a set of hieroglyphs for single consonants only, to be combined with any vowel. The earliest evidence of alphabetic writing derives from Serabit el-Khadim, a site in the Sinai with strong Egyptian influence in the early second millennium. In the second half of the second millennium, various alphabetic scripts coexisted. The system that survived into later periods had a set of characters whose reading was based on the acrophonic principle: e.g., the drawing of a house represented the sound /b/, the first in the Semitic word for house, *baytu*. A handful of such alphabetic inscriptions of the second millennium are known, most of them with a few characters only. The forms of the letters show a great deal of variation, but a common basic system can be recognized. These texts were mainly carved on stone or metal or drawn with ink on pottery shards.

In the thirteenth century, a much better-attested cuneiform alphabet was used in the Syrian city of Ugarit and its territory alongside the cuneiform system from Babylonia. Written on clay tablets, the Ugaritic alphabetic signs were shaped like the syllabic cuneiform ones, but there is no obvious formal connection between the two. A large variety of texts was written in the alphabetic script, including letters, contracts, and literature. Very few texts do not record the local Semitic language, however. It seems that local affairs were recorded in Ugaritic alphabetic writing, while Babylonian was preferred for international affairs. In total, some 1400 tablets with the Ugaritic script are preserved. Interestingly, both for the cuneiform and the other alphabetic systems, abecedaries of this period were found, which shows that the sequence of letters was well established.

Ugarit did not survive after 1200 BC, nor did its script. The Phoenicians adopted the linear alphabet and developed it further during the first millennium to write the Semitic languages of Syria-Palestine. With the spread of the Aramaic language in the Assyrian empire in the first millennium, and its adoption as an official language in the Persian empire in the fifth century, the alphabet became the dominant script of the Near East and far beyond. The date of transmission to Greece is controversial. Most scholars believe this took place from the Phoenician or Syrian area in the ninth or eighth centuries, but some suggest a date before 1200. The Greeks reserved a number of the signs to indicate vowels, thereby enabling the use of the alphabetic script for non-Semitic languages.

to bronze, could be produced without the need for an elaborate trade network. Once again, the regions where the palaces remained strong, Mesopotamia and Egypt, lagged behind. Iron became common there only in the ninth century, and even then was mostly reserved for the palaces.

During the Dark Age an almost complete restructuring of society took place over most of the Near East. The crisis of the states enabled foreign peoples to migrate into the region and internal population movements were numerous. There was a flux between semi-nomadic and settled people. Many urban residents turned to a pastoralist lifestyle, while some previously semi-nomadic people gained political power in cities. The situation was very confused and the movements cannot be traced accurately. We can see, however, that when the tenth- and ninth-century records indicate the presence of peoples, many regions were inhabited by populations previously unknown.

Some came from outside the Near East. In central Anatolia, for example, Phrygians seem to have arrived from the Balkans in the twelfth century, and by the eighth they had formed a unified state. Some of the Sea People identified by the Egyptians settled down in the region of Syria-Palestine. There is much scholarly speculation about the destination of these groups, all based on a comparison of the names listed by the Egyptians with toponyms and the names of tribes in later texts. It is very often stated that the Peleset of the Sea People became the Philistines, who inhabited the coastal area just north of Egypt in the early first millennium. But, besides the similarity in names, there is nothing to confirm this hypothesis. Other identifications are even less clear: the Sea People called Denyen, for example, have been associated with the Israelite tribe of Dan and with the north Syrian region Danuna around modern Adana. The evidence, purely based on name similarity, is tenuous. Whatever the origin of the Sea People and their final destinations, they did participate in the general movement of populations and the restructuring of societies. Even if the Peleset were not the Philistines, we can say on the basis of archaeological evidence that a new material culture appeared in southern Palestine, a region later called Philistia.

The most prominent among the groups who gained in importance were the Arameans. Most probably pastoralists in northern Syria for a long time before 1200, they took advantage of the weakening of the states to spread out over large parts of the Near East and to acquire political power, including in cities. They kept their tribal organization and were subdivided into groups identified as belonging to the "house of so-and-so," in Akkadian *Bit* and the name of a person, who was considered to be the tribal ancestor. Some of the states they founded were referred to in the first millennium by this designation, for instance Bit-Adini. In northern Syria, Arameans took control of many cities, including some that were inhabited by people who maintained Hittite cultural and political traditions. In such places certain kings had Luwian names, others Aramaic. Other cities were completely Aramean and became the core of states, such as Aram-Damascus. By the ninth century these people politically dominated the whole of Syria.

In the first millennium, Arameans also migrated into Assyria and Babylonia. In many respects they were just one of the succession of north Syrian peoples that did so, and their presence had similar results. Culturally, Mesopotamian traditions continued to dominate. Akkadian remained the official language, found in royal inscriptions, letters, administrative texts, and so on. But a large part of the population spoke Aramaic, and traces of its influence in the grammar and lexicon of Akkadian are clear. First-millennium Assyrian reliefs represent two types of scribes: those writing on clay tablets and those writing on a leather scroll. The profession of a "scribe on leather" is also attested in the texts. These scribes would have written Aramaic in alphabetic script on parchment, but this material has not survived in the archaeological record, so we have no evidence of their work. The names of people remained predominantly Akkadian, yet it is clear that Aramaic speakers did take on Akkadian names, or even had distinct names in both languages. The latter is shown by a later literary tale in Aramaic regarding a man called Ahiqar. The earliest manuscript is from late fifth-century BC Elephantine in southern Egypt, but references to Ahiqar are found in earlier texts. In the tale he was adviser to the seventh-century Assyrian kings Sennacherib and Esarhaddon, and he helped his masters acquire a fabulous amount of gold in a competition with the king of Egypt. According to this story, the Aramean Ahiqar was a highly placed member of the Assyrian court. We would not have recognized him in the contemporary record as an Aramean, however, since he also had an Akkadian name. This is revealed by a cuneiform text from second-century Babylonia, which lists as adviser to King Esarhaddon "Aba-Enlil-dari, whom the Arameans call Ahiqar." Many of the high court officials with Akkadian names recorded in the Assyrian documentation could thus have been Arameans.

The Arameans started to raid Babylonia in the eleventh century, but occupied territories along the Tigris River only in the ninth century. They were joined by people called Chaldeans, also with a tribal organization but of a different kind, who settled primarily along the Euphrates and in the south. Both groups remained distinct and used separate tribal designations, but together they controlled most of the Babylonian countryside. Also in the first millennium, Arabs from the peninsula entered central Babylonia, while until the mid-ninth century remnants of the Kassites remained in the area, especially in the Diyala Valley, and they kept their own tribal organization. Often opposed to these groups were the inhabitants of the remains of the great cities of the past, such as Babylon, Nippur, and Ur, who held on to ancient Babylonian traditions. For almost five centuries, the political situation in the region was extremely volatile, and rarely did a succession of men from the same family hold royal power. Chaldeans, Babylonians, Kassites, Elamites, and Assyrians fought incessantly over the throne, until the Neo-Babylonian dynasty was established in 626. There thus existed a stark opposition between cities and the countryside, with the former having little influence outside their walls. Often urban residents sought military support from the kings of Assyria, who had great difficulty in the eighth and seventh centuries in controlling Babylonia. But at other times the cities were opposed to Assyria, and their rebellions were sometimes violently crushed.

During the Dark Age there also occurred a technological change that brought new populations into contact with Near Eastern states: the domestication of the camel. This happened in the Arabian Peninsula in the later second millennium and has to be related to the beginning of overland incense trade to Mesopotamia and the Levant. Consequently, Arabs became part of the documented Near Eastern world. On the fringes of the settled societies, they were mostly seen as enemies. Anti-Assyrian coalitions in Syria often included Arab warriors and their camels. Only during the late Assyrian empire, when it experienced its greatest expansion, did kings attempt to subdue them in their own territories, but Assyrian warfaring techniques were not suitable for a desert environment. Camels enabled a new type of nomadism. Instead of sheep and goat pastoralism that utilized areas in between permanent settlements, camel nomads could traverse long stretches of the desert using oases as resting places. The latter thus became connected to the better-known Near Eastern lands, and much later the sixth-century Babylonian King Nabonidus temporarily moved his capital to one of them.

The Dark Age was, therefore, of fundamental importance in Near Eastern history, connecting two very different worlds. The radical changes that took place during this period will always remain difficult to study, since there was so much upheaval and consequently a lack of records. When the historian next becomes able to comprehend the situation, the Near East can be said to develop into an age of empires.

NOTES

1   M. Dietrich and O. Loretz, "Das 'seefahrende Volk' von Sikala (RS 34.129)," *Ugarit Forschungen* 10 (1978), pp. 53–6.
2   John A. Wilson, in *Ancient Near Eastern Texts Relating to the Old Testament*, third edition (Princeton: Princeton University Press, 1969), p. 262.

Part III
Empires

11

The Near East at the Start of the First Millennium

3000	2500	2000	1500	1000	500

853	Battle of Qarqar between Assyrian King Shalmaneser III and western coalition
ca. 850	Sarduri I unifies Urartian state
ca. 740	Elamite resurgence
714	Raid by Sargon II of Assyria ends Urartian threat
691	Battle of Halule between Sennacherib of Assyria and Humban-nimena of Elam
646	Assurbanipal of Assyria sacks Susa
626	Nabopolassar founds Neo-Babylonian dynasty

With the start of the first millennium, the political situation in the various parts of the Near East had settled and an entirely new network of states arose. Consequently, records were written again and the historian's comprehension of events increases. The process took time, however, and it is only in the ninth century that sources start to shed light on a wide geographical region. At this time one power, Assyria, began to dominate in military terms, though we have to wait until the seventh century before it became so encompassing that the entire Near East can be studied through its sources. Despite Assyria's dominance in historical reconstructions, we have to keep in mind that a variety of states coexisted with it. To study their histories we often have to take into account somewhat earlier and later evidence. These states included Babylonia in

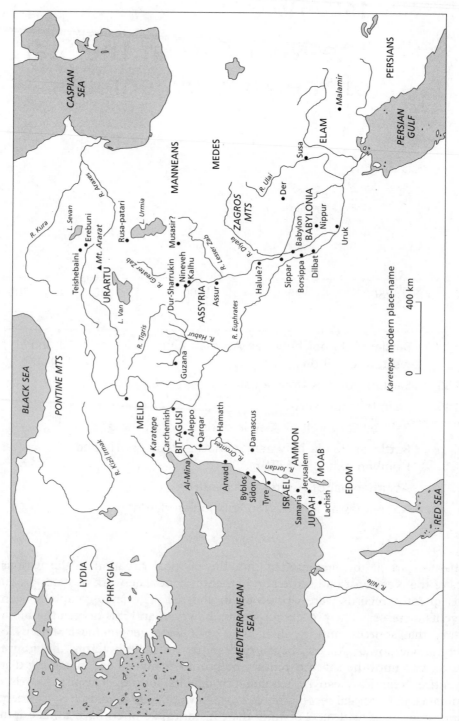

Map 11.1 The Near East in the early first millennium

Mesopotamia, and Urartu, which developed in eastern Anatolia in the early first millennium. Elam in western Iran became a crucial actor in the eighth century only. Outside the Near East as defined in this book, Egypt remained important. In the Syro-Palestinian region and Anatolia, a large number of smaller states existed. Some were a continuation of those of the second millennium: the Phoenician harbor cities and the Neo-Hittite states. Others were entirely new: the Aramean states in Syria, and those of Israel, Judah, and their eastern neighbors. In Anatolia, Phrygians and Lydians created new political entities, while in the Zagros Mountains a set of peoples formed small states. These states will be discussed in this chapter, while the rise of the Assyrian empire within this context will be described in the next.

11.1   The Eastern States

In the east of the Near East, three states already known in the second millennium, Assyria, Babylonia, and Elam, continued to be important in the early first, while a newcomer, Urartu, developed at this time. Our ability to reconstruct their respective histories is uneven and very much biased toward an Assyrian point of view. Still, a study of the development of the Assyrian empire has to take its neighbors into account, and a survey of their histories is provided first.

The entire period from 1000 to 626 was a difficult one for Babylonia. Politically, the region was in disarray with various groups vying for power, and economically it was weak because of a collapse of the agricultural infrastructure and a loss of access to trade routes. In political terms, power passed from the Kassites to the Chaldeans during a long period of instability. The shift was much more complicated than before because other groups, both inside and outside Babylonia, were determined to control the region. After the end of the Kassite dynasty in 1155, two successive dynasties with their power base in different parts of the country sat on the throne of Babylon: the long-lasting second Isin dynasty from central Babylonia and the short second Sealand dynasty from the extreme south. The latter was made up of Kassites and was succeeded by three Kassite men from another region, the Bazi dynasty. Then men of various backgrounds were kings of Babylon, rarely two from the same family in succession. They included Babylonians and Chaldeans, as well as someone who claimed distant Elamite descent. After 722 the Assyrians became involved, and their attempts to rule Babylon will be described in a later chapter. Most of these men accomplished little, and a political history of this period can easily read like a mere succession of names (for a list of rulers, see pp. 312–13).

The main challenge to the kings was to control their territory. The newly arrived Arameans and Chaldeans dominated the countryside and certain regions were de facto independent. The Aramean tribes were most prominent along the Tigris River and seem to have settled primarily in small village communities on the fringes of the agricultural zone. Assyrian military accounts list many tribal names, most important among them being the Gambulians and the Puqudians. The Arameans did not seek integration in Babylonian society, and mostly did not seek political power. By 850, the Chaldeans were firmly established along the Euphrates and in the south, including in fortified cities, but we do not know where they came from. Some scholars state that they were very closely related to the Arameans, but the ancient sources always keep them distinct, so this is far from certain. The Chaldeans were organized in three leading tribes, Bit-Amukani, Bit-Dakkuri, and Bit-Jakin, and these affiliations remained important throughout their history. They did try to gain political control over Babylon and were often successful in capturing its throne. Consequently, they were often the leading opposition to Assyrian expansion in Babylonia. Their greater integration into Babylonian society is visible in the fact that they often adopted Babylonian names. Because of their control of the area at the head of the Persian Gulf, the Chaldeans cut off Babylonia from the trade routes there. The land of Dilmun, which had been part of the Kassite zone of influence, became a distant region that rarely appeared in the texts from the first millennium, and the Babylonian king could not exercise control there.

The few texts we have from this period mention violence and warfare, not only between cities and tribal groups, but also between different cities. For instance, Nabu-shuma-imbi, governor of Borsippa in northern Babylonia in the early eighth century, wrote:

> Disorders, disturbances, revolt, and turmoil occurred in Borsippa, the city of truth and justice. During the reign of king Nabu-shuma-ishkun, the Dakkurian, the Babylonians, the Borsippians, (the people of) the town Duteti (which is on) the banks of the Euphrates, all the Chaldeans, Arameans, (and) the people of Dilbat *sharpened*(?) their weapons for many days (to fight) with one another (and) slew one another. Moreover, they fought with the Borsippians over their fields.[1]

References to warfare against tribal groups are plentiful in other texts. Part of the anti-tribal rhetoric, accusing them of purely hostile and destructive behavior, probably resulted from the usual negative attitude toward newcomers of the residents of ancient cities. But the highly unstable nature of the period and its warlike character cannot be denied.

Within this volatile situation the Assyrians often meddled with military actions. Already in the second half of the ninth century they campaigned in the region, sometimes against tribes in support of cities, sometimes against the Babylonian king. In the mid-ninth century, the Babylonian King Marduk-zakir-shumi I asked for the help of Shalmaneser III to quell a rebellion by his younger brother. That Shalmaneser III regarded him as an equal is clear from a representation on the base of his throne at Kalhu in which he is shown grasping the Babylonian king's hand. The latter helped Shalmaneser III's successor to come to the throne of Assyria, forcing on him an unfavorable treaty. But Babylonian power was too ephemeral to maintain this attitude for long, and by 813 the Assyrian Shamshi-Adad V had captured and deported two Babylonian kings in succession. A chronicle mentions that there were no kings in Babylon for more than a decade,[2] although king lists give some names. Assyrian intervention thus often thwarted the power of Babylonian kings.

Within this disarray, cities stood out as isolated areas where a traditional political and cultural life was preserved. In political terms, they seem to have been important as a support for royal power, which retained its urban character of the past. The ancient cities of Babylonia were greatly reduced in size and economically weak. They did, however, provide the king with points of control in an unruly countryside. In return, the citizens could demand special privileges, which, while their precise characteristics are unclear, seem to have been very encompassing. Kings were not allowed to tax or demand corvée labor and military service; they could not arrest someone or seize property. These privileges seem to have been renewed after the accession of each new king as a personal agreement, and they survived into the period of Assyrian domination. The list of cities awarded them included Babylon, Borsippa, Nippur, Sippar, and Uruk, all of them important religious centers. The gods were considered to be the guardians of the agreement, and a literary text we call "The Advice to a Prince" (date of composition unknown) clearly sets out that the king would be severely punished were he to break it. Although men acted as royal governors in the cities and owed allegiance to the king in Babylon, they must have had substantial autonomy at many times during the period.

These cities continued the cultural and religious traditions of Babylonia, although not much wealth could be devoted to this activity. Until Assyria's conquest of the region, very little building work was undertaken, for instance, and it was mostly restricted to the restoration of older structures and city-walls. In religious practices, the role of the god Marduk had substantially increased in the late second millennium, especially under King Nebuchadnezzar I, who brought back his statue from Elam. In the early first millennium Marduk's son, Nabu, the scribe of the gods, rose in prominence, as did Nabu's cult-city, Borsippa. His statue had to visit Babylon during the New Year's festival, which had become the most important royal ritual, and when Nabu's statue failed to participate in the festival it was reported. Scribal activity was also limited because of the lack of economic and building activity. The number of legal and administrative records is paltry, and official inscriptions are rare and mostly very short. Yet, earlier literary and scholarly texts continued to be copied out. When in the seventh century King Assurbanipal of Assyria compiled his library at Nineveh, he ordered his officials to go into the Babylonian temples and private houses of priests and scholars to collect tablets that were rare or unavailable in Assyria. This seems to indicate that the temples had become the patrons of scribal activity.

From the late eighth century on, the state of Elam in the east regularly supported Babylonian and Chaldean opposition to Assyria. The marshes of the south linked the two areas together and rebels could easily flee from Babylonia to Elam to escape Assyria's army. Moreover, the Babylonians easily persuaded Elamite armies to do battle with Assyria, and often paid for these services. We know the history of Elam in the first millennium almost exclusively through Assyrian and Babylonian sources. Although some Elamite kings left inscriptions, these are few in number and contain little information. For the period of Elamite resurgence on the international scene from about 740 to 647, we know of only five kings from native sources, while sources from Mesopotamia record fifteen men who claimed the throne. Despite Elam's political instability – fifteen kings in one hundred years – the state was able to cause trouble for Assyria and to acquire wealth that made it the envy of its neighbors.

After the sack of Susa by Nebuchadnezzar I around 1100, we hear almost nothing about Elam until it joined Babylonia in its struggles against Assyria. The first attested ruler was Humban-nikash, who helped in the fight against Sargon II (ruled 721–05). His successor Shutruk-Nahhunte II, in his own name and with the title "King of Anshan and Susa," referred back to the glorious past of the Middle Elamite kingdom. He started to leave royal inscriptions at Susa and at Malamir, a site on the way to Fars where Anshan was located. It is unclear whether he controlled the latter area as well, despite his official claim to it. The prolonged war with Assyria led to victories and defeats on both sides, and often an indeterminate outcome. The various witnesses regularly differ on who won individual battles. For example, for the battle at Der in 720 between Assyria and a coalition of Babylonians and Elamites, the Assyrian Sargon II and the Chaldean Marduk-apla-iddina both claimed victory in their own inscriptions, while the Babylonian Chronicle credited it to the Elamite king, stating that the Chaldean did not even arrive on time. In 691, Sennacherib of Assyria confronted a coalition of Iranian states led by Humban-nimena of Elam at Halule on the Tigris. Again the Assyrian claimed victory, while the Babylonian Chronicle gave it to the Elamite. The battle was not decisive, as it did not prevent Sennacherib from devastating Babylon, though it did stop him from invading Elam. Afterwards there was a period of relative peace, which only ended in 664 when Elam invaded Babylonia. Ten years later the Assyrian Assurbanipal invaded Elam and fought a battle at the river Ulai, which runs near Susa. During this battle the king of Elam, Tepti-Humban-Inshushinak, was killed and decapitated. Assyrian reliefs illustrate how his head was transported to Nineveh for display in the royal garden. When Assurbanipal and his brother became engaged in a civil war in Babylonia from 652 to 648, Elam supported Babylonia. Assurbanipal defeated his brother and turned against Elam, ransacking the countryside. In 647 he devastated Susa and all other remaining centers. The destruction of the capital was as thorough as possible: the Assyrians salted the fields to make them useless and deported the population wholesale to Samaria in the west of the empire. They even emptied the royal tombs of their bones. Yet, a small and weak state remained in existence, and Elam survived longer than Assyria, until the Persians integrated it into their empire.

Elamite internal political life was characterized by great instability. Various families contended for the throne and those who failed often sought support in Assyria for their claims. The power of the local lords seems to have been great, and they acquired wealth that seemed fabulous in the eyes of the Assyrians.

Such wealth must have partly derived from the control of trade routes, but we have no documents to study this in detail.

Elam probably controlled only the plain of Khuzestan on the western flank of the Zagros Mountains. The highlands of Anshan were home to the Persians, and groups that had only recently entered the area inhabited the Zagros Mountains further north. They formed various states that were at first very loose coalitions of peoples, with names only known to us from Assyrian sources. These mention Medes, Manneans, Persians, and others, originally with large numbers of kings, later as consolidated states. It is out of this complex political situation that the principal opponents to Assyria would later develop.

To the north of Assyria in eastern Anatolia there existed one of the most enigmatic important states of the ancient Near East: Urartu. While it is clear that it played a crucial role in the first half of the first millennium, and at one point was the most powerful state in the region, the reconstruction of its history is extremely difficult. Most information needs to be culled from Assyrian accounts, which also provide the only chronological framework we have. They mention Urartian rulers only in conflict situations. The Urartians themselves left inscriptions, at first in the Assyrian language, script, and formulary, and from the late ninth century on in the Urartian language. These are primarily building inscriptions with mentions of military campaigns and they provide little insight into the history of the state. The textual information is thus biased toward an Assyrian view. Archaeological exploration in Urartu has focused solely on the mountain fortresses, and so, again, stresses military aspects of the state.

High mountains and narrow valleys, with rivers that do not form a sequential system, dominate Urartu's territory (document 11.1). The headwaters of many rivers originate there, but they flow in all directions, and only the Euphrates is navigable. The original center of the state was Lake Van, whose waters are too saline for drinking and agriculture. The people lived in villages in the valleys, which they often could not leave during the winter because of snow. Traffic through the region was difficult, and this fact protected it from the advances of the Assyrian army, among others. The state extended in all directions and clashed with Assyria in southern Anatolia and north-west Iran, where it came close to the Assyrian heartland. Its northern and eastern borders are not clear to us, but in its heyday Urartu incorporated the region of the modern state of Armenia. Modern Yerevan is located where ancient Urartian Erebuni used to be. The name of the city is the same after more than 2000 years.

The first references to a political organization in this region come from the thirteenth century, when Assyrian kings campaigned to the north of Syria and encountered what they called Nairi and Uruatri, a variant of the later name Urartu. The separate political entities joined forces most likely as a reaction to Assyrian aggression. From the ninth century on, Assyrian kings mention fewer and more formidable opponents in the region of eastern Anatolia. The ruler who unified the state of Urartu and initiated its royal dynasty was Sarduri I, attested in the accounts of Shalmaneser III (ruled 858–24). His immediate successors turned the state into an important power. They campaigned incessantly in all

Document 11.1   *An Assyrian description of the Zagros Mountains*

To the Assyrians who lived in the lowlands, the Zagros and Taurus mountains to the east and north presented formidable barriers and an unfamiliar natural environment. Military campaigns with regular armies were very difficult there, and Assyrian expansion was constrained. In this region they faced the Urartian state, however, and when Sargon II decided to attack it in 714, he needed to enter the inhospitable mountains. In his report on the campaign, a letter to the god Assur written in high literary language using many metaphors from the animal world, he describes the challenges he faced in these words:

Mount Simirria, a great mountain peak that points upwards like the blade of a lance, and raises its head over the mountain where the goddess Belet-ili lives, whose two peaks lean against heaven on high, whose foundations reach into the midst of the netherworld below, which, like the back of a fish, has no road from one side to the other and whose ascent is difficult from front or back, ravines and chasms are deeply cut in its side, and seen from afar, it is shrouded in fear, it is not good to climb in a chariot or with galloping horses, and it is very hard to make infantry progress in it; yet, with the intelligence and wisdom that the gods Ea and Belet-ili destined for me and who broadened my stride to level the enemy land, I made my engineers carry heavy bronze axes, and they smashed the peaks of the high mountain as if it were limestone and made the road smooth. I took the head of my army and made the chariots, cavalry and battle troops that accompany me fly over it like eagles. I made the support troops and foot soldiers follow them, and the camels and pack mules jumped over the peaks like goats raised in the mountains. I made the surging flood of Assyrians easily cross over its difficult height and on top of that mountain I set up camp.

Translation after François Thureau-Dangin, *Une relation de la huitième campagne de Sargon* (Paris: Librairie Paul Geuthner, 1912), pls. I–II.

directions from the heartland at Lake Van, and annexed territories as far north as Erebuni. In the west they reached northern Syria, and in the south-east they occupied the Zagros Mountains just to the east of Assyria. This expansionist policy was made possible by the internal weakness of Assyria in the late ninth to early eighth centuries. An Assyrian official in northern Syria, Shamshi-ilu, often led the opposition to Urartian expansion rather than the king himself. The Urartians solidified their territorial gains by building a system of mountain fortresses, such as Rusa-patari, "Small city of King Rusa," or Teishebaini, "City of the god Teisheba." Perched on top of natural heights, they controlled the agricultural plains and the trade routes that ran through them. They were administrative centers containing huge storage areas for grain and wine. Agriculture was further developed by the construction of hydraulic works, including aqueducts. This work required a large labor force and it is likely that many of the military expeditions were intended to gather people for these tasks.

In the mid-eighth century, under King Sarduri II, Urartu was at the height of its power. It controlled the trade routes from northern Mesopotamia and Iran to the Mediterranean and to metal sources in Anatolia. Northern Syria itself was within its military reach. The reorganization of Assyria and its subsequent expansion led thus to immediate confrontations with Urartu. These are detailed in Assyrian accounts, naturally with a strong bias. Tiglath-pileser III (ruled 744–27) fought the Urartians in the west, where they had made alliances with Syrian states such as Bit-Agusi, just north of Aleppo. Sargon II attacked the south of Urartu by moving his troops through the Zagros Mountains east of Assyria and plundered the city of Musasir, an important religious center of that state. Subsequently, Urartu was no longer a target of Assyrian campaigning but was closely watched by its spies, who sent reports to Nineveh. Assyria had contained the threat on its northern flank and did not intend, or was unable, to strike the final blow.

Urartu's later fate may have been determined more by people from the north. Scholars have suggested various groups as being responsible for its demise. Among them are the Cimmerians from northern Anatolia, who in the early to mid-seventh century seem to have controlled the central Zagros and may have annihilated Urartu on the way. The Medes and Scythians have also been suggested, but there is no solid evidence. The end of Urartu was violent, however, as many of its fortresses were burned down. Certainly, by the late sixth century, the Armenians had replaced the Urartians and the region was part of the Persian empire.

Urartian culture and religion are relatively poorly known. The language has no known cognates except for the Hurrian of the second millennium. The two languages had a common ancestor and Urartian was spoken somewhere when we have only Hurrian evidence. The textual record from Urartu consists mostly of royal inscriptions, some of which are also known in an Assyrian version. A small number of economic documents and hundreds of royal sealings have been found, indicating that the state had a central administration. Many names of gods are attested in the inscriptions, but few are otherwise known. Three deities headed the pantheon, two of whom were known to the Hurrians as well: Teisheba, who is the Hurrian stormgod Teshub, and Shiwini, the Hurrian sungod Shimiki. The most important god in battle accounts was Haldi, probably a god of war and not known elsewhere in the Near East. His main cult center was Musasir, which was sacked by Sargon II in 714. The excavated fortresses show remains of temples, perhaps originally shaped as square towers. Urartu's most impressive material remains are its metalwork, especially bronze, which was cast as vessels, furniture attachments, armor, statuettes, and so on. The location of the state gave it direct access to many mines, and it controlled trade routes from central Anatolia and Iran where other mineral resources were found. The focus on metalwork is therefore not surprising. Unfortunately, many of the remains were illicitly excavated and we do not know their context.

Consequently, our understanding of Urartu remains weak. What is undeniable, however, is that it was one of the most powerful states of the Near East in the first three centuries of the first millennium, and that it played an important role in the early development of the Assyrian empire.

11.2   The West

The western part of the Near East was characterized in political terms by a set of small states with varied cultural backgrounds. They were inhabited and governed by groups who spoke different languages and had varied traditions and ancestries. The states were still mostly quite small, dominated by one city that acted as the political capital. We can distinguish between those that continued the political and cultural traditions of the late second millennium, primarily the Neo-Hittite and Phoenician states, and those that were newcomers, principally the Aramean states. It is, however, clear that political power increasingly shifted toward the Arameans, until the Assyrians conquered the region in the late eighth century.

The so-called Neo-Hittite states were located in southern Anatolia and north-western Syria, from the Upper Euphrates Valley to the Mediterranean coast. Assyrian accounts call the region Hatti, acknowledging thus a connection with the second-millennium Hittite state. Continuity is visible in the script and language, and in the organization of political power. The Neo-Hittite states used for their official records a writing system that had been of limited use in the second millennium: the so-called Hittite hieroglyphs. It rendered the Luwian language, which was similar to the Hittite of the second millennium. Most of the texts were monumental inscriptions in stone, recording military deeds and building activity, and there were also some letters and economic documents. Politically, the rulers of some of the states presented themselves as descendants of the Hittite kings. Crucial in this transmission was the city Carchemish, where a viceroy of the king of Hattusa, often a prince, had resided in the second millennium. With the collapse of the Hittite state the "King of Carchemish," Kuzi-Teshub, became independent and filled the power vacuum in northern Syria. His state was soon fragmented, however, and a set of successors developed along the Euphrates and to its west. Most prominent was Melid around the city Malatiya, where rulers claimed descent from Kuzi-Teshub. Further west, on the southern Anatolian plateau, there were a number of states where kings with names such as Mursili proclaimed themselves "Great Kings," in second-millennium tradition. These states were likely to be remnants of Tarhuntassa, a state that had coexisted with the Hittite state in the late second millennium.

Very little is known about the political organization of these states. The cities had citadels with palaces and temples surrounded by massive walls, and in that sense they continued second-millennium practices. Although there are no written records to demonstrate how the elites ruled, there are indications that they lived

Figure 11.1   Neo-Hittite orthostat from Guzana (Tell Halaf). The Metropolitan Museum of Art, Rogers Fund (1943.135.1). Photograph, all rights reserved, The Metropolitan Museum of Art

in a luxury that was the envy of others. The Assyrians admired a typical element of the north Syrian palaces, a portico with columns, so much that they integrated it within their own royal architecture, and referred to it explicitly as an imitation of the style from Hatti. The royal citadels of northern Syria were decorated with orthostats set up on gates and walls, carved with scenes in a style that is typically Neo-Hittite (figure 11.1). These reliefs often contained hieroglyphic inscriptions celebrating the king's acts, and they may have inspired the Assyrians, who saw in the palaces of the Neo-Hittites an example of the expression of royal power. The social rebellions that contributed to the collapse of the second-millennium system seem thus to have bypassed the Neo-Hittite states.

The wealth of the Neo-Hittite region probably derived from its control over east–west trade routes and of mining areas. Several of the prominent cities, such as Carchemish and Malatiya, commanded passages over the Euphrates, and traffic from Anatolia to Syria also had to go through the region. The strategic location and the wealth of these states made them appealing targets for their powerful neighbors. When Assyria expanded westward, it encountered them as soon as the Euphrates was crossed. Neo-Hittite states were thus forced in the ninth century to pay tribute to Shalmaneser III, and in the mid-eighth century Tiglath-pileser III gradually incorporated them into his empire. In the period in between, the Urartian kings extended their influence over these states when Assyria was weak. Moreover, the Aramean tribes increasingly made their influence felt and were able to seize political power in some of the Neo-Hittite states. For example, Hamath, the southernmost Neo-Hittite kingdom in central Syria, was by the eighth century ruled by Arameans.

Another region where late second-millennium political entities survived was the Levantine coast. The Phoenician harbor cities of Tyre, Sidon, Byblos, and Arwad were not destroyed around 1200 and continued to function as before, even though their wealthy customers had disappeared. The change in the status of the latter is vividly portrayed in the Egyptian tale of Wen-Amun. It relates how a priest of the god Amun of Thebes in Egypt around 1100 traveled to Byblos to obtain cedar wood. Robbed on the way, he was unable to pay for the wood, and when he appealed to the customs of gift exchange that had regulated trade in luxury items in the second millennium, the ruler of Byblos told him he was no servant of Egypt and demanded payment. Only after Wen-Amun procured payment from Egypt did he receive the wood. The Phoenicians were famous for their control of luxury goods, such as hardwoods, metals, and craft products, and their highly skilled craftsmen. Thus, when the Biblical authors wanted to portray Solomon as a wealthy and powerful king, they imagined him as receiving wood and specialist builders from Hiram, king of Tyre.

The greatest distinction of the Phoenicians, however, was their ability as seafaring merchants. With technically improved ships that had a large loading capacity, they sailed as far west as Morocco and Spain, where they established colonies from the tenth century on. These were true trading ports, where merchants collected resources from the interior and shipped them home. Likewise, in the Near East itself groups of Phoenicians resided in other cities and states in order to conduct business. Unlike the records of early second-millennium Assyrian merchants in Anatolia, those of the Phoenicians are no longer extant, as they were written on perishable parchment and papyrus. At first the Neo-Hittite and Aramean states provided lucrative markets, as their elites desired luxury goods; later on the growing Assyrian empire continued the demand. When the Assyrians came to control Syria in the eighth century, they exacted large amounts of tribute but left the Phoenician cities independent. This arrangement provided them with the foreign goods they wanted without having to manage a trade infrastructure in distant lands. The Phoenician colonization of north Africa became more intense with the establishment of Carthage on the Tunisian coast in the early eighth century. The increased Phoenician focus on the west caused intense competition there, at first with the Greeks who founded colonies along the northern Mediterranean, and centuries later with emergent Rome, which sacked Carthage in the mid-second century BC.

Despite the fame of Phoenician arts and crafts in antiquity, relatively few examples are preserved. This is partly due to the fact that the cities have been continually occupied to this day and are very difficult to explore archaeologically. Only portable items are known from outside Phoenicia, and it is not always certain whether they were Phoenician imports or local imitations. The art is best known from carved ivories, where Egyptian motifs were often employed (figure 11.2). They present a good example of the high level of

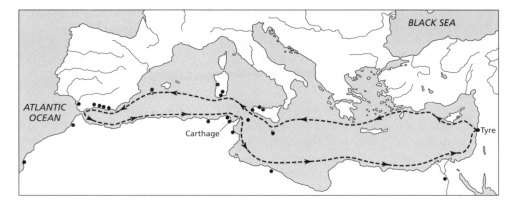

Map 11.2 Phoenician settlements along the Mediterranean coast and the main shipping route (after Barry Cunliffe, *Facing the Ocean* [Oxford: Oxford University Press, 2001], p. 266)

Figure 11.2 Syrian ivory in the Phoenician style. The Metropolitan Museum of Art, Rogers Fund, 1961 (61.197.5). Photograph, all rights reserved, The Metropolitan Museum of Art

craftsmanship, which one can assume was visible in the other work as well. Phoenician textiles were extremely prized – the Greek name Phoenicia was also used to indicate the purple color used in cloth-dyeing – but no examples are preserved. Also the written remains of these people are scarce, though they were of seminal importance for the development of writing throughout the ancient world. Since they used the linear alphabet on papyrus and parchment, all records of daily activities have disintegrated over time, and few monumental inscriptions carved in stone have survived. Classical sources make reference to Phoenician histories, but the Greek and Roman accounts seem extremely garbled. The longest Phoenician inscription was found in the southern Anatolian site of Karatepe and has a Luwian translation written in Neo-Hittite hieroglyphs. It is an account by Azatiwata, a servant of the king of Danuna, who commemorated the building of the city, named Azatiwataya after him. It dates to the late eighth or early seventh centuries, and we can therefore be certain that the Phoenician language and alphabet had expanded into the rest of Syria and southern Anatolia by then.

The role of the Phoenicians in the spread of the alphabet is their most renowned accomplishment. Having preserved the use of the script in the Dark Age after 1200, the Phoenicians inspired all the alphabetic writing systems of their neighbors. In the Near East, the Hebrew and Aramaic scripts derived from the Phoenician. Of major importance to Europe was the adoption of the Phoenician alphabet by the Greeks, either directly from Phoenicians or through intermediaries in Syria or Anatolia. The classical sources were clear about this debt: the Greeks called their letters Phoenician. The date of the borrowing is controversial, however, and scholarly arguments are based almost solely on the forms of individual letters, which were notoriously diverse. The earliest Greek inscriptions can be dated to the first half of the eighth century, but considering the scarcity of earlier inscriptions in the Near East, it would hardly be surprising if earlier Greek ones have not yet been found. So some scholars have suggested a date of transmission of the alphabet to the Greeks as early as the thirteenth century, which seems unlikely.

The Phoenician city-states were thus very important for the preservation of second-millennium traditions into the first millennium, and were perhaps the least affected by the events of 1200. Other states inland may also have adhered to Canaanite traditions. In Israel and Judah the language, Hebrew, was similar to what was spoken in the region in the second millennium. Gods, myths, and cultic practices attested in the Ugaritic texts, for example, found their way into the Biblical account, most likely because in certain localities they survived into the first millennium. The two kingdoms of Israel and of Judah had separate, yet closely related, histories. These are always reconstructed on the basis of the Hebrew Bible, a very difficult source for the historian to use (see box 11.1). It was written from a Judean point of view, and used religion as its primary point of reference to represent people's actions. In post-exilic times, that is, after the fifth century BC, the religious ideology of the area of Judah was a monotheistic devotion to the god Yahweh, the god of the temple in Jerusalem. At that time

Box 11.1 *The Hebrew Bible as a historical source*

All historians of the Near East in the first millennium are confronted with the question of the historicity of the account in the Hebrew Bible. The text provides a detailed and engaging narrative of the history of two states, Israel and Judah, from their formation in the tenth century to their disappearance in the late eighth and early sixth centuries respectively. It also presents a reconstruction of the earlier histories of the region's inhabitants from the time of creation to the establishment of a large unified kingdom under David and Solomon in the tenth century. Scholars have written countless books and articles on whether or not material can be used in historical reconstructions, and what Biblical passages are more reliable than others. They have produced numerous histories of Israel and Judah, ranging from a paraphrase of the Bible to an almost complete rejection of any of its information as historically useful, and have engaged in bitter and unforgiving disputes over the issue, which cannot be resolved from the Biblical text itself.

There are many elements that make the use of the Bible as a historical source suspect. We do not know the date of composition of most of the component books, and it seems safe to assume that, in the format known to us, they are from the period after the Babylonian exile in the late sixth century. The anonymous authors used earlier works, but we cannot date those accurately, nor establish how they were reworked. More importantly, the authors did not intend the writing to be historically objective but as a polemic in defense of a people and its religion. They saw the history of humankind through the lens of how one related to the god Yahweh. Many of the facts stated in the Bible can be confirmed through extra-Biblical sources, textual and archaeological. But, even here, one has to be careful not to force interpretation to coincide with the Biblical text. The names of kings, queens, and others can be found in the sources of Israel and Judah's neighbors or in short inscriptions from those states themselves. But the context in which they appear is often vague outside the Bible. Scholars have become increasingly critical about the use of the Biblical text in historical reconstructions. For instance, they now often no longer regard the accounts of the Patriarchs as reflective of a second-millennium reality. But many scholars still give great credence to other parts where no outside confirmation is available. For example, many believe in the existence of a large kingdom under David and Solomon, but this cannot be ascertained and seems unlikely in a setting where all Syro-Palestinian states were very small.

However critical the scholar's attitude toward the Biblical text, it is impossible to ignore it completely as it is such a powerful narrative. Many ideas and customs can be derived from it, but the histories of Israel and Judah need to be based on other sources. On the other hand, certain Biblical books provide us with insights about the Assyrian, Babylonian, and Persian empires not available elsewhere. They show the perspective of people living in the shadows of, and conquered by, these empires. For example, the Assyrian meddling with the succession of kingship in Israel and Judah, and its military campaigns there, can be studied through Biblical and Mesopotamian sources. While there are often discrepancies between the two, they clearly deal with the same events and confirm the basic outlines of the interactions between the empires and Israel and Judah. Such information is not available from other Syro-Palestinian states.

all earlier history was judged by how people related to that god, but it is clear that prior to the exile other gods were tolerated as well. Archaeology has revealed, for example, the existence of the cult to Yahweh's wife Asherah both in Israel and in Judah. The Biblical text suggests that the two states were quite different. Its portrayal of Israel before its conquest by Assyria in the late eighth century is as a country where Canaanite cults and traditions flourished. Israel's rulers were in much closer contact with their neighbors than were those of Judah, and they were more open to Canaanite cults like those of Ba'al and El. It is thus possible that Israel was a survivor of a second-millennium state, while the archaeological record of Judah reveals greater changes at the beginning of the first millennium. That state was probably made up of new populations that had settled in the region and introduced new social and cultural practices.

The Biblical text and the intensive archaeological research in the territories of ancient Israel and Judah may suggest that these states were unusual for their time. That was not the case, however. Like all their neighbors, Israel and Judah were small kingdoms centered on their capital cities. According to the Biblical account, which cannot be checked fully from independent sources, Israel had 19 rulers in the two centuries preceding its conquest by the Assyrians in 722. The kings were members of various families, who often relied on out-side support for their claims to the throne. The kingdom was most powerful in the first half of the ninth century. Omri (ruled ca. 885–74), the creator of a new dynasty, founded a capital city at Samaria and strengthened Israel's ties with the Phoenician city Tyre. The Assyrians referred to Israel as "the house of Omri" even after his dynasty had ended. Omri's son and successor, Ahab (ruled ca. 874–53), contributed 2000 chariots and 10,000 troops to the coalition that fought Shalmaneser III at Qarqar in 853, the second largest contingent. Twelve years later a man called Jehu (ruled ca. 841–14) put a violent end to Omri's dynasty by massacring the entire family. Later on in his reign he is represented on the Black Obelisk of Shalmaneser III as submitting to the Assyrian king, the only representation of an Israelite ruler in existence today.

Rule in the kingdom of Judah was more stable and a dynasty, called the "house of David" in an Aramaic inscription of the late ninth century, stayed in power from the state's creation, probably in the ninth century, to its annexation by the Babylonians in 587. The only exception was a seven-year period (ca. 841–35) when Athaliah, the daughter of Omri and wife of the deceased Judean king, ruled on her own. The Bible lists 19 kings for the 350-year period of Judah's existence, who all used Jerusalem as their capital. Judah was smaller and weaker than Israel and in the late ninth century the history of both states became dominated by the kingdom of Damascus, a situation that lasted until Assyria invaded the west in the mid-eighth century. The subsequent history of Israel and Judah was determined by the Mesopotamian empires and will be discussed in later chapters.

It was the Arameans who formed the most important new population group that held political power in the west. During the centuries of the Dark Age, they took control over states throughout Syria and expanded their political influence, at the expense of the Neo-Hittites and others, up until the eighth century. Their states were often referred to as the "House of" an ancestor, and the inhabitants were identified as his sons, acknowledging a tribal background. Some of these ancestors are attested as historical figures. For example, Gusu, the ancestor of Bit-Agusi, was the opponent of the Assyrian Assurnasirpal II around the year 870. But the territorial claims of the tribes and their control of urban centers led to different designations of the states at the same time. When the Bit-Agusi turned Arpad, some 30 kilometers north of Aleppo, into a major city, their kingdom was also called Arpad. Another designation of certain Aramean states, especially in the Bible, included the term Aram, usually coupled with the name of a region or a city, for example Aram-Damascus. When that state became the strongest opponent of Assyria in the area, it was sometimes just given the name Aram, including in the texts of its Aramean neighbors. The multitude of designations shows that the ideological basis of these states was varied. They could be regarded as belonging to a tribe (Bit-X), as territories around a city (e.g., Arpad), or as governed by a particular people (Aram-X).

Despite the variety in designations of the states, the idea that a king, with the support of the local god, held supreme power in them was preeminent. The pictorial arts regularly show the king on the throne or as making an offering to the gods. The concept of inherited rule was firmly established. When Assyria expanded into the west, the local rulers at first remained in place, but as Assyrian vassals. This led to a dual status: to the people of the state they were kings, to the Assyrian overlords they were officials. This duality is expressed in the statue of Hadad-yith'i, ruler of Guzana in northern Syria, probably in the mid-ninth century. On it was carved a bilingual inscription in Aramaic and Akkadian. The first calls him "king of Guzana," the second "governor" (see document 11.2).

The political histories of these states are usually reconstructed on the basis of testimonies from outsiders, especially the Hebrew Bible and Assyrian military accounts. Local inscriptions are very limited in number. All sources attest to a great deal of internecine warfare. While the states would unite against the common enemy of Assyria, they turned against each other when there was no outside threat. It seems likely that smaller states formed coalitions to protect themselves within these conflicts, and that in general larger polities developed over time. Power seems to have shifted from the Neo-Hittites to Arameans in northern Syria, and in the south Damascus became dominant.

To the south of Syria new states, with closely related histories, arose under people with non-Aramean backgrounds. In Israel, Judah, Ammon, Moab, and Edom, people spoke Canaanite languages instead of Aramaic. On the southern Mediterranean shore, Philistines controlled five city-states that regulated access into Egypt and were at the end of overland trade routes from the Arabian Desert. Arabs from the peninsula, who were camel nomads, were in close contact with the Syro-Palestinian region and provided luxury goods such as incense from Yemen.

Document 11.2   *The Akkadian–Aramaic bilingual inscription of Hadad-yith'i*

In northern Syria the life-size statue of a standing man was found, on which was carved a bilingual Akkadian–Aramaic inscription of Hadad-yith'i, ruler of Guzana, probably dating to the mid-ninth century. The two versions are closely related in the first half of the text, while in the second half they differ more extensively. The basis of the translation here is the Akkadian version.

To Adad, the canal inspector of heaven and earth, who causes it to rain abundance, who gives well-watered pastures to the people of all cities, and who provides portions of food offerings to the gods, his brothers, inspector of the rivers who makes the whole world flourish, the merciful god to whom it is sweet to pray, he who resides in the city Guzana.

Hadad-yith'i, the governor of the land Guzana, the son of Sassu-nuri, governor of the land Guzana, has dedicated and given (this statue) to the great lord, his lord, for his good health and long days, for making his years numerous, for the well-being of his house, his descendants and his people, to remove his body's illnesses, and that my prayers will be heard and that my words will be favorably received.

May whoever finds it in disrepair in the future, renew it and put my name on it. Whoever removes my name and puts his own on it, may Adad, the hero, be his judge.

Statue of Hadad-yith'i, the governor of Guzana, Sikani, and Zarani. For the continuation of his throne and the lengthening of his reign, so that his words will be agreeable to gods and men, he has made this statue better than before. In front of Adad who resides in the city Sikani, lord of the Habur River, he has erected his statue.

Whoever removes my name from the objects in the temple of Adad, my lord, may my lord Adad not accept his food and drink offerings, may my lady Shala not accept his food and drink offerings. May he sow but not reap. May he sow a thousand (measures), but reap only one. May one hundred ewes not satisfy one spring lamb; may one hundred cows not satisfy one calf, may one hundred women not satisfy one child, may one hundred bakers not fill up one oven! May the gleaners glean from rubbish pits. May illness, plague and insomnia not disappear from his land!

Translation after Jonas Greenfield and Aaron Shaffer, "Notes on the Akkadian–Aramaic Bilingual Statue from Tell Fekherye," *Iraq* 45 (1983), pp. 109–16.

The history of the entire west was determined by its relationship to Assyria, which from the ninth century on campaigned there with great regularity, a process we will study in the next chapter. The numerous states would ally themselves to meet the threat, although some would seek support in Assyria to remain independent of their neighbors. Yet, the alliances could be massive.

When Shalmaneser III crossed the Euphrates in 853 and engaged in a major battle at Qarqar, by his own account he was confronted with:

> 1200 chariots, 1200 cavalry, and 20,000 troops of Hadad-ezer of Damascus; 700 chariots, 700 cavalry, and 10,000 troops of Irhuleni, the Hamathite; 2000 chariots and 10,000 troops of Ahab, the Israelite; 500 troops of Byblos; 1000 troops of Egypt; 10 chariots and 10,000 troops of the land of Irqanatu; 200 troops of Matinu-ba'al of the city of Arwad; 200 troops of the land of Usanatu; 30 chariots and [ ],000 troops of Adon-ba'al of the land of Shiannu; 10,000 camels of Gindibu' of Arabia; [ ] hundred troops of Ba'asa of Bit-Ruhubi, the Ammonite.[3]

While this coalition was most likely successful in holding Assyria back, it did not last long and local competition soon resurfaced.

The entire west from southern Anatolia to the Egyptian border has to be seen as a multicultural zone where people with many different backgrounds interacted closely, mixing languages, cultures, and devotion to various gods. Some maintained second-millennium traditions – the kings of Hamath had Hurrian names until 800 – but there was no resentment of, or resistance to, new ones. A king could write inscriptions in Luwian and Phoenician at the same time. Artistic styles mixed various influences without difficulty. People seem to have maintained an international spirit and were outward-looking. They welcomed merchants from abroad. In coastal towns, such as Al-Mina at the mouth of the Orontes River, the Greeks were allowed to set up trading settlements. East Arabian traders entered Philistine cities. People of the Near East also sought goods in distant places, traveling there themselves, with the Phoenicians playing a primary role in this activity.

It is thus no surprise that the cultural contact between the Near East and the emerging Greek world was extensive. The transmission of the alphabet has been mentioned above. But many works of art, especially metalwork and ivories, also entered Greece from the Near East and influenced local production to such an extent that Greek art of the seventh century is called "Orientalizing." Other, less tangible, influences on Greek culture are clear, yet it is often difficult to demonstrate that they were directly borrowed, and, if so, when. Greek material may also have contained survivals from the second millennium, when the Aegean was clearly integrated in the regional system of the Near East. The elements where Near Eastern influence on Greek culture has been suggested include loan words, literary motifs, ideals of kingship, diplomacy, astronomy, divination, cultic procedures, mathematics, measures and weights, economic practices such as interest, and so on. The enthusiasm of scholars for finding connections depends largely on whether they see Greece as the beginning of western civilization or as located in a cultural evolution that dates much further back in time. It is usually difficult, if not impossible, to prove that Greeks were aware of a particular Near Eastern practice and consciously copied it. For example, Hesiod's *Theogony*, written around the year 700, has close parallels with second-millennium Hittite mythology. Did he personally know those texts, which would then have been preserved in Anatolia into the first millennium, or was he influenced by traditions that at some distant moment in time had inspired Hittite tradition as well? The influence of the Near East on early first-millennium Greece has certainly been underrated in classical scholarship, but it is also easy to go too far in the other direction and find a Near Eastern background too readily. Be that as it may, the Syrian cultures of the early first millennium were not provincial or self-centered. The region flourished in many respects, economically and culturally. A new urban culture had arisen, and there was great artistic activity. Mesopotamia was no longer seen as the source of all civilized life, but local tastes were preferred. The region was so successful that it presented an inviting target for the emergent Assyria.

NOTES

1 Grant Frame, *Rulers of Babylonia: From the Second Dynasty of Isin to the End of Assyrian Domination (1157–612 BC)* (*The Royal Inscriptions of Mesopotamia. Babylonian Periods*, volume 2) (Toronto: University of Toronto Press, 1995), p. 124.
2 A. K. Grayson, *Assyrian and Babylonian Chronicles* (Locust Valley: J. J. Augustin, 1975), no. 24.
3 K. Lawson Younger, Jr., "Kurkh Monolith," in W. W. Hallo, ed., *The Context of Scripture* (Leiden: E. J. Brill, 2000), volume 2, pp. 263–4.

12

The Rise of Assyria

3000	2500	2000	1500	1000	500

ca. 880–830	Sustained Assyrian military expansion under Assurnasirpal II and Shalmaneser III
ca. 878	Assurnasirpal chooses Kalhu as his new capital
827–823	Rebellions in Assyrian heartland
823–745	Period of Assyrian decline
717	Sargon II founds new capital at Dur-Sharrukin
704	Sennacherib moves Assyrian capital to Nineveh

The history of the Near East in the first millennium until the late seventh century was dominated by one power: Assyria. Through its military might, this state gradually expanded its control over a vast area from western Iran to the Mediterranean and from Anatolia to Egypt, dominating political and economic life. The development of this empire was accomplished by a series of powerful rulers who led their army on campaigns almost every year. Progress was neither smooth nor linear. Two phases can be distinguished: the first in the ninth century, and a second, much more expansive, phase starting in the mid-eighth. While there are many similarities in Assyria's behavior in these two periods, only the second phase displays a conscious and systematic approach toward the formation of a unified empire. These centuries in Assyrian history are often referred to as the Neo-Assyrian period. This chapter will highlight some of the patterns of behavior that characterized the entire period, and focus on the first phase of Assyrian expansion. The next will discuss the empire at its height.

12.1 Patterns of Assyrian Imperialism

Assyria was a militaristic society. The army provided its basic structure and hierarchy. All men could be called up for military service and all state offices were designated as military ones, even if they had non-military duties. The king was at the top of this structure and his primary role was to conduct war for the benefit of the god Assur and the state. Thus there existed an ideology that the king in person should lead his army into battle annually: in theory, every campaign was headed by the king and every year of his reign was identified with a campaign. While it is clear that military activity was constant, the idea that every year a major campaign took place under the leadership of the king was a fiction. That he was actively involved is clear, however, as is shown by the death on the battlefield of King Sargon II, which traumatized his son, who saw it as a punishment of the gods. Beneath the king was a large, pyramid-shaped hierarchy of officers, who between them took care of all state responsibilities. Those with the highest ranks were also governors of provinces in the interior of Assyria. For example, the commander-in-chief was governor of the strategic province that stretched over northern Syria from Harran to the Upper Euphrates Valley. These men were originally members of prominent Assyrian families, but in the mid-eighth century they were replaced by eunuchs appointed by the king in order to curb local powers.

Campaigns were at first only fought during the summer, in the period after the harvest when agricultural tasks were limited and men were available, and when mountain passes were open and rivers could be easily crossed. In the late phase, when a standing army had been created, it could fight at any time. The number of soldiers is sometimes estimated at several hundreds of thousands for the seventh century, as accounts of the deaths among opponents can number above 100,000. This figure seems unreasonably high, however. At the battle of Qarqar in 853, Assyria's opponents fielded some 50,000 men, so the Assyrian army was probably similar in size. In any case, the number of men required for military service surpassed the resources of Assyria's heartland, and conquered people had to be integrated into the army. Texts from the armory at Kalhu indicate, for instance, that soon after the conquest of Samaria in Israel, chariot teams from there were incorporated into the Assyrian army. Since Assyria had no navy, it engaged Phoenician ships and sailors for battles in the Mediterranean and at least in one attempt to subdue Chaldean rebels in the marshes near the Persian Gulf. Deportees from conquered regions were also regularly used in especially mobile forces that could be moved around the empire at short notice. So the army contained a diverse group of men speaking different languages and with multiple origins.

We know very little about how troops were levied and organized. The responsibility for recruitment at first was given to governors, but with the reorganization of the state in the eighth century it was directly in the hands of the central government. Soldiers were grouped into units of fifty men each. We have no information on how these units were integrated into larger ones to make up the entire army. The provisioning of these men with uniforms and weaponry must have been a major enterprise requiring the labor of a large number of craftsmen. The cities in the heartland had large armories where troops and horses were trained and equipment was stored. A few records give us some insight into the quantities of barley needed to feed the troops and animals. In the time of Sargon, those stationed in the eastern city of Kar-Assur required daily 70,500 liters of barley for rations and 57,800 liters for fodder, a monthly outlay of 3,849,000 liters. And that was only for one segment of the army. Royal granaries provided most of the barley, but about a fifth was the responsibility of the government officials. Although there are a few records that provide information, we know remarkably little about the organization and support of the army, despite its prominence in Assyrian society.

Notwithstanding the royal rhetoric, the army rarely moved out in full force or engaged in large battles in the open field. Its tactic was often one of terrorizing the enemy into submission. Territories were approached with massive forces and, if they did not yield immediately, cities and villages that presented easy targets were attacked. When conquered, the inhabitants were severely punished as examples. They were tortured, raped, beheaded, and flayed, and their corpses, heads, or skins were publicly displayed. Houses were razed, fields were covered with salt, and orchards cut down. If this did not convince the capital city to give in, a siege was laid (figure 12.1). Emissaries were sent to address the population directly and to urge it to capitulate against the ruler's wish. As sieges were expensive, they were carried out selectively. The Assyrian king, never willing to admit failure in the official record, stated that he locked up the enemy like a bird in a cage. The royal accounts describe complete destruction after a tenacious city had been conquered, but probably use a great deal of hyperbole. The psychological edge of Assyria's behavior was important. This has been called "calculated frightfulness," the idea being that the results of defeat would be so calamitous that it was better to yield immediately.

As a direct result of their campaigns, the Assyrians acquired huge quantities of resources from all over the Near East. The royal inscriptions were eloquent about the spoils that were taken from the treasuries, palaces, and temples of conquered cities. The influx of precious goods, metals, artifacts, weaponry, and so on was enormous, as many of Assyria's victims had been extremely wealthy. In addition, cattle, sheep and goats, horses, and camels were taken. Accounts sometimes boast that the result was a glut that made exclusive items available to commoners. After the submission of a foreign state, the Assyrians set a level of tribute, to be paid annually, which often included specialties of the region. For example, the Phoenicians had to provide purple cloth and cedar logs, the Zagros people horses. The amounts were not set out in the few Assyrian treaties we have, so we do not know their size. But the burden must have been a heavy one, as tributary states often rebelled despite Assyria's clear military superiority. Massive resources were thus drawn to the heartland.

The same was true for manpower. Assyria had a desperate need for labor to work in agriculture and on the great building projects it undertook, to replace

Figure 12.1 Assyrian relief from Nineveh depicting a city under siege.
The Metropolitan Museum of Art. Purchase, Joseph Pulitzer Bequest, 1955
(55.121.4a,b). Photograph, all rights reserved, The Metropolitan Museum of Art

Assyrians who were enlisted in the army. It also required inhabitants for the cities
that were built. Throughout ancient Near Eastern history victorious armies had
deported defeated populations, but the Assyrians of the first millennium greatly
expanded this practice, especially after the mid-eighth century. Again, the royal

inscriptions are explicit about the numbers moved. It has been estimated that 4.5 million people were deported in the three centuries of the Assyrian empire.[1] Entire communities of men, women, and children were moved from one corner of the empire to another. Different levels of deportation existed. At first only specialist craftspeople were chosen, in order to assist in the building projects. But if a region remained defiant, the majority of the population could be moved. This practice had several strategic benefits for Assyria, while it provided labor and people to inhabit its new cities. It reduced opposition in peripheral territories as rebellious populations were resettled in foreign environments where they needed imperial protection against local hostility. Moreover, they would not escape, as they were unfamiliar with the country. The threat of deportation could be used when the army was approaching an area in order to encourage immediate submission.

The territories of deported people were selectively resettled with other groups when they were crucial for trade or the production of materials and goods. When there was no clear benefit, they were left with only a minimum of people. For example, the northern parts of the ancient state of Israel were almost completely deserted after the Assyrian conquest. A side-effect of the deportations was a mixture of populations throughout the Near East, including the spread of the Arameans with their language and alphabetic script. If our estimates of the numbers of people involved are correct, they must have caused great demographic changes. Those who were deported were forced to walk the entire distance from their homeland to their destination, the men often in chains. Part of the population from Samaria in Israel, for example, was resettled in Media in the Zagros Mountains, some 1200 kilometers away. The supervision and feeding of large numbers of people during a voyage of several months must have required enormous organization, surprisingly not recorded for us.

The Assyrian heartland was the main beneficiary of the massive resources of labor and goods acquired. There was a direct correlation between campaigns and major building projects. Successful military leaders were also great builders, and the largest projects were undertaken after they returned with their immense spoils. The construction projects of this period included several new capital cities. Assur, the traditional capital, was too small for the enormous state apparatus and soon after Assyria initiated its first phase of expansion the capital was moved. The builder, Assurnasirpal II (ruled 883–59), chose the site of a Middle Assyrian city, Kalhu, but completely rebuilt it, a task that took some fifteen years. He laid out a city-wall 8 kilometers long and enclosing an area of 360 hectares, and on top of the large citadel in the south-west corner constructed his palace, several temples, and a ziggurat. The palace was over 200 meters long and at least 120 meters wide, built around a vast courtyard. Not only was its architecture monumental, but the state rooms were also decorated with stone wall reliefs depicting battles, royal hunts, and cult scenes. Huge human-headed bulls in stone guarded the entrances. A text commemorates the inauguration of the palace with a banquet to which 69,574 people were invited:

When I consecrated the palace of Kalhu, 47,074 men and women, who were invited from every part of my land, 5000 dignitaries and envoys of the people of the lands Suhu, Hindanu, Patinu, Hatti, Tyre, Sidon, Gurgumu, Malidu, Hubushku, Gilzanu, Kummu, and Musasiru, 16,000 people from Kalhu, and 1500 palace officials, all of them – altogether 69,574 (including) those summoned from all the lands and the people of Kalhu – for ten days I gave them food, I gave them drink, I had them bathed, I had them anointed. (Thus) I did honor to them and send them back to their lands in peace and joy.[2]

Later kings constructed additional palaces and Assurnasirpal's immediate successor, Shalmaneser III, built a large arsenal in the south-east corner of the city. Kalhu remained Assyria's capital for 150 years, when Sargon II (ruled 721–05) decided to build an entirely new one on virgin soil, and called it Dur-Sharrukin, "Fortress of Sargon." (document 12.1) This again was an immense city, with a wall of some 7 kilometers enclosing 300 hectares, and contained two citadels with monumental buildings decorated with reliefs and bull statues. This city was abandoned upon Sargon II's death and his successor, Sennacherib (ruled 704–681), entirely refurbished the old city of Nineveh as his capital. He extended it to 750 hectares enclosed by a 12-kilometer-long wall, and developed two citadels with public buildings, again all decorated. These massive cities were clear markers of the wealth of Assyria. Although we cannot estimate their populations with any degree of certainty, it is likely that they greatly surpassed what could be supported by the surroundings and had to be fed and maintained using the resources of the whole empire. They were also much too large to be populated only by inhabitants from the region, so people were imported from all over to live there and to serve the state bureaucracy.

Simultaneously, public buildings in other cities of the heartland were restored and expanded, and provincial centers in the territory near Assyria, such as Dur-Katlimmu, were completely redesigned. Moreover, when the Assyrians conquered Aramean cities in western Syria, for example, they turned them into Assyrian cities. Til-Barsip of the land of Bit-Adini on the Euphrates, renamed Kar-Shalmaneser in 856 after its conqueror Shalmaneser III, was probably expanded in size and provided with Assyrian public buildings and residences. The state thus displayed its power by constructing highly visible symbols of its presence.

The building activity required manpower and wealth that only the empire could provide. The cities and palaces were certainly also lavishly decorated and became the depositories of precious goods from all over the Near East. The archaeological record is much less complete for movable items, rugs, carpets, jewelry, and so on, but there are some indications of the wealth that was displayed in the Assyrian court. Ivory attachments to furniture, carved in the various styles of the western part of the empire, were found in great abundance at Kalhu. Most spectacular has been the find in the same city during the 1980s of the undisturbed tombs of queens from the ninth and eighth centuries. Their bodies were covered with an abundance of gold jewelry, some 35 kilograms in

---

Document 12.1 *King Sargon and Dur-Sharrukin*

The major building project Sargon II undertook was the construction of a massive new capital, called Dur-Sharrukin, "fortress of Sargon." He celebrated its foundation in inscriptions that showed his personal involvement: he developed the idea, laid out the plans, and oversaw the construction. That he was heavily immersed in the project is clear from his official letters, preserved in the cities of Nineveh and Nimrud. A total of 113 letters can be associated with the building of Dur-Sharrukin, a tenth of all preserved letters from his reign. They involve twenty-six provincial governors, which shows how resources from the entire empire were used. Six letters seem to have been written by the king himself, demanding materials or labor.[1] Three of them are translated here.

1 Letter found in Nineveh

The king's word to the governor (of Kalhu): 700 bales of straw and 700 bundles of reed, each bundle more than a donkey can carry, must arrive in Dur-Sharrukin by the first of the month Kislev. Should one day pass by, you will die.

Translation after Simo Parpola, *The Correspondence of Sargon II, Part I. Letters from Assyria and the West* (Helsinki: Helsinki University Press, 1987), no. 26.

2 Letters found in Kalhu

a) The 1100 limestones that Bel-lishir-talaktu is loading, let them be brought to me in Dur-Sharrukin quickly! [   ]. (Addressed to the) second vizier.
b) 700 limestones that Bel-lishir-talaktu is loading, quickly bring them to me in Dur-Sharrukin! (Addressed to the) eunuchs.

Translation after Barbara Parker, "Administrative Tablets from the North-West Palace, Nimrud," *Iraq* 23 (1961), pp. 37 (ND 2606) and 41 (ND 2651).

[1] Simo Parpola, "The Construction of Dur-Sharrukin in the Assyrian Royal Correspondence," in A. Caubet, ed., *Khorsabad, le palais de Sargon II, roi d'Assyrie* (Paris: Louvre, 1995), pp. 47–77.

---

total, which displays the great skills of the craftsmen and gives some idea of the incredible wealth that was available to the royal family. If we remember that most of the luxury items were lost over time, we can only vaguely imagine how spectacular this must have been.

Wealth trickled down to the elite members of Assyrian society, a group whose size we cannot determine. The almost exclusive focus of archaeological research on monumental architecture has led to a paucity of detail concerning private citizens, even those from the upper classes. A few houses have been excavated, but there is scant information about their contents. Textual information from contracts and deeds shows that the high officials of the state had access to considerable wealth in silver and landed property. Unfortunately, the extent of an entire holding cannot be reconstructed. Men are known to have lent large amounts of silver, perhaps more than 500 kilograms at one time. They also were given large landed estates by the king for their services, which they could expand through acquisition of more land, but the sizes of these estates are also a matter of pure guesswork. The donations included entire villages, houses, fields, orchards, and the populations to work them, and were often located in different regions, so they did not form one large, coherent domain. The kings regularly granted tax exemption to the owners of these estates, which certainly increased their disposable wealth. There is little doubt, then, that the upper echelons of Assyrian society benefited from the empire.

Large parts of the population were not in that situation, however. Assyria always remained a fundamentally agricultural society, and the majority of its people lived on the land they worked. Again, we are not directly informed about conditions here and scholars disagree on the status of the lower classes. The Assyrian policy of developing the countryside agriculturally by establishing villages and settling deportees there must have led to a substantial number of people being directly dependent on the state. Next to them seem to have existed free peasants, but the degree of their freedom is often thought to have been so limited as to make them no different from state dependents. Since entire villages could be sold, their residents probably had little freedom.

A group of seventh-century texts, often called census lists, although their purpose is enigmatic, gives detailed inventories of rural families, seemingly all part of the properties of wealthy men. For example:

> Idranu, farmer; his brother; one son; three women, twenty hectares of arable land; one house; one threshing floor; one garden. Total, in the town of Badani, near Harran.[3]

The families recorded are small, with one wife and, on average, fewer than two children accounted for (others had probably already left the household). They worked small plots of land, tended vines and vegetable gardens, and had a few oxen, sheep, and goats. These lists may reflect the condition of most of Assyria's population. The social structure of the state probably had great inequalities, therefore, with a small and extremely wealthy upper class and numerous families living at subsistence level.

12.2 The Historical Record

Since there is a direct correlation in Mesopotamian history between the strength of the state and the size of the documentary record it produced, it is no surprise that the sources for the Assyrian empire are plentiful. They derive almost exclusively from the palace and focus principally on the activities of the king, especially as a warrior and a builder. Military actions also figure prominently in the pictorial record carved on reliefs that were displayed in the palaces (see box 12.1), so we have access to much factual data in that aspect of history. This tends to underrate the Assyrians' other endeavors and leads to a primarily military history of the period.

The most detailed record is provided by the royal annals, year-by-year accounts of military campaigns (see chapter 9). For each year they present a sequence of opponents defeated by the king, sometimes merely giving a list of names, sometimes describing the Assyrian actions in great detail. The yearly campaign became such a fundamental concept in the Neo-Assyrian period that it came to structure the chronology of a king's reign. In his annals he did not

---

Box 12.1 *Assyrian relief sculpture*

The enormous building activity of the Neo-Assyrian kings led to the existence of another type of record available to the historian: the pictorial relief. The palaces at Kalhu, Dur-Sharrukin, and Nineveh were decorated with wall reliefs representing cult activities and military campaigns undertaken by the rulers. Often, short inscriptions identify the persons and cities represented, so that we know what events are depicted and have a record parallel to that from the annalistic accounts.

While Assyrian relief sculpture dates back to the second millennium, it is with Assurnasirpal II that the decoration of the palaces we have excavated becomes more expansive. Carved limestone slabs some two meters high lined the walls of public spaces. In antiquity the reliefs were painted, but only traces of this have remained. Sennacherib's palace at Nineveh has the most extensive record available to us. In it were represented such military campaigns as the siege of Lachish in Judah and attacks on the marshes in southern Babylonia. Why these campaigns were chosen is not clear, as they are not the most important military actions in his reign. While some of the images depicting the siege of Lachish, for example, can be related to archaeological information from that site, we cannot see the reliefs as intended to be accurate historical records. At the same time as the siege is going on, people and goods are represented as being deported as well. The historian thus has to interpret these scenes with the same analytical techniques as those applied to the textual accounts.

Besides war scenes, the reliefs also contain representations of cultic acts and of the king as a hunter. The decorative layout of the palace rooms was carefully planned to portray the idea that the king ruled the entire universe and that he excelled in other areas as well. Moreover, the reliefs had the function of protecting the palace rooms. Integrated within them were massive bull sculptures that were invoked to ward off evil. In order to understand the individual scenes, we have to study them within their architectural context and in relation to the other scenes that surround them.

state "in my fifth year," for example, but "in my fifth campaign." Simultaneously, the ancient Assyrian custom of naming each year after an eponymous
official was continued and lists of these names were made up, some of them
with an indication of where the army campaigned that year (document 12.2).
We have a full sequence for the years 910 to 649. It is chronologically anchored
by the statement that "in the year of Bursagale from Guzana, there was an
uprising in the inner city, and in the month Simanu there was an eclipse of the
sun."[4] This eclipse can be dated to June 15, 763 BC, and we have thus a firm
absolute chronology for the entire period. The Assyrians provided some other
chronological sources, such as a "Synchronistic King List," where the names
of Assyrian and Babylonian kings are listed in parallel from the nineteenth
to the seventh centuries, and a "Synchronistic History," a review of, usually
hostile, exchanges between the two states in certain reigns from the fifteenth
to the eighth centuries.

As the state bureaucracy was large, it produced many records. Some of the
imperial archives, albeit surprisingly few, have been recovered in the cities of
Assur, Kalhu, and Nineveh. The more than three thousand letters written to
the kings by officials throughout the empire provide a rich source of information. They discuss mostly administrative and military matters. It is certain that
in addition to clay tablets inscribed with cuneiform, the Assyrians also produced papyri and parchments with alphabetic writing. These have not survived
in the archaeological record owing to the Near Eastern climate, and we are thus
denied access to what may have been a substantial part of the bureaucratic
apparatus. Moreover, the nature of our record is almost totally palatial, as
archaeologists have concentrated on the spectacular architectural works of the
kings. In the capital cities Kalhu, Dur-Sharrukin, and Nineveh, only the citadels
have been explored, while the immense lower towns have been left untouched.
There is thus virtually no knowledge about people outside the palace sector.
Even though the palace was certainly dominant, our documentation's exclusive
focus on it is undoubtedly misleading.

12.3   Ninth-Century Expansion

The troubles of the twelfth through tenth centuries had forced Assyria to
surrender control over the north-east Syrian area that it had colonized in the
Middle Assyrian period. The administrative centers they had established then
did not disappear, however, and local rulers who showed some affiliation with
Assyria remained in power. How dependent they were on the heartland is a
point of scholarly debate, with many arguing that Assyria had lost all influence.
The countryside was certainly dominated by the Arameans, however, who had
gained power in certain cities as well. The records suggest that into the ninth
century, permanent settlement in north-east Syria was limited. Assyrian armies
campaigning in the Habur Valley, for example, encountered virtually no villages,
so tribal groups must have been the primary inhabitants of the region. The

Document 12.2 *Excerpt from the Eponym Chronicle*

Ten manuscripts found in various sites in Assyria contain lists of years identified by the eponym, with a summary note about what happened then, most often the goal of the major military campaign. Such lists provide us with an accurate way to date a long stretch of Neo-Assyrian history, and give us an idea of the military exploits that were considered most important. In the translation here, which includes information from Eponym lists as well, the years BC are added.

719	[In the year of]	Sargon, king [of Assyria]	[ent]ered
718	[In the year of]	Zer-ibni, governor of Ra[sappa]	[to Ta]bal
717	[In the year of]	Tab-shar-Assur, chamberlain	[Dur-Sharru]kin was founded
716	[In the year of]	Tab-sil-Eshara, governor of the citadel	[to] Mannea
715	[In the year of]	Taklal-ana-beli, governor of Nasibina	[ ] governors appointed
714	[In the year of]	Ishtar-duri, governor of Arrapha	[to Ur]artu, Musasir, Haldia
713	[In the year of]	Assur-bani, governor of Kalhu	[the] nobles in Ellipi, he entered the new house, to Musasir
712	[In the year of]	Sharru-emuranni, governor of Zamua	in the land
711	[In the year of]	Ninurta-alik-pani, governor of Si'mme	[to] Marqasa
710	[In the year of]	Shamash-belu-usur, governor of Arzuhina	to Bit-zeri the king stayed at Kish
709	[In the year of]	Mannu-ki-Assur-le'i, governor of Tille	Sargon took the hands of Bel
708	In the year of	Shamash-upahhir, governor of Habruri	Kummuhi conquered and a governor was appointed
707	In the year of	Sha-Assur-dubbu, governor of Tushan	the king returned from Babylon, the vizier and nobles, the booty of Dur-Jakin was carried off, Dur-Jakin was destroyed, on the 22nd of Teshrit, the gods of Dur-Sharrukin entered the temples
706	In the year of	Mutakkil-Assur, governor of Guzana	the king stayed in the land, the nobles [ ], on the 6th of Ayar, Dur-Sharrukin was completed
705	In the year of	Nashur-Bel, governor of Amidu	the king [ ] against Qurdi the Kullumean, the king was killed, the camp of the king of Assyria [ ], on the 12th of Ab, Sennacherib [became] king

Translation after Alan Millard, The Eponyms of the Assyrian Empire, 910–612 *(Helsinki: University of Helsinki Press, 1994), pp. 46–8, 60.*

kings of Assyria always maintained control over the plains to the east of the Tigris from Assur northward somewhat beyond Nineveh, a region the size of Wales. In the last third of the tenth century, the situation began to be reversed when the Assyrians initiated a policy of regular military campaigns. Their primary target was the area to the west, which they considered to have been taken from Assyria by the Arameans. This reconquest was accompanied by a resettlement of the region. For example, Assur-dan II (ruled 934–12) stated in his annals:

> I brought back the exhausted people of Assyria who had abandoned their cities and houses in the face of want, hunger, and famine, and had gone up to other lands. I settled them in cities and houses that were suitable and they dwelt in peace. I constructed palaces in the various districts of my land. I hitched up plows in the various districts of my land and thereby piled up more grain than ever before.[5]

The cities Assyrians had controlled in the late second millennium were turned into centers from which the region could be ruled permanently through the construction of palaces and official buildings. There was a conscious policy of developing the north Syrian territory: canals were built along the Habur River, for instance, in order to facilitate the transport of heavy goods, and the Middle Assyrian road system was repaired to maintain direct contacts with the heartland of Assyria.

This policy culminated in the reign of two kings who laid the basis for the Neo-Assyrian empire over a period of some sixty years: Assurnasirpal II (ruled 883–59) and Shalmaneser III (ruled 858–24). They consolidated control over the region from the Zagros Mountains to the Euphrates and from the foothills of the Taurus Mountains to the Babylonian border. This area then became the platform from which to campaign in more distant parts. The first ruler carried out a systematic conquest in all directions of the zone that immediately surrounded Assyria, relying on the positions that his predecessors had secured. His troops never covered the same area twice unless a rebellion forced them to do so. Assurnasirpal campaigned in the upper valleys of the Diyala and Lesser Zab controlling access to the Zagros Mountains and Babylonia, in the north-east up to the Taurus Mountains, in the north along the Tigris, where he built a fortress at the point where that river enters Mesopotamia, and in the west. From there he marched first on the Middle Euphrates, then turned against the powerful state of Bit-Adini. He secured the areas by building Assyrian centers in strategic locations, such as river crossings. At the end of his reign, Assurnasirpal had conquered all of the regions that had been considered to be part of Assyria from the late second millennium on. He had only once crossed the Euphrates in the west to obtain booty there.

His son and successor, Shalmaneser III, had a thirty-five-year reign that was filled with military campaigns, especially in the west and the north. In the west, he regularly crossed the Euphrates in order to gain access to the Mediterranean Sea and to the wealth of the small states in the region. Political fragmentation made Syria militarily weak and thus an easy target, but under the leadership of

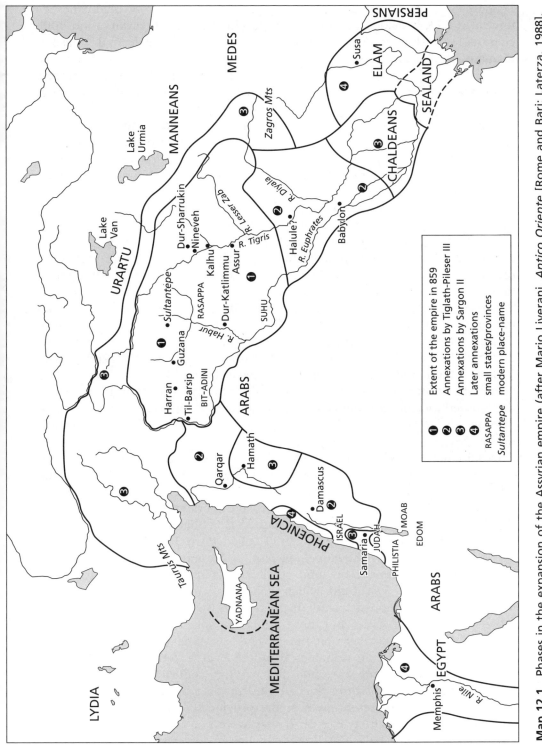

Map 12.1 Phases in the expansion of the Assyrian empire (after Mario Liverani, *Antico Oriente* [Rome and Bari: Laterza, 1988], p. 793)

Legend:

1 Extent of the empire in 859
2 Annexations by Tiglath-Pileser III
3 Annexations by Sargon II
4 Later annexations

RASAPPA small states/provinces
Sultantepe modern place-name

Damascus it formed a major coalition against the advance of Shalmaneser's forces. In 853, it fielded an army of 40,000 infantry, 2000 cavalry, and 4000 chariots, according to Assyrian sources. The troops came from Damascus, Hamath, Israel, and the Phoenician cities, with support from the Arabs and Egyptians, and they seem to have been able to push the Assyrians back in a battle near Qarqar. In the next few years, Shalmaneser had to reestablish control closer to home. But the Damascus coalition fell apart on the death of the king of Damascus, Hadad-ezer, and by 841 Shalmaneser III seems to have removed all southern Syrian opposition. This enabled him to turn his attention to the north, where he subdued the Neo-Hittite states and gained access to southern Anatolian mines. The aim of these military actions was not the incorporation of Syria into Assyria. The states there remained independent, keeping their original rulers, and only had to provide tribute. There was thus no attempt at this time to expand the boundaries of the Assyrian state.

To the north of Assyria the state of Urartu had developed as a formidable opponent. From the beginning of his reign Shalmaneser III had probed its resistance, but only after he had subdued the west did he give it his full attention, organizing five campaigns in quick succession in the years 832 to 827. Shalmaneser stopped leading the army himself, leaving that role to his highest military official, the commander-in-chief (Akkadian *turtanu*) Dayyan-Assur. The expeditions aimed primarily at obtaining spoils and reducing the military threat of Urartu. They led Assyria into distant lands in the Zagros, where it first encountered peoples such as the Medes and Manneans, who would later become important opponents. Similarly, there was no attempt to control the southern neighbor of Babylonia. Shalmaneser campaigned there only twice, in order to intervene in a civil war that had erupted between the king and his brother.

Despite the high level of military activity, Assyria under Shalmaneser III was not an expansionist state. The borders established by Assurnasirpal were maintained, and campaigns beyond them were to protect them and to obtain booty and tribute (figure 12.2). The east bank of the Euphrates was fully Assyrianized: the Aramaic city of Til-Barsip was renamed Kar-Shalmaneser after the king, and guarded the river crossing. A center called Pitru 30 kilometers upstream across the river became the launching pad for Syrian campaigns. On the east bank of the Euphrates and on some small islands in the river, a string of well-defended fortresses was built which delineated and protected the border. The Assyrians maintained a clear distinction between two types of territories, those of the land of Assur and those under the yoke of Assur, a system they inherited from Middle Assyrian times. The first type was considered to be Assyria proper, the region stretching from the Zagros to the Euphrates, which by Shalmaneser III's time was under full Assyrian control. That land was uniformly organized under a provincial administration: men appointed by the king acted as his direct representatives in the provinces. They resided in palaces constructed in Assyrian style, even if they were not as grand as those in the central capitals. The palace at Kar-Shalmaneser, for example, was decorated

Figure 12.2 Tribute bearers, detail on the Black Obelisk of Shalmaneser III.
Photo © Trustees of the British Museum, London

with frescoes representing the same type of scenes as were found in stone reliefs at Kalhu. The provinces were integrated into a system of maintenance of the god Assur, whose sole temple was in the city Assur, and who functioned as the god for the entire land of Assyria. Every province had to supply basic foodstuffs to support him. This may be seen as an ideological expression of the fact that the economies of the entire region were integrated into a single system in order to feed the central state bureaucracy. In political terms, the provinces were equivalent in status, although in practice Assyrian kings allowed some of them a greater degree of autonomy. "Dynasties" of governors, with the office passing from father to son, existed for example in the Middle Euphrates province of Suhu. As long as they obeyed the Assyrian king, there was no need to reorganize them to fit the provincial system.

Outside these boundaries, the Assyrians dominated a number of states that remained nominally independent but whose rulers were vassals. These were considered to be "under the yoke of Assur." Their duties included the delivery of annual tribute in the form of valuable items. This was given to the king, not to the god Assur, and there is no evidence that the deity's cult was imposed. As vassals the tributary rulers had to adhere to treaties, as was the case in the second millennium, and any breach was considered a grave transgression that gave the Assyrians the right to impose a military punishment. The clear distinction between Assyria proper and the outside shows that, in the first phase of its empire, Assyria wanted only to recreate the state it had in the Middle Assyrian period. Beyond the borders was a world that had to obey, but did not need to become part of Assyria.

Even within these boundaries Assyria was a large entity, and the king, who was personally responsible for the proper functioning of the state, had to rely on an extensive bureaucracy. The power of the higher administrators and military officers was considerable and they became more independent as Shalmaneser III grew older. The fraying of central power was already visible late in Shalmaneser's reign. The commander-in-chief, Dayyan-Assur, openly led military campaigns starting in 832, and in 827 a rebellion broke out involving the heartland of Assyria. Princes felt aggrieved at Dayyan-Assur's power and also fought one another for the right of succession. The confusion lasted for seven years, including the first three of the reign of King Shamshi-Adad V, who had gained the throne in 823 with the help of Babylonia.

12.4 Internal Assyrian Decline

Because of the highly centralized structure of the Assyrian state, the dynastic struggles at the end of Shalmaneser III's reign had a disastrous impact on the entire state system. Although Shamshi-Adad V ruled for thirteen years (823–11) and portrayed himself as a victorious warrior, the dominance over Syria had disappeared and states there refused to pay tribute. At first he was forced by the Babylonians to accept a treaty on unfavorable terms, a situation he reversed by attacking the region late in his reign. Within Assyria itself royal power also slipped. This became clearer after Shamshi-Adad's reign, but the process had already started under Shalmaneser III. Local governors and officials within Assyria became virtually independent. They commissioned inscriptions, some of them bilingual Assyrian and Aramaic, in which they portrayed themselves as kings, even if they sometimes paid homage to the Assyrian ruler. These men included governors of provinces close to Assyria's heartland, such as Rasappa and Guzana. The commander-in-chief Shamshi-ilu was perhaps the most powerful man of his time. He was active under four kings for most of the first half of the eighth century and, from Kar-Shalmaneser, campaigned west of the Euphrates on his own behalf. He used his prestige to arbitrate conflicts between local north Syrian rulers without reference to the king in Assyria. On the Middle Euphrates around ancient Mari, a dynasty of governors left royal-style inscriptions without acknowledging the Assyrian king. Instead, they claimed descent from Hammurabi of Babylon! Governors and officials from cities such as Kalhu and Assur arrogated royal powers to themselves. The king, who was nominally owner of all the land of Assyria, gave them large estates in order to keep them on his side. Even in the palace itself, competition for power was rife. In this context we have to see the importance of Queen Sammuramat, who was the inspiration for the legendary Semiramis. The wife of Shamshi-Adad V, she remained so influential in the reign of her son Adad-nirari III (ruled 810–783) that official inscriptions mentioned the two as acting together. Special emphasis on dynastic succession may have been needed to affirm the king's status. These internal problems put an end to the emergence of Assyria as the major Near Eastern power in the ninth century. The state's initial success seems to have overwhelmed its administrative capacities and the center was insufficiently unified to function properly under a ruler who was not particularly forceful. The dynasty survived, with rule passing from father to son, but the kings had to buy officials' favors in order to remain in place.

What Assyria had accomplished in the ninth century was a recreation and consolidation of the territorial state it had had in the late second millennium. It had started to use it as a platform for campaigns farther afield, especially in the west. There are no statements from the Assyrians themselves, or reports from their victims, that explain why they mounted such huge military operations annually, at great expense of manpower and resources. Assyrian kings only state that they did so at the command of the god Assur. Scholars are mystified as to why the Assyrians behaved in this way, suggesting mainly ideological, economic, and defensive reasons as an explanation. Most likely the reasons for the expansionism changed as the nature of the state evolved. The first phase was one of reconquest in order to control groups, such as the Arameans, and to gain access to agricultural lands in northern Syria. When the Euphrates was reached, the wealth of western Syria provided an appealing target for the Assyrian elites, who had become used to living off the income from Assyria's conquests. It was also an easy target, as there was no unified territorial state to mount an opposition. There was no attempt to integrate these regions into Assyria, only a demand for goods, and Assyria tolerated the existence of independent neighbors as long as they did not threaten its interests. The official records, both textual and pictorial, paint an image of the Assyrian king forcing all others into submission, through battle or the threat of it, and then being presented with their goods. The whole of the external world supplied his needs, enabling the king to display his enormous wealth through acts such as large building projects. The system of extracting resources from the surrounding area may have functioned in the ninth century, but when central power was weakened, it came to a halt. Assyria had to develop another approach, systematic expansion, which was to characterize the second phase of its empire.

NOTES

1 B. Oded, *Mass Deportations and Deportees in the Neo-Assyrian Empire* (Wiesbaden: Harrassowitz, 1979), p. 20.
2 A. Kirk Grayson, *Assyrian Rulers of the Early First Millennium BC. Volume 1: 1114–859 BC* (*The Royal Inscriptions of Mesopotamia. Assyrian Periods*, volume 2) (Toronto: University of Toronto Press, 1991), p. 293.

3 F. M. Fales and J. N. Postgate, *Imperial Administrative Records*, part 2 (*State Archives of Assyria* 11) (Helsinki: University of Helsinki Press, 1995), p. 138.

4 Alan Millard, *The Eponyms of the Assyrian Empire, 910–612* (Helsinki: University of Helsinki Press, 1994), p. 41.

5 Grayson, *Assyrian Rulers of the Early First Millennium* BC. *Volume 1: 1114–859* BC, pp. 134–5.

13

Assyria's World Domination

3000	2500 2000 1500 1000 500

744	Tiglath-pileser III initiates structural changes in Assyria
722	Conquest of Samaria
689	Sennacherib sacks Babylon
671	Esarhaddon captures Egyptian capital Memphis
664–3	Assurbanipal captures Egyptian capital Thebes
652–49	Babylonian rebellion under Shamash-shuma-ukin
626	Independent dynasty in Babylonia
612	Sack of Nineveh by Medes and Babylonians

From 745 to 612, Assyria extended its military dominance over the entire Near East and, at times, Egypt. It eliminated all opposition from its rivals and gradually incorporated more territories into a centrally controlled administrative system. This late Assyrian period can be considered to form the true empire phase in Assyrian history, when a territorial unit from western Iran to the Mediterranean and from southern Anatolia to Egypt was created. As before, the king played a crucial role in the activities of the empire and its military successes, and the six men who occupied the throne in succession were strong and able rulers (for a list, see p. 317). The imperial project was flawed, however, and frictions and instabilities undermined the state. Although the six rulers belonged to the same family, they often had difficulties establishing control, as they were not first in line for succession. Assyria's internal weakness may explain why the kings after Assurbanipal lost their grip on the state, and why the collapse of the Assyrian empire was so sudden.

13.1 The Creation of an Imperial Structure

In the first half of the eighth century Assyria had lost its ability to campaign outside its borders, and internally local officials had usurped some of the royal powers. Provincial governors were able to act with a great deal of independence, although they still had to acknowledge their subservience to the king. Scholars disagree about the extent of internal weakness: some see the local officials as virtually autonomous, others consider them as fully integrated within the Assyrian state structure and their activities as coordinated with those of the king. Their proclaimed independence would then have been more a rhetorical device for local audiences than a lack of obedience to the king. Whatever the case, the early eighth-century Assyrian rulers were not powerful military leaders and the influence of the state on its surroundings was less significant than it had been in the mid-ninth century. Moreover, Urartu was able to extend its influence over northern Syria, thereby threatening Assyria's access to the Mediterranean. Finally, in the years 762 to 759, a number of cities, including the ancient capital of Assur, rebelled against the royal power.

This situation was reversed starting with Tiglath-pileser III (ruled 744–27). He and his second successor, Sargon II (ruled 721–05; figure 13.1), restructured the Assyrian state internally, campaigned almost annually outside its borders, and started to incorporate foreign territories into Assyria. The internal restructuring focused on thwarting the powers of local officials. The kings replaced the old provinces under powerful governors with smaller ones, and increased their number from twelve to twenty-five. Similarly they made the most important military and administrative offices less powerful by assigning them to two persons rather than one. For example, instead of one commander-in-chief (*turtanu*), two men shared that post, one "of the left" and one "of the right." They often appointed eunuchs in high government positions so that there was no pressure for duties to be passed on from father to son. The "land of Assur" was thus restructured in order to limit the powers of officials and increase the king's control.

Simultaneously, Tiglath-pileser III initiated a policy of territorial expansion far beyond the borders that had been maintained since Middle Assyrian times. He may have reorganized the army and replaced the annual levy of troops from the Assyrian population with a standing professional army, using conquered people for the infantry and Assyrians as the core of the cavalry and chariotry. Tiglath-pileser III crossed the Euphrates, as his ninth-century predecessors had done, but the policy toward the region changed fundamentally. Instead of merely forcing the local states there to pay tribute, their existence was gradually abolished and the regions were incorporated into the empire as provinces. This policy actually may not have been Assyria's initial intention but was forced upon it by the resistance of the local populations.

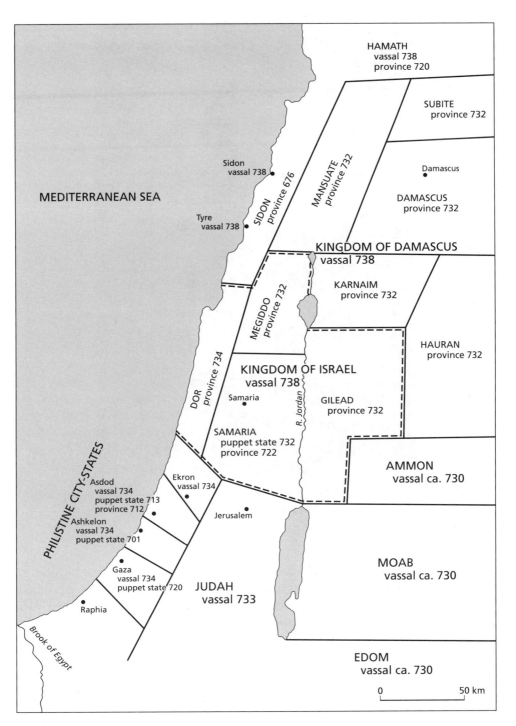

Map 13.1 Assyrian annexation of western states in the eighth century (after Benedikt Otzen, "Israel under the Assyrians," in M. T. Larsen, ed., *Power and Propaganda* [*Mesopotamia* 7, Copenhagen: Akademisk Forlag, 1979], p. 252)

Figure 13.1 Relief from Dur-Sharrukin depicting King Sargon II and an official, Louvre Museum, Paris. Photo: Hevre Lewandowski. © Réunion des Musées Nationaux/Art Resource, NY

   Ideally, Assyria did not want to exert direct control over regions beyond its traditional borders. The intention was to exact tribute and to enforce political obedience, and local rulers were left in power as long as they complied with Assyrian demands. We can distinguish three types of political arrangements with the states in the west, reflecting three stages toward their full incorporation into the empire: (1) vassal states where the local ruler remained in charge but was to deliver annual tribute; (2) puppet states where a local man considered to be more faithful to the Assyrians was placed on the throne; and (3) provinces, ruled by a governor directly under Assyria's control. Acts of disobedience usually precipitated the progression from one stage to the next: only if the arrangement failed to produce the desired results did the Assyrians reduce local autonomy further. They planned the creation of provinces strategically to maximize control and reduce direct confrontation with surrounding enemies. For example, Tiglath-pileser III at first expanded the number of provinces along the Mediterranean coast and stopped at the Philistine city-states, which he left independent. Access to the sea and control of the north–south route running along it were thus guaranteed, but there was still a buffer with the state of Egypt. Only later did he turn inland Syro-Palestinian states into provinces as a reaction against their disobedience, but the entire region was never fully incorporated within the empire's provincial system (see map 13.1).

The history of the state of Israel provides a good example of how this policy operated and shows the various stages of Assyrian control as well as local reaction to it. The Biblical account allows us to see the non-Assyrian point of view, while the Assyrian annals give the empire's version of events. Early in Tiglath-pileser's reign, the Israelite Menahem provided tribute voluntarily and was left in peace. After his death, his son Pekahiah was almost immediately assassinated by the anti-Assyrian Pekah in 735, supported by Damascus and by the population, who resented the heavy payments. In 734, Tiglath-pileser III campaigned along the Syrian coast and turned the regions there into provinces. Only in 732 did he advance against Damascus, the focus of opposition to Assyria, which he incorporated into the empire. At the same time, the northern parts of Israel were likewise made Assyrian provinces. Tiglath-pileser III claims that the people of Israel overthrew Pekah and replaced him with a pro-Assyrian ruler, Hoshea, an act certainly prompted by his military presence nearby. When Tiglath-pileser died, Hoshea at first remained loyal to Assyria, but later on, possibly as part of a general rebellion, he stopped paying tribute. This led to a military campaign by Shalmaneser V (ruled 726–22), who laid siege to Israel's capital for three years and conquered it just before his death. His successor Sargon II claimed the victory for himself and turned the region into the province of Samaria.

The repercussions for Israel were great. The Assyrians deported a substantial number of people – 27,290 according to Sargon – and settled them in northeastern Syria and western Iran. People from other parts of the empire resettled the region of Samaria, creating a less homogeneous population that was more docile toward Assyria. While the northern parts of the original state, the provinces of Megiddo and Karnaim, were left almost unpopulated, Samaria was developed economically through the creation of small villages and agricultural estates. The administration was restructured to fit Assyria's needs. The capital was rebuilt and, along with a few other cities, it came to be the seat of governors, who lived in residences built in the Assyrian style. Fortresses were constructed along the border to protect the province against incursions from the south and east. Legal transactions were now recorded in the Assyrian language and cuneiform script.

Israel provides a good example of how Assyrian rule in the Syro-Palestinian area changed, and many other states were similarly affected. But the Assyrians' policy was flexible. They left states outside the provincial system when this was better for the empire's interests. Local vassal or puppet rulers continued to govern Judah and all other states to the south and east of Israel, although their territories were often much reduced in size. The Assyrians adopted this policy to create a buffer between their empire and the Egyptians and Arabs, and probably also to enable trade with these peoples. They similarly preserved the political structures of the Phoenician cities, as their trade was important to Assyria. They fully exploited the economic assets of regions, even of those not turned into provinces. In the Philistine area, for example, Assyria's influence changed the production of olive oil from a cottage industry to a centralized system that guaranteed supply to Assyria. Thus the empire cannot be considered as driven by a mere desire to acquire territory. It was a structure that aimed at maximizing resources for its core. The policies described here were ideal for interactions with smaller political units at Assyria's borders and were applied from southern Anatolia to Palestine, and in the mountain areas to Assyria's east. In its interactions with the great states Assyria used different policies, and we will explore this below.

13.2 The Defeat of the Great Rivals

Assyria was surrounded by a number of great states at its borders: Babylonia in the south, Elam in the south-east, Urartu in the north, and Egypt beyond the Syro-Palestinian region. They were too large and powerful to be completely controlled, or, in the case of Babylonia, special considerations prevented full incorporation into the Assyrian empire. All kings from Tiglath-pileser III to Assurbanipal were preoccupied with these states, and once again adopted a flexible approach in dealing with them.

The Assyrians never solved the question of how to control Babylonia. While they could not accept the existence of a disobedient neighbor at their southern border, they seem to have been reluctant to take over the country openly. Probably an acknowledgment that Babylonia had fundamentally influenced Assyria's culture and religion led to a sense of respect that prevented similar treatment to that meted out to other regions. Furthermore, Babylonia was not a homogeneous area: the ancient cities preserving cultural and political traditions were surrounded by a countryside inhabited by tribal groups. The extreme south of the region was impossible to control as it was covered with marshes where traditional military tactics could not be deployed. These areas provided refuge to the Chaldeans, who competed with the Assyrians for the throne of Babylon (figure 13.2).

During the reigns of the six major late Assyrian kings, some twenty transitions of power took place in Babylon (for a list of kings, see p. 313). The kings there could belong to one of five groups:

1 the Assyrian king himself;
2 a family member of Assyria's king;
3 a native Babylonian, put on the throne by Assyria;
4 a Babylonian independent from Assyria; or
5 a Chaldean who was anti-Assyrian.

Figure 13.2 Assyrian representation from Nineveh showing refugees in southern marshes. Photo © Trustees of the British Museum, London

The numerous changes show both Assyria's inability to find an effective way of controlling Babylonia and the strength of local opposition. The king of Elam often supported the opposition, requesting payment for his services.

The frustration with Babylonia, and the various attempts to rule it, are well documented in the reign of Sennacherib, who was king of Assyria from 704 to 681. In those years the rule of Babylon changed hands seven times. When Sennacherib came to the throne of Assyria, he did what his three most recent predecessors had done: he also became king of Babylonia, which remained a separate kingdom. After two years he lost that kingship to a native Babylonian, Marduk-zakir-shumi II, who a few weeks later was himself overthrown by the fiercely anti-Assyrian Marduk-apla-iddina II. In succession they ruled Babylon for only ten months in 703, and Sennacherib devoted his first formal campaign to the reconquest of the south. He drove Marduk-apla-iddina into the marshes and this time placed a native Babylonian on the throne, probably in an effort to appease the urban population. The man, Bel-ibni, is described as having grown up in Sennacherib's palace "like a young puppy," so his loyalty should have been great. Babylonia was thus reduced to a puppet kingdom. Assyrian governors soon assisted Bel-ibni to counter the Chaldean threat in the south, however. Sennacherib had to mount another campaign to deal once and for all

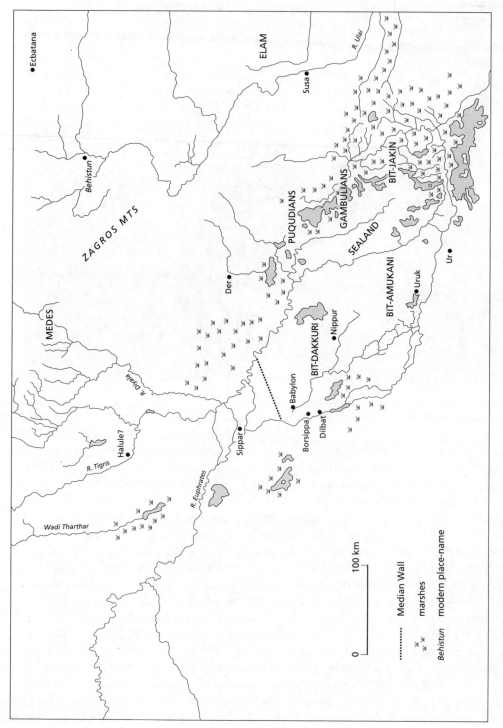

Map 13.2 Babylonia in the first millennium

with Marduk-apla-iddina during which he replaced Bel-ibni with his own eldest son, Assur-nadin-shumi. Six years later, the Babylonians took advantage of an Elamite military raid in the region to capture Sennacherib's son and hand him over to the Elamite king. He was taken off and disappeared for good. A new native Babylonian was made king but was quickly removed by Sennacherib, who failed however to take the city. Then a Chaldean leader, Mushezib-Marduk, seized the throne and formed another large coalition against Assyria, including Chaldeans, Arameans, Babylonians, and Elamites whose support he bought using the temple treasury. In 691, the coalition engaged Sennacherib in a major battle, which was probably indecisive, near Halule on Assyria's border. The next year Sennacherib started a fifteen-month-long siege of Babylon, and when he was finally successful he took revenge for the problems it had caused him. His description of the destruction details the razing of temples and houses, the looting of treasuries, and the deportation of the population. Having exhausted all other possibilities, Sennacherib left Babylonia in disarray. Very little activity took place, and the handful of records preserved either name Sennacherib or his deceased son, Assur-nadin-shumi, as king.

Babylonia was too important to be left in this state of decline for long, so its reconstruction was immediately begun by Sennacherib's successor, Esarhaddon. He rebuilt Babylon and made a concerted effort to portray himself in the official record as a king who unified the two states. The idea that Babylonia and Assyria were united does not seem to have been comfortable, however, and before he died Esarhaddon appointed two of his sons as future kings of the separate kingdoms. The younger, Assurbanipal, received Assyria, the older, Shamash-shuma-ukin, Babylonia. The dominance of the first was clear, and he treated his brother as a vassal, albeit a favored one. In 652 Shamash-shuma-ukin rebelled, joining forces with Chaldeans, Arameans, and Elamites. Resistance to Assyria was successful and Assurbanipal had to campaign for four years before Babylon fell. The effort drained the resources of both states. Babylonia's subsequent king was Kandalanu. As he died at the same time as Assurbanipal in 627, it is sometimes thought that Kandalanu was a Babylonian throne-name of the Assyrian king. But no solid evidence for this connection exists and it is probably best to see the Babylonian and Assyrian kings at this time as two men, the former being a puppet ruler controlled by Assyria. Despite the proximity of Babylonia to Assyria and all the effort expended to control it, the region was never fully integrated into the empire. Assyria gave it special treatment because of the respect it deserved, but equally important was Babylonia's resilience and its ability to maintain its opposition.

The respect shown to Babylonia did not exist in the cases of Urartu and Elam. They were detested enemies who continued to make Assyria's life difficult. Both were the targets of many extensive campaigns, described in chapter 11, which ended up reducing their threat, although Assyria did not annihilate them. Sargon II dealt with Urartu in 714, while Assurbanipal, exasperated by Elam's support for his brother's rebellion, sacked Susa in 647. The two weakened states were only later absorbed into the Persian empire.

The final important rival to Assyria was Egypt, which from the ninth century on had supported Syro-Palestinian rebels. Its distance and the weakness of Assyrian control over the adjacent region had made an invasion impossible in the early phase of the empire. But Egypt's great wealth made it an appealing target. Nubians from Sudan had conquered the country in the mid-eighth century and had direct access to gold mines. Their control over Egypt was probably indirect and local Egyptians were mostly in charge of administration. The idea of conquering Egypt must have been tempting to Esarhaddon, and when the Assyrian king had sufficiently consolidated his hold over southern Palestine through a system of loyal vassals, he invaded. Already advanced in years, he organized three campaigns, defeating the Nubian Taharqa and conquering the northern capital of Memphis. The Assyrian captured a Nubian prince and an enormous quantity of spoils, which he used partly to fund Babylon's reconstruction. In order to maintain influence over the land, Esarhaddon made vassals of a number of rulers of the Nile Delta region.

Assyria's control was weak, however, and by the time Esarhaddon died, the Nubian Taharqa had reasserted rule over the entire country of Egypt. Assurbanipal sent out a successful expedition, but its advance was interrupted by a rebellion of the Delta vassals. The Assyrian king defeated the rebels with the assistance of an army recruited from the Syro-Palestinian vassals, such as Judah, Edom, and Moab, and with ships obtained in Phoenicia and Cyprus in order to sail down the Nile. He punished the vassals, but reinstated one of them, Necho, and gave him special prominence (document 13.1). When Assyria's army departed, the new Nubian king, Tantamani, returned, forcing a final major attack by Assurbanipal in 664 and 663. This time he reached the capital of Thebes in central Egypt, which provided huge spoils. Nubian influence in the country was finally brought to an end. The system of vassals under Assyrian control lasted a short time only, however. By 656 a son of Necho, Psamtik, who had been educated in Assyria and installed on a local throne, proclaimed himself sole king of the whole of Egypt with full independence. Egypt in this era was thus an area contended over by two outsiders, Assyria and Nubia, and ultimately local rulers themselves gained enough strength to become independent. In the last years of the empire, Egypt started to help Assyria against the threat from the east, and together they tried to prevent the Babylonian conquest of Syria. This was to no avail, however, and the conquest of Egypt became a goal of the Babylonian empire.

The resilience of the states surrounding Assyria shows that the empire was not always fully dominant and could be successfully opposed. Beyond this world of well-established and ancient states, there were other people, often nomadic, who could cause Assyria serious trouble. These included the Scythians and Cimmerians in Anatolia, who had to be kept at bay by military and diplomatic means. In the Arabian Desert east of Syria-Palestine, the Assyrians clashed repeatedly with Arabs, who were able to escape easily in the desert and were never fully controlled. There were also a number of states outside the reach of Assyria but in contact with it. In the Persian Gulf, a king of

Document 13.1 *Assurbanipal and Egypt*

Excerpt from Assurbanipal's account written after 664

Tarqû,[1] the godless, came out in order to take Egypt and [ ]. He forgot about the power of Assur, my lord, and trusted his own strength. The harsh things, which my father had done to him, did not occur to him, so he came and entered Memphis, and turned the citizens to his side. He sent an army to kill, destroy, and plunder against the people of Assyria who were in Egypt, my servants, whom Esarhaddon king of Assyria, my father, had entrusted with kingship there.

A fast messenger came to me in Nineveh and informed me of this. I became infuriated at these deeds and was enraged. I called the commander-in-chief and the governors with the men under them, my mighty force, and ordered them to hurry and go help the kings and governors, my servants. I ordered them to go to Egypt. They marched fast and came to the city of Kar-Banite. Tarqû, the king of Kush,[2] who heard of the coming of my army in Memphis, raised his army to do battle in the open field. Under the protection of Assur, Sin, and the great gods, my lords who go at my side, they defeated them in open battle. They cut down with the sword the troops in which he had trusted.

Fear and terror fell upon him, and he went insane. He left Memphis, his royal city, which he had trusted, and boarded a ship in order to save his life. He left his camp, fled alone, and entered the city Ni'.[3] All the warships that were with him and his battle troops they seized. A messenger described to me the happy events that he had witnessed. To my mighty troops (there) I added strength by sending the chief-cupbearers, the governors and the kings of the areas across the River, all of them my servants, and the kings of Egypt, my servants, together with their forces and ships, in order to chase Tarqû from Egypt and Kush. To Ni', the fortress of Tarqû, king of Kush, they went in a march of one month and ten days. When Tarqû heard of the approach of my army, he left Ni', his fortress, crossed the Nile, and set his camp up at the other side.

Nikkû,[4] Sharru-lu-dari and Paqruru, the kings whom my father had established in Egypt, violated the oath of Assur and the great gods, my lords, and broke their word. They forgot the good my father had done to them and planned evil in their hearts. They spoke false words, and they counseled each other in a counterproductive way. "If they chase Tarqû out of Egypt, where shall we stay?" They sent their emissaries to swear an oath of peace, saying: "We want to establish peace and be in agreement amongst ourselves. We want to divide the land amongst ourselves. Let there be no lord among us."

They repeatedly planned evil against the mass of the troops of Assyria, the strength of my rule. They plotted to take their lives, and endeavored to do unheard evils. My officials heard of these things and played a trick on them. They captured their messengers with their messages, and saw their treacherous doings. They captured Sharru-lu-dari and Nikkû, and shackled their hands and feet. The curse of Assur, king of the gods, came upon them, they who had sinned against their mighty oath. Those to whom I had done good deeds, I called to task. The people of the cities, all who had joined them and had plotted evil, great and small, they cut down with their weapons, and not a single person inside these cities was saved.

To him, whom they brought to me in [Nineveh], my royal city, I Assurbanipal, king of Assyria, the broad-minded, the well-doer who seeks goodness, to Nikkû, my servant, to whom had been entrusted the city Kar-Bel-Matati, I showed mercy, although he had sinned. I laid upon him a loyalty oath that was stricter than what existed before. I encouraged him, put bright garments on him, and gave him a golden hoe, the symbol of his kingship. I put golden rings on his fingers, and gave him an iron dagger with a sheath inlaid with gold on which I had written my name. Chariots, horses and mules I granted to him for his royal journeys. I sent to him my officials and governors to help him. I sent him back to Sais, which is now called Kar-Bel-Matati, where my father had made him king. I showed him kindness even greater than my father had done.

Translation after Hans-Ulrich Onasch, *Die assyrischen Eroberungen Ägyptens* (*Ägypten und Altes Testament* 23) (Wiesbaden: Harrassowitz Verlag, 1994), pp. 104–15.

[1] Taharqa, king of Nubia, ruled Egypt 690–64.
[2] Nubia.
[3] Thebes.
[4] Necho, king of Sais.

Dilmun ruled, but we do not know much about his state. In central Anatolia was the kingdom of Lydia, attested in the classical sources, which is known to have sent envoys to Assyria and to have aided anti-Assyrian rebellions. The Assyrians portrayed such countries as being subservient to them, but the reality of that claim is doubtful.

13.3 The Administration and Ideology of the Empire

The vast empire the Assyrians had created required a large and well-oiled administration. With the expansion of the provincial system, the earlier distinction between the "land of Assur" and the "yoke of Assur" disappeared, and throughout the entire Near East direct Assyrian control was exercised. Beyond the provinces were located vassal and puppet states, which were administered indirectly and whose control was a matter of diplomacy.

The structure of Assyria's administration is poorly known, although we have a large array of attested titles. One of its basic characteristics was that there was no separation of duties among officials: their positions were simultaneously administrative, military, and religious. Men with titles that we translate in a military sense were also governors of provinces, for instance. Assyrian society in general can be regarded as a pyramid-like structure with the king at its apex and the mass of the population at the bottom. The multitude of officials was placed in between, as they regulated the interactions between the two. There is still a great deal of uncertainty about the hierarchy of offices. As in all other courts in history, men held titles that said little about their duties. Thus the cupbearer (*rab shaqe*), for instance, was a highly placed official who led diplomatic missions. A trio of officers assisted the king: the *turtanu*, *ummanu*, and *rab sha muhhi ekalli*. Our translations of commander-in-chief, chancellor, and majordomo respectively probably limit the extent of their duties too much. Scholars often compare the Assyrian court to later Middle Eastern ones, especially the Ottoman court, but we have to be careful not to let such a comparison determine the details of how we see Assyria's administrative structure.

Personal loyalty was crucial in the interactions between king and officials. Duties were not formulated in legal terms, but officials were expected to serve the king loyally and he trusted them in return. He requested tax payments and the like by letter as if this were a personal arrangement between the king and his official. Similarly, the king granted tax exemptions as if they were personal favors. Such a system led to the need for an army of scribes to maintain contacts. The large quantity of letters found at Nineveh and Kalhu, some 2300 in number, probably constitutes only a small part of what was originally written. As a reward for loyalty the subject remained in office, a position that was granted and withdrawn at the king's pleasure, not on the basis of hereditary rights. In any case, many officials seem to have been eunuchs, so offices reverted to the crown upon death or retirement. Moreover, officials received estates that could be very extensive, but these remained the king's property.

The idea that loyalty was owed to the king extended to all people of Assyria and to the subject rulers. At times the entire population was made to swear an oath before the gods that they accepted a royal decision – or at least the kings claimed that all had sworn the oath. This happened, for example, when Esarhaddon appointed his younger son Assurbanipal as his successor. According to the latter, "Esarhaddon convened the people of Assyria, great and small, from coast to coast, made them swear a loyalty oath by the gods and established a binding agreement to protect my crown-princeship and future kingship over Assyria."[1] If anyone opposed the new king, they would break their oath and invoke divine retribution. Loyalty oaths were also at the basis of the interactions between the Assyrian king and his vassals. The latter had specific responsibilities to the person of the king, such as providing troops in case of war, and shirking them would mean the breach of an agreement supervised by the gods.

The empire's central administration was paralleled in the provincial system of government. Each province was headed by a governor (Akkadian *shaknu*) whose residence was the equivalent of the royal palace in Assyria itself. The governors were high officials in the empire's administration, army commanders, cupbearers, and so on, and it is unclear how they divided their time between central and provincial duties. The provinces had to produce resources for the empire and to provide laborers and soldiers. Sometimes the production of certain goods, such as olive oil in the Philistine area, was restructured in order to increase supply. Most often, however, it seems that the Assyrians relied on the structures in place and did not interfere. The provincial administration was the only one with which the people came into contact. Similarly, cities in the heartland, such as Assur and Kalhu, were headed by an official, the mayor (Akkadian *hazannu*), whose duty it was to represent those people not directly dependent on the palace. Some larger cities had more than one mayor, probably to prevent their power from becoming too great, as we know that at times cities rebelled against royal power.

The full focus on the person of the king in these interactions was a result of the ideological basis of rule in Assyria. The king, as representative of the god Assur, represented order. Wherever he was in control, there was peace, tranquility, and justice, and where he did not rule there was chaos. The king's duty to bring order to the entire world was the justification for military expansion. This idea pervaded royal rhetoric. All that was foreign was hostile, and all foreigners were like non-human creatures. Images of swamp-rats or bats, lonely, confused, and cowardly, were commonly applied to those outside the king's control. This message was communicated through a variety of means. Royal inscriptions are the most eloquent to us today, but in Assyrian times they were incomprehensible to the mostly illiterate population. The people were informed through events such as victory parades, and there is evidence that certain campaign accounts were read aloud in the cities. Moreover, the new cities themselves, with their planned layout and great walls and gates, instilled an idea of safety and order in their residents and visitors. When Sargon II described the building of his capital Dur-Sharrukin, he used language that resembled the description of the god Marduk's organization of the universe in the Epic of Creation. The royal palaces, inaccessible to most people but visited by foreign dignitaries, were decorated with wall-reliefs that portrayed the king as master of the world. Stelae and rock-reliefs representing the king were established in the empire's periphery, as far afield as Egypt, to indicate the same idea. There was no doubt in the Assyrians' minds that military campaigning was justified and for the good of all.

The gods of Assyria benefited from the empire in that their cults were well provided with tribute and booty. As main priest of the god Assur the king supported that cult, and other temples were probably also entirely dependent on the state for their maintenance. Provincial taxes were often collected as temple offerings. There is no evidence, however, that Assyrian cults were imposed upon conquered populations, certainly not at the expense of existing religions. Foreign temples were sacked for their treasuries. There was no religious intolerance and vassal treaties, for instance, were sworn in the names of the vassal's gods as well as those of Assyria.

13.4 Assyrian Culture

Most studies of Assyria focus on the military aspects of the society as a logical result of the dominance of that topic in the official accounts. But

Assyrian remains also show a strong interest in literature and scholarship under the auspices of the palace. Most revealing in this respect is the library that Assurbanipal collected in his capital, Nineveh. Unfortunately, the tablets were excavated in the early days of Mesopotamian exploration in the mid-nineteenth century, so little information is available on what items were found together and where. Moreover, the bulk of these tablets are now stored in the so-called Kuyunjik collection at the British Museum in London, where they are mixed with finds made at other sites both in Assyria and Babylonia. The mass of tablets that derive from Assurbanipal's library is enormous: some 5000 literary and scholarly texts were found together with the letters and administrative documents that detail the daily affairs of the state. Many of the literary and scholarly texts were found in up to six manuscripts, and in total some 1000 to 1200 compositions were preserved. It is estimated that these represent an accurate reflection of all Mesopotamian learning and literature up to that time. Successive kings consciously brought the library together, but Assurbanipal was most active in this enterprise. A now fragmentary record of texts that were acquired in the year 648 probably listed some 2000 tablets and 300 writing boards, that is, wooden or ivory boards covered with wax and inscribed with a cuneiform text.[2] These were bought or confiscated mostly from the private libraries of Babylonian priests and exorcists, and Assurbanipal's recent defeat of Babylon probably made the task easier. A letter found at Nineveh and written by an unnamed king to his representative in the Babylonian city Borsippa (perhaps a literary fiction rather than an actual letter) states that he should take tablets from specialists' homes and temples. "I have already written to the temple overseer and the chief magistrate that you are to place the tablets in your storage house. No one shall withhold a tablet from you. In case you should see a tablet or ritual that I have not mentioned to you and that would be good for my palace, take it as well and send it to me."[3]

The manuscripts were not merely collected but were copied out according to a standard format for the library. The cuneiform script and tablet layout were uniform, and at the end of each tablet an identification was provided stating that it belonged to Assurbanipal's library. These subscripts or colophons could be simple stamps with the text "palace of Assurbanipal, king of the universe, king of Assyria," but often indicated at length that the preceding texts were copied carefully from an original tablet, and that the copy was reviewed and checked. Indeed, the scribes were careful in their work. They indicated in their copies when they found a break in the original tablet and when they restored a lacuna. They corrected mistakes and, very rarely, indicated the variants they found in different original manuscripts.

The purpose of the library is indicated by the colophons, that is, a statement at the end that gives information on the nature and place of preservation of the tablet. The texts were kept in order to provide authorized versions that diviners and exorcists could use. Many of the manuscripts contained omens, and it was important that a correct version was on record. Also literary and scholarly texts were kept, as specialists whose duty it was to protect the king and the state sometimes needed to quote them in their reports, and the accuracy of these quotes was important. That Assurbanipal took personal pride in his library is indicated by statements such as: "the wisdom of Ea, the art of the learned priests, the knowledge of the sages, and that which provides solace to the great gods, I (Assurbanipal) wrote on tablets according to texts from Assyria and Babylonia, and I reviewed and checked."[4] The king clearly wanted to set himself apart from others by claiming knowledge of writing and of secret lore, and presented the library as something compiled for his own interests.

The compositions preserved in Nineveh were of a very varied nature. About 300 tablets contain omens, 200 lexical lists, 100 bilingual Sumerian-Akkadian texts of varied characters, sixty medical texts, and only some thirty-five to forty contain the epics and other compositions we consider to be purely literary. The predominance of omens does reflect the preoccupation of the library, but it also shows the importance these texts had in Assyria and in Mesopotamia in general. They were meant to predict the future based on the observation of everything in the surrounding world. The entries were all phrased according to the pattern, "if . . . , then . . ." The second part of the statement, the apodosis, indicated what the observation foretold. The first part, the protasis, could be anything in the world that was readily observable or realized through special procedures. Any occurrence in the natural world was ominous, such as the flight of birds or the physical aspects of animals in the house. Unusual events were, of course, even more important. There were omens that interpreted the appearance of malformed births, such as lambs with more than one head. In addition to observations of spontaneous events, specialist diviners would cut open sheep to examine their livers, and all discolorations, protuberances, and anomalies were considered ominous. For example, "If the left lobe (of the liver) is covered by a membrane and it is abnormal – The king will die from illness."[5] They would interpret the patterns rising smoke made, the configurations of oil poured on water, and so on. The scribes used to expand the list of observations by including potential occurrences and determining the outcome by means of analogy. For example, the appearance of a cat was spun out into a list of good and bad omens depending on its color:

> If a white cat is seen in a man's house – hardship will seize the land.
> If a black cat is seen in a man's house – that land will experience good fortune.
> If a red cat is seen in a man's house – that land will be rich.
> If a multicolored cat is seen in a man's house – that land will not prosper.
> If a yellow cat is seen in a man's house – that land will have a year of good fortune.[6]

In the first millennium, astronomical omens became increasingly widespread and the series describing and interpreting planetary alignments, eclipses, the appearance of stars and many other celestial events became extremely lengthy. One popular series was called Enuma Anu Enlil and was copied out on seventy tablets. It contained omens dealing with the moon, its visibility, eclipses, and conjunction with planets and fixed stars, the sun, its corona, spots, and eclipses, the weather, namely lightning, thunder, and clouds, and the planets and their visibility, appearance, and stations. For example: "If the moon makes an eclipse in Month VII on the twenty-first day and sets eclipsed – they will take the crowned prince from his palace in fetters."[7]

The observations were not simply made to determine whether the omens were propitious or not, but so that actions could be taken to change the gods' minds. Specialist priests would recite prayers to make the gods alter the future, or actions were taken to guarantee that the king would not be hurt. A practice repeatedly attested in the Neo-Assyrian period was the appointment of a substitute king. When it was determined that the king's life was in danger, a man was selected to replace him temporarily and the true king was hidden away. Once the danger had passed, and the substitute king probably murdered, the king reappeared. The idea was not that the future was unalterable, but that steps could be taken to avoid the evil the future held or to change it into something positive. Omens were important for every level of society, and numerous people paid diviners to ascertain the future and exorcists to implore the gods to take evil away.

The lexical texts in Assurbanipal's library similarly had practical uses. They were expansions of lists that had first appeared in the late fourth millennium and contained within them a full record of the Sumerian lexicon with Akkadian translations. They included lists of signs and sign combinations, and of Sumerian words for animals, stones, woods, implements, city-names, and so on. All of these texts had already been compiled in the second millennium, and the versions we find in Assurbanipal's library are copies. Knowledge of the Sumerian terms was important to the scholars who needed to read cultic texts in Sumerian and had to understand difficult cuneiform signs for their interpretative work.

The third largest group of tablets in the library consisted of incantations and prayers in Sumerian, which had died out as a spoken language many centuries earlier. The texts were provided with a line-by-line translation into Akkadian. Similarly, some Sumerian epics and myths were preserved with Akkadian translations, not necessarily the ones that had been the most popular in the early second millennium when most of Sumerian literature was recorded. Incantations, that is, lists of spells to ward off evil, and manuals for exorcists were also an important part of the monolingual Akkadian texts.

Medical texts were very similar in format to the omen texts and were based on the same concept that any observation determined the outcome of the disease. Even things that happened when the physician walked to the patient's house were indicative. For example, "If the *âšipu* (Akkadian term for diagnostician) sees a black dog or a black pig, the ill man will die. If he sees a white pig, the ill man will get well, or he will be seized by distress."[8] The diagnosis was based on whether parts of the body were hot or cold, the color of the skin and urine, and other elements that we would consider medically relevant. But others that seem trivial to us, for example whether the patient's chest hair curled upwards or downwards, were also important.

Finally, the smallest group of compositions in Assurbanipal's library was made up of Akkadian literary texts, often preserved in several manuscripts. Modern scholars regularly consider the version of these compositions found at Nineveh to have been the standard, but there is no indication that the format found there was later regarded as authoritative. Today the most famous composition from the library is the Epic of Gilgamesh (box 13.1), but this is only

---

Box 13.1   *The Epic of Gilgamesh*

The most famous literary composition from ancient Mesopotamia today is the Epic of Gilgamesh, a tale of the hero's search for immortality after the death of his friend Enkidu. The quest takes him to the edge of the world, where he meets the only survivor of the flood, Utnapishtim, who tells Gilgamesh that he will never obtain physical immortality. But the version found at Nineveh indicates that a king can be remembered for eternity through his deeds, including building. The epic begins and ends with praise of the walls of Uruk, through which Gilgamesh will be known forever:

> Go up, pace out the walls of Uruk,
> Study the foundation terrace and examine the brickwork.
> Is not its masonry of kiln-fired brick?
> And did not seven masters lay its foundation?[1]

At the library of Assurbanipal several copies of a version written on twelve tablets were found, and its author was said to be Sin-leqe-unninni. This name places him in the Kassite period and Sin-leqe-unninni was regarded by many Babylonian scribes of the first millennium as their ancestor. The Gilgamesh story underwent a long development before the version found at Nineveh. At its basis lay a number of Sumerian tales from the early second millennium, and in the Old Babylonian period the first Akkadian version is attested. It was one of the Babylonian literary works known in Syria-Palestine and Anatolia in the late second millennium. The version from Nineveh incorporated previously independent literary works such as the Flood story, also known from the Old Babylonian period on. After the sack of Nineveh, the epic remained popular in Babylonia, although the known manuscripts are exceedingly fragmentary. The figure of Gilgamesh survived in first-millennium AD classical, Aramaic, and possibly Arabic sources, but he seemed to have been confused with other heroic figures.

1 Translation from Benjamin R. Foster, *The Epic of Gilgamesh* (New York: W. W. Norton, 2001), p. 3.

one of a group of narrative poems that revolved around the gods and heroes of Babylonia. Gods were the sole characters in myths such as the Descent of Ishtar into the Netherworld, a summary of a lengthy Sumerian text known from the early second millennium, where the goddess tries to extend her powers over the netherworld but is trapped there until a substitute can be found. Mortals played important roles in stories like that of Adapa, a primordial sage who visited the gods in heaven and failed to obtain immortality. A flood story was preserved in the story of Atrahasis, the man whom the god Ea saved so that humans could continue to provide offerings to the gods. These were compositions whose origins went back to the early second millennium, some with Sumerian antecedents. More recent were Akkadian compositions such as the Creation myth, describing the organization of the universe by the god Marduk, who in some Assyrian versions was replaced by the god Assur. The poem was probably composed in the late second millennium. Of first-millennium date was the Erra Epic, describing the violent destruction of Babylonia (see document 10.2). Similarly pessimistic were wisdom texts, such as the laments of a virtuous man suffering hardship at the hands of the god Marduk for no apparent reason, and a dialogue between a master and his slave, who argues that any decision taken is as valuable as its direct opposite.

The scholars in Assurbanipal's library also collected commentaries on other texts (document 13.2). These explained passages in lexical lists, medical and omen texts, and in literary compositions such as the Babylonian Creation myth. They clarified antiquated and technical terms, listed attributes of the gods, or elaborated on their acts in mythological texts. The function of the library was practical. The scholarship undertaken was focused on understanding the signs of the gods that could be seen everywhere in the surrounding world and which had to be properly read. In order to further their knowledge, scholars all over the empire reported what they observed, such as astronomical occurrences, and interpreted events based on their understanding of the omens. The palace archives contain numerous letters written to the king in order to help him with problems such as illness, making a decision to go to war, and royal succession. The final goal of all this work was to protect the king and the state, and to ensure that he was not unaware of any impending danger.

While Assurbanipal's palace library was by far the most extensive in Assyria, it was not alone. In Nineveh itself there was another library in the Nabu-temple, and temples in other cities, such as Kalhu, contained collections of literary and scholarly tablets. In addition, private houses could hold libraries. At Sultantepe in southern Turkey, one was found in the house of a priest called Qurdi-Nergal and his son Mushallim-Baba, which contained incantations, medical texts, prayers, epics, and wisdom literature. These libraries suggest the importance of literary culture in Assyria. There was a clear awareness that it derived from Babylonia, which probably led to that region's unique position in the Assyrian empire. The Assyrians made no attempt to incorporate the literature of any other cultural area they occupied into their own culture.

Document 13.2 *Scholarly commentaries*

By the seventh century, when the Library of Assurbanipal had its greatest growth, the literature of Mesopotamia was already very old and many literary and scholarly texts had a history of more than a thousand years. As any other language, Akkadian had developed in its use of grammar and vocabulary, and certain words and expressions were no longer clear. In the Nineveh library, and elsewhere in Assyria and later Babylonia, appeared scholarly texts that provided help to clarify such difficulties. They mostly explained omen texts, whose understanding was especially important to scholars in the king's employ.
Also for some literary texts, difficult words were explained with synonyms. The scholar wrote out a line with a difficult term and then gave an explanation of it. This example from Assurbanipal's library lists unconnected verses of a composition we call "The poem of the righteous sufferer," possibly created in the thirteenth century, and elucidates some words. The example here discusses lines 11, 21, 24, and 43 of the second tablet of the composition. I provide the difficult Akkadian words and their ancient explanations in parentheses.

I look behind: persecution, harassment (Akkadian *ip-pe-e-ri*)
harassment (Akkadian *ip-pi-ri*) = weariness (Akkadian *ma-na-aḫ-tum*) = illness (Akkadian *murṣu*)
Like one possessed(?) (Akkadian *im-ḫu-ú*), who forgot his lord: possessed(?) (Akkadian *im-ḫu-ú*) = cumbersome (Akkadian *ka-ba-tum*)
Prayer to me was the natural recourse, sacrifice my rule (Akkadian *sak-ku-ú-a*): rule (Akkadian *sak-ku-u*) = cultic rite (Akkadian *par-ṣi*)
What (the gods) intend for people changes in a twinkling (Akkadian *ki-i pi-te-e ù ka-ta-me*) = day and night (Akkadian *u₄-mu ù mu-ši*)

Translation based on W. G. Lambert, *Babylonian Wisdom Literature* (Oxford: Clarendon Press, 1960), pl. 15 and Benjamin R. Foster, *Before the Muses*, third edition (Bethesda: CDL Press, 2005), pp. 398–9.

13.5 Assyria's Fall

By 640, Assyria was at the height of its powers and controlled a vast landmass from western Iran to Egypt, having eliminated all potentially significant forces of opposition. Thirty years later the Assyrian empire was finished. What exactly happened is unclear. We have to piece together events primarily from terse Babylonian sources and from attestations of royal names in documents. Why it occurred is open to several interpretations: most likely, however, we have to search for the reasons within the structure of the Assyrian empire itself.

Assurbanipal was one of the longest reigning kings of Assyria, but we are uncertain about when exactly his rule ended and how. The last royal inscription dates to 639, and the last attestation of Assurbanipal on an administrative document to 631. The control over certain peripheral areas of the empire started to slip late in his reign. By 630 there was no longer an Assyrian presence in the southern Levant, for example, and the Egyptians had filled the power vacuum there. Most likely Assurbanipal continued to rule until his death in 627. He had designated his son Assur-etel-ilani as successor, but this was contested by another son, Sin-shar-ishkun. While such succession problems were not unusual in the Neo-Assyrian empire, they may have been more divisive than before. Assyria lost its hold over Babylonia, where the disappearance in 627 of Assurbanipal's appointed ruler, Kandalanu, created great political confusion. In 626, a native dynasty arose under a former Assyrian official, Nabopolassar. Various cities proclaimed allegiance to the different Assyrian claimants to the throne, and the Babylonians laid siege to and conquered several, causing great hardship among the inhabitants. By 616 Nabopolassar had sufficiently extended his powers throughout the region to be able to invade Assyria.

Simultaneously, in western Iran a mountain people called the Medes had strengthened its army, probably taking advantage of the power vacuum caused by Assurbanipal's eradication of Elam. The Medes had served the Assyrians in the past as mercenaries and may have learned advanced military techniques from their masters. In 615, they attacked cities in Assyria's heartland, and concluded an alliance with Babylonia, possibly selling their services as mercenaries to them. In 612, the combined forces, aided by groups like the Scythians, attacked the capital Nineveh and sacked it. The Assyrian ruler at the time, Sin-shar-ishkun, may have perished, and his successor, Assur-uballit II, took a last stand in the north-Syrian city of Harran, relying on support from Egypt. How long he lasted is unclear, but soon after 610 Assyria existed no more. Babylonia took over control of Assyrian territories in Mesopotamia, Syria, and Palestine, while the peoples of the Zagros Mountains, western Iran, and Anatolia regained their independence.

The conquerors set out to destroy the cities of Assyria, taking revenge for the humiliations they had suffered at Assyria's hands. On wall-reliefs of kings Sennacherib and Assurbanipal in Nineveh, for example, they identified the representations of the kings with the help of the inscriptions accompanying them, and ritually destroyed them by cutting out the eyes and ears. These were not random acts of mutilation. In the detailed depiction of Assurbanipal's defeat of the Elamites, for example, only the face of a soldier cutting off the head of the king of Elam was similarly destroyed, probably by the Medes, who saw the Elamites as their ancestors. Likewise, the records of loyalty oaths that King Esarhaddon had forced Median bodyguards to swear and which had been stored at Kalhu were smashed. The palaces were burnt down only after the lengthy task of defacing images and destroying symbols of submission to Assyria had been completed. The Babylonian king returned home with some of the ashes of Nineveh to avenge Sennacherib's destruction of Babylon. Assyria's heartland lost its urban characteristics and the remaining population resided in small settlements on top of massive mounds. In certain Syrian cities Assyrian administrative practices were continued, but the king of Babylon was acknowledged as the new master.

The causes of Assyria's swift collapse were probably rooted in problems inherent in the empire's basic organization. The concentration of power in the hands of one man was effective when there was an able king, but the task of government could easily exceed an individual's capabilities. While we do not know how old Assurbanipal was when he ascended the throne, he must have been advanced in age late in his 42-year-long reign Moreover, succession to the throne was always problematic in the late Assyrian period, and the ensuing conflicts caused great instability. Sennacherib had been killed by two of his sons, and his selected heir Esarhaddon had to eliminate them and other contenders before he could take a firm hold on power. The struggle between Assurbanipal and his brother Shamash-shuma-ukin that led to the devastating war in Babylonia must have been extremely disruptive to the state. Likewise, upon Assurbanipal's death, several Assyrians claimed power. The functioning of the empire was always disturbed when these internal problems occurred.

Indeed, Assyria's rapacious attitude toward the territories it conquered, with deportations and heavy demands for tribute, made any opportunity to rebel appealing. Tributary states constantly revolted despite heavy-handed Assyrian responses, and in the last decades they may have been successful in withholding tribute. Cut off from the empire's supply base, the core could not continue to maintain its massive cities and enormous army. Moreover, as many of the inhabitants of the heartland were deportees, their loyalty to the state was probably minimal and Assyrians by themselves could not continue to exercise the control needed to preserve their empire. In essence, that empire had always been built on a weak basis, and fissures could undermine the whole system. The combination of external pressure and internal conflict led to the sudden collapse of the entire structure.

As no Assyrian power was ever again to emerge, there are no native reflections on these events as there were, for example, after the Ur III state. Later traditions of people conquered by Assyria did examine the empire's fall, however, and attributed the sack of Nineveh, for instance, to divine retribution. Sennacherib's sack of Babylon was avenged this way, as was the conquest of Israel and the attacks on Judah by successive Assyrian rulers. Assyria had been arrogant, and its victims reveled in its destruction. The fourth-century Greek historian Ktesias presented the downfall in the context of the perceived opposition between Greeks and easterners. Sardanapallos, the Greek name for Assurbanipal, was doomed to fall because of his effeminate life of luxury. That tradition inspired nineteenth-century European images of the ancient Near East, which judged Assyria as the paradigm of oriental decadence. That was surely an inaccurate evaluation of this powerful empire, which was highly successful for some three centuries.

NOTES

1 Translation from Simo Parpola and Kazuko Watanabe, *Neo-Assyrian Treaties and Loyalty Oaths (State Archives of Assyria* 2) (Helsinki: Helsinki University Press, 1988), p. xxix.

2 F. M. Fales and J. N. Postgate, *Imperial Administrative Records, Part 1 (State Archives of Assyria* 7) (Helsinki: Helsinki University Press, 1992), no. 49.

3 Translation after Robert H. Pfeiffer, *State Letters of Assyria* (New Haven: American Oriental Society, 1935), no. 256.

4 After H. Hunger, *Babylonische und assyrische Kolophone* (Kevelaer: Verlag Butzon & Bercker, 1968), p. 102, no. 328.

5 After Ulla Koch-Westenholz, *Babylonian Liver Omens* (Copenhagen: Carsten Niebuhr Institute of Near Eastern Studies, 2000), p. 169.

6 After A. Guinan, in W. W. Hallo, ed., *The Context of Scripture* (Leiden: E. J. Brill, 1996), volume 1, p. 424.

7 David Brown, *Mesopotamian Planetary Astronomy: Astrology* (Groningen: Styx, 2000), p. 135.

8 After René Labat, *Traité akkadien de diagnostics et prognostics médicaux* (Paris: Académie internationale d'histoire des sciences, 1951), volume 1, pp. 2–3.

14

The Medes and Babylonians

3000	2500	2000	1500	1000	500

670s	Esarhaddon of Assyria queries sun god about Median ruler Kashtaritu
626	Nabopolassar founds Neo-Babylonian dynasty
612	Sack of Nineveh by Medes and Babylonians
605	Nabopolassar defeats Egyptians at Carchemish
587	Sack of Jerusalem by Nebuchadnezzar II
585	Median expansion in Anatolia halted
ca. 553	Rise of the Persian King Cyrus
552	Nabonidus moves to Teima
539	Cyrus captures Babylon

The military defeat of Assyria was primarily the work of two peoples, the Medes and Babylonians, who were relative newcomers to the Near Eastern scene and represented two very different political organizations and livelihoods. The Medes were pastoral mountain people from the central Zagros, where it was only in the eighth century that fortified cities appeared in strategic locations. To our knowledge they had no native written tradition, and their history must be pieced together from references in external sources. The Babylonian dynasty rose to power in the late seventh century, and became heir to the urban traditions that

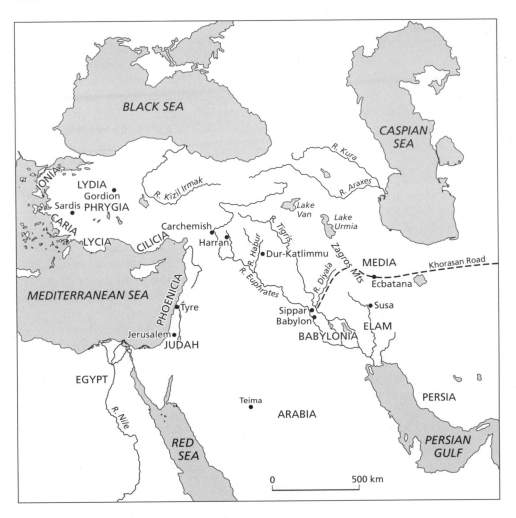

Map 14.1 The Near East in the sixth century

had long existed in Southern Mesopotamia. The kings continued earlier political, cultural, and administrative practices and emphasized connections with the second millennium. They left rich records of their accomplishments, primarily as builders. The Babylonians ruled an empire as dominant in the Near East as the Assyrian had been, but they were not alone. They confronted a resurgent Egypt, various states in Anatolia, and the nascent Persia in south-west Iran. Moreover, marauding groups such as Scythians and Cimmerians entered the area from the north and often caused serious disturbances. The history of the sixth century is determined by these various states and peoples until the Persians totally changed the organization of the region.

14.1 The Medes and the Anatolian States

Throughout their history the Assyrians had encountered various population groups in the Zagros Mountains to the east of Mesopotamia. These are only known to us from Assyrian sources as no indigenous written tradition is preserved, and the information provided is confused. Often the Assyrians seem to have jumbled names and they were unclear about what group resided exactly where. One of these groups was called the Medes, and because they would defeat the Assyrian empire they gained special attention in the ancient historical tradition. They should be seen as a typical example of a mountain people, however, who turned against their wealthy lowland neighbors. Rare references to the Medes appear in Assyrian records from the mid-ninth century on, suggesting that they inhabited the central Zagros region along the Khorasan road, east of the sources of the Diyala River. This road provided the main connection between lowland Mesopotamia and the regions of central Iran and beyond, and all overland traders in luxury goods such as metals and semi-precious stones had to use it. The desire to control the route may explain why the Assyrians in the late eighth century turned the region into three provinces, unlike other parts of the Zagros where they kept vassals in place. They established a string of fortified cities and collected taxes, mostly consisting of horses. Assyria's political control was not complete, however. Many Medes remained independent, although in small groups, and Sargon II mentions that he received tribute from some twenty-two of their chiefs (figure 14.1).

The Assyrians and Medes interacted with one another in the same way as other lowland and mountain peoples throughout Near Eastern history. On the

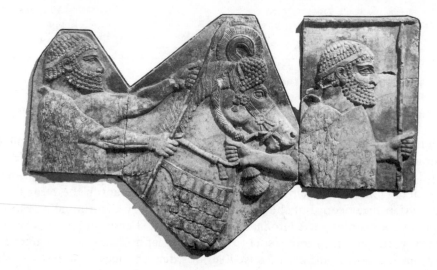

Figure 14.1 Assyrian relief from Dur-Sharrukin depicting Medes, Louvre Museum, Paris. Photo: Hevre Lewandowski. © Réunion des Musées Nationaux/Art Resource, NY

one hand, the Assyrians, who were settled farmers and city-dwellers, feared the Medes as unruly enemies; on the other hand they used their services. In the archives of King Esarhaddon (ruled 680–69) at Nineveh appear about 130 queries directed to the sun god Shamash, asking advice on how to deal with perceived threats. He implored the god to answer through messages inscribed in the organs of slaughtered rams, a typical way in which omens were communicated. Among those, twenty-three deal with Media, especially the local ruler Kashtaritu. They ask, for example:

> I ask you, Shamash, whether from this day, the 3rd day of this month, the month Iyyar, to the 11th day of the month Ab of this year, either Kashtaritu and his troops, or the troops of the Cimmerians, or the troops of the Manneans, or the troops of the Medes, or of any other enemy, will capture that city, Kishassu, enter that city, Kishassu, conquer that city, Kishassu, and whether it will be delivered to them.[1]

At the same time, Esarhaddon made several Median leaders swear allegiance to himself and the successors he had selected as kings of Assyria and Babylonia. Seven of these vassal treaties are preserved, smashed into pieces by the Medes who sacked the city Kalhu where they had been kept.[2] The Medes who swore loyalty were probably mercenaries, maybe even part of the royal bodyguard.

Assurbanipal's annihilation of the state of Elam in 646 probably permitted the Medes to expand their influence over the Zagros, and in 614 one Umakishtar attacked Assyria and soon destroyed that empire with Babylonian help. Umakishtar may have been temporarily selected as the leader of the Medes, but there is no indication he was king of a unified state. With the end of the empire, the Assyrian fortifications were abandoned and the Medes and other Zagros people continued their raids in neighboring areas. To counter them the Babylonians built a massive wall connecting the Tigris and Euphrates rivers just north of Babylon, which was later called the Median wall. The Persians, who lived in the southern Zagros, ended this situation of political fragmentation and instability. Their king, Cyrus, profited from a rebellion of the Median army against their leader Ishtumegu, and in 550 took over control over the entire Zagros, using this as a base to create the Persian empire. The Medes had been important in the history of the ancient Near East, because of their role in Assyria's overthrow, but were not unusual among the people of the Zagros Mountains.

They did play a very prominent role, however, in later reflections on this period as they are preserved in classical sources, especially the Greek historian Herodotus (box 14.1). In the first book of his *Histories* he wrote a story of state formation, where disparate groups selected a king to judge and guide them and built him a capital. The new Median state grew into a great empire with the defeat of Assyria and the conquest of eastern Anatolia, where it faced the powerful Lydian state at the Kizil Irmak River. Herodotus describes how a full solar eclipse, which we can date to May 28, 585, stopped their battle, and how

Box 14.1 *Classical sources and the history of the*
ancient Near East

With the development in fifth-century Greece of a rich literary tradition, and especially that of narrative history, a whole new perspective on the Near East becomes available through the eyes of these outsiders. Most prominent is the fifth-century work by Herodotus, who sought to explain the origins of the Persian wars by studying the histories of the people involved, both Persians and Greeks. He provides numerous stories about the Medes, Babylonians, and Egyptians as well as of people outside the Near East with whom the Persians interacted, such as the Scythians and Ethiopians. Other Greek authors included Xenophon, a mercenary commander who fought on one side of the Persian civil war in 401, and Ktesias, a physician at the Persian court around the same time. Their focus was on Persian history. A third-century Babylonian priest, Berossus, wrote a history of Babylonia in Greek for his Greek ruler, but his text is only poorly preserved in later excerpts. Altogether the record remains small. The evidence is richest on the Persians, since their powerful empire and the threat it posed to Greece spurred the Greeks to write about them. References to earlier Near Eastern history are scanty. Herodotus pays attention to Babylonia mostly because Babylon was known to him as a grand city of fabulous wealth and proportions, but gives very little historical data. He fails to fulfill his promise to write a history of Assyria.

The stories provided in these works have great appeal to a modern audience as they are structured in the style of contemporary history writing and give a coherent narrative on topics such as the history of the Medes. The accounts can only be used with great caution, however, and have to be critically evaluated. A fundamental difficulty lies in the fact that the Persians were the archenemies of the Greeks, and thus the negative bias toward them was very strong. Often Greeks portrayed Persians as the incarnation of all that was evil. They became a mirror image displaying all the opposites of Greek virtues (sobriety–excess, masculinity–femininity, etc.). Moreover, many of the stories were based on hearsay and confused names and events. In the fifth century, Herodotus knew little about seventh-century Assyrians except that they had ruled the Near East and had been very wealthy. His history of the Medes reads like a smooth and detailed account, but seems to be mostly fictional and based on Persian tales about them. The classical authors are thus not a reliable source for Near Eastern history, which needs to be reconstructed from native evidence.

they concluded a peace agreement negotiated under the auspices of the kings of Babylonia and of Cilicia. According to him, the Median empire was overthrown by one of its vassals, the Persian Cyrus. While elements of Herodotus' story agree with the bits of information we have on the Medes from Assyrian and Babylonian sources, the whole is a fictional account. No Median empire ever existed. Why was it concocted then? Herodotus imagined there had been a sequence of world empires in Asia before the Persian one that the Greeks confronted. He knew about Assyria and Persia, but in between them was a void. This he filled with the Medes, and thereby he created a phantom empire whose image is still widely accepted today.

If we can believe Herodotus, the Medes raided central Anatolia and threatened regions further west. The Assyrians had incorporated only the southern part of Anatolia into the empire, and launched sporadic campaigns further north and east. Assyria's main opponent there was Phrygia, a central Anatolian state that was famous in later Greek tradition for the enormous wealth of its king, Midas. Sargon II campaigned against a Mita of Mushku, who must be the same man. Together with the king of Urartu, Midas supported anti-Assyrian rebellions in northern Syria and southern Anatolia, but finally he concluded a peace treaty with Sargon. His nemesis came from the north. In 695, nomadic Cimmerian warriors overran Phrygia and sacked the capital Gordion. Together with another northern nomadic group, the Scythians, they caused great disruption in many parts of the Near East. Urartu and Assyria were repeatedly engaged in battle against them or tried to keep them at bay through diplomacy, while, according to Herodotus, the Medes were temporarily dominated by the Scythians. Both groups participated in the final defeat of Assyria and remained present in Anatolia, although they never formed a state. The homeland of the Scythians seems to have been the region north of the Black Sea, and it is there that the Persian king, Darius, would unsuccessfully campaign against them.

When Phrygia was severely reduced in strength, its western neighbor, Lydia, became the main power in the west of Anatolia. King Gyges established contacts with the Assyrians and wanted to be included among the great kings of the time. Access to gold and silver mines made the state famous for its wealth. In the sixth century, Lydia under King Alyattes (ruled ca. 610–560) expanded in all directions, bringing it in direct contact with the Greek settlers on the west coast of Anatolia. The close interactions between the two peoples led to a dramatic expansion of the use of coinage, a Lydian invention originally minted in electrum. Moreover, the Greeks became interested in Lydia, and Herodotus describes Lydian history in detail, seeing the origin of the animosity between Greeks and easterners in the Greek cities' conflict with the Lydian state. Alyattes' successor Croesus (ruled 560–47) wanted to extend firm dominion from the Aegean sea to the Kizil Irmak River, and constantly put pressure on Greek cities in the west of Anatolia. His attack on Persia brought about his downfall. Crossing the Kizil Irmak River with a vast army, he was held back by Cyrus of Persia, who chased him into his own territory and took the capital Sardis as well as the entire Lydian state. Other states existed in Anatolia, such as Cilicia, Caria, and Lycia, whose histories can be similarly reconstructed from Near Eastern and classical sources. Their remains, textual and archaeological, demonstrate the survival of some of the second-millennium traditions in language and culture and the adoption of influences from the surrounding world, especially of the maritime Phoenicians and Greeks. There was a great diversity of cultures and intense interaction and cross-fertilization in western Anatolia. The fact that much of pre-classical Greek culture was influenced by the civilizations of the Near East should not, therefore, come as a surprise. The literature and arts of eighth- through sixth-century Greece were part of the cultural *koine* of the eastern Mediterranean world that was imbued by Near Eastern traditions.

14.2 The Neo-Babylonian Dynasty

Once Assyria's control over southern Mesopotamia had slipped following the death of Assurbanipal, a local official, Nabopolassar, took the throne of Babylon in 626, and by 616 he united the entire area under his rule. He founded a dynasty, often called Neo-Babylonian in modern scholarship, and was instrumental in overthrowing the Assyrian empire (for a king list, see p. 313). Babylonia took over most of the territory that Assyria had ruled. Already in the last decades of its existence, the Assyrian empire's grasp over the Syro-Palestinian area had disappeared and Egypt had filled the void there. Thus soon after Assyria's defeat, Babylonia and Egypt faced one another for control over the region. Nebuchadnezzar II led the Babylonian forces, first as crown-prince, then as king, and in 605 he inflicted a serious defeat on the Egyptians near the north Syrian city of Carchemish. Soon afterwards his father died and Nebuchadnezzar had to rush to Babylon to secure his hold on the throne. He returned to the west immediately, and although battles were fought close to Egypt, Babylonia had a hard time asserting its authority there. States constantly rebelled in support of Egypt. Best known is the situation in Judah, which was turned into a province of the Babylonian empire following the pattern Assyria had established centuries before. In 597, Nebuchadnezzar removed the local king and replaced him with a puppet ruler, while he deported a large part of the population to Babylonia. The newly installed king turned against his master, however, and after a siege the capital Jerusalem was destroyed and more people were deported in 587. In 582 the Babylonian governor was assassinated during a rebellion and Nebuchadnezzar had to intervene again, deporting even more Judeans. He annexed other previously independent states, such as Tyre, whose siege lasted thirteen years. Nebuchadnezzar wanted complete dominion over Syria-Palestine, perhaps because he intended to invade Egypt. After several inconclusive battles with that state, he seems to have given up, however, and a border was agreed upon in 567.

Nebuchadnezzar stands out as the great military leader of the Neo-Babylonian dynasty, but that image is probably exaggerated by the nature of the documentation available. Unlike the Assyrians, the Babylonian kings did not leave lengthy accounts of their campaigns and the information on Nebuchadnezzar derives from two chronicles and from external sources, especially the Hebrew Bible whose authors bore the brunt of Babylonian military action. For later Neo-Babylonian kings only vague references to military successes exist, but their accomplishments in that area might not have been minor. Neriglissar, for instance, annexed Cilicia, the leading state in south-west Anatolia, and

Nabonidus conquered several oases in the north of the Arabian Desert. Also in contrast to the Assyrian situation, we have virtually no idea about how the empire was administered. We know that governors were appointed but not the names and extent of the provinces, the way in which taxes were collected, and so on. The archives of the Babylonian state are not preserved. This lack of information should not lead to the conclusion that the Babylonian empire was fundamentally different from its predecessor. On the contrary, it is best regarded as the successor to Assyria. In the Syrian city of Dur-Katlimmu the Babylonians continued Assyrian administrative practices, now with an acknowledgment of the king in Babylon as supreme ruler. As the example of Judah shows, they deported entire populations, and the fact that people continued to rebel shows that imperial rule must have been harsh. One could even say that the Babylonian attitude toward conquered territories was more oppressive. Unlike the Assyrians, they did not develop the southern Levant after they conquered it, but left the region uninhabited and the cities destroyed. This was probably due to the fact that the core was so rich that it did not need supplies from the periphery, and led to more devastation in the latter areas.

The focus of royal inscriptions of the period is on building activity, and indeed in this area the Babylonian kings were extremely active, as archaeology confirms. Nebuchadnezzar wanted Babylon to express in its physical layout and monuments the idea that it was the center of the universe, bringing order in a world of chaos and constantly renewing the primordial act of creation. His rebuilding of the city caught the imagination of the ancient world. Both the city-walls and the elusive hanging gardens were among the seven wonders of the ancient world. The awe in which Babylon was held is evidenced by Herodotus' description (Book I, 178–83). Scholars strongly disagree about whether the Greek historian visited the city, a question that will never be settled. More important than establishing that fact is the clear indication that he saw the city as the epitome of wealth and majesty. Excavations there, which started at the end of the nineteenth century, have substantiated some of this image. At 900 hectares, the city was gigantic in size. The outer walls formed a triangle with a perimeter of 18 kilometers, the inner city was a rectangle surrounded by three sets of walls, two of them of baked bricks (figure 14.2). The gates were especially monumental. Most famous is the Ishtar gate, an entrance that was entirely decorated with glazed colored tiles forming images of bulls, lions, and dragons in low relief (figure 14.3). The ziggurat of Marduk, removed by Alexander of Macedon, was so massive that it inspired the Biblical tale of the tower of Babel. While Nebuchadnezzar was not the only Babylonian king responsible for these construction projects, his extensive involvement is clear from the thousands of bricks and stone tiles inscribed by him. Many other cities of Babylonia were similarly restored and their temples embellished. As in the case of Assyria, the spoils of the empire seem to have financed a huge building programme at home.

Nebuchadnezzar's succession was extremely problematic; three kings ruled for a total of six years only, and two of them were assassinated. Finally, a man

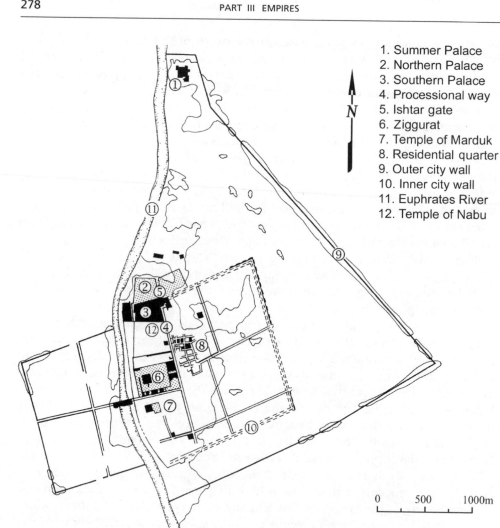

1. Summer Palace
2. Northern Palace
3. Southern Palace
4. Processional way
5. Ishtar gate
6. Ziggurat
7. Temple of Marduk
8. Residential quarter
9. Outer city wall
10. Inner city wall
11. Euphrates River
12. Temple of Nabu

N

0   500   1000m

Figure 14.2 Plan of Babylon in the sixth century, from Marc Van De Mieroop, "Reading Babylon," *American Journal of Archaeology* 107 (2003), p. 262

of non-royal descent, Nabonidus (ruled 555–39), was placed on the throne. He is one of the most intriguing figures in Mesopotamian history, an image certainly determined by the pro-Persian propaganda literature composed against him by the Marduk priesthood. Nabonidus is one of the few individuals in Near Eastern history whose mother we know. Adad-guppi was a devotee of the moon god Sin in the north Syrian city of Harran, and she left an autobiography in which she states that she was born in the twentieth year of King Assurbanipal and cared for the god for ninety-five years (document 14.1). The transition from Assyrian to Babylonian rule did not affect her situation. Devotion to the moon god was one of Nabonidus' characteristics too, which caused the enmity of the Marduk priesthood. He gave special attention to the

Figure 14.3 Lion relief from the Ishtar gate at Babylon. Courtesy of The Metropolitan Museum of Art. Fletcher Fund, 1931 (31.13.12). Photograph, all rights reserved, The Metropolitan Museum of Art

Document 14.1 *Excerpts from Adad-guppi's autobiography*

The text was found in two copies on paving stones at the entrance to the mosque of Harran, the city commemorated here as the center of the moongod Sin's cult. It starts with a first-person account by Adad-guppi and ends with a description of her burial.

I am Adad-guppi, mother of Nabonidus, king of Babylon, a servant of Sin, Ningal, Nusku, and Sadarnunna, my gods, for whose divinity I have cared since my youth. . . .

From the twentieth year of Assurbanipal, king of Assur, in which I was born, until the forty-second year of Assurbanipal, the third year of Assur-etel-ilani, his son, the twenty-first year of Nabopolassar, the forty-third year of Nebuchadnezzar, the second year of Evil-Merodach, the fourth year of Neriglissar – for ninety-five years I cared for Sin, the king of the gods of heaven and earth, and for the sanctuaries of his great divinity. He looked upon me and my good deeds with joy. Having heard my prayers and agreeing to my request, the wrath of his heart calmed. He was reconciled with Ehulhul, Sin's house, located in the midst of Harran, his favorite dwelling.

Sin, the king of the gods, looked upon me. He called Nabonidus, my only son, my offspring, to kingship. He personally delivered the kingship of Sumer and Akkad, from the border of Egypt and the upper sea, to the lower sea, all the land. . . .

When, in my dream, Sin, the king of the gods, had set his hands on me, he said thus: "Through you I will bring about the return of the gods (to) the dwelling in Harran, by means of Nabonidus your son. He will construct Ehulhul; he will complete its work. He will complete the city Harran greater than it was before and restore it. He will bring Sin, Ningal, Nusku, and Sadarnunna, in procession back into the Ehulhul.

I was attentive to the word of Sin and I saw it come true! Nabonidus, (my) only son, my offspring, completed the neglected rites of Sin, Ningal, Nusku, and Sadarnunna. He constructed the Ehulhul anew. He completed its work. He completed Harran better than before, he restored it; he brought Sin, Ningal, Nusku, and Sadarnunna from Babylon, the royal city, into the center of Harran, into Ehulhul their favorite dwelling. He made (them) dwell there in joy and in happiness.

What Sin, the king of the gods, had not done before and had not granted to anyone, for love of me who worshipped his divinity, (who) beseeched him, the king of the gods – he raised my head; he gave me a fine reputation in the land, long days and years of well-being he added to me. From the period of Assurbanipal, king of Assur, until the ninth year of Nabonidus, king of Babylon, my offspring, they established me for 104 years in the worship of Sin, the king of the gods. He kept me alive and well. My eyesight is clear and my mind is excellent. My hands and my feet are healthy. Well chosen are my words; food and drink still agree with me. My flesh is vital; my heart is joyful. My little ones living four generations from me I have seen. I have reached a ripe old age.

In the ninth year of Nabonidus, king of Babylon, she [died]. Nabonidus, king of Babylon, her son, her offspring, buried her corpse, . . . , fine (clothing), a [bright] mantle, gold . . . [bright] beautiful stones, (choice) stones, precious stones . . . her corpse with fine oil they placed in a hidden location. He sl[aughtered] fattened sheep before her. He gathered together Babylon and Borsippa [with the people] dwelling in distant regions, [kings, princes], and governors, from the [border] of Egypt, the [upper] sea, to the lower sea he [caused to arise] . . . mourning and [ ]. They cried out [bitter]ly. They threw down their [ ] seven [days] and seven nights [ ]. They piped; they cast down [their] clothes. On the seventh day, the troops of the entire land cut [their] hair [ ] their garments [ ] their clothes chest [ ] in food [ ] he [colle]cted perfume [ ] fine oil on [their] heads he poured. He caused their hearts to rejoice. . . .

Translation by Tremper Longman III, *Fictional Akkadian Autobiography* (Winona Lake: Eisenbrauns, 1991), pp. 225–8, reproduced with the author's permission.

temples of Sin in Harran and Ur and made his daughter high priestess in the latter city, reviving an office that had lapsed many years before. More disturbing to the Marduk priesthood, however, was his decision in 552 to abandon the capital Babylon and move to the oasis of Teima in the Arabian Desert, leaving his son Belshazzar in charge. This resulted in the cancellation of the New Year's festival in which the king in person had to lead the ceremonies. The annual introduction of Marduk's statue into his temple, which indicated the beginning of the year, did not take place, and this disrupted the entire cultic cycle. Furthermore, when Nabonidus returned after about ten years from Teima, he turned several temples, including Marduk's at Babylon, into sanctuaries for Sin. Both the texts commissioned by Nabonidus and those written about him portray a man who sought to change Babylonian culture, looking at the ancient written traditions in order to put his personal mark on them. These acts made him highly unpopular with the priests and traditional scholars of

Babylon, and possibly already during his reign they composed texts portraying his behavior as a crime that Marduk would avenge. A text written when Cyrus of Persia was king of Babylon states:

> By his own plan, he did away with the worship of Marduk, the king of the gods; he continually did evil against Marduk's city . . . Daily, [ ] he imposed the corvée upon its inhabitants unrelentingly, ruining them all.[3]

Nabonidus' move to the desert was probably informed by an astute understanding of the international political situation rather than by purely religious motives. The cult of the moon god was indeed prominent in Arabia, but there is no clear indication in Nabonidus' inscriptions that he promoted it there. Probably more important in his decision to move the court to Teima were the political changes that were taking place in Iran. By 559, Cyrus had become the leader of the Persians and in 550 he had established full control over the Zagros region. The expansionist aims of the new king may have been clear to Nabonidus. Northern Mesopotamia and Syria were easy targets for armies coming from Anatolia, and the loss of these territories would have cut off Babylonia from the Mediterranean Sea. Nabonidus may have been exploring new routes through the desert from Babylon to the west to secure access to that sea. Moreover, north Arabia was known for its wealth, which must have appealed to the king. The move to the desert was thus not frivolous, although it may have exacerbated hostility toward him at home.

Possibly because of the Babylonian population's resentment of their king, the Persian conquest of the region seems to have been straightforward. In 539, Cyrus entered the country from the east. After a major battle near the confluence of the Diyala and Tigris rivers, won by the Persians, he took over cities without resistance. On October 12, 539, Babylon fell and native rule over the area was ended for many centuries. With the capital, Persia received the entire territory of the Babylonian empire and profited from Babylonia's earlier achievements in its unprecedented expansion. Cyrus used Nabonidus' negative image in support of his claim to kingship in Babylonia and portrayed himself as a savior selected by Marduk to restore order and justice. This image of Nabonidus survives in later Jewish tradition. In the first century BC, he appears in the Dead Sea scrolls as having been struck by an evil disease while in Teima. In the Biblical book of Daniel, written in the Hellenistic period, this image is shifted to Nebuchadnezzar, better known and more hated in Jewish tradition. It says about him: "He was driven from among men, and ate grass like an ox, and his body was wet with the dew of heaven till his hair grew as long as eagles' feathers, and his nails were like birds' claws" (Daniel 4: 33).

The Neo-Babylonian period initiated twelve centuries of great economic prosperity for Babylonia whose basis was agriculture. Peaceful conditions after centuries of often devastating wars enabled the irrigation system to be expanded, and a grid pattern of canals was laid out throughout the countryside. Large tracts of land could now be cultivated, although water was an expensive commodity. Labor was also difficult to obtain and the Neo-Babylonian rulers continued the Assyrian practice of deportations, settling many people in Babylonia itself. This may reflect a policy of internal colonization, the organized development, with coerced labor, of territory within the state itself.

There was a great deal of exchange of goods, both within Babylonia and with other regions of the empire and abroad. The canals provided an easy way to transport agricultural produce by boat, and many documents record shipments of barley, dates, and other bulk items. Those ventures were financed by trading houses such as the house of Egibi from Babylon. They accepted deposits, provided loans, paid off clients' debts, and enabled the acquisition of goods for future payment by providing credit. The family was very successful in its trade of agricultural products, which enabled it to acquire large tracts of land, and some of its members became leading officials in Babylon. In the cities, small-scale peddlers sold salt, beer, cooking wares, and so on. Long-distance trade was conducted between the regions of the empire and beyond: Egypt, Cyprus, Anatolia, Syria-Palestine, Babylonia, and western Iran made up a world where goods such as iron, copper, tin, lapis lazuli, textiles and the products of textile manufacture (natron, dyes, etc.), wine, honey, and spices were exchanged in great quantities. Merchants were attached to the palace and the temples, or could act independently. Political boundaries did not seem to affect their work. Greek pottery from Athens, for example, was found in Babylon. Also the change in political regimes did not negatively affect this activity, and the Egibi house continued its business without interruption when the Persians captured Babylonia.

The extensive economic activity required detailed recordkeeping, and the Neo-Babylonian and subsequent Achaemenid periods provide us with the greatest abundance of documents from Babylonia after the Ur III period. Some 15,000 tablets have been published and many more are known to exist in museums. They derive almost exclusively from temple and private archives. The palace's role in the economy is thus not directly documented, which certainly biases our view of affairs. Many temples owned large and self-contained agricultural estates with fields, orchards, and animal herds. A substantial part of their wealth derived from "tithes" paid by all who owned land or another source of income and lived nearby the temple estates. While the figure was not always exactly 10 percent, all people, including the king, had to give a share of the profits they made on fields, orchards, herds, and so on to the temple. These were paid in kind or in silver, and were collected by special officials. If people were unable to pay, they had to take out loans from private moneylenders or give their children to the temple as slaves. As hired labor was rare, slaves were very useful for performing menial tasks. Another source of slaves was prisoners of war given by the king to the temples. Yet the majority of temple land was farmed by non-slave laborers who were assigned plots for which they were required to pay a share of the harvest as rent. The palace and private landowners used the same arrangement on their estates. They provided seed grain, tools, and plow animals when these were needed, so the farmers had little invested in the land. Yet they were not allowed to leave without permission, and runaways were arrested and returned in shackles.

The collection of rents and the distribution of seed and tools, as well as marketing the harvests, required complex organization. Landowners, both institutional and private, were reluctant to undertake this themselves so they relied on entrepreneurs, as was done in earlier Babylonian history from the early second millennium on. These middlemen were often organized in business houses that administered such affairs for various owners in the same region and continued to do so under different political regimes. Their access to silver allowed them to purchase in advance of the harvest, to finance transport to cities, and to issue loans to defaulting tenants. They also used their assets to finance trade. Private archives provide the second largest source of documentation from the Neo-Babylonian period, and contain records of many activities beyond the entrepreneurs' businesses. Anything that involved a transfer of property was recorded in a detailed contract witnessed by several people (document 14.2).

Document 14.2 *Neo-Babylonian private contracts*

The Neo-Babylonian period has provided one of the richest textual records for the study of ancient Near Eastern society and economy, and thousands of cuneiform tablets with documents of daily life are preserved. Among them is a group of marriage contracts that stipulate agreements made between a husband and his wife's family. Contracts of this type often contain a direct speech, where one party asks the other to initiate a transaction.

Mr. Dagil-ili, son of Mr. Zambubu, spoke to Ms. Hamma, daughter of Mr. Nergal-iddin, descendant of Mr. Babutu, as follows: "Please give me Ms. La-tubashshinni, your daughter. Let her be my wife."

Ms. Hamma agreed with him and gave Ms. La-tubashshinni, her daughter, to him as wife. And Mr. Dagil-ili voluntarily gave to Ms. Hamma, in consideration of Ms. La-tubashshinni her daughter, Mr. Ana-muhhi-bel-amur, a slave who was bought for one-half pound of silver, and in addition another one and one-half pounds of silver.

Should Mr. Dagil-ili take another wife, Mr. Dagil-ili will give one pound of silver to Ms. La-tubashshinni, and she may go wherever she pleases.

(This agreement was concluded) in the presence of Mr. Shum-iddin, son of Mr. Ina-teshi-etir, descendant of Mr. Sin-damaqu. The witnesses (were): Mr. Bel-ahhe-iddin, son of Mr. Nabu-bel-shumati, descendant of the priest of Ishtar of Babylon; Mr. Marduk-sharrani, son of Mr. Balatu, descendant of the potter; Mr. Marduk-etir, son of Mr. Nergal-iddin, descendant of Mr. Babutu; and the scribe Mr. Nabu-mukin-zeri, son of Mr. Marduk-zer-ibni, descendant of the priest of Ishtar of Babylon.

(Written in) Babylon, month Marchesvan, day 9, year 13 of Nebuchadnezzar, king of Babylon.

Translation after Martha T. Roth, *Babylonian Marriage Agreements 7th–3rd Centuries BC* (Kevelaer: Butzon & Bercker, 1984), pp. 42–3.

Numerous private family archives are preserved today: they documented all assets, such as real estate, slaves, and animals, and outstanding debts. The records were often kept for several generations and they show that relatives such as cousins and in-laws regularly worked together and owned property in common.

Neo-Babylonian society was very much concentrated in cities. The level of urbanization was substantially higher than at any time in the preceding centuries, although it did not reach early second-millennium levels. Places such as Babylon became enormous in terms of their size and number of inhabitants and had to be fed by a large hinterland. Agricultural production was probably partly specialized by region to satisfy demand. The relationship between cities and the state was similar to that in Neo-Assyrian times. Kings had to grant special privileges to certain ancient cities, exempting them from military and labor services. The cities were self-governing organizations centered on the temple, which is the source of most of our documentary evidence. Cities had their own law courts and cases were often decided in assemblies. We do not know who was allowed to sit in them, however. The temples provided the social structure of these cities, as an individual's position in the temple hierarchy determined his social status and authority in the urban government. Free laborers, such as skilled craftsmen, could negotiate their rights as a group. Rural populations were not in such a privileged position. Tied to the land they worked, they were forced to provide labor and rent to the landowners. High state officials were given estates, which changed hands repeatedly during political crises such as the succession problems following Nebuchadnezzar II. The owners were absentee landlords with little connection to their properties, who left the management to local entrepreneurs and were only interested in profits. Many of the farmers were deportees brought in from distant parts of the empire and housed together in villages.

The policy of deportation to the heartland of the empire and extensive contacts with foreign states resulted in cities such as Babylon becoming multiethnic. People from Syria-Palestine, Phoenicia, Elam, Persia, Media, Ionia, Cilicia, and Egypt lived in close proximity. The deported upper classes were allowed to live at the royal court. People from enemy states were welcome, too: Egyptians, for example, are attested all over Babylonia, often as scribes of cuneiform tablets.

A multitude of languages and customs must have been present in Babylon. However, the kings pursued a policy of maintaining, and even reviving, ancient Babylonian culture and traditions. Akkadian was probably no longer widely spoken and was replaced by Aramaic as the main vernacular, but it was preserved as the language of culture and administration. As in the Neo-Assyrian period, ancient literature was copied out and preserved. But the interaction with the past went further. In inscriptions, outdated Akkadian expressions and Sumerian words were used. Sometimes the cuneiform script was made to look like that of the third millennium. Interest in the past was not limited to texts. When ancient artworks were discovered they were preserved. Nabonidus found a statue of Sargon of Akkad, set it up in a temple, and provided it with regular offerings. In the temple of Shamash at Sippar modern excavators discovered objects dating back as far as the Jemdet Nasr period, from Babylonia and from neighboring regions, including inscribed stone bowls, statues, boundary stones and so on. Similar collections were kept in other cities as well. When temples were restored it was important that the earliest foundations were located, so something resembling modern archaeological research took place. Nabonidus recounts how Nebuchadnezzar had failed to determine where the foundations of the Sippar temple were located, and that his restoration had been unsteady as a result. So he repeated the excavations until a foundation deposit from the time of Naram-Sin of Akkad was found, and only then was the temple properly rebuilt. Nabonidus even determined that Naram-Sin had ruled 3200 years before him, a gross miscalculation but an indication that he saw himself as heir to a very old tradition. Such an attitude explains how he could revive the office of high priestess of the moon god at Ur, which had originally been created by Sargon. Notwithstanding the innovations Nabonidus attempted, the religious practices in the Neo-Babylonian period were traditional and continued to focus on the age-old gods of the region. As in the past, each city was considered to be the home of a particular deity and the main temple was that god's residence. Because of the central role of temples in the economy, many of them were very wealthy and cults flourished. Some of the oldest cults of Babylonia experienced a revival, for example those of gods Anu and Ishtar at Uruk. In the city of Babylon the god Marduk was pre-eminent, and his leading status in the pantheon was confirmed annually in the New Year's festival. At that time the statues of other gods visited the god and entered the city in a public procession leading to the main sanctuary where Marduk's kingship over them was renewed.

The Neo-Babylonian dynasty was the last native Mesopotamian dynasty in ancient Near Eastern history and therefore its end may be seen by us as a momentous event, although it probably was not by the people at the time. The kings saw themselves as very much part of an old tradition of Babylonian greatness going back to the third millennium, and promoted an awareness of that tradition. Babylonian culture was extremely strong by the time the dynasty was overthrown, and survived unscathed in the following historical era.

NOTES

1   Translation by Ivan Starr, *Queries to the Sungod* (State Archives of Assyria 4) (Helsinki: Helsinki University Press, 1990), no. 43.
2   Simo Parpola and Kazuko Watanabe, *Neo-Assyrian Treaties and Loyalty Oaths* (State Archives of Assyria 2) (Helsinki: Helsinki University Press, 1988), no. 6.
3   Translation by Mordechai Cogan, in W. W. Hallo, ed., *The Context of Scripture* (Leiden: E. J. Brill, 2000), volume 2, p. 315.

15

The Persian Empire

3000	2500	2000	1500	1000	500

559   Cyrus rises to power in Persia

547   Cyrus conquers Lydia

539   Cyrus conquers Babylonia

525   Cambyses conquers Egypt

521   Darius usurps the throne

490   Battle of Marathon in Greece

331   Defeat of Darius III by Alexander of Macedon

323   Death of Alexander in Babylon

In a few decades of the second half of the sixth century, the Persians of south-west Iran created an enormous empire covering the entire Near East and regions beyond from the Indus Valley to northern Greece, from Central Asia to southern Egypt (for a king list, see p. 314). It was to last more or less intact for two hundred years, a long time when compared to previous and subsequent empires in the region. It successfully brought together areas with different languages, cultures, economies, and sociopolitical organizations, and was the first in Near Eastern history to acknowledge the variety among its people. Its swift expansion was halted when Persia failed to conquer mainland Greece despite several attempts, and those wars dominate the historical record available to us. Classical sources provide the greatest detail on Persian history, but as they are written from the perspective of a people threatened by the empire, they are exceedingly biased. On the one hand, they often portray Persians in a stereotyped negative light, although the approach of some authors is surprisingly nuanced at times. Herodotus, for example, may depict Cambyses as a raving madman, but he portrays Xerxes both as a wise ruler with good strategic insight and as a tyrant. Xenophon presents Cyrus as the example of the ideal king. On the other hand, the Greeks primarily cared about the western part of the empire and provide virtually no information on the extensive eastern dominions. This situation is exacerbated by the scarcity of historical inscriptions from Persia itself. Only isolated texts, most prominently the description of Darius' rise to power, deal with anything but building activity. There are no accounts of the numerous campaigns that are known to us from Greek references. While economic practices in various parts of the empire were continued, including in Egypt and Mesopotamia where records were meticulously kept, few archives have been used for historical reconstructions. Our view of Persia is thus focused on western regions and emphasizes its negative aspects. This should not prevent us from seeing in it a successful imperial structure that kept together an enormous territory until it was defeated by Alexander of Macedon. During its existence, it established patterns of rule and administration that influenced the Near East for many centuries to come.

15.1 The Rise of Persia and its Expansion

The heartland of Persia was located in the south-west of Iran, in the region today called Fars, south of the earlier state of Elam and of Media. Starting in the early sixth century, a local dynasty traced its ancestry back to a man called Achaemenes, and the term Achaemenids is often used to refer to the Persians. In 559 Cyrus came to power, and in 550 he defeated the Median ruler Ishtumegu. Herodotus claims he was a vassal who overthrew his master, while Babylonian sources report a conquest of one state by another. With this act Cyrus took over the entire territory the Medes had controlled, and he and his immediate successors pursued rapid military expansion, creating an enormous empire. In 547 Cyrus defeated King Croesus of Lydia, thereby reaching the Aegean Sea and Greek cities on the Anatolian coast. From 546 to 540 he probably campaigned in eastern Iran, but the details are unknown. In 539 he marched against Babylonia, a war he seemingly won easily because of the population's dissatisfaction with King Nabonidus. The capture of Babylon's throne made Cyrus ruler of the entire Neo-Babylonian empire, although Arabia and Cilicia were lost. The end of Cyrus' reign was taken up with military activity in Central Asia where, according to Herodotus, Cyrus died in battle in 530.

His successor Cambyses (ruled 529–22) had already been active in the campaigns in the west as crown prince and co-regent, and his greatest military accomplishment as king was the conquest of Egypt in 525. He overextended himself, however, by attempting to expand along the north African coast and into the oases and Nubia, enterprises that were doomed to failure. The

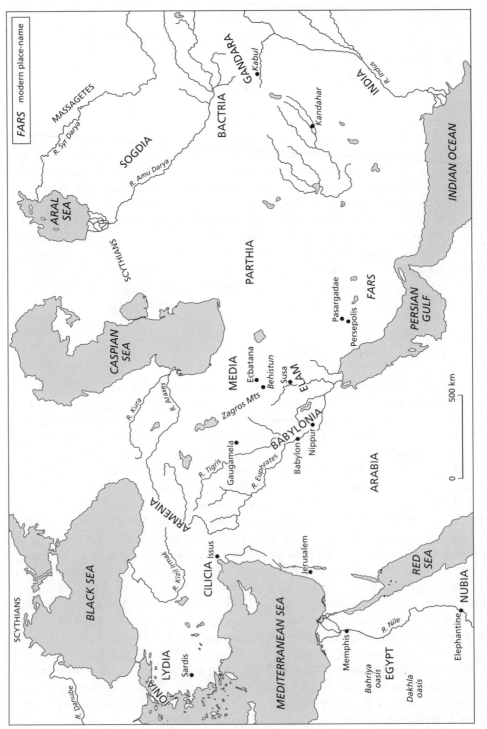

Map 15.1 The Persian empire (after Josef Wiesehöfer, *Das antike Persien* [Zurich: Artemis and Wickler, 1993])

annexation of Egypt was not a raid, as it had been under the Assyrians, but a true incorporation of the country into the Persian empire. Cambyses became king of Egypt and seems to have stayed there for most of his reign until 522. Expansion did not end there, however. Darius (ruled 521–486) was able to conquer Libya and to exact tribute from Nubia. He also invaded Scythia, an unsuccessful project according to Herodotus, but he did subject some of its people. Western India was also annexed.

Perhaps in revenge for a rebellion by Greek cities on the Aegean coast and in Cyprus that took from 499 to 494 to subdue, Darius decided to invade Greece itself, but was rebuffed in 490 at the battle of Marathon. The conquest of Greece became a primary goal of his successor Xerxes (ruled 485–65), or at least it is depicted as such by the classical authors. They saw the Persian wars as testimony to the steadfast Greek desire for independence and portrayed them as a battle between eastern slavery and western freedom. Several Persian attacks by land and by sea were repelled and in 478 Xerxes abandoned his attempt at conquest, which may indicate the end of the empire's expansion. Persia had to remain militarily alert, however, as rebellions in its territory occurred regularly, including a successful revolt by Egypt, which became independent from 404 to 343.

The Persian military had thus been extremely effective in bringing together numerous earlier states and empires under one rule, and had done so quite swiftly. Its main strength seems to have been its size, an aspect that Greek authors certainly exaggerated. Herodotus (Book VII, 185) states that Xerxes led 2,617,610 men into Greece, a truly fantastic number. The army could draw on an enormous population for its soldiers and successfully coordinated the different populations with their specific military skills. Arabian camel drivers fought next to Libyan charioteers. Phoenicians manned the navy with Egyptians, Cypriots, and Ionians. Closest to the king as his personal bodyguard was the corps of 10,000 lancers, also called "Immortals." Made up of native Persians, their number remained exactly the same as each fallen man was immediately replaced.

The system of recruitment is known from Babylonian sources. State-owned land was rented out to groups of men who, in return, had to provide a type of military service, as charioteers, cavalrymen, or archers. Over time they may have become professional soldiers who had their fields managed by specialized business houses, such as the Murashu family in the Nippur region. They found tenants, provided seed grain and access to water, and collected rents and taxes. Babylonia's system need not have been universally applied throughout the empire, but it is clear that the vast manpower available, as well as the resources to pay for the soldiers, gave the king access to an immense army. Classical sources depict a situation in which the use of mercenaries, especially Greek, increased over time, and suggest that by the fourth century they alone made up the army's true strength. It is undeniable that mercenaries were used. The Greek author Xenophon, for example, was a mercenary commander who in 401 led 10,000 Greek soldiers in the service of Cyrus the younger in an unsuccessful bid to seize the throne. He left a detailed account of the men's march from the Aegean Sea to the battle in northern Babylonia and back. The importance of mercenary forces is overstated, however, and forms part of the Greek portrayal of Persia as a decadent society after Xerxes. It should not be taken at face value, as the Persian army remained a formidable opponent. It did indeed collapse between 334 and 330 under Macedonian attacks, but this seems to have been the result of Alexander's skillful use of the phalanx rather than of a gradual decline in Persian military might.

15.2   Political Developments

The swift expansion of the empire and its vast size presented one of its greatest challenges. Local desires for independence led to rebellions, which remained a constant feature throughout the history of Persia. A more serious threat to stability, however, was the competition for power within the Persian royal house itself. The earliest attestation of this already appears in the reign of Cambyses. Our main source of information about events is the description by the final victor, Darius, who was not a legitimate successor to the throne. His account was carved in three languages (Old Persian, Elamite, and Akkadian) on a rock facade at Behistun in a Zagros Mountain valley connecting Babylonia and Iran (document 15.1 and figure 15.1). It was also spread throughout the empire in Aramaic translation on papyri, and possibly Herodotus used one of these as the basis for the story he told in his *Histories*. We have thus a severely biased description by a usurper who justifies his actions in the text, and it is not easy to determine what really happened.

Cambyses' prolonged stay in Egypt gave his brother Bardiya a chance to claim kingship at home. The latter abolished taxes and military levies for three years in order to gain popular support. Cambyses returned from Egypt but was probably assassinated either by Bardiya or by Darius, a high military commander who subsequently killed Bardiya. When these dynastic struggles occurred, various parts of the empire rebelled, including Persia, Media, Elam, Babylonia, Assyria, and Egypt. The rebels often proclaimed themselves descendants of the last independent ruler of their states. In Babylon a Nebuchadnezzar, son of Nabonidus, appeared, in Media a Hashatritu, descendant of Umakishtar. Darius goes into these matters in great detail: he calls the local men liars and not of royal blood, since he had to become the legitimate heir to these various thrones. The insurrections lasted several years, from 522 to 518, and Darius was often forced to return to a region many times to deal with successive rebels. The whole empire was involved, including Persia, and Darius' real task was to make himself accepted as ruler by all the populations.

Probably as a result of these troubles, Darius regularized imperial control once he was fully in charge. Instead of a number of polities with different systems of rule but headed by the same person, the empire was turned into a uniform structure of about twenty provinces. These are often called satrapies

Document 15.1   *The Behistun Inscription of Darius*

This long inscription, carved in three languages (Old Persian, Elamite, and Akkadian) on the cliff at Behistun in the Zagros Mountains on the road from Babylon to Ecbatana, contains the explanation of how Darius came to be king of Persia. The translation of some excerpts here is based on the Akkadian version.

I am Darius the king, the son of Hystaspes, the Achaemenid, the King of Kings, the Persian, the king of Persia. . . .

Thus says Darius, the king: These are the countries that listen to me – it is under the protection of the god Ahuramazda that I am their king: Persia, Elam, Babylonia, Assyria, Arabia, Egypt, the Sealand, Sardis, Ionia, Media, Urartu, Cappadocia, Parthia, Drangiana, Aria, Choresmia, Bactria, Sogdiana, Gandhara, Scythia, Sattagydia, Arachosia, and Maka, in total twenty-three countries. . . .

Thus says Darius, the king: This is what I have done in one year under the protection of the god Ahuramazda. After becoming king, I have fought nineteen battles in one year, and under the protection of Ahuramazda I have won them. I have captured nine kings: The Magian named Gaumata, who lied saying: "I am Bardiya, son of Cyrus, king of Persia," and who caused the lands of Persia and Media to rebel; an Elamite called Atrina, who lied saying: "I am the king of Elam," and who caused Elam to rebel; a Babylonian called Nidintu-Bel, who lied saying: "I am Nebuchadnezzar, son of Nabonidus, the king of Babylon," and who caused Babylonia to rebel; a Persian called Martiya, who lied saying: "I am Immanieshu, the king of Elam," and who caused the Elamites to rebel; a Mede called Parmartish, who lied saying: "I am Hashatritu, descendant of Umakishtar," and who caused Media to rebel; a Sagartian called Shitirantahmu, who lied saying: "I am the king of the Sagartians, descendant of Umakishtar," and who caused the Sagartians to rebel; a Margian called Parada, who lied saying: "I am the king of Margia," and caused Margia to rebel; a Persian called Umizdatu, who lied saying: "I am the son of Cyrus, king of Persia," and who caused Persia to rebel; an Urartian called Arahu, who lied saying: "I am Nebuchadnezzar, son of Nabonidus," and who caused Babylonia to rebel.

Translation after Florence Malbran-Labat, *La Version akkadienne de l'inscription trilingue de Darius à Behistun* (Rome: GEI, 1994), pp. 93–103.

in modern scholarship after the Greek rendering of the Old Persian term for "protecting the kingdom." Darius did not invent the idea of provinces but probably accelerated the extension of their use. When needed, he redrew political boundaries. For example, a new province of "Beyond the River," that is, west of the Euphrates, was established separately from Babylonia, with its capital probably at Damascus.

Figure 15.1 Detail of the Behistun relief. Courtesy of Columbia University, Department of Art History and Archaeology

While there was a smooth succession from Darius to his son Xerxes, competition for the throne among different branches of the royal family became a prevailing problem later on. We have to be careful as our only sources on this issue are classical authors who seem to have enjoyed painting a court plagued by intrigues, with concubines and eunuchs plotting behind the scene. However, dynastic struggles did occur. For example, the Greek Xenophon was involved as a mercenary in the failed attempt by Cyrus the younger to overthrow his brother Artaxerxes II in 401. Several kings executed potential rivals when they ascended the throne. As owners of large estates, members of the royal house had access to considerable resources in manpower and goods, which they could use in a bid for power. A king thus had to be careful not to allow them to recruit an army.

Local populations may have taken advantage of the dynastic instability by revolting. Best known are the rebellions Darius had to squash. His restructuring of the empire did not end such disturbances, however. For example, Xerxes had to deal with two Babylonian uprisings, and on the death of Darius II Egypt

successfully gained independence for some sixty years. There is great disagreement among scholars about the strength and stability of the Persian empire
after the reign of Xerxes. Originally the image in classical sources of an empire
in decline, gradually disintegrating as a result of infighting and the decadent
enjoyment of excessive wealth, was readily accepted. More recently, some
scholars have stressed the continuity and longevity of the empire, which they
claim was well organized and strong. A closer analysis of regional data will be
needed before the picture can be clarified.

15.3 Organization of the Empire

The Persian empire was at the same time highly centralized and respectful of
the multiplicity of the people it governed. It was the first empire that acknowledged the fact that its inhabitants had a variety of cultures, spoke different
languages, and were politically organized in various ways. In contrast, the
Assyrians had incorporated numerous peoples and cultures, but their ideology
had erased the differences and made them all Assyrians once they were conquered. The most telling demonstration of Persia's novel approach comes from
the city of Persepolis (see box 15.1). In the center of Fars was constructed a
massive stone platform with palaces and audience halls on the top. The complex had a primarily ceremonial function connected to the collection of tribute
from the empire's provinces. On the sides of the platform was carved a long
procession of people bringing specialties of their regions: Bactrians bringing
vessels, hides, and a camel, Arabs robes and a dromedary, Nubians elephant
tusks and a giraffe, and so on. The groups were clearly differentiated by their
clothing, hairstyles, and weapons, showing their varied origins (figure 15.2).
On several other reliefs the throne of the king is carried by people identified by
trilingual inscriptions as Persian, Mede, Babylonian, Assyrian, and so on. Some
of these lists include up to twenty-nine groups, representing the multitude of
the empire's people and recognizing that they differed from one another.
     A variety of languages and scripts was equally embraced. The Persians
themselves spoke an Indo-European language and had no written tradition
of their own until they created the empire. When they conquered countries
with ancient bureaucratic traditions, they adopted them for local use. In Persia
itself they introduced the Elamite language and cuneiform script for administrative records, as is documented by the archives found at Persepolis, of
which some 25,000 tablets were excavated. In Mesopotamia they continued
the use of Babylonian recordkeeping, and in Egypt they adopted local scripts
(hieroglyphic and demotic) and papyrus scrolls. As the administrative language
for the whole empire they chose Aramaic, written on parchment or papyrus in
an alphabetic script. This shows that centralizing forces were at work, but not
to the extent that they erased local variation. At the same time, several languages
and scripts were adopted for the monumental inscriptions, which were virtually
always multilingual. In addition to the ancient Elamite and Akkadian languages

Box 15.1 *Persian capital cities*

Before the defeat of Babylonia the Persians did not have major cities or a tradition of monumental architecture. One of the necessities of the empire was a capital city, and the Persians constructed several of them in succession. Cyrus built the earliest capital at Pasargadae in central Fars. It was a large walled area in which were placed at considerable distance from one another a number of palaces and audience halls, with extensive gardens in between them irrigated with special channels. The Greeks called those gardens *paradeisos*, the basis for our word paradise. Gardens were especially popular among the Persians and were laid out throughout the empire. At Pasargadae there was also a fortified citadel and a cultic area including a fire altar, while Cyrus' tomb was built nearby in a separate building.

Darius moved the capital to Persepolis some 40 kilometers to the south. Construction of the city started in 518 and continued under his two immediate successors. At its center was an enormous platform, 450 by 300 meters, on which were placed several palaces, audience halls, and a treasury. All buildings were of stone, and prominent in them were tall columns with capitals carved in the shape of griffins and bulls carrying the wooden roof-beams. The columns of the largest building, the *apadana* or reception hall, were almost 20 meters high. Another building contained a hall of one hundred columns. On the sides of the platform was carved a large procession of royal servants, soldiers, and representatives from all satrapies bearing gifts for the king, who was shown seated on his throne. Oftentimes the winged sundisk, probably depicting Ahuramazda, was carved above the king. Persepolis was extended far beyond the monumental stone buildings that have been excavated. It was one of the main administrative centers of the empire and contained its greatest treasury. It lay at the heart of a fully developed agricultural area with numerous settlements. The tablets found at Persepolis derive from two locations. In the fortifications were found thousands of records of food disbursements to people of widely differing social status, from royal family members to laborers. In the treasury a smaller group records payments to workers. We do not have the imperial archives, however. The city was burned down by Alexander, either deliberately or in an accident when he was drunk. Near the city, at Naqsh-i-Rustem, the tomb chambers of Darius and three of his successors were cut into the cliff.

Together with Persepolis, Darius also developed Susa as a capital, because it had direct access to the western parts of the empire. An immense palace was also built here, decorated with glazed brick representations of Persian soldiers and servants (figure 15.3). Among the finds was a monumental statue of King Darius, represented according to Egyptian sculptural traditions but in Persian garb. Carved on the statue were trilingual inscriptions (Old Persian, Elamite, Akkadian) invoking Ahuramazda, and hieroglyphic inscriptions rendering traditional Egyptian texts. All of these constructions reveal a mixture of architectural and artistic influences, Assyrian, Babylonian, Greek, Egyptian, and local. The Persians used materials from different parts of the empire and employed specialist workmen from the various regions, not to work in their local styles but to contribute to an imperial form of expression that showed Persia as a multicultural unit.

Figure 15.2   Syrian tribute bearers represented at Persepolis. Courtesy of Columbia University, Department of Art History and Archaeology

and cuneiform scripts, an alphabetic cuneiform to write the Old Persian language was developed under Darius. These three languages and scripts became used for almost all royal inscriptions, while Egyptian hieroglyphic writing was sometimes added. The text was also occasionally translated into Aramaic and written on scrolls distributed throughout the empire.

Moreover, the Persians were aware of and respected the different political traditions of the people they had conquered, and adapted them to facilitate their overall control. When Cyrus captured Babylon, he became a traditional Babylonian king, took part in the religious rituals, and left building inscriptions. When Cambyses conquered Egypt, he appointed a local official to teach him how to behave like an Egyptian king, and adopted an Egyptian throne-name, Mesutire (offspring of the god Re). The early Persian rulers protected local cults and even presented themselves as restoring traditions that had been disrupted. Cyrus describes the conquest of Babylon as a liberation from Nabonidus at the request of the god Marduk:

> Marduk ordered Cyrus to march to his city Babylon. He set him on the road to Babylon and like a companion and friend, he went at his side. His vast army, whose number, like the water of the river, cannot be known, marched at his side fully armed. He made him enter his city Babylon without fighting or battle; he saved Babylon from hardship. He delivered Nabonidus, the king who did not revere him, into his hands.[1]

Similarly, the Hebrew Bible states that Cyrus was chosen by the god Yahweh to rebuild the temple of Jerusalem (Isaiah 44:28–45:4), repeating what must have been Persian propaganda. To most people the fact that their country was under Persian rule must have made little difference from when they were under a native dynasty, as the king's behavior did not change. Also cultural traditions continued uninterrupted. In Babylonia, for example, the temple library at Sippar in use under Cambyses collected the important literary and scholarly works of the region without any restrictions from the royal house (document 15.2). The willingness to adopt local customs and to insert the Persian king into existing traditions of rule made it possible to bring unity to the vast empire created in a short time-span. The king in person provided the bond that tied the various regions together. The succession problems after Cambyses seriously endangered this arrangement, and the occurrence of several rebellions at this time then presents no surprise. In response, the Persians developed a more systematized

---

Document 15.2 *The Persian library at Sippar*

The tolerance of the Persians toward the traditions of the regions they conquered is visible in many ways, and Babylonian culture continued to flourish under them. Because the empire brought together an enormous landmass that had previously been divided, it enabled activities impossible before. This is vividly demonstrated in the remains of a library excavated in the Babylonian city of Sippar. The library was located in the temple of the sun god Shamash, and contained many manuscripts of earlier Babylonian literature and scholarship. Those were mostly copied from locally available exemplars, but not all. In its collection was a copy of the prologue to the code of Hammurabi carved on the famous stele now in the Louvre Museum (see figure 6.1). This stele had been carried off to Susa in Elam in the twelfth century (cf. chapter 9) and had thus been inaccessible to people from Babylonia for many centuries. With the unification of Elam and Babylonia under the Persian empire, this was no longer a problem, and someone had gone there to copy the inscription from the original stele. He identifies the inscription by its first words (When the august god Anu), as was the common practice in ancient Mesopotamia, and declares at the end of his tablet:

> First tablet of the composition called "When the august god Anu," not complete.
> Written in accordance with the wording of the original old stele that Hammurabi, king of Babylon, set up in Susa. A clay tablet of Marduk-shumu-usur, son of Mushallim of the city Agade.

Translation after Abdulillah Fadhil, "Der Prolog des Codex Hammurapi in einer Abschrift aus Sippar," *XXXIV. International Assyriology Congress* (Ankara: Turkish Historical Society, 1998), p. 726.

form of governance: from a union of states held together by the person of the king, it evolved into an empire with provinces. Darius is usually credited with instituting drastic reforms, but he probably regularized a system that had gradually grown under his predecessors.

The centralized nature of the Persian empire is clear from its tribute collection. All provinces were forced to contribute set amounts annually, and the Persepolis complex was probably built to host the ceremonial aspect of that event. Herodotus gives a detailed list of what each province was supposed to deliver (Book III, 90–94), primarily silver but also horses, grain, and eunuch boys. For example, Babylonia contributed the largest amount of silver, 1000 talents, and India paid 360 talents of gold dust. While this list is not necessarily accurate, it is certain that vast amounts of silver and gold were collected and stored in the royal treasuries. Classical sources tell that Alexander of Macedon captured some 180,000 talents of Persian gold, and when he released them on the market it caused inflation. The gold:silver ratio dropped from 1:13 to 1:10 and both metals lost half their value compared to copper. Other goods and services were also drawn to the core of the empire. When Darius built a palace in Susa, he used materials from all over the empire: timber, gold, lapis lazuli, carnelian, turquoise, silver, ebony, and ivory. Craftsmen from Ionia, Lydia, Egypt, and Media were engaged, and Babylonians made bricks. The entire empire's resources in goods and labor were at the court's command (figure 15.3).

Certainly by the early fifth century the empire was divided into satrapies, which provided administrative uniformity. Usually the satrap was a Persian nobleman and his local residence was like a royal palace, with a treasury, an archive, and a chancellery. He coordinated local systems of rule so as to make them most beneficial to the state, allowing indigenous upper classes to preserve their earlier status. Classical sources report a system of personal royal emissaries, the "eyes" of the king, and these men kept the local powers in line. The satrapies were connected to the capital by a system of royal roads with rest-houses at regular intervals, where precedence was given to the king's emissaries. The most famous road is that from Sardis to Susa, a distance of some 2500 kilometers, which could be covered by a man in ninety days, according to Herodotus.

Persian aristocrats were sent throughout the empire to direct the satrapies. They were rewarded with estates whose income they could keep, although the land remained in royal possession. These estates were located in different parts of the empire and administered by local agents. We know, for example, that Arsames, the governor of Egypt in the late fifth century, had large estates in Babylonia, and his correspondence deals regularly with other noblemen's lands in Egypt. These estates increased awareness of imperial rule throughout the empire at the regional level.

The person of the king was central in this arrangement. He appointed governors, granted estates as rewards, and made all decisions. He was king of Babylon, Egypt, and so on, but first and foremost he was the Great King and

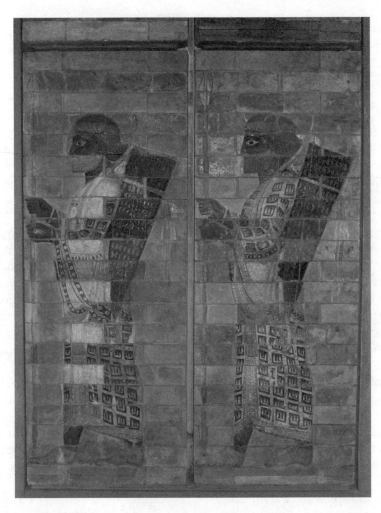

Figure 15.3 Glazed brick representations of soldiers at Susa, Louvre Museum, Paris. Photograph by the author

King of Kings. The ruler had to be a descendant of the distant ancestor Achaemenes. When Darius usurped the throne he demonstrated that he also had that ancestry, as had the man he replaced. The throne had to pass along that line, even if the eldest son was not necessarily appointed as heir. One of the heir's responsibilities was the burial of his predecessor, conducting the corpse to the royal tombs near Persepolis with great ceremony. By doing this for Darius III, Alexander of Macedon declared himself inheritor of the throne and thus a legitimate Persian king. The Achaemenid family was selected by the god Ahuramazda, who was the supreme deity of Persian royal inscriptions. Whether or not this makes the royal house Zoroastrian is subject to debate, and the issue cannot be decided on the basis of the meager evidence we have.

The god and the king guaranteed order and they represented justice and truth. This message is clear in the royal texts and imagery, but it was not imposed at the expense of other cults.

The invention of the Old Persian cuneiform script was probably similarly used to emphasize the king's identity as ruler of Persia. It is usually thought that Darius was instrumental in bringing this about and that Old Persian inscriptions of earlier kings were carved under his rule. Its development may have been part of his efforts to strengthen the cohesion of the state. The king was essential for economic growth throughout the empire, and these were good times for many regions as well. He sustained and extended irrigation systems, thereby making him owner of the water, for which all users were obliged to pay a tax. Several kings are known to have tried to promote trade with distant regions. Darius, for instance, dug a canal from the Nile to the Red Sea. Trade in this period must have flourished, as the world from the Nile to the Indus was under one political regime. Because Persia controlled the Phoenician harbor cities, it had access to resources from the western Mediterranean. Moreover, the coastal areas of the empire from western Anatolia to Egypt were connected by sea trade. Ships from Ionia and the Levant imported oil, wine, metals, wood, wool, and other products into Egypt, for instance, and exported natron, a chemical needed for textile production, and other Egyptian goods in return. The Persian state levied a tax on these shipments, which was to be paid in gold and silver coins. Clearly, overseas trade crossed political boundaries. Greek merchants were active in Egypt under Persian rule, for instance, and Syro-Palestinian traders traveled all over the Mediterranean. In the eastern territories sea trade must also have existed across the Arabian and Indian seas, but the available evidence is extremely slim.

Over time Persian rule started to influence local cultures and Persian customs spread. Local coinage and seals show Persian motifs, while high officials may have changed their clothing and habits to reflect Persian practice. While respect for local traditions was a Persian characteristic, this did not prevent local people from trying to imitate imperial styles. We see that the two poles, local and central, interacted in various ways with each other throughout the empire. There was no eradication of local traditions, religious or otherwise, but rather a respect for them. On the other hand, the longevity of Persian control over the region had its unifying effects over time.

15.4 Alexander of Macedon

Possibly because of the pressure exerted by the Persian empire, at its margins there developed centralized territorial states, the Mauryan empire in northern India, and Macedon to the north of Greece. The latter brought about Persia's downfall. In 336, the twenty-year-old Alexander became king, and after having reestablished Macedon's control over Greece, he marched his army into Anatolia. A continuous ten-year-long campaign followed in which he led his troops throughout the Persian empire, annexing all its satrapies. The Persian King Darius III offered fierce resistance in the battles of Issus in north-west Syria (333) and Gaugamela in northern Iraq (331), but was finally defeated. In classical sources Alexander's conquest is portrayed as a liberation from oppressive Persian rule, and the people of Egypt and Babylonia, for example, are supposed to have welcomed him eagerly. This is to a great extent Macedonian propaganda, however, and most people probably saw little difference between the old and new regimes. Alexander did appeal to the political and religious elites in order to be accepted as the local king, just as the Persians had done. He promoted cults, as an earlier ruler would have. At Babylon, for example, he initiated extensive reconstruction of the Marduk temple, including the (unfinished) rebuilding of the ziggurat. He also wanted to be accepted as the legitimate king of Persia, and buried Darius III with full ceremony after the latter had been assassinated by some of his own courtiers. Alexander married a local princess, Roxane, and urged his generals to find local wives likewise. When in 324 his soldiers refused to campaign farther, he returned to Babylon, where he set up his capital. He seems to have adopted the ceremonial habits of the Persians, including their duty to prostrate themselves in front of him. He was certainly very impressed by Near Eastern customs and traditions and, for instance, saw himself as the son of the Egyptian god Amun. This behavior may have led to the disenchantment of his Macedonian men, and it is possible, though not widely accepted among scholars, that his death in Babylon in 323 may have been an assassination.

Soon afterwards the enormous empire he had created was carved up among his generals. The Near East, Iran, and parts of central Asia came to be ruled by the dynasty of Seleucus, which used northern Babylonia as its political and administrative center. The extent of the Seleucid empire, which was to last for two hundred years, was originally similar to that of the Persians, except for Egypt. Until recently, scholars subscribed to the classical image of the Near East as tired and decadent by the fourth century, and that Alexander and his successors brought new life to it. This image of revitalization provided an example of, and justification for, nineteenth-century European colonial enterprise in regions that had known a glorious past but had not modernized. Although Hellenism was seen as the merging of European and Asian traditions, its vitality was thought to derive from Greek cultural and political practices (e.g., philosophy, literature, the city-state, etc.), introduced into regions with huge resources that had stagnated. Today, closer examination of the documentary evidence from the Near East has started to change this opinion. The Persian system, itself an amalgam of earlier traditions, was continued in many respects. Satrapies and political arrangements with local populations endured; kings used the local cults and their rituals to further their political interests; administrative practices survived. New political offices did indeed develop, new administrative languages replaced older ones such as Babylonian, Greek buildings appeared in old cities and new cities were founded that followed a Greek layout, but these changes were gradual. Alexander has been called "the last of the Achaemenids,"[2] but his death in 323 did not present a clear end or a new beginning in the long history of the Near East.

NOTES

1 Translation by Mordechai Cogan, in W. W. Hallo, ed., *The Context of Scripture* (Leiden: E. J. Brill, 2000), volume 2, p. 315.
2 Pierre Briant, *From Cyrus to Alexander: A History of the Persian Empire* (Winona Lake: Eisenbrauns, 2002), p. 876.

King Lists

All dates indicate the period of rule and are to be considered as approximate. They do not take into account detailed adjustments made in recent years, but are based for rulers of Mesopotamia (Sumerian, Babylonian, Assyrian) on J. A. Brinkman's list in A. Leo Oppenheim, *Ancient Mesopotamia*, second edition (Chicago: University of Chicago Press, 1977), pp. 335–48. Descent is not always clear: when it is certain, successive kings are connected with a solid downward rule (|); when possible, by ?; when no direct family connection existed, successive rulers are separated by a blank space.

1 Akkad Dynasty

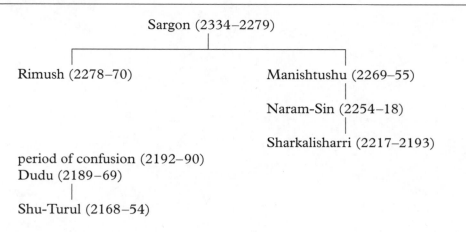

Sargon (2334–2279)

Rimush (2278–70)

Manishtushu (2269–55)

Naram-Sin (2254–18)

Sharkalisharri (2217–2193)

period of confusion (2192–90)
Dudu (2189–69)

Shu-Turul (2168–54)

2 Third Dynasty of Ur

Ur-Namma (2112–2095)
|
Shulgi (2094–47)
|
Amar-Suen (2046–38)
|
Shu-Sin (2037–29)
|
Ibbi-Sin (2028–04)

3 First Dynasty of Isin

Ishbi-Erra (2017–1985)
|
Shu-ilishu (1984–75)
|
Iddin-Dagan (1974–54)
|
Ishme-Dagan (1953–35)
|
Lipit-Ishtar (1934–24)
|
Ur-Ninurta (1923–1896)
|
Bur-Sin (1895–74)
|
Lipit-Enlil (1873–69)

Erra-imitti (1868–61)

Enlil-bani (1860–37)

Zambija (1836–34)

Iter-pisha (1833–31)

Ur-dukuga (1830–28)

Sin-magir (1827–17)

Damiq-ilishu (1816–1794)

1793: Larsa conquers Isin

4 Larsa Dynasty

Naplanum (2025–05)
?
Emisum (2004–1977)
?
Samium (1976–42)
|
Zabaja (1941–33)
?
Gungunum (1932–06)
?
Abi-sare (1905–1895)
?
Sumu-el (1894–66)

Nur-Adad (1865–50)
|
Sin-iddinam (1849–43)
?
Sin-iribam (1842–41)
|
Sin-iqisham (1840–36)
?
Silli-Adad (1835)

Warad-Sin (1834–23)   Rim-Sin I (1822–1763)

Rim-Sin II (1741–40)   1763: Babylon conquers Larsa

5   Eshnunna

The absolute dates for most rulers are unknown.

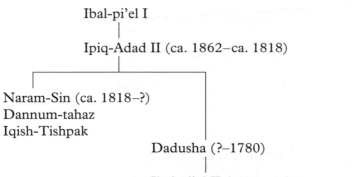

Ibal-pi'el I
|
Ipiq-Adad II (ca. 1862–ca. 1818)

Naram-Sin (ca. 1818–?)
Dannum-tahaz
Iqish-Tishpak

Dadusha (?–1780)
|
Ibal-pi'el II (1779–65)
1766: conquest by Babylon, Mari, and Elam

Silli-Sin

6   Mari

Yahdun-Lim
|
Sumu-Yaman

Yasmah-Addu (ca. 1795–76)

Zimri-Lim (ca. 1775–62)

1761: Babylon conquers Mari

7 Yamkhad

All dates are approximate.

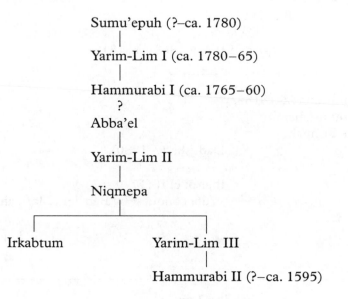

Sumu'epuh (?–ca. 1780)

Yarim-Lim I (ca. 1780–65)

Hammurabi I (ca. 1765–60)
?
Abba'el

Yarim-Lim II

Niqmepa

Irkabtum   Yarim-Lim III

Hammurabi II (?–ca. 1595)

8 First Dynasty of Babylon

Sumuabum (1894–81)
?
Sumulael (1880–45)
?
Sabium (1844–31)
?
Apil-Sin (1830–13)
?
Sin-muballit (1812–1793)

Hammurabi (1792–50)

Samsuiluna (1749–12)

Abi-eshuh (1711–1684)

Ammiditana (1683–47)

Ammisaduqa (1646–26)
?
Samsuditana (1625–1595)

9 Old Hittite Kingdom

All dates are approximate.

Hattusili I (1650–20)
|
Mursili I (1620–1590)

Hantili I (1590–60)

Zidanta I (1559–)
|
Ammuna

Huzziya I (–1526)

Telipinu (1525–1500)

10 Mittani

Shuttarna I

ca. 1500   Parrattarna

Saustatar
?
Artatama I
|
ca. 1380   Shuttarna II
               ?

Artashumara   Tushratta   Artatama II
                   | |
ca. 1340   Shattiwaza   Shuttarna III
                   |
Shattuara I
|
Wasashatta
?
Shattuara II

ca. 1250

11   Hittite New Kingdom

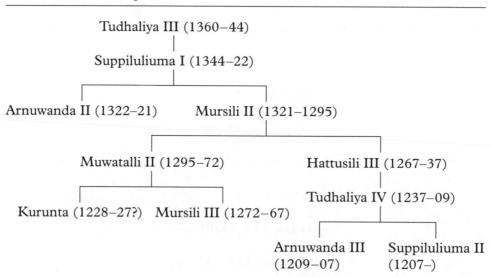

Tudhaliya III (1360–44)
|
Suppiluliuma I (1344–22)

Arnuwanda II (1322–21)   Mursili II (1321–1295)

Muwatalli II (1295–72)   Hattusili III (1267–37)
|
Tudhaliya IV (1237–09)

Kurunta (1228–27?)   Mursili III (1272–67)

Arnuwanda III   Suppiluliuma II
(1209–07)   (1207–)

12   List of Selected Kings of the Syro-Palestinian Area

Ugarit

Ammistamru I (?–1354)
|
Niqmadu II (ca. 1353–18)

Niqmepa (ca. 1313–1251)   Arhalba (ca. 1317–14)
|
Ammistamru II (ca. 1250–10)
|
Ibiranu (ca. 1209–1200)
|
Niqmadu III (ca. 1199–92)
?
Ammurapi (ca. 1191–82)

Amurru

Abdi-Ashirta
|
Aziru (ca. 1340–15)
|
Ari-Teshub (ca. 1315–13)
|
Tuppi-Teshub (ca. 1313–1280)
|
Benteshina (ca. 1280–75; 1260–30)
|
      Shapili (ca. 1275–60)
|
Shaushga-muwa (ca. 1230–10)

13 Babylonia in the Late Second Millennium

Kassite dynasty

Kadashman-Enlil I (1374?–60)
|
Burnaburiash II (1359–33)

Kara-hardash (1333)   Kurigalzu II (1332–08)
Nazi-Bugash (1333) |
                                       Nazi-Maruttash (1307–1282)
                                       |
                                       Kadashman-Turgu (1281–64)
                                       |
                                       Kadashman-Enlil II (1263–55)
                                       ?
                                       Kudur-Enlil (1254–46)
                                       ?
                                       Shagarakti-Shuriash (1245–33)
                                       |
                                       Kashtiliashu IV (1232–25)

Enlil-nadin-shumi (1224)
Kadashman-Harbe II (1223)
Adad-shuma-iddina (1222–17)

                                       Adad-shuma-usur (1216–1187)
                                       |
                                       Meli-Shipak (1186–72)
                                       |
Zababa-shuma-iddina (1158)   Marduk-apla-iddina I (1171–59)
Enlil-nadin-ahi (1157–55)

Second dynasty of Isin

> Marduk-kabit-ahheshu (1157–40)
> |
> Itti-Marduk-balatu (1139–32)
>
> Ninurta-nadin-shumi (1131–26)
> ┌─────────────────────────────┴─────────────────────────────┐
> Nebuchadnezzar I (1125–04)   Marduk-nadin-ahhe (1099–82)
> |
> Enlil-nadin-apil (1103–1100)
>
>   Marduk-shapik-zeri (1081–69)
> Adad-apla-iddina (1168–47)
> Marduk-ahhe-eriba (1046)
> Marduk-zer-x (1045–34)
> Nabu-shumu-libur (1033–26)

14 Middle Elamite Rulers

(a)   Between 1500 and 1400 with uncertain affiliation

> Kidinu
> Tan-Ruhurater II
> Shalla
> Tepti-ahar
> Inshushinak-sunkir-nappipir

(b)   Between 1400 and 1200

All dates are uncertain.

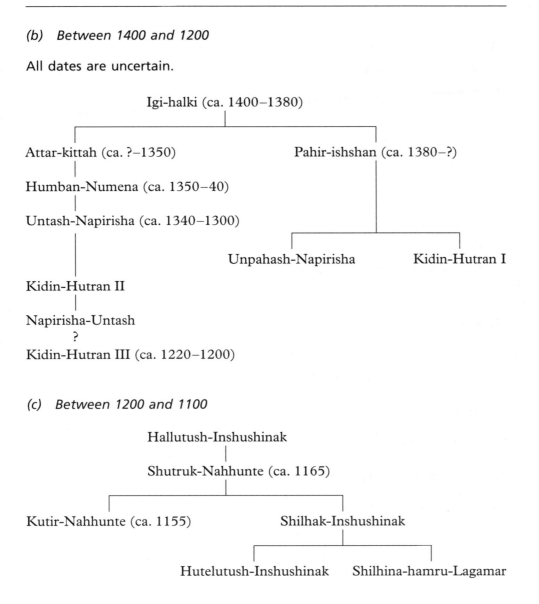

(c)   Between 1200 and 1100

15 Babylonia in the Early First Millennium

Second Sealand dynasty

Simbar-Shipak (1025–08)
?   Ea-mukin-zeri (1008)
Kashshu-nadin-ahhe (1007–05)

Bazi dynasty

Eulmash-shakin-shumi (1004–988)
┌──────────────?──────────────┐
Ninurta-kudurri-usur I (987–85)   Shirikti-Shuqamuna (985)

Elamite dynasty

Mar-biti-apla-usur (984–79)

Uncertain dynasties

Nabu-mukin-apli (978–43)
├──┐
Ninurta-kudurri-usur II (943)   Mar-biti-ahhe-iddina (942–?)

Shamash-mudammiq (?–?)
?
Nabu-shuma-ukin I (?–?)
│
Nabu-apla-iddina (?–?)
│
Marduk-zakir-shumi I (?–?)
│
Marduk-balassu-iqbi (?–ca. 813)

Baba-aha-iddina (?–?)
Ninurta?-apl?-[ ]
Marduk-bel-[zeri]
Marduk-apla-usur
Eriba-Marduk
Nabu-shuma-ishkun (?–748)

Uncertain dynasties (continued)

Nabu-nasir (747–34)
|
Nabu-nadin-zeri (733–32)
Nabu-shuma-ukin II (732)
Nabu-mukin-zeri (731–29)
Tiglath-pileser III (728–27)
|
Shalmaneser V (726–22)
Marduk-apla-iddina II (721–10)
Sargon II (709–05)
|
Sennacherib (704–03)
|
| Marduk-zakir-shumi II (703)
| Marduk-apla-iddina II (703)
| Bel-ibni (702–700)
|
Assur-nadin-shumi (699–94)
Nergal-ushezib (693)
Mushezib-Marduk (692–89)
Sennacherib (688–81)
|
Esarhaddon (680–69)
|
Assurbanipal (668)   Shamash-shuma-ukin (667–48)
Kandalanu (647–27)

16   Neo-Babylonian Dynasty

Nabopolassar (626–05)
|
Nebuchadnezzar II (604–562)
|
Evil-Merodach (561–60)

Neriglissar (559–56)
|
Labashi-Marduk (556)

Nabonidus (555–39)

17 Persian Empire

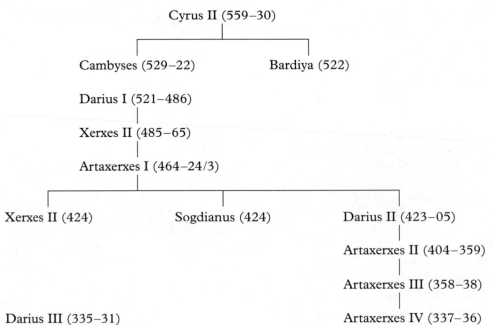

Cyrus II (559–30)

Cambyses (529–22)   Bardiya (522)

Darius I (521–486)

Xerxes II (485–65)

Artaxerxes I (464–24/3)

Xerxes II (424)   Sogdianus (424)   Darius II (423–05)

Artaxerxes II (404–359)

Artaxerxes III (358–38)

Darius III (335–31)   Artaxerxes IV (337–36)

Alexander of Macedon (330–23)

18 Assyria

Aminu
|
Sulili

Kikkija

Akija

Puzur-Assur I

Shalim-ahum

Ilushuma
|
Erishum I
|
Ikunum
|
Sargon I
|
Puzur-Assur II
|
Naram-Sin
|
Erishum II

Shamshi-Adad I (ca. 1808–1776)
|
Ishme-Dagan (1775–?)

Assur-uballit I (1363–28)
|
Enlil-nirari (1327–18)
|
Arik-den-ili (1317–06)
|
Adad-nirari I (1305–1274)
|
Shalmaneser I (1273–44)
|
Tukulti-Ninurta I (1243–07)
┌──────────────────────┴──────────────────────┐
Assur-nadin-apli (1206–03)   Enlil-kudurri-usur (1196–92)
|
Assur-nirari III (1202–1197)

Assyria (continued)

Ninurta-apil-Ekur (1191–79)
|
Assur-dan I (1178–33)
├─────────────────────────────────┐
Ninurta-tukulti-Assur   Mutakkil-Nusku
                                   |
                                   Assur-resha-ishi I (1132–15)
                                   |
                                   Tiglath-pileser I (1114–1076)
        ┌──────────────────┬────────────────────┐
Asharid-apil-Ekur   Assur-bel-kala (1073–56)   Shamshi-Adad IV (1053–50)
(1075–74) | |
                     Eriba-Adad II (1055–54)   Assurnasirpal I (1049–31)
        ┌──────────────────┐ |
Shalmaneser II (1030–19)   Assur-rabi II (1012–972)
        | |
Assur-nirari IV (1018–13)   Assur-resha-ishi II (971–67)
                                                    |
                                                Tiglath-pileser II (966–35)
                                                    |
                                                Assur-dan II (934–12)
                                                    |
                                                Adad-nirari II (911–891)
                                                    |
                                                Tukulti-Ninurta II (890–84)
                                                    |
                                                Assurnasirpal II (883–59)
                                                    |
                                                Shalmaneser III (858–24)
                                                    |
                                                Shamshi-Adad V (823–11)
                                                    |
                                                Adad-nirari III (810–783)
                                        ┌───────────────────────┐
                                Shalmaneser IV   Assur-dan III
                                (782–73)   (772–55)

Assyria (continued)

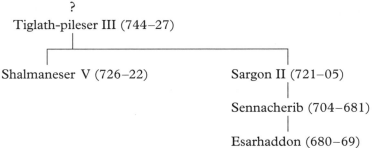

Assur-nirari V (754–45)
?
Tiglath-pileser III (744–27)

Shalmaneser V (726–22)   Sargon II (721–05)

Sennacherib (704–681)

Esarhaddon (680–69)

Assurbanipal (668–27)

Assur-etel-ilani (627–23)   Sin-shar-ishkun (622–12)
?
Assur-uballit II (611–?)

Guide to Further Reading

The scholarly literature on the histories and cultures of the Near East is very substantial in size, and ranges from short paragraph-long notes to multi-volume books. They are mostly written in English, French, and German, while some very important work has been published in Italian and other languages. A small selection of works, mostly in English, is provided here. I have given special attention to recent publications, where further up-to-date bibliography is available.

For ancient Near Eastern history and culture in general, *Civilizations of the Ancient Near East*, edited by Jack M. Sasson (New York: Charles Scribner's Sons, 1995) in four volumes is very useful. The numerous contributions, dealing with a wide array of subjects on history, archaeology, art, language, literature, etc. and written by many scholars, are all in English. *A Companion to the Ancient Near East*, edited by Daniel C. Snell (Oxford: Blackwell, 2005) is less encompassing, but contains many interesting contributions. The *Dictionary of the Ancient Near East* edited by Piotr Bienkowski and Alan Millard (London: British Museum Press, 2000) provides brief explanations of key terms and concepts with handy bibliographies.

English surveys of history include Amélie Kuhrt, *The Ancient Near East c.3000–330 BC*, 2 volumes (London and New York: Routledge, 1995), and the much shorter William W. Hallo and William K. Simpson, *The Ancient Near East: A History*, second edition (Forth Worth: Harcourt Brace College Publishers, 1998). A very authoritative multi-authored account is provided in *The Cambridge Ancient History* (Cambridge: Cambridge University Press), edited by John Boardman and others. The first four volumes, some with multiple parts, cover the history of the ancient Near East. The contributions were written from the 1960s to the early 1990s, and some of them are outdated. They do provide the most detailed factual account of most historical periods, however. In German appeared recently, D. O. Edzard, *Geschichte Mesopotamiens: von Sumerern bis zu Alexander dem Grossen* (Munich: C. H. Beck, 2004). A revised edition of a French two-volume history was also published in recent years: Paul Garelli, Jean-Marie Durand, Hatice Gonnet, and Catherine Breniquet, *Le Proche-Orient asiatique. Volume I: Des origins aux invasions des peuples de la mer* (Paris: PUF, 1997) and Paul Garelli and André

Lemaire, *Le Proche-Orient asiatique. Volume II: Les empires mésopotamiens, Israël* (Paris: PUF, 2002). An excellent history in Italian is Mario Liverani, *Antico Oriente. Storia, società, economia* (Rome and Bari: Laterza, 1988).

There exist some detailed long-term studies of specific regions of the Near East. For Syria: Horst Klengel, *Syria: 3000 to 300 BC* (Berlin: Akademie Verlag, 1992) and Peter M. M. G. Akkermans and Glenn M. Schwartz, *The Archaeology of Syria. From Complex Hunter-Gatherer to Early Urban Societies (ca. 16,000–300 BC)* (Cambridge: Cambridge University Press, 2003). For Anatolia: Trevor Bryce, *The Kingdom of the Hittites*, new edition (Oxford: Oxford University Press, 2005). For western Iran: D. T. Potts, *The Archaeology of Elam* (Cambridge: Cambridge University Press, 1999). For the Persian Gulf: D. T. Potts, *The Arabian Gulf in Antiquity* (Oxford: Clarendon Press, 1990). The Assyrians and Babylonians were the subject of one recent book in German each: Eva C. Cancik-Kirschbaum, *Die Assyrer: Geschichte, Gesellschaft, Kultur* (Munich: C. H. Beck, 2003) and Michael Jursa, *Die Babylonier: Geschichte, Gesellschaft, Kultur* (Munich: C. H. Beck, 2004).

Michael Roaf, *Cultural Atlas of Mesopotamia and the Ancient Near East* (Oxford: Equinox, 1990), contains very informative maps for the various periods of ancient history, and a good summary discussion of ancient Near Eastern history. The book also contains numerous excellent illustrations. D. T. Potts, *Mesopotamian Civilization. The Material Foundations* (Ithaca: Cornell University Press, 1997) is a good discussion of the material world of the Mesopotamians, organized by topics. A. Leo Oppenheim, *Ancient Mesopotamia*, second edition (Chicago: University of Chicago Press, 1977) is the only true intellectual history of the region, also organized around different topics. Thorkild Jacobsen provides a history of Mesopotamian religion in *The Treasures of Darkness* (New Haven and London: Yale University Press, 1976).

Some illustrated websites with general information are: www.mesopotamia.co.uk from the British Museum in London; http://oi.uchicago.edu/OI/default.html from the Oriental Institute at the University of Chicago; and www.metmuseum.org/Works_of_Art/department.asp?dep=3 from the Metropolitan Museum of Art, New York. www.arch.ox.ac.uk/archatlas contains interesting satellite maps and discussions of issues such as the origins of agriculture and trade routes.

In addition to the books mentioned above which contain important information on almost all periods of Near Eastern history, the reader can consult the works below for further information on topics discussed in specific chapters here. The list is far from complete and provides only a guide to further reading.

Chapter 1 Introductory Concerns

What is the ancient Near East?: Marc Van De Mieroop, "On Writing a History of the Ancient Near East," *Bibliotheca Orientalis* 54 (1997), pp. 285–306.

Sources: Marc Van De Mieroop, *Cuneiform Texts and the Writing of History* (London: Routledge, 1999); Roger Matthews, *The Archaeology of Mesopotamia. Theories and Approaches* (London: Routledge, 2003); Jean-Jacques Glassner, *Mesopotamian Chronicles* (Atlanta: Society of Biblical Literature, 2004); Paul Zimansky, "Archaeology and Texts in the Ancient Near East," in S. Pollock and R. Bernbeck, eds., *Archaeologies of the Middle East. Critical Perspectives* (Oxford: Blackwell, 2005), pp. 308–26.

Role of the environment: Andrew Sherratt, "Climatic Cycles and Behavioural Revolutions: The Emergence of Modern Humans and the Beginnings of Farming," *Antiquity*
71 (1997), pp. 271–87; P. J. Richardson et al., "Was Agriculture Impossible During
the Pleistocene but Mandatory During the Holocene? A Climate Change Hypothesis,"
American Antiquity 66 (2001), pp. 387–411.

Prehistoric developments: Hans J. Nissen, *The Early History of the Ancient Near East.
9000–2000 BC*, translated by E. Lutzeier and K. Northcutt (Chicago and London:
University of Chicago Press, 1988); Jean-Daniel Forest, *Mésopotamie. L'Apparition
de l'état* (Paris: Paris-Méditéranée, 1996); Marcella Frangipane, *La nascita dello stato
nel vicino oriente* (Rome and Bari: Laterza, 1996); Petr Charvát, *Mesopotamia Before
History* (London and New York: Routledge, 2002).

Absolute chronology: H. Gasche et al., *Dating the Fall of Babylon: A Reappraisal of Second-
Millennium Chronology* (Ghent: University of Ghent, 1998); *Just in Time. Proceedings
of the International Colloquium on Ancient Near Eastern Chronology*, M. Tanret, ed.,
Akkadica 119–20, Sept–Dec. 2000.

PART I   CITY-STATES

For prehistory and the early periods of Near Eastern history, see Hans J. Nissen,
The Early History of the Ancient Near East. 9000–2000 BC, translated by E. Lutzeier and
K. Northcutt (Chicago and London: University of Chicago Press, 1988); Susan Pollock,
Ancient Mesopotamia. The Eden that Never Was (Cambridge: Cambridge University Press,
1999). Many aspects of society and culture are discussed by J. N. Postgate, *Early
Mesopotamia: Society and Economy at the Dawn of History* (London: Routledge, 1992),
and Harriet Crawford, *Sumer and Sumerians*, second edition (Cambridge: Cambridge
University Press, 2004). The art of the third millennium is extensively illustrated in
Joan Aruz, ed., *Art of the First Cities. The Third Millennium BC from the Mediterranean to
the Indus* (New York: The Metropolitan Museum of Art, 2003).

Chapter 2   Origins: The Uruk Phenomenon

Sources: Josef Bauer, Robert K. Englund, and Manfred Krebenik, *Mesopotamien.
Späturuk-Zeit und Frühdynastische Zeit* (Freiburg: Universitätsverlag, 1998), pp. 13–
233 [in English]; www.cdli.ucla.edu.

General: Mario Liverani, *Uruk: The First City*, translated by Z. Bahrani and M. Van De
Mieroop (London: Equinox, 2006).

Origins of cities: Marc Van De Mieroop, *The Ancient Mesopotamian City* (Oxford:
Oxford University Press, 1999): chapter 2.

Texts and administrative tools: Hans J. Nissen, Peter Damerow, and Robert K. Englund,
*Archaic Bookkeeping. Early Writing and Techniques of Economic Administration in
the Ancient Near East* (Chicago and London: University of Chicago Press, 1993);
Dominique Collon, *First Impressions. Cylinder Seals in the Ancient Near East* (London:
British Museum Publications, 1987). For lexical texts, see http://cuneiform.ucla.edu/
dcclt.

Origins and development of writing: C. B. F. Walker, *Cuneiform* (London: British Museum, 1987); Denise Schmandt-Besserat, *Before Writing* (Austin: University of Texas Press, 1992); Jean-Jacques Glassner, *Writing in Sumer. The Invention of Cuneiform*, edited and translated by Z. Bahrani and M. Van De Mieroop (Baltimore: The Johns Hopkins University Press, 2003); Jerrold S. Cooper, "Babylonian Beginnings: The Origin of the Cuneiform Writing System in Comparative Perspective," in S. D. Houston, ed., *The First Writing. Script Invention as History and Process* (Cambridge: Cambridge University Press, 2004), pp. 71–99.

The Uruk expansion: P. R. S. Moorey, *From Gulf to Delta and Beyond* (*Beer-Sheva* 8) (Beer-Sheva: Ben Gourion University of the Negev Press, 1995); Mitchell S. Rothman, ed., *Uruk Mesopotamia & Its Neighbors* (Santa Fe: School of American Research Press, 2001); Pascal Butterlin, *Les temps proto-urbains de Mésopotamie* (Paris: CNRS Editions, 2003); Guillermo Algaze, *The Uruk World System*, second revised edition (Chicago and London: University of Chicago Press, 2005).

Chapter 3   Competing City-States: The Early Dynastic Period

Sources: Jerrold S. Cooper, *Reconstructing History from Ancient Inscriptions: The Lagash-Umma Border Conflict* (Malibu: Undena, 1983); id., *Sumerian and Akkadian Royal Inscriptions, I. Presargonic Inscriptions* (New Haven: American Oriental Society; 1986); Roger Matthews, *Cities, Seals and Writing: Archaic Seal Impressions from Jemdet Nasr and Ur* (Berlin: Gebr. Mann, 1993); Josef Bauer, Robert K. Englund, and Manfred Krebenik, *Mesopotamien. Späturuk-Zeit und Frühdynastische Zeit* (Freiburg: Universitätsverlag, 1998), pp. 237–585 [in German].

Political organization: Piotr Steinkeller, "Archaic City Seals and the Question of Early Babylonian Unity," in Tzvi Abusch, ed., *Riches Hidden in Secret Places. Ancient Near Eastern Studies in Memory of Thorkild Jacobsen* (Winona Lake: Eisenbrauns, 2002), pp. 249–57, and "More on Archaic City Seals," *NABU* 2002/2, p. 29.

The wider Near East: For Ebla, see Giovanni Pettinato, *Ebla. A New Look at History* (Baltimore: The Johns Hopkins University Press, 1991); Alfonso Archi, "Fifteen Years of Studies on Ebla: A Summary," *Orientalistische Literaturzeitung* 88 (1993), pp. 461–71; Paolo Matthiae et al., *Ebla. Alle origini della città urbana* (Milan: Electa, 1995).

Early dynastic society: Kazuya Maekawa, "The Development of the é-mí in Lagash during Early Dynastic III," *Mesopotamia* 8–9 (1973–4), pp. 77–144; Giuseppe Visicato, *The Bureaucracy of Shuruppak* (Munster: Ugarit Verlag, 1995); Richard L. Zettler and Lee Horne, eds., *Treasures from the Royal Tombs at Ur* (Philadelphia: University of Pennsylvania Museum of Archaeology and Anthropology, 1998).

Later literary reflections: Claus Wilcke, "Genealogical and Geographical Thought in the Sumerian King List," in H. Behrens et al., eds., *DUMU-E₂-DUB-BA-A: Studies in Honor of Åke W. Sjöberg*, (Philadelphia: University of Pennsylvania Museum of Archaeology and Anthropology, 1989), pp. 557–71; Andrew George, *The Epic of Gilgamesh* (London: Penguin, 1999), chapter 5; Douglas Frayne in Benjamin R. Foster, *The Epic of Gilgamesh* (New York and London: Norton, 2001), pp. 99–154; Jean-Jacques Glassner, *Mesopotamian Chronicles* (Atlanta: Society of Biblical Literature, 2004); H. L. J. Vanstiphout, *Epics of Sumerian Kings: The Matter of Aratta* (Atlanta: Society of Biblical Literature, 2004).

Chapter 4   Political Centralization in the Late Third Millennium

Sources: Douglas R. Frayne, *Sargonic and Gutian Period (2334–2113 BC)* (Toronto: University of Toronto Press, 1993); Piotr Michalowski, *Letters from Early Mesopotamia* (Atlanta: Scholars Press, 1993); Douglas R. Frayne, *Ur III Period (2112–2004 BC)* (Toronto: University of Toronto Press, 1997); Dietz O. Edzard, *Gudea and His Dynasty* (Toronto: University of Toronto Press, 1997); Walther Sallaberger and Aage Westenholz, *Mesopotamien. Akkade-Zeit und Ur III Zeit* (Freiburg: Universitätsverlag, 1999) [in English and German].

The Akkad dynasty: Mario Liverani, ed., *Akkad, The First World Empire* (Padua: Sargon, 1993).

The Ur III state: Piotr Steinkeller, "The Administrative and Economic Organization of the Ur III State: The Core and the Periphery," in McGuire Gibson and R. D. Biggs, eds., *The Organization of Power. Aspects of Bureaucracy in the Ancient Near East* (Chicago: The Oriental Institute, 1987), pp. 19–41, and "Archival Practices at Babylonia in the Third Millennium," in M. Brosius, ed., *Ancient Archives and Archival Traditions* (Oxford: Oxford University Press, 2003), pp. 37–58; Tonia M. Sharlach, *Provincial Taxation and the Ur III State* (Leiden: Brill, 2004).

Later literary reflections: Joan Westenholz, *Legends of the Kings of Akkade* (Winona Lake: Eisenbrauns, 1997); Marc Van De Mieroop, "Literature and Political Discourse in Ancient Mesopotamia. Sargon II of Assyria and Sargon of Agade," in B. Böck et al., eds., *Munuscula Mesopotamica. Festschrift für Johannes Renger* (Munster: Ugarit Verlag, 1999), pp. 327–39 and "Sargon of Agade and his Successors in Anatolia," *Studi Micenei ed Egeo-Anatolici* 42 (2000), pp. 133–59; Timothy Potts, "Reading the Sargonic 'Historical-Literary' Tradition. Is There a Middle Course?," in T. Abusch et al., eds., *Historiography in the Cuneiform World* (Bethesda: CDL Press, 2001), pp. 391–408.

Chapter 5   The Near East in the Early Second Millennium

Sources: Douglas R. Frayne, *Old Babylonian Period (2003–1595 BC)* (Toronto: University of Toronto Press, 1990); Dominique Charpin, Dietz Otto Edzard, and Marten Stol, *Mesopotamien. Die altbabylonische Zeit* (Friburg: Academic Press, 2004) [in French and German].

Nomads and sedentary people: Mario Liverani, "Half-Nomads on the Middle Euphrates and the Concept of Dimorphic Society," *Altorientalische Forschungen* 24 (1995), pp. 44–8; Daniel E. Fleming, *Democracy's Ancient Ancestors: Mari and Early Collective Governance* (Cambridge: Cambridge University Press, 2004).

Babylonian society in the Isin-Larsa period: Marc Van De Mieroop, *Society and Enterprise in Old Babylonian Ur* (Berlin: Dietrich Reimer Verlag, 1992); Johannes Renger, "Royal Edicts of the Old Babylonian Period – Structural Background," in M. Hudson and M. Van De Mieroop, eds., *Debt and Economic Renewal in the Ancient Near East* (Bethesda: CDL Press, 2002), pp. 139–62.

Old Assyrian history and trade: Mogens Trolle Larsen, *The Old Assyrian City-State and Its Colonies* (Copenhagen: Akademisk Forlag, 1976); Klaas R. Veenhof, "Archives of Old Assyrian Traders," in M. Brosius, ed., *Ancient Archives and Archival Traditions* (Oxford: Oxford University Press, 2003), pp. 78–123. Cécile Michel translated a rich selection of letters into French in *Correspondance des marchands de Kanish* (Paris: Les Editions du Cerf, 2001).

Mari: Jean-Marie Durand translated a vast number of letters into French and gave very up-to-date general introductions to many topics in *Les documents épistolaires du palais de Mari* I–III (Paris: Les Editions du Cerf, 1997–2000); Dominique Charpin and Nele Ziegler, *Florilegium marianum* V. *Mari et le Proche-Orient à l'époque amorrite. Essai d'histoire politique* (Paris: SEPOA, 2003); Wolfgang Heimpel, *Letters to the King of Mari. A New Translation with Historical Introduction, Notes, and Commentary* (Winona Lake: Eisenbrauns, 2003).

Chapter 6   The Growth of Territorial States in the Early Second Millennium

Sources: see chapter 5.

Kingdom of Upper Mesopotamia: see Mari in chapter 5; Klaas R. Veenhof, *The Old Assyrian List of Year Eponyms and Its Chronological Implications* (Ankara: Turkish Historical Society, 2003).

The Old Babylonian dynasty: Jean Bottéro, "The 'Code' of Hammurabi," in *Mesopotamia. Writing, Reasoning, and the Gods* (Chicago: University of Chicago Press, 1992), pp. 156–84; Dominique Charpin, *Hammu-rabi de Babylone* (Paris: PUF, 2003); Marc Van De Mieroop, *King Hammurabi of Babylon: A Biography* (Oxford: Blackwell, 2005). For a translation of the Code of Hammurabi, as well as all other law codes from Mesopotamia and the Hittites, see Martha T. Roth, *Law Collections from Mesopotamia and Asia Minor*, second edition (Atlanta: Scholars Press, 1997). For extensive translations of Sumerian literature, see Jeremy Black et al., *The Literature of Ancient Sumer* (Oxford: Oxford University Press, 2004), and www-etcsl.orient.ox.ac.uk. For the school curriculum, see Steve Tinney, "Texts, Tablets, and Teaching. Scribal Education in Nippur and Ur," *Expedition* 40/2 (1998), pp. 40–50.

Old Hittite state: Trevor Bryce, *The Major Historical Texts of Early Hittite History* (Brisbane: University of Queensland Press, 1983), and *The Kingdom of the Hittites*, new edition (Oxford: Oxford University Press, 2005), pp. 1–107.

Aftermath: Karel Van Lerberghe, "Kassites and Old Babylonian Society. A Reappraisal," in K. Van Lerberghe and A. Schoors, eds., *Immigration and Emigration within the Ancient Near East. Festschrift E. Lipinski* (Louvain: Uitgeverij Peeters, 1995), pp. 381–93; Mirjo Salvini, "The Earliest Evidences of the Hurrians Before the Formation of the Reign of Mittanni," in G. Buccellati and M. Kelly-Buccellati, eds., *Urkesh and the Hurrians. Studies in Honor of Lloyd Cotsen* (Malibu: Undena, 1998), pp. 99–115; Amanda Podany, *The Land of Hana* (Bethesda: CDL Press, 2002).

PART II   TERRITORIAL STATES

Chapter 7   The Club of the Great Powers

Sources: William L. Moran, *The Amarna Letters* (Baltimore and London: The Johns Hopkins University Press, 1992) translates all Amarna letters into English. Gary Beckman, *Hittite Diplomatic Texts*, second edition (Atlanta: Scholars Press, 1999) contains translations of a large selection of treaties and other diplomatic material from the Hittite court.

The international system: Raymond Cohen and Raymond Westbrook, eds., *Amarna Diplomacy. The Beginnings of International Relations* (Baltimore and London: The Johns Hopkins University Press, 2000); Mario Liverani, *Prestige and Interest* (Padua: Sargon, 1990), and *International Relations in the Ancient Near East, 1600–1100 BC* (New York: Palgrave, 2001); Marian H. Feldman, "Luxurious Forms: Redefining a Mediterranean 'International Style,' 1400–1200 BCE," *Art Bulletin* 84 (2002): pp. 6–29; Trevor Bryce, *Letters of the Great Kings of the Ancient Near East: The Royal Correspondence of the Late Bronze Age* (London: Routledge, 2003); Marc Van De Mieroop, "The Eastern Mediterranean in Early Antiquity," in W. V. Harris, ed., *Rethinking the Mediterranean* (Oxford: Oxford University Press, 2005), pp. 117–40.

Chapter 8   The Western States of the Late Second Millennium

Sources: Harry H. Hoffner, "Histories and Historians of the Ancient Near East: The Hittites," *Orientalia* 49 (1980), pp. 283–332; Mario Liverani, *Myth and Politics in Ancient Near Eastern Historiography* (London: Equinox, 2004).

Mittani state: Gernot Wilhelm, *The Hurrians* (Warminster: Aris & Phillips Ltd, 1989).

Hittites: Oliver Gurney, *The Hittites* (London: Penguin Books, 1990); Horst Klengel, *Geschichte des hethitischen Reiches* (Leiden: Brill, 1999); Trevor Bryce, *Life and Society in the Hittite World* (Oxford: Oxford University Press, 2002), *The Kingdom of the Hittites*, new edition (Oxford: Oxford University Press, 2005). http://www.asor.org/HITTITE/hittiteHP.html.

Levant: Itamar Singer, "A Concise History of Amurru," in Shlomo Izre'el, *Amurru Akkadian*, volume II (Atlanta: Scholars Press, 1991), pp. 134–95; Wilfred G. E. Watson and Nicolas Wyatt, eds., *Handbook of Ugaritic Studies* (Leiden: Brill, 1999).

Chapter 9   Kassites, Assyrians, and Elamites

Sources: J. A. Brinkman, *Materials and Studies for Kassite History, vol. I: A Catalogue of Cuneiform Sources Pertaining to Specific Monarchs of the Kassite Dynasty* (Chicago: Oriental Institute, 1976); A. Kirk Grayson, *Assyrian Rulers of the Third and Second Millennia BC (to 1115 BC)* (Toronto: University of Toronto Press, 1987); Friedrich W. König, *Die elamischen Königsinschriften* (Graz, 1965).

Kassites: J. A. Brinkman, "Kassiten," *Reallexikon der Assyriologie* 5 (Berlin and New York: Walter de Gruyter, 1976–80): pp. 464–73 [in English]; Kemal Balkan, *Studies in Babylonian Feudalism of the Kassite Period* (Malibu: Undena, 1986).

Middle Assyria: Peter Machinist, "Provincial Governance in Middle Assyria," *Assur* 3/2 (1982), pp. 1–37.

Chapter 10   The Collapse of the Regional System and Its Aftermath

J. A. Brinkman, "Settlement Survey and Documentary Evidence: Regional Variation and Secular Trend in Mesopotamian Demography," *Journal of Near Eastern Studies* 43 (1984), pp. 169–80; W. W. Ward and M. S. Joukowsky, eds., *The Crisis Years: The 12th Century BC from Beyond the Danube to the Tigris* (Dubuque: Kendall/Hunt Publishing Company, 1992).

Mario Liverani, "Ramesside Egypt in a Changing World. An Institutional Approach," in *L'impero ramesside* (Rome: Università degli studi di Roma "La Sapienza," 1997), pp. 101–15; Seymour Gitin, Amihai Mazar, and Ephraim Stern, eds., *Mediterranean Peoples in Transition. Thirteenth to Early Tenth Centuries BCE* (Jerusalem: Israel Exploration Society, 1998).

PART III   EMPIRES

Several contributions in M. T. Larsen, ed. *Power and Propaganda* (Mesopotamia 7) (Copenhagen: Akademisk Forlag, 1979) are important for the Assyrian empire. The whole first millennium is surveyed in Francis Joannès, *The Age of Empires: Mesopotamia in the First Millennium BC*, translated by Antonia Nevill (Edinburgh: Edinburgh University Press, 2004).

Chapter 11   The Near East at the Start of the First Millennium

Sources: Grant Frame, *Rulers of Babylonia. From the Second Dynasty of Isin to the End of Assyrian Domination (1157–612 BC)* (Toronto: University of Toronto Press, 1995).
Babylonia: J. A. Brinkman, *Prelude to Empire* (Philadelphia: Occasional Publications of the Babylonian Fund, 1984).
Elam: Matthew W. Waters, *A Survey of Neo-Elamite History* (Helsinki: The Neo-Assyrian Text Corpus, 2000).
Urartu: Mirjo Salvini, *Geschichte und Kultur der Urartäer* (Darmstadt: Wissenschaftliche Buchgesellschaft, 1995); Charles Burney and David Marshall Lang, *The Peoples of the Hills. Ancient Ararat and Caucasus* (London: Phoenix Press, 2001), chapter 5.
Phoenicia: Sabatino Moscati, ed., *The Phoenicians* (Milan: Bompiani, 1988); Glenn E. Markoe, *Phoenicians* (Berkeley and Los Angeles: University of California Press, 2000).
Arameans: Edward Lipinski, *The Aramaeans. Their Ancient History, Culture, Religion* (Louvain: Uitgeverij Peeters, 2000).
Israel and Judah: Israel Finkelstein and Nadav Na'aman, eds., *From Nomadism to Monarchy. Archaeological and Historical Aspects of Early Israel* (Jerusalem: Israel Exploration Society, 1994); Israel Finkelstein, "State Formation in Israel and Judah," *Near Eastern Archaeology* 62 (1999), pp. 35–62; J. Alberto Soggin, *An Introduction to the History of Israel and Judah*, third edition (Philadelphia: Westminster Press, 1999).

Chapter 12   The Rise of Assyria

Sources: A. Kirk Grayson, *Assyrian Rulers of the Early First Millennium BC I (1114–859 BC)* (Toronto: University of Toronto Press, 1991). The letters, administrative records, legal documents, and sundry other texts found in the Assyrian archives at Nineveh are being fully re-edited by members of a project housed in Helsinki. Thus far 18 volumes have appeared in a series called *State Archives of Assyria* under the general editorship of Simo Parpola. F. Mario Fales, *L'impero Assiro: storia e amministrazione, 9.–7. secolo a.C.* (Rome and Bari: Laterza, 2001) contains a very good analysis of these sources.

The army: F. Mario Fales, "Preparing for War in Assyria," in *Économie antique. La guerre dans les économies antiques* (Entretiens d'archéologie et d'histoire. Saint-Bertrand-de-Comminges, 2000), pp. 35–62.

Expansion of the empire: Mario Liverani, "The Growth of the Assyrian Empire in the Habur/Middle Euphrates Area: A New Paradigm," *State Archives of Assyria Bulletin* 2 (1988), pp. 81–98; J. N. Postgate, "The Land of Assur and the Yoke of Assur," *World Archaeology* 23 (1992), pp. 247–63.

The capital Kalhu: Joan and David Oates, *Nimrud. An Assyrian Imperial City Revealed* (London: British School of Archaeology in Iraq, 2001). On the palace of Assurnasirpal: www.learningsites.com/NWPalace/NWPalhome.html.

Chapter 13   Assyria's World Domination

Many contributions in Simo Parpola and R. M. Whiting, eds., *Assyria 1995* (Helsinki: Helsinki University Press, 1997) are important for the study of this period.

Sources: Andreas Fuchs, *Die Inschriften Sargons II. aus Khorsabad* (Göttingen: Cuvillier Verlag, 1993); Daniel David Luckenbill, *The Annals of Sennacherib* (Chicago: The Oriental Institute, 1924); Eckart Frahm, *Einleitung in die Sanherib-Inschriften* (Horn: Institut für Orientalistik der Universität Wien, 1997); Riekele Borger, *Die Inschriften Asarhaddons Königs von Assyrien* (Graz, 1956); id., *Beiträge zum Inschriftenwerk Assurbanipals: die Prismenklassen A, B, C = K, D, E, F, G, H, J und T sowie andere Inschriften* (Wiesbaden: Harrassowitz Verlag, 1996).

The western areas: Ephraim Stern, *Archaeology of the Land of the Bible. II: The Assyrian, Babylonian, and Persian Periods, 732–322 BCE* (New York: Doubleday, 2001), pp. 1–300.

Babylonia: Grant Frame, *Babylonia 689–627 BC. A Political History* (Istanbul: Nederlands Historisch-Archaeologisch Instituut, 1992); Barbara N. Porter, *Images, Power, and Politics. Figurative Aspects of Esarhaddon's Babylonian Policy* (Philadelphia: American Philosophical Society, 1993).

Ideology: Zainab Bahrani, "Assault and Abduction: The Fate of the Royal Image in the Ancient Near East," *Art History* 18 (1995), pp. 363–82.

For the contents of Assurbanipal's library, see A. Leo Oppenheim, *Ancient Mesopotamia*, second edition (Chicago: University of Chicago Press, 1977), pp. 14–23. English translations of numerous Akkadian literary texts can be found in Benjamin R. Foster, *Before the Muses. An Anthology of Akkadian Literature*, third edition (Bethesda: CDL Press, 2005), with a concise version published as *From Distant Days: Myths, Tales, and Poetry of Ancient Mesopotamia* (Bethesda: CDL Press, 1995). The same author published a translation of *The Epic of Gilgamesh* (New York: W. W. Norton, 2001). Another recent translation of that epic is by A. R. George, *The Epic of Gilgamesh* (London: Penguin, 1999), who also published an authoritative full edition, *The Babylonian Gilgamesh Epic: Introduction, Critical Edition and Cuneiform Texts* (Oxford and New York: Oxford University Press, 2003). For astronomy, see David Brown, *Mesopotamian Planetary Astronomy – Astrology* (Groningen: Styx, 2000) and Francesca Rochberg, *The Heavenly Writing. Divination, Horoscopy, and Astronomy in Mesopotamian Culture* (Cambridge: Cambridge University Press, 2004).

Assyria's fall: Mario Liverani "The Fall of the Assyrian Empire: Ancient and Modern Interpretations," in S. Alcock et al., eds., *Empires: Perspectives from Archaeology and History* (Cambridge: Cambridge University Press, 2001), pp. 374–91.

Chapter 14   The Medes and Babylonians

Sources: Stephen Langdon, *Die neubabylonischen Königsinschriften* (Leipzig: Hinrichs'sche Buchhandlung, 1912); Paul-Richard Berger, *Die neubabylonischen Königsinschriften* (Kevelaer: Butzon & Bercker, 1973); Hanspeter Schaudig, *Die Inschriften Nabonids von Babylon und Kyros' des Großen* (Munster: Ugarit Verlag, 2001).

Medes: Mario Liverani, "The Medes at Esarhaddon's Court," *Journal of Cuneiform Studies* 47 (1995), pp. 57–62; Giovanni B. Lanfranchi et al., eds., *Continuity of Empire(?) Assyria, Media, Persia* (Padua: Sargon, 2003).

The Neo-Babylonian empire: David S. Vanderhooft, *The Neo-Babylonian Empire and Babylon in the Latter Prophets* (Atlanta: Scholars Press, 1999); Ephraim Stern, *Archaeology of the Land of the Bible. II: The Assyrian, Babylonian, and Persian Periods, 732–322 BCE* (New York: Doubleday, 2001), pp. 301–50.

Individual rulers: Ronald H. Sack, *Images of Nebuchadnezzar*, second edition (Selingsgrove: Susquehanna University Press, 2004); id., *Amel-Marduk 562–560 BC* (Kevelaer: Butzon & Bercker, 1972); Paul-Alain Beaulieu, *The Reign of Nabonidus, King of Babylon 556–539 BC* (New Haven: Yale University Press, 1989); Piotr Michalowski, "The Doors of the Past," *Eretz Israel* 27 (2003), pp. 136–52 [on Nabonidus].

The city of Babylon: Marc Van De Mieroop, "Reading Babylon," *American Journal of Archaeology* 107 (2003), pp. 257–75.

Interest in the past: Irene J. Winter, "Babylonian Archaeologists of The(ir) Mesopotamian Past," in P. Matthiae et al., eds., *Proceedings of the First International Congress on the Archaeology of the Ancient Near East* (Rome: Università degli studi di Roma "La Sapienza", 2000), pp. 1785–800.

Chapter 15   The Persian Empire

Sources: Old Persian inscriptions: Roland G. Kent, *Old Persian*, second edition (New Haven: American Oriental Society, 1953); *Corpus Inscriptionum Iranicarum*, Part I *Inscriptions of Ancient Iran* volumes I–V (London: School of Oriental and African Studies, 1978–2000); http://oi.uchicago.edu/OI/PROJ/ARI/ARI.html; www.avesta.org/op/op.htm.

The empire: Josef Wiesehöfer, *Ancient Persia from 550 BC to 650 AD* (London and New York: Tauris Publications, 1996); Amélie Kuhrt, "The Achaemenid Persian Empire (c.550–c.330 BCE): Continuities, Adaptations, Transformations," in S. Alcock et al., eds., *Empires: Perspectives from Archaeology and History* (Cambridge: Cambridge University Press, 2001), pp. 93–123; Pierre Briant, *From Cyrus to Alexander: A History of the Persian Empire* (Winona Lake: Eisenbrauns, 2002); Lindsay Allen, *The Persian Empire: A History* (London: British Museum Press, 2005); Maria Brosius, *The Persians* (London: Routledge, 2006).

Economy: Matthew W. Stolper, *Entrepreneurs and Empire* (Istanbul: Nederlands Historisch-Archaeologisch Instituut, 1985).

Index

References to the terms on maps are in *italics*.